Contents

List of Maps and Illustrations

THE HISTORY OF HAVANA

Dick Cluster and
Rafael Hernández

OR Books
New York • London

Published for the book trade by OR Books in partnership with Counterpoint Press.
Visit our website at www.orbooks.com

All rights information: rights@orbooks.com

First printing 2018.

Cataloging-in-Publication data is available from the Library of Congress.
A catalog record for this book is available from the British Library.

British Library Cataloging in Publication Data: A catalog record for this book is available from the British Library.

ISBN 978-1-94486-967-0
ISBN 978-1-94486-968-7 e-book

Typeset by Lapiz Digital Services, Chennai, India.

Acknowledgements

"What seemed like mystery," sang Jimmy Cliff on an island not far from Cuba, "were only untold history." Many people have initiated us into Havana's mysteries, far too many to thank them all individually here. Among those who contributed leads and sources that helped us shape this book in particular, we wish to acknowledge Antolín Bárcenas, Luisa Campuzano, Mario Coyula, Denia García Ronda, Antonio José Ponte, Reina María Rodríguez, Daniel Taboada, and those who generously agreed to be interviewed about their family histories: Raquel Cañizares, Carlos Larrinaga, Verónica Loynaz, Daniel Motola, and Juan Valdés Paz. In the Office of the City Historian, we received valuable contributions from Zenaida Iglesias and Yamira Rodríguez, researchers in the Dirección de Arquitectura Patrimonial, and from Magda Resyk, director of Habana Radio. Cuban historians Oscar Zanetti Lecuona, Gustavo Placer Cervera, and Oscar Loyola read and commented on parts of this manuscript. In the José Martí National Library, Eliades Acosta and Teresita Morales aided our research, and staff members Olga Vega, Ana Gloria Valdés, and Martha Haya, as well as Marisel Caraballo, collaborated in our search for information and illustrations. We are also grateful for help from specialists at the archives of the Institute of History.

For their aid in turning our project into an actual book, we are indebted to Tom Hallock and Gayatri Patnaik at Beacon Press for their advice; to our editor for the original edition at Palgrave, Gabriella Pearce; and to our new editor at OR Books, John Oakes. Nancy Falk supported this goal throughout, contributed her own perspective on the city, consulted on many drafts, and put up with the U.S. author's servitude to the project and all the obsessions that came with it. Daybel Pañellas lent her critical judgment, and Ileana Gonzalez supported the Cuban author's research on original sources and illustrations.

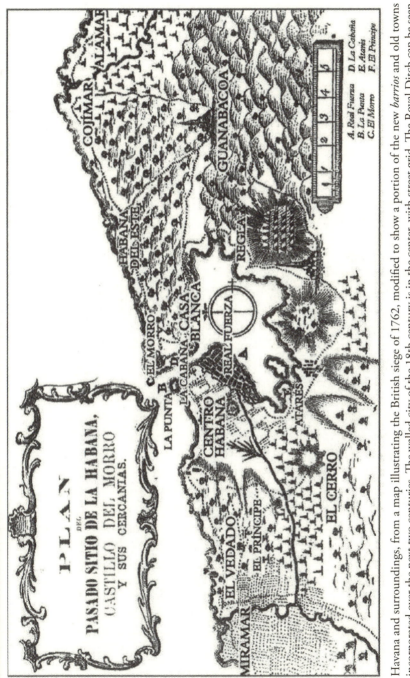

Havana and surroundings, from a map illustrating the British siege of 1762, modified to show a portion of the new *barrios* and old towns incorporated over the next two centuries. The walled city of the 18th century is in the center, with street grid. The Royal Ditch can be seen bringing water from the Almendares or Chorrera River (at left separating the modern neighborhoods of Miramar and El Vedado). Locations of Spanish fortresses built before and after the British invasion are labeled.

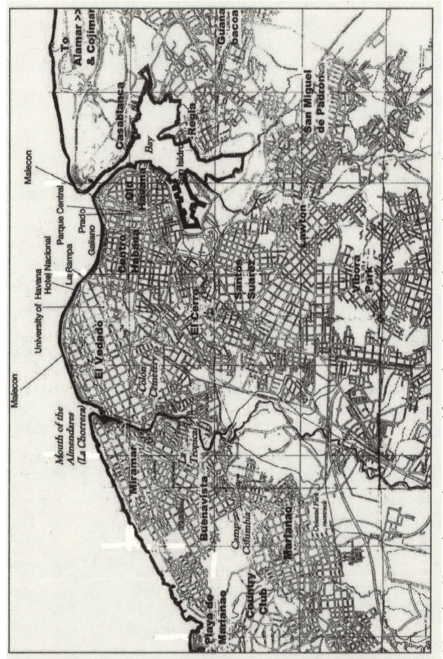

Metropolitan Havana showing places mentioned frequently in the text, with the names they bore at the time.

Introduction: *Un tipo muy popular*

Near the docks and custom house of Old Havana, in front of the meticulously restored basilica of the convent of San Francisco de Asís, stands the life-size bronze statue of a figure with long, flowing hair and beard, wrapped in a D'Artagnan-style cape which seems to drift in the wind as he walks. This is one of the very few statues erected in Havana since the revolution of 1959. It does not portray a rebel hero, a patriotic general, a famous writer, a great architect, or the composer of some unforgettable song dedicated to this city on the bay. Rather, it is the statue of the Parisian Gentleman, El Caballero de París.

The French themselves would have called him a *clochard*, a vagabond. From the 1920s to the 1970s he slept where he could, on one corner or another as he moved about the city, feeding himself on what he found or was offered by street vendors or passers-by, holding up his pants with a rope belt from which dangled pencils secured by strings. Yet, dressed in his signature cape over a tattered set of tails, the self-styled Parisian Gentleman projected an aura of dignity and majesty. This European aristocrat washed up on the shores of this New World—or so he presented himself—made speeches to the crowds in seventeenth-century Spanish or busied himself arranging his mysterious bags and bundles and masses of newspapers and magazines.

He was, by most accounts, a Spanish immigrant who had come to Cuba as a teenager and who found work in Havana's sophisticated stores and hotels. Some said he had gone crazy for love, while others said he'd been jailed for a murder or a robbery that he did not commit. Over the course of decades, he became an institution. Ageless, capable of appearing at any hour of day or night, attached to no neighborhood in particular, white but poor, both comic and tragic, he became a sort of essential citizen of Havana, to whom the city's residents have dedicated songs, poems, memoirs, imagined biographies, and plays. "*Un tipo muy popular,*" one such song calls him—which suggests "popular" and "of the people" all at once.

The Caballero died in 1985 and was buried in an obscure grave on the city's outskirts. When the ruined colonial church and convent of San Francisco (turned to civilian uses since the mid-nineteenth century) was restored in the year 2001, the city historian requested the transfer of the Caballero's ashes to that sanctuary beside the city's earliest marketplace. The reception this vagabond received sums up the spirit of his adopted city: throughout his lifetime on the streets, even those who laughed at him protected him. They conversed with him and accepted the quill pens and colored papers he gave out as gifts to those who offered him alms. He once buttonholed a Cardinal, who listened politely as the Caballero explained that the church should sell all its goods and distribute the proceeds among the poor. By the 1940s, he was such an institution that he was interviewed in the press. In the 1950s, he appeared on television alongside two similar itinerant characters, La Marquesa and Bigote de Gato. In the 1960s, he was given carte-blanche for free food from the kitchens of the newly state-run restaurants.

The courtesy and protection afforded to the Caballero testifies to something about Havana that every visitor notes—this city is the most welcoming place. The people of Havana welcomed the Caballero as they welcome almost everyone, with hospitality and compassion. It doesn't take much to strike up a conversation, even if you are a stranger, or strange.

We believe this characteristic stems from the city's origins. Havana began as a port and a crossroads, and it has been that way ever since—a melting pot of transients and immigrants and refugees, of slaves and freedmen and freedwomen, as well as of conquistadors and plutocrats, a confluence of the four points of the compass, of Spain, Africa, China, and the Levant, of the Caribbean islands and the Americas on both sides of the Rio Grande. The name of the city, La Habana or La Havana, comes from the Spanish transcription of an indigenous word. But in ensuing years many came to believe that the name derived from haven and harbor, which the city has always been in both a physical and a social sense. Exiles adding to city's mix in various eras have included Irish Catholics, French Protestants, Bonapartists, South American royalists and revolutionaries, Haitian ex-planters and ex-canecutters, Indonesian communists, South African guerrillas, and American fugitives ranging from Black Panthers to gangsters and millionaires. Through it all, Havana has been a city that takes what comes—and assimilates it. Comparisons of the Cuban capital to the French one have been frequent, but what made El Caballero de París beloved was that he was quintessentially Havana—and being quintessentially Havana did not rule out naming himself after someplace else.

At the same time, the Caballero's popularity had to do with the way he spoke out for his city. We will come, eventually, to the story of the Caballero's arrest for defaming a president, part of a long tradition of protest against endemic corruption and graft. For now, we note that mixing defense with hospitality is another characteristic of Havana. The narrow neck of the bay that welcomed so many immigrants and visitors was closed up every night in the seventeenth and eighteenth centuries by a chain of logs pulled tight between its two flanking fortresses. At the same nine o'clock hour, a cannon shot was fired and the gates of the city's walls were shut tight. In the tense days of May and June of 1586, when the threatening fleet of the privateer Francis Drake tacked back and forth along the coastline, citizens and subjects from the city and surrounding farms gathered to keep watch and drill with the scarce arms available to them. In 1762, when British forces besieged Havana from the land, local guerrillas attacked behind their lines. In 1961 and 1962, when an invasion from the north was—with reason—expected at any moment, the seaside Malecón drive filled with sandbag barriers, cannons, militia men and women, and antiaircraft guns.

We have opened this book with the Caballero for one more reason. We, just like him, have adopted the city and have been adopted by it. Both of us have been its residents without having been bred there, and in this we are hardly unique. A popular joke in Havana in the 1990s involved Fidel Castro seeking advice about the perennial issue of the capital's overcrowding. For counsel about this vexing problem, he summoned Pepito, the proverbial bad boy of generations of Cuban jokes. "No problem, *comandante*," Pepito replied. He advised the President to line up twenty *camellos* (camels), the popular name for the giant, crowded, lurching, two-humped tractor-trailer buses invented to cope with the transport crisis that ballooned in those years. "Twenty *camellos*," repeated Pepito, "and one Mercedes-Benz." He said to fill up the buses with recent migrants from Oriente—the island's easternmost region—and send them back where they belong. "Very good, Pepito," answered the President, a graduate of the University of Havana but originally an immigrant from Oriente himself. "I think I'll do that, send them back as you say. I can provide the twenty buses. But why do we need the Mercedes-Benz?" "*Comandante*," Pepito demanded, "You're not planning to ride in one of those *camellos* yourself?!"

It is partly because neither of us is any more indigenous than the late commander-in-chief that we believe our viewpoints can help North American readers see this crossroads as it needs to be seen, from both within and without. Having lived its daily life (one as a temporary resident and the other as a permanent one) we see it in a way that travel writers, chroniclers, and tourists of past and present centuries do not. Having lived outside, we perhaps have a better sense of what makes it special than those who have always lived within it. Thus we are as Havanan, and as foreign, as tens of thousands of others who live there today or who were born there and have held onto its memory while living in other parts.

Further, we have tried to use our double authorship to offer readers in the United States a binocular, three-dimensional account. In the late nineteenth century and the first half of the twentieth, panoramic views of Havana were a staple not just of American picture postcards but of three-dimensional double-image devices from the Stereopticon to the Viewmaster. In the years since, visions of the Cuban capital have often been one-sided, monocular, for political reasons above all. In the course of writing this book we have argued with each other and learned from our arguments. At the same time, we have often let the impressions of our two distinct viewpoints stand side by side, not saying a given moment was solely fish or solely fowl, or its most representative figure was solely *fulano* or *mengano*, Peter or Paul.

The *yanqui* in our authorial pair first saw Havana in the predawn light of late November, 1969, through the windows of a Hungarian bus carrying him from the José Martí International Airport to a cane-cutting camp in the countryside to the east. He had come to check out the new post-revolutionary Cuba, and at that moment a mammoth sugar harvest was where the action was. Over the next few months, the capital loomed tantalizingly in the distance, tasted in short weekend visits and above all in the stories of the Cubans with whom he worked in those fields, almost all of them from Havana. Then and in subsequent visits in the 1970s and the 1980s, he took in distinct spots and routes that did not yet add up to a coherent map—eating rabbit at the restaurant across from where he would later live, getting eyeglasses at the ophthalmological hospital across from where he would later teach, taking buses that by the time he returned had ceased to run—all the while hearing stories and more stories from old and new friends and random residents on the street. He finally got the chance to live and work in Havana over a four-year period in the 1990s, during which he explored the city by foot, bicycle, bus, and very occasionally by car. One day early in his stay a friend-to-be said, on their first meeting, "Are you sure you're a North American? You listen too well." He does not believe his fellow Americans are incapable of listening, but he took the warning to heart. He goes back whenever he can, asks a lot of questions, and listens to the rhythms of Havana's never-silent citizens. He realizes that never-silent is an exaggeration. Unlike his countrymen and women, most residents of Havana keep quiet while they eat.

The Cuban of our pair was born in the capital but grew up in a town in the center of the island. His first conscious impression of Havana was thus a product of his imagination, aroused by an uncle who worked in a toy store on the Calle Galiano and would arrive in the provincial town laden with gifts and fabulous tales. He discovered the capital for real in December of 1961, descending from a train full of literacy teachers returning from the mountains, to take up residence as a boarding student in

in ways that allowed no going back. But in the lives of cities, as in other lives, continuities are as important as ruptures. There is no going forward, either, without them. In this history of Havana we have also looked for and found the things that remain the same.

Finally, a note about language.

In what follows, translations from Cuban Spanish are almost always our own. We've kept Spanish words and Havana slang to a minimum, but at times they are essential to flavor the stew, and we hope readers will learn some of them. In the process we have grappled with what to do about an adjective missing from the English language, whose job would be to accurately describe things from or pertaining to the United States. José Martí used the term "Our America" to describe the many American nations south of the Rio Grande, but what do we call the influential residents and products and colloquial language of the nation that lies to the north? Even in Spanish, the adjective *estadounidense* (United-States-ian), though it exists, is rarely used. Cubans often say *norteamericano*, but Canadians and Mexicans rightly point out that they are North Americans too. So we have reluctantly gone with the usage "American," even though Brazilians are American people, Chilean wines are American products, and Mexican speech is American language as well.

Whatever word we use, we have called attention to the ways that New York, Tampa, Miami, and other U.S. cities have influenced Havana since at least the eighteenth century, and have made some mention of Havana's considerable influence on them. We hope that recognition of these cultural ties will contribute to a long-delayed restoration of unhindered contact between U.S. cities and Cuban ones, especially the capital, in a climate of equality and mutual respect.

What follows is a new edition of our book, which was originally published in 2006. We have made minor corrections and additions to Chapters 1-16, covering the period from the city's founding to 2005. But principally, what we have done is to add an epilogue that covers the momentous developments of the decade from 2006 to 2016, including the social effects of the restoration of diplomatic relations between Cuba and the United States and other steps toward full normalization. We are still waiting for fully unobstructed contact, but are happy to see that there has been some progress, even in fits and starts and with backsliding, since our first edition appeared.

—Dick Cluster and Rafael Hernández, Oakland, California, and Havana, Cuba, 2017.

1 Key to the Indies

When Christopher Columbus explored the northern coast of Cuba on his first voyage to America, he mistook the territory for a peninsula extending from the mainland of China, inhabited by subjects of the Great Khan. After the inhabitants convinced him—temporarily—that this was not so, he turned back, eastward toward home. Thus he missed his chance to lay eyes on the dramatic break in Cuba's coastline that would become Havana: the high cliff, narrow channel, protected bay, and sweeping oceanfront where the city would later rise. Yet this part of the island did not altogether escape his notice. In his letter to the Spanish sovereigns who had sponsored his voyage, he reported, "There are in the western part of the island two provinces which I did not visit; one of these is called by the Indians 'Avan,' and its inhabitants are born with tails."

Born with tails? The Admiral's letter and journals are full of half-truths, lies, delusions, wishful thinking, and mysteries. On his second voyage, a native chief told him (as best as he could make out) that Cuba was "an island without end." Centuries later, his bones finally made it to the fabled Avan, to be buried in the city's new cathedral—or so everyone believed, but it now appears that they may have been his brother's remains, by mistake. So let us just note that even before the city was settled, foreign sensibilities found in it the stuff of fantasies—the unknown, the exaggerated, and a whiff of the devil as well.

When Spanish soldier-settlers finally reached and conquered the western part of the island some twenty-five years after Columbus's voyage, they were still calling it "La Avana" or "La Abana," a name which they took from a word often repeated by the inhabitants, a word recorded by the Spaniards as Havaguanex or Habaguanex, which they thought to be the name of a local chief. In 1515 or 1516 they founded a town on the southern coast in an ill-chosen, swampy, mosquito-ridden spot with a poor harbor. This town they named in honor of St. Christopher (and perhaps also the Admiral) as San Cristóbal de La Habana. The blending of Habaguanex and St. Christopher established another precedent. In Havana, distinct cultures and creeds would always cross and mix.

Geographically, however, a better site already beckoned: the fine bay on the north coast that Columbus had not seen, but Sebastian de Ocampo had. Ocampo was a veteran of Columbus's second voyage, dispatched later by the Spanish crown to establish Cuba's true shape once and for all. Circumnavigating the long thin body of land, he concluded it was indeed an island. In the course of this circumnavigation, he landed his two ships in a bay he called Carenas, where he stopped for the process called "careening," or scraping the hulls and recoating them with natural tar or pitch which he found oozing in abundance from the rocks.

Sometime thereafter, the place was visited by Father Bartolomé de las Casas, who had already participated in the conquests of Hispaniola and eastern Cuba as a military officer, a chaplain, a settler, a landowner, and a master of indigenous serfs or slaves. The horrors he had observed— the decimation of the native population by massacre, disease, and being forced to pan local streams for scant quantities of gold—would later be recorded in his justly famous *Brief History of the Destruction of the Indies* and in the petitions for an end to Indian slavery that he filed with the King. Of the Bay of Carenas, he wrote, prophetically, "There are few harbors in Spain, and perhaps not in any other parts of the world, that may equal it." Thus he too predicted the future of Havana. For five centuries it would be a strategic location and an international port.

It took one more ingredient, though, to secure Havana's destiny. Venturing to the New World in search of a short route to China and India, the Spaniards stumbled instead on a new continent, with civilizations possessed of more silver and gold than they had ever seen before. These civilizations, as Columbus had noted, "have no iron or steel or weapons," and a small number of Spanish troops "would suffice to destroy all that land." The first to find and conquer such riches was Hernán Cortés, a Spanish law school dropout turned military adventurer, briefly deputy governor of Cuba, who in 1519 slipped out of Santiago de Cuba in defiance of the governor's orders with eleven ships under his own command. He picked up some additional recruits from among the disgruntled settlers of the original San Cristóbal de La Habana, and soon made landfall in Veracruz to begin the conquest of Mexico. When he sent a ship full of Aztec gold to the King, his emissaries sailed along Cuba's north coast and stopped for provisions in the Bay of Carenas or someplace nearby. It soon became clear that the harbor offered an ideal spot for assembling and provisioning the treasure fleets returning to Spain, from which they could take advantage of the Gulf Stream and the Bahama Channel for a speedy voyage to Seville.

In the meantime, refugees from the original San Cristóbal de La Habana settled here. They did not choose the shore of the bay at first, but rather the mouth of a river some four miles to the west, which the native inhabitants called Casiguaguas and the Spaniards called La Chorrera, the spout. This spot is now well within metropolitan Havana, the mouth of the river today called the Almendares. It would be the site of bombardment and landing by British invaders in the eighteenth century, and the terminus of a train line to the secluded bathing and vacation spots of Vedado in the nineteenth. In the twentieth century, a Secretary of Public Works would use the fruits of corruption to build his pleasure dome there, complete with bronze lions and live ones—an estate later to be sacked by a crowd celebrating a Cuban revolution that nearly triumphed when Fidel Castro was only five years old. Today that estate is a restaurant and night club frequented mostly by foreign tourists, and the nearby end of Havana's seawall is a gathering point for Cuban youth. But in 1518 the settlement was just a small gathering of *bohíos*, the thatch-roof huts of palm leaves, mud, and branches that the settlers copied from the native Taino Indians—a settlement which most of the Spaniards soon abandoned, yet again, for new quarters on the bay. There is no historical record of exactly when they moved, or how they marked the city's third founding, if at all. But modern Havana takes it as an article of faith that on St. Christopher's Day of 1519, those Spaniards celebrated this third and final move with a town council meeting followed by a mass, both held in the open air under a towering ceiba tree close by the shore of the bay. The roots of this legend are so deep that already in 1754, when the allegedly historic tree died, governor Francisco Cagigal de la Vega ordered the carving of a commemorative column to be placed at its foot. "Stop here, passerby," his inscribed proclamation commanded in Latin, a language which very few of the residents of the city could read. He enjoined future pilgrims to imagine "a tree, a leafy ceiba, or shall I say a memorable sign of the prudence and the ancient religion of the young city." He ordered a new tree planted from a cutting of the old.

The column is still there, at the edge of Old Havana's Plaza de Armas, standing before a small commemorative neoclassical temple built in 1828. But it's the tree, not the column or the temple, that forms a strand of the web of popular culture in Havana. Ceibas are powerful trees in Cuban lore, which draws from the traditions of both Africa and Spain. When the Virgin came to the palm tree, one myth has it, the tree would not step aside, and so it was condemned to absorb the full rays of the sun. The ceiba, which did not make the same mistake, was blessed with the spreading foliage that crowns its tall, bulbous, elephant-leg trunk. For the Africans brought to Cuba as slaves, the ceiba took the place of a species of baobab, and so became the deity Iroko, uniter of heaven and earth, and the dwelling place of many more deities. When Chinese traditions were added to the Yoruba-Catholic mix, the ceiba tree also became the body of Sanfán Kon, now identified with the *orisha* Changó and his alter ego, Santa Bárbara. Every November 16, hundreds of *habaneros* come to circle the ceiba, three times, in silence. On each circuit they make a wish.

We do not know what the founders wished for, this small group of Spaniards, almost all of them men, seeking their fortunes in the Indies far from home. We do know something of what they did. Once again, they built *bohíos*, which they laid out along a few crooked dirt lanes. Some waited for their chance to join other expeditions to the American mainland. When Cuban governor Hernando de Soto set sail from Havana for

Florida in 1538 with a flotilla of ships and a thousand troops to pursue the chimeras of the Fountain of Youth and the Seven Cities of Cibola made of solid gold, he took most of the town's citizens with him. He left his wife Doña Isabel de Bobadilla behind in at least nominal command. Four years later, a few survivors of his expedition brought news of his death on the shores of the Mississippi, the great river he had found. Meanwhile, in Havana, others had set out to make a living by provisioning the passing ships and fleets.

The ships needed fresh water, which was brought in small boats from La Chorrera. They needed dried meat and leather, both secured from livestock raised on the settlers' land grants on the city's outskirts, and they needed durable wood for repairs, which could be felled from the forests of caoba, mahogany, cedar, and ebony that surrounded the city on all landward sides. But most of all, they needed bread. If Cuba was no place for growing wheat, making do without wheat flour was something else the Spaniards had learned from the native inhabitants before they disappeared. The root of a plant the Tainos called *yucay* could be ground into a kind of flour, which in turn could be baked into a dry round bread called *casabe*, with the texture of a thin cracker, which could be sold to the passing crews. The surviving Indians were put to work cultivating this food in the settlers' land grants. Soon, this labor passed to small numbers of newly imported African slaves.

Yuca, boiled and then drenched in garlic sauce, remains a proud staple of the dinner table. *Casabe*, however, is now rare in Havana, though it can still be found on the eastern part of the island. The native word for this substitute bread found its way into Spanish and then French, so that the European colonizers, by the time they took the yuca plant to Africa, called it "cassava." But the problem for Havana's handful of landowning citizens was how to capitalize on it. Though the prices of *casabe* and dried meat doubled or even tripled when significant numbers of ships were in port, Havana was still a poor place at best. In the 1550s, when the imports of gold and silver from the Americas reached the unprecedented level of 2 million ducats a year (the equivalent of some 16,000 pounds of gold), Havana could boast only fifty landowners, four streets with scattered lots and houses of boards and thatch, an adobe church with a small, half-completed bell tower, and a ruined earthenwork fort that De Soto had left behind. The total population of the town and surrounding area was probably well under a thousand, perhaps half Spaniards and the rest Indians, Africans, mestizos, and mulattos, some slave and some free. The grandest house—belonging to the farmer, real estate developer, butcher-shop owner, and public official Juan de Rojas—was the only two-story building and one of the few to boast masonry rather than bare cedar boards and palm thatch.

The threat of piracy, more than the sale of *casabe*, led to the town's first real spurt of growth. As a safe port en route to and from Spain's New World empire, Havana developed a unique strategic position. By the end of the sixteenth century, Havana would acquire the honorific title "Key to the Indies," primarily because rival empires were intent on picking the Spanish lock. French pirates and privateers were the first to begin menacing Spanish shipping, not only in European waters, but in the seas of the American colonies (the so-called Spanish Main). They picked off isolated ships on the high seas, and they set out to attack the poorly defended ports.

In 1537, a French pirate exacted 700 ducats in gold as his price for not putting Havana to the torch. The residents paid, but when three ships opportunely arrived from Mexico after the Frenchmen left, the local authorities ordered them to deposit their gold and silver ashore, and give chase. However, the pirates instead captured the Spanish pursuers, returned to Havana, and confiscated the town's replenished stock of treasure. In 1555, another Frenchman, the privateer Jacques de Sores, approached at the head of a fleet of four ships. De Sores had already raided Santiago de Cuba, kidnapping the archbishop and leading citizens, whom he freed for a ransom of eighty thousand pesos and the silver ornaments of the church. Guided by a Portuguese pilot who had once lived in Havana, he proceeded to that harbor where he expected to find valuable cargoes at the docks.

When there turned out to be no treasure ships, de Sores and his crew occupied the town for nearly a month, during which time the pirate used Juan de Rojas's two-story house as his fortress, repelled an attack by a hastily gathered militia, and demanded a ransom of hidden gold and silver plus *casabe* and meat. When the residents couldn't or wouldn't comply, he ordered the buildings smeared with pitch (the same local natural substance that had so entranced Sebastian de Ocampo) and set afire. All told, seventeen of Havana's fifty-one landowners and an unknown number of other Spaniards, Africans, and native inhabitants lost their lives in battle or reprisals. In a final act of farewell, de Sores raided the surrounding farms, taking further prisoners whom he held for ransom. Six male slaves whose masters did not pay up were hanged.

The town council, reporting to the King, insisted that de Sores was "a terrible Lutheran heretic, as were all of those who came with him," as could be seen from their words and deeds. "His Divine Majesty" must have had a reason for chastising the city, the local authorities concluded sorrowfully, but the King, unconvinced, decided to take action. Faced not only with the French threat but with the beginnings of a still more dangerous English one, the Spanish court decided that the American trade needed protection. Thenceforth, the vital cargoes would not travel in small groups but in great convoys, accompanied by warships. From the 1560s on, two fleets left Seville each year, one in April or May for the Caribbean islands and Mexico, one in August for Cartagena and Panama. The following spring both return fleets would assemble, bit by bit, in Havana. There the treasure ships of Spanish America gathered, assembling gold and silver, pearls and plumage, precious hardwoods and hardy potatoes, the astonishing flavors of pineapple and chocolate—and there, too, the ceramics and silks and spices that came across the Pacific in special galleons from Manila to Acapulco, crossed Mexico overland, and were again loaded onto ships in Veracruz.

In Havana, everything worth shipping back to fill the coffers of Spain and its legion of creditors was assembled. In Havana, too, the armed galleons of the Spanish military awaited this treasure, availing themselves of services of refitting and repair, while their crews took shore leave in the town. So for weeks and often months, as the fleet gathered, Havana would become home to galleons, cargo ships, merchants, soldiers, sailors, commanders, and crews—most of them with considerable money to spend.

To protect the newly strategic town, a permanent military garrison was established. On the high cliff or *morro* on the east side of Havana Bay, a tall stone watchtower was built, from which sentinels could watch for hostile ships and warn the town. In the town itself rose a solid stone fortress, a four-pointed star designed to withstand a lengthy siege, with drawbridge, moat, high parapets, and walls fifteen feet thick. The Castillo de La Real Fuerza, completed in 1577 a stone's throw from the famous ceiba, is the oldest construction that still stands in Havana today. Its rough utilitarian walls contrast with the elegant portals and colonnades of two centuries later, but its strategic location and design can still be appreciated at a glance. The Real Fuerza's cannon commanded a new town square, the Plaza de Armas, as well as the waters of the port. There were seven cannon to begin with, a quantity soon doubled by purchases from passing warships, though this did not keep governors and fort commanders from begging Madrid for more and better ones.

La Fuerza proved only a beginning. Despite the new fortification, in 1586 Havana received a visit from the English arch-privateer Francis Drake. On previous expeditions, Drake's ships had ravished the sea lanes and coasts of the Caribbean and South America, and even made their way into the Pacific, capturing rich prizes of the coasts of Peru. In this new incursion, they had already attacked Santo Domingo and Cartagena de Indias. In May, Drake's armada was observed rounding Cape San Antonio on Cuba's western tip, where it stopped to take on water and firewood. Now lookouts were posted along the seafront from La Chorrera to the village of Cojímar far to the east of the bay, and the town council assembled all available Spanish settlers from the countryside around Havana and put them to work, along with slaves, free blacks, and Indians, digging trenches and manning observation posts.

After five days of tacking back and forth along the coastline, Drake turned northward to raze the Spanish settlement at St. Augustine, in Florida, instead. That Havana escaped English attack this time, however, did not ease the fear of future attempts. A new governor, the field marshal Juan de Tejada, and an Italian military engineer, Giovanni Battista Antonelli, were dispatched to Havana to render the port impregnable.

Antonelli had been in Spanish service for many years, and this was his second American journey. All we know of his first one is that it got him as far as the Straits of Magellan, from which he had returned "naked and poor" and inclined to enter a monastery until this new commission beckoned him westward once again. His charge was to construct a pair of forts at the mouth of the bay, as well as a canal to bring the fresh water of the Chorrera to the harbor where it could safely supply ships.

The canal opened first, in 1592, discharging its current "as wide as the body of an ox" in the area then known as the Plaza of the Swamp and two other waterfront sites. It was called the Royal Ditch (*zanja*), and a part of its route is still followed by the street called Zanja that passes through Central Havana and Chinatown. The ditch's terminus is marked today by the half-block Callejón del Chorro that leads from the Plaza de la Catedral to the artists' printmaking cooperative at its end. "The Field Marshall Jvan de Texada brought this water in 1592" reads a very old inscription above an old spout-hole in a seashell design, while a few blocks south, near the Plaza Vieja, recent restoration efforts have exposed a section of the ditch itself, revealing the combination of rock and coral out of which it was laboriously built by slaves.

On the flat western shore of the bay's narrow neck, north of the town itself, meanwhile, gradually rose the Castillo de San Salvador de la Punta, today a maritime museum, which forms the starting point of the modern Malecón. On the great cliff opposite, Antonelli laid out the fortress that has become the backdrop for every foreign newscaster reporting from Havana, and the site, over the years, of garrisons, battles, and dungeons, book fairs, art expositions, and more: el Castillo de los Tres Reyes del Morro. The Morro Castle, its walls and turrets rising directly out of the rock, is connected on the landward side by a flying bridge and topped by a lighthouse (then a tall tower with a signal fire) whose beam can be seen from the hills and rooftops of Havana and from miles out to sea. Across the slim channel between the forts was strung a chain of wood and iron, anchored to a buried cannon at either end, that could be drawn up at night or in the face of attacking ships. Thus ships in the harbor were protected not only by the artillery of the forts but by this physical barrier as well.

It took forty years to complete both fortresses, financed like the Real Fuerza by taxes on shipping and sales in Havana and by a series of subsidies from the viceroyalty of New Spain (Mexico), for which the fleets continued to be a lifeline. When these immense construction projects were finally complete, Havana became, by royal Spanish decree, a city, "the key to the New World and bulwark of the Indies," soon to be granted an official seal bearing the likeness of the three forts, as silver towers in a blue field, ranged around a golden key. Between 1575 and 1650, shipments of gold and silver alone from Spain's American colonies averaged an incredible 6 million ducats a year. As guardian of this trade, Havana became a city still rude but at the same time cosmopolitan, a city of wharves and warehouses and all manner of nautical workshops for repairing or manufacturing ships' equipment, instruments, supplies, and maps. It was a city where viceroys in transit rubbed shoulders with itinerant vendors, where priests worked alongside prostitutes, where Andalusian soldiers and sailors shared the streets with Chinese traders and African slaves.

On the one hand, a sixteenth-century governor, sounding rather like Columbus, wrote with true or mock horror of his new post, "All the criminals banished from Peru and New Spain and other parts, those sent back to Spain for failing to fetch their wives, the bankrupt merchants, the wives fleeing their husbands—all come in the fleets, as do to friars in lay clothes and vagabonds and rascals and sailors jumping ship, all of whom roam through the citizens' properties and fear neither royal justice nor God." On the other hand, we can only guess what excitement must have been provoked when Havana received its most exotic visitor of these years, the samurai Hasekura Tsunenaga, the first Japanese emissary to cross the Pacific. He arrived from Mexico in 1614 with thirty retainers and a Dominican priest en route to Madrid and Rome on a secret mission to establish direct trade between Japan and the Spanish Empire. His global trade mission failed when the Tokugawa shogunate decided to close Japan to outside influence, but Tsunenaga returned to Havana quite recently, at the beginning of the twenty-first century, in the form of a life-sized statue, a gift from his native province of Sendai, in a small Japanese garden halfway between the Real Fuerza and La Punta flanked by two rows of tall, sinuous royal palms.

Noble visitors and nascent industries aside, however, Havana's residents lived chiefly off of what supported most shipping towns and military ports: supplying drink, cheap lodging, food, gambling and sex. And customs duties (and their attendant corruption), and slavery, though of a type significantly different from the later plantation sort.

In 1594, Governor Juan de Maldonado decreed closure of any tavern that refused to make a forced loan for the completion of the two new forts—and he counted eighty that did contribute, in a city whose irregular populated streets could not have equaled more than thirty square blocks. This number, he added "would not be a small one, even in Madrid." The town council, some three decades before, had estimated total annual sales at fifty-two barrels of wine a year, approximately twenty thousand bottles of modern size. To keep down "disorder" (and probably to limit competition), an early regulation limited tavern keepers to one open barrel at a time, and stated they could not be resupplied until they displayed the disassembled staves of the previous barrel in their yards. The wine, of course, had to be imported just like its consumers. Principally from the Canary Islands, it came in the outbound ships, so the town's legion of tavern operators were operating on slender margins between what they bought and what they sold. Most of them operated out of their own houses, where many also sold lodging (with or without hammocks or beds) and prepared food. Others sold food on the streets, either prepared dishes or fruits picked from trees within the town or carried in from the outlying farms.

In all of these trades, Africans and mulattos were active as well as Spaniards, and possibly more so, though they were always subject to regulations to keep their competition down:

> Because many black women and other persons go about on the streets selling sausage and pastries of yuca flour and ground corn without authorization . . . it is ordered that sausages shall be sold only at a price of one real for the length of one yard and a half, and all the other goods should not be sold unless the *regidor* or his deputy should declare a price for it.

> Because many black slave women of this town have
> taken up the business of having a house in which to
> sell lodging or wine or tobacco at much prejudice to
> the public good, it is proclaimed that from today on
> no black slave woman shall dare live in a house of her
> own nor have a tavern nor sell tobacco on the pain of
> fifty lashes for any of said black women who act to the
> contrary, and any owner who allows this shall incur a
> fine of two pesos.

At the same time, larger business in the wine trade was done from the top, and like other opportunities for economic favoritism, it engendered constant feuds. Fort commander Diego Fernandes de Quiñones, in 1584, accused the current governor and his wife of profiteering on wine and oils, buying them directly from incoming ships at pretax prices, restricting the supply available to others, and then operating their own taverns that sold drink at twice the normal rate.

As for bulk food supplies, *casabe* still fed the soldiers of the forts, but the ships often took on sea turtle, butchered on the outskirts of the town and cut into long thin slices, salted, and hung in the sun and wind to dry. "And so it serveth the mariners in all their voyage to Spain," wrote Thomas Gage, who sailed back to Europe from Havana in 1637, "which they eat boiled with a little garlic, and I have heard them say that to them it tasted as well as any veal." Being a ship's passenger rather than a sailor, he dined on chickens and pigs that were taken on board live, and slaughtered en route.

Rivaling provision of drink, food, and lodging were the industries of gambling and prostitution, in which the military garrisons, among others, were intimately involved. Gambling was not only permitted but officially authorized, with the governor, fort commanders, and other officials running games in their houses, from which they extracted a sizable take. One governor's attempt—sincere or not—to outlaw games of chance failed because, as he informed the King, he had jurisdiction over the games in citizens' houses but not the areas under control of the most important figures, the generals of the fleets. The crown responded by conceding the right to run gaming inside the forts to an official called the sergeant major, who surely appreciated the monopoly, to the extent that it endured. Fernandes de Quiñones, quoted above, boasted to the King of his own efforts regulating gambling: he prohibited cursing during the games, set a penalty for interfering with the roll of the dice or the deal of cards, and barred the soldiers from betting the uniforms off their backs.

Francisco de Calona, master of public works, was accused by four of his Spanish stonecutters of gambling "day and night" and owing more than his entire salary of 800 ducats a year. Gambling bred robbery. Practically all the white males of the city went into the streets armed with sword or dagger, though such weapons were prohibited for those of darker skin. Don Martín Calvo de la Puerta, town counselor and court official, obtained a royal decree authorizing him to carry a small arsenal of two swords, two daggers, and a musket when he ventured onto the streets. His servants, "to protect their persons," were authorized to go about similarly armed to the teeth. One way or another, the city was hard to govern—there were too many characters in the drama, with too many sources of power, and it has been that way ever since.

Prostitution was of course a major industry in a city whose economy was based on periodic protracted stays by transient men, and a relative shortage of women as well. Cuban historian Manuel Moreno Fraginals has pointed out how the city's sexual slang developed a strongly maritime flavor: the streetwalker was called a *fletera*, derived from the term for rented ships or cargo space, and the term for coitus became *singar* (to row with a single oar protruding from the stern). Other such maritime sex slang was later displaced by slang derived from the processing of sugar.

Given the shortage of free white women (and their resultant value in the marriage market), prostitution was closely bound up with slavery, as well. Aside from a few mines and the military construction projects, in which the slaves were royal property imported for the purposes, slavery in Cuba's first two centuries was a small-scale affair. Havana's wealthier citizens owned a few slaves who acted as household servants, worked on the owners' small farms or ranches on the outskirts of the city, or were hired out as day laborers in construction and other trades. When masters assigned their slaves to work as day laborers, they often provided incentive for them to develop new (more profitable) skills or to work hard without much supervision, by allowing them to keep part of the daily pay. The luckier male slaves were apprenticed to skilled craftsmen, and often succeeded in eventually buying their freedom. The unlucky ones were rented for the crueler work of laboring on the huge forts, alongside the slaves belonging to the crown.

Females often ran small eateries for sailors, as noted above, but they were especially earmarked for sexual services. Governor Juan de Salamanca, in 1658, suggested that it might be advisable "to require the owners of black women and mulattas to keep them within their houses and not give them permission to live outside nor to go to the mills and corrals . . . because these slaves thus earn for their owners wages much greater than those that are [otherwise] earned," but he did not find that such a prohibition had much effect.

It was common for soldiers in the forts to buy one or two female slaves, and supplement their military earnings (generally delayed) with their earnings as pimps. "Andrea, twenty-five, of the Mandinga nation" was sold by a local citizen to an artilleryman in 1588 for 250 ducats, far more than a soldier could normally afford. That same year, the royal notary Melchor Casas bought the slaves Juan and Esperanza for 500 ducats, then shortly resold Esperanza, a twenty-year-old Biafran, to Pedro de Campos, "a soldier of the fort" for a sum not recorded, of which 140 ducats was a loan which Campos would later pay back.

This practice was not limited to soldiers. A contract from 1579 has a Spaniard renting his female slave to Alonso Rodriguez, *moreno* (black), for a year at a price of five ducats a month, with the stipulation that, while the fleet was in port, the renter had to pay to the owner "what other women of the town would bring in during this time." Churchmen were also involved in the traffic in one way or another, if another section of Governor Salamanca's report to the crown is to be believed:

> I have found many [of these women] who maintain
> friendship with clergy, and in God's service I have tried to

banish some for their dissolute behavior and require others to abstain from illicit friendships, but I had to stop
because the clergy began to mutiny under protection of a
judge . . . When the bishop Don Juan de Montiel received
notice of such things, and began to visit his subjects, he
died most rapidly and, according to the rabble (as perhaps
Your Majesty may have heard by other means), his dying
was assisted, as often happens in these Indies.

The use of urban slaves as day laborers who could buy their freedom
was rooted in part in the scarcity of white wage workers, and in part in
medieval Spanish legal codes from a time when slaves were more likely
to be Moors than Africans. In any case it contributed to the growth in
Havana's numbers of free mulattos and blacks. So too did the gender
imbalance among Spanish settlers, which resulted in the male settlers coup-
ling first with indigenous women, and then with African slaves.

Generally speaking, the offspring of the Spanish-Indian unions were
legitimized, and frequently they were *blanqueado* (bleached), or considered white. The classic example is the progeny of one Anton Recio, whose
slaves raised cattle in various locations in the outskirts of the city and
who owned some urban lots as well. In 1567 he bought for 800 ducats
the office of depository general, otherwise known as "keeper of the box
with three keys." The office charged him with safekeeping of the funds
from tax collections and from the estates of those who died without heirs
on this side of the sea, for which service he was rewarded not only with
a commission of 2.5 percent but also with the privilege of investing the
funds in enterprises of his choosing. His will listed items valued at 20,000
ducats, including assets in livestock, land, buildings, and slaves, a gold-
handled sword and dagger, and a set of silver tableware. His son Juan, by
his Indian mistress, inherited his estate and—despite a protest by the rival
landowners and officeholders of the de Rojas family—the job of keeper
of escrow funds as well.

The offspring of African-Spanish unions, often the only children of
their fathers, were frequently granted their freedom, or allowed to buy

it at least. Of Havana slaves who obtained their freedom at young age in this period, the records show a majority being described as mulatto. One Spaniard who purchased the freedom of a mulatto slave in 1604 said he did so to serve God and because the slave's father was "an honorable man and my friend." This seems to have been particularly true of girls. A survey of documents from the seventeenth and early eighteenth centuries shows that female slaves were more likely to be granted their freedom either for services rendered or at the time of the owner's death. The survey also shows that slave women were more likely than men to buy their freedom, and generally this too at an earlier age.

One way or another, by the seventeenth century, the free blacks and mulattos began to be of considerable numbers, and they—some of them owning a few slaves themselves—worked not only as laborers, laundresses, prostitutes, and street vendors, but also as skilled artisans, small merchants, and operators of established inns and taverns. They had their own religious fraternities that marched in the city's religious processions, and as of 1638 they had a church, the Church of the Holy Spirit, which (after much remodeling) is the oldest in Havana today. Town council minutes began to complain of blacks and mulattos dressing in vibrant colors too rich for their station and blood.

One further testimony to their rise, dating from the end of this period, is the will of Doña Lorenza de Carvajal, who in 1700 left her single-story adobe house facing the moat of the Real Fuerza to her former house slave, the mulatta Juana Carvajal "for the care and friendship with which she has attended me." Juana had already been granted her freedom under the condition that she should continue in service until her mistress's death. She inherited enough money from Doña Lorenza that she soon set about improving the house, where she lived for the next thirty-three years, remodeling it and adding a second story much as white families were starting to do to theirs. She in turn left the house to her two nieces, Margarita and Mónica de Ribera, one of whom lived in a smaller building next door, while a mulatto carpenter named Lúcas Gómez lived on the other side. The nieces sold Juana's house, presumably at some profit, to Don Pedro José Calvo de la Puerta, who was buying up property on the block. Don Pedro was the great-grandson of the Don Martín Calvo of two-sword, two-dagger, and musket fame.

All the same, city ordinances continued the longstanding practice of listing separate penalties according to race. Where a white resident might have to pay a fine, those from "other spheres" received physical punishment: lashes, confinement in stocks, or worse. Colored bakers of *casabe* could have their earthenware grilles smashed or confiscated if they could not name a white landowner they had bought the yuca from.

Across the moat from Juana Carvajal, at the pinnacle of Havana society, the governors enjoyed the distinction, views, and breezes of Real Fuerza's upper story. They were transients in Havana, generally career Spanish military men awarded the post as a plum. Pedro de Valdés, governor and captain general from 1602 to 1607,[1] was a former naval commander who had led several Indies fleets and skippered a prominent warship in the ill-fated Spanish Armada of 1588. He'd been captured in the English Channel by Francis Drake, of whom Valdés later testified that his "valour and felicity was so great that Mars and Neptune seemed to attend him in his attempts." Ransomed from his English captivity, Valdés returned to the King's service and was later awarded the Cuban governorship, which came with attendant luxuries: a budget of 3000 gold pesos for wardrobe, other personal effects, and tableware, plus three house slaves and fourteen paid servant staff. Those 3000 pesos would have bought the captain-general more than his share of the silks and velvets, the fine linens and taffetas, the contrasting emerald greens, blacks, pinks, and yellows preferred by the upper crust. No wonder that an early visitor wrote of the "birds of brilliant plumage" who emerged from the city's "rudely crafted nests." Valdés left ample record of the rivalries for social position that grew up between governors, fort commanders, and local officials. At the base of such disputes was always money: who had the authority to inspect incoming ships for both taxable goods and contraband, with the opportunities for control of public funds and private payoffs that this implied. The conflict flared most visibly, however, over small symbols of precedence such as who sat where in ceremonial occasions, or who got to ease his bones with a pillow while sitting on the hard benches or sarcophagi in the church. As the old sea dog Valdés reported to the King:

> I ordered a velvet cushion taken away from Juan de Villaverde, captain of the Morro, and it came about in this way: Villaverde decided to carry publicly and in my presence a formal staff with insignia of general, the same as I carry in this city in your name. Besides, he took to carrying a velvet cushion into church and sat at my side with both staff and cushion as if there were no difference between us. Though I warned him not to do this, so as not to fall into an act of rebellion, he did it again and so I had the cushion taken from him.

In another letter to the King, Valdés spoke about his own unpopularity with the colonists. He attributed that problem to his insistence that the *naturales* (natives) treat him with the deference that his superior standing deserved. This is the first instance in the Archives of the Indies in which a Spanish official uses such a term to apply to Cubans of European origin. It was a sign of a gap that would loom larger and larger from then on.

Meanwhile, the city grew slowly, and began to cover its roughness with some signs of grace. Where Valdés had needed to parade in his finery on horseback or slave-carried sedan chair over the muddy streets, in the 1620s governor Lorenzo de Cabrera lurched through the streets in the city's first carriage, along with his relative Don Juan de Benavides, a general of the fleet. Atop the Real Fuerza, ten years later, was built a slender and largely ornamental watchtower, giving the utilitarian fort a fairy-tale castle touch. The tower was topped by a weathervane cast in bronze, the nearly life-sized figure of a woman holding the military cross of Calatrava in one hand and an olive branch in the other and gazing (when the wind was right) out to sea. This figure became known as La Giraldilla, the little sister to the larger-than-life female figure which topped La Giralda, the 300 foot high bell tower of the Cathedral of Seville. But once again differences between Spaniards and *naturales* appeared. La Giralda's weathervane is a representation of the Catholic faith, a demure if triumphant figure, standing straight upright, decorously cloaked, with head bowed. La Giraldilla stands with her hand on her hip, right knee bent as if in motion, her skirt hiked halfway up her right thigh and, in counterpoint, flying in the breeze behind her left foot. She wears a form-fitting top, she is crowned with a tiara, and her chin tilts proudly up into the air. La Giraldilla became and remains as much a symbol of Havana as the Morro Castle. Whatever the intent of her sculptor (a local craftsman by the name of Martín de Pinzón), Havana legend soon had her depicting Doña Isabel de Bobadilla, the wife and deputy of Hernando de Soto, gazing seaward for a glimpse of his long-delayed return.

Little by little, Havana and its environs produced more than just victuals for troops and passing ships. Cannons for the forts were cast in a short-lived foundry alongside the bay, between La Punta and the town, where now stands a children's playground behind Tsunenaga's monument, called "La Maestranza" (armory) in recognition of that fact. In the wake of the foundry came shipyards, built further south along the bay near the Alameda de Paula, which used Cuban hardwoods to turn out frigates and galleons and cargo ships for the protection of the coasts, the pursuit of pirates and smugglers, and the annual Indies fleet. The forest of ebony, mahogany, cedar, and oak that had surrounded the city disappeared into ships and the holds of ships, until there were no trees fit for cutting within a twelve mile radius of the city, and the shipbuilders began to feud with the cattle ranchers over who had the right to exploit the forests further out. Tobacco cultivation began (adopted from the native Tainos and Sibonneys) as did construction of small mills to grind the dried tobacco into snuff. Production of sugar began in a minor way, encouraged in part by construction of the *zanja,* whose current south and west of the city was enough to power primitive mills. Among the first in the sugar business were the Recio family, the descendants of Antón, who established their small plantation in the town of Regla across the bay.

Though Havana would never be a city of great cathedrals, ten churches and convents had been built or begun by the end of the seventeenth century. The pealing of their bells now added to the chants of stevedores and food vendors, the appeals of streetwalkers and taunts of sailors, the rolling of dice and drilling of troops, and the signal cannon shots from the Morro to announce the comings and goings of ships. Two hospitals (one of them for soldiers) also operated under the auspices of the church.

Religious festivals, royal births, and other important occasions were marked with processions and masquerades, parades including candles and lanterns, artillery barrages from ships and shore, floats with music and dancing, jousting, and running of bulls. Town council records detail spending for "inventions" for such celebrations, which include giants, dragons, monkeys, midgets, and Moors, and complain of women mixing too freely in processions and entertainments of this type. Of popular music in the city at this date, nothing reliable is known. Still, it must have been in these first centuries that Spanish ballads and guitar strings learned to live in creative tension with African drums and call-and-response, and that Havana made its first great contribution to Cuba's polyrhythmic, Afro-Euro-Caribbean musical instrumentation: the *claves*, the rhythm sticks derived from the pegs of wooden sailing ships.

The city suffered the growing pangs of all early modern cities: a fire of 1622 destroyed nearly a hundred houses, and a plague that lasted from May to October of 1649, probably yellow fever, carried off as many as one third of the residents, according to one report. The population in 1660, according to a census, totaled 8000, which was one third of that of the island as a whole. In the 1670s began the last of the military constructions of this period, the erection of a wall around the landward boundaries of the city. Every night and every morning, a cannon blast from one of the warships in the harbor signaled the closing and opening of the gates, and the drawing up or lowering down of the chain strung between the forts at the neck of the bay.

The Italian traveler Giovanni Gemelli Careri, in the chronicle of his round the world voyage, has left us the first extensive description of the Cuban capital, where he stayed for two-and-a-half months during the winter of 1698, waiting for a fleet to leave in the spring. He describes a compact, round, walled city a mile and a half in circumference, of mostly single-story houses, populated by "beautiful women and agreeable looking men." He reports a high cost of living, especially when the fleets are in, with wheat bread available for those who can pay the high price of imported flour, and *casabe* eaten not only by the poor, but also by the "extensive families" among the well to do. The workforce is, to his eye, entirely slave, rented out at four *reales* a day, or six when the fleet is in, and he is interested by a large group of blacks and mulattos preparing for a procession in carnival.

Gemelli Careri's social visits while in Havana are mostly with travelers—Flemish noblewomen returning home from South America as rich widows, or university graduates from Peru looking to buy themselves royal posts in Madrid. By contrast, what interests him in Havana itself (devoid, still, of university or nobility) are the tropical fruits brought in from outlying farms—he encounters, for the first time, the *guanabana* and the *caimito*—and the exotic birds that may be hunted or collected, from parrots to hummingbirds, as well as a shipload of cardinals which has just arrived from Florida. He notes how the sailors of the fleet, who have just been paid their back salaries, rush to invest in these strange red birds.

When the fleet finally sails, Gemelli Careri travels on the lead galleon, which fires six ceremonial cannonades when it passes the Real Fuerza, which are answered by the guns of the fort, and six more when it passes the Morro, answered in the same way. After the warship clears the channel, there is a surprising discovery on board—a woman dressed as a man. As it is too late to turn back, she is lodged among the women, whoever she is, and Havana, why ever she is leaving it, is left behind. But not all the travelers have departed. Despite stern commands that all members of the fleet must leave with their ships, on pain of death, a sizeable number of sailors are missing, having jumped ship after receiving their pay. The Key to the Indies must be more attractive to them than Spain.

2 The Hour of the Mameys

Around the year 1740, Brook Watson, a fourteen-year-old orphan apprenticed to a Boston merchant, had the luck or misfortune to descend from
his ship for a swim in Havana Bay to escape the oppressive and unaccus-
tomed heat while accompanying some cargo of his master's. There he was
attacked by a shark, which took off his leg before he could be rescued.
Years later, as a successful London businessman, he told the story to the
American portraitist John Singleton Copley. The painter responded with
the first famous American vision of Havana. In Copley's canvas *Watson
and the Shark*, the shores of the bay are framed by tall convent towers and
the unmistakable bulk of the Morro Castle, and ringed by a forest of three-
masted ships. At the center of the painting a naked, pale-skinned youth
flails on his back among wind-whipped green swells, while an immense
open-jawed shark twice his size, staring out of one cold baleful eye, closes
in for the kill. A white officer in knee-britches jabs a spear in the shark's
direction. A black sailor, next to him, tosses the desperate youth a rope.

Copley had never seen Havana (or, quite possibly, a shark) but by this
time engravings of the city were in wide circulation in England and its
trading partners, because in 1762–63, between the moment of Watson's
boyhood adventure and Copley's stay in London during the American
Revolution, there passed a ten-month period when Havana was a British
possession. The Taking of Havana by the English, as this event is always
called in Cuba, provided Anglo-Saxon eyes and boots with their first large-
scale exposure to a city that would continue to draw them forever more.
Equally important, it provided Havana with new realities and new myths

that would define Cuban nationality, and it set a contradictory pattern for relations with foreign powers and foreign peoples in the times to come.

The reasons for the British attack, in the last year of the great-power conflict known as the Seven Years' War, were mixed. Above all, to British imperial and military planners in London, Havana was still the center of Spanish military control in the Caribbean and by extension in Spain's entire American realm. The English increasingly disputed control of the Caribbean, undermining Spain's monopoly on settlement and trade. In the seventeenth century, Britain had begun colonizing small islands unoccupied by the Spanish, and a British naval expedition had succeeded in wresting Jamaica from Spain. But Havana, boasting at least thirty thousand residents, remained the most important port in the Americas, ranking in both population and riches behind only Lima and Mexico. In 1762, it was significantly larger than Philadelphia and about three times the size of New York. Besides strategic goals, the lure of booty from the city and its transient cargoes beckoned the British military as strongly as it had tempted Francis Drake.

To merchants in England and its North American colonies, meanwhile, Havana meant a market in which to sell slaves, textiles, and machinery, and from which to buy the products of industries still in their infancy in Cuba, but of growing importance to European and colonial tastes. Molasses refined from West Indian sugar cane was crucial to the rum distilleries of New England, and the outskirts of Havana by now contained about a hundred small plantations with primitive mills. Tobacco was likewise being produced and ground into snuff, but its export from Cuba was strictly controlled by a royal monopoly conceded only to merchants of the port of Cádiz in Spain. Contraband trade between Cuba and the British Empire was an established tradition, but it was mostly limited to remote coastal areas of the countryside, outside of strict Spanish control. Regla, the small harbor across the bay from Havana that housed the patron saint of sailors, also had a longstanding reputation as a smuggler's haven. Perhaps the ship carrying Brook Watson had been making a quiet visit there.

For both strategic and commercial reasons, then, in 1762 secret plans were drawn up for a naval force of unprecedented size—some two hundred ships and twenty thousand men—to converge on Havana from Britain, Jamaica, and New England. A seventeen-year-old Connecticut volunteer named Levi Redfield enlisted with the hopes of defending his homeland from the French, and of marching through Vermont to Lake Champlain "over a fertile country, the whole of which I had long wished to view." He found instead that he had "left the peaceful abode of my childhood, and commenced a scene of troubles that I had never anticipated." He was shipped to New York, where the troops were confined to their ships for fear of desertion until the fleet set sail for Havana. Though weather, sea battles, and the grounding of some ships delayed the arrival of Redfield and the 4000 regular and provincial troops departing from New York, still on June 6, 1762, the rest of the invasion fleet of 50 warships, 100 or more transports, and 15,000 soldiers, sailors, and slave laborers appeared off Havana, to the consternation of the Spanish governor who had scoffed at rumors of their approach.

Rather than attempt to force entrance to the harbor past the cannons of the Morro and Punta and through their connecting barrier chain, the British chose to land thousands of their troops some miles to the east of the bay, just beyond the fortress at the outlying harbor of Cojímar, which they bombarded until its defenders fled. Cojímar was the same small anchorage where an American writer two centuries later would moor his motor launch, drink, talk with Cuban fishermen, and set his last novel, *The Old Man and the Sea.*

The invading troops encamped on the empty stretch of coast beyond Cojímar, where residents of the housing development of Alamar (to which we will return in the 1970s) today go to swim. Then they made their way overland to the heights of La Cabaña, a ridge overlooking the bay, which the governor and captain-general Juan de Prado Portocarrero had begun to fortify too late. On these heights, the English set up a gun battery to threaten the Morro Castle from the landward side.

There followed two months of siege, cannon duels from ships and shore, and bloody skirmishes bringing heavy loss of life on both sides. A British cannonball exploded alongside a powder magazine near where the art-deco Bacardi building stands today. By some miracle the powder depot did not ignite, but the street was called for many years Calle de la Bomba in commemoration of this narrow escape (it is now the western end of Calle San Juan de Dios), and a nearby market was called The Powderhouse (El Polvorín). Thousands of civilians, including the nuns from the convents and many other women, were evacuated from the city; so were great quantities of the prominent families' cash. Male slaves, on the other hand, were brought in from surrounding farms and mills to participate in the defense.

The British made a second landing, to the west of the city at the mouth of La Chorrera, after cannonading the squat, square fortress there into submission. The British then occupied the rugged coral seacoast between La Chorrera and the city. Inland, they diverted the waters of the Royal Ditch into the Bay and attempted to cut the walled city off from the countryside, reinforcements, and supplies.

Responsibility for feeding the beleaguered populace fell to the city's hereditary chief magistrate, Pedro José Calvo de la Puerta, whose townhouse was the former dwelling of the ex-slave Juana de Carvajal, now much expanded by combination with other properties on the same block. Don Pedro's office carried the duty of regulating the slaughterhouse and meat distribution, previously a lucrative task compensated with a fee called the "right of the knifethrust," three silver *reales* for every slaughtered cow. As the siege tightened, food became scarce. Spanish authorities issued an order instructing citizens to throw all their dogs into the sea, so as not to compete for scarce supplies.

While the British overwhelmed Spanish troops and the local white, mulatto, and black militia units in conventional fighting, some of the militias turned to guerrilla warfare under independently operating chiefs, in the same spirit that had animated the settlers who counterattacked the French pirate occupiers of two centuries before. These guerrillas inflicted new casualties, took prisoners, and threatened the supply lines of British forward troops. The most famous was the group from Guanabacoa led by the mayor of that village, José Antonio Gómez de Boullones. Relieved of his command and confined to the defensive encampment on the hill of Jesús del Monte by a jealous Spanish colonel, Gómez de Boullones died before the end of the siege. Some versions have him perishing of apoplexy, others of melancholy, others of exhaustion after his feats. All record that he became a hero, the nascent nation's very first one, who has passed into Havana legend under his nickname Pepe Antonio, no last name required.[1]

Still more damaging to the English were the effects of another native enemy—tropical fevers. Given the exposure to midday sun and evening mosquitoes, the lack of fresh water in the trenches, and the effect of guerrilla action on food supplies, illness took such a toll that the majority of the besieging troops were out of action much of the time. The result of the massive expedition hung in doubt.

Finally, the New England contingent arrived, including both the regular army units and the 2000 provincial volunteers from New York, Rhode Island, Connecticut, and New Jersey, including Levi Redfield, the seventeen-year-old who had hoped to march through Vermont toward Canada and fight against the French. These reinforcements, coupled with the efforts of sappers who at last succeeded in blowing up a section of the Morro's seaward wall, allowed the English to storm the castle. They were then able to reduce La Punta fortress to submission with the Morro's guns. Twelve days later, Spanish authorities surrendered the city, and the British occupiers marched in. The prize yielded the victors a booty of some 3 million British pounds in funds from the royal treasury, goods and cargoes belonging to Spanish merchants, Spanish naval ships and supplies, and reparation levies extracted from the civilian elite and the church. Terms of the capitulation allowed Spanish troops to be repatriated and city authorities to administer local affairs after swearing loyalty to George III. Local residents had four years to decide whether they would become British subjects or emigrate to Spain.

"I walked over the hill a way to see the fighting and there was a very grand affair to be seen," reports the journal of Roswell Park of Preston, Connecticut, who like Redfield arrived in the siege's final days. "The city of Hivanna with all its fine buildings, churches, nunneries, the great battery, the governor's fort in town, the many batteries round the famous place for to bait the bull for diversion. There was the finest land to look to I ever saw. Coconut trees, cabbage trees [palms], canaries, grapes, the cattle, the ass, the mule." He did not get to see much more. On August 13, he records the capitulation, and on August 16, his journal ends. He took sick, his wife's postscript to his diary says, and "was buried at the Havannah where they made a burying place to bury those who died there." Deaths on the Spanish side may have reached 2000, though some reports say less. British losses totaled about 5000, the great majority from disease.

There are few surviving testimonies from Havana residents, but these few show how the defense, capture, and occupation of the city heightened the distinction between Spaniards and *naturales*. Only eleven days after the English victory appeared a memorandum, addressed to the Spanish king Carlos III, signed by the "*señoras de La Habana*." In this letter, the ladies of Havana's aristocracy recount the events of the attack and siege, accusing the captain-general and his top aides of having intended the city's surrender all along. They cite the Spanish commanders' refusal to use guerrilla tactics to stop the British advance through unfamiliar territory; their having failed to either fortify La Cabaña hill or clear it of anything providing shelter for the English; their abandoning that height without an organized defense; their sinking three warships in the mouth of the harbor to prevent a British entry which had the result of keeping all the rest of the King's navy bottled up inside; their holing up within the walls of the city rather than risking their lives in an attempt to relieve the Morro; their failing to recognize the importance of the English preparations to mine the castle; and, finally, their deciding on the capitulation of the city without consulting the city council, citizens, or bishop.

In contrast, the letter lauds guerrilla leader Pepe Antonio and also Luis de Aguiar, a city councilor who defended La Chorrera fortress and harried the English gun emplacements and supply lines thereafter. It takes pains, more surprisingly, to remember "a large number of slaves, released by us their owners" who mounted cannon and other defenses, as well the members of a free mulatto militia unit who, without pay, did attempt to fortify La Cabaña, and a contingent of twenty black militiamen who sallied forth from the Morro to attack the British with machetes in hand. It further takes to task, in a generalized denunciation, the "despotism of the governors of these parts of the Indies who, when any of your vassals take the legitimate measure of complaining to your Majesty or making you aware of any important news, trample upon them and close all doors by use of the word *sedition*."

Most historians attribute the composition of this remarkable letter—indeed seditious of contemporary authority and ideology, if brimming with declared loyalty to the King—to the Marquesa Beatriz de Jústiz y Zayas, then twenty-nine years old. The marquesa's family was typical of Havana's new aristocracy. Her mother came from a landed Cuban family, while her father was a Spanish colonel and former fort commander. She had married a Havana-born city councilor, treasury official, and possessor of one of the first titles of nobility to be sold to rich Cubans by the Spanish crown. The Jústiz house was one of the city's finest, representative of Havana's growing prosperity as its production of ships, sugar, and tobacco slowly increased. Close to the sea by the Plaza de Armas, the mansion boasted a Moorish-style watchtower that rose four stories above the street. Not limiting herself to the Memorial, the Marquesa de Jústiz wrote and published (again anonymously) a poem likewise addressed to the King. "A Sorrowful Metrical Expression of the Siege and Surrender of Havana" echoes many of the same criticisms and praises, while glossing them with biblical references, baroque verbal dexterity, and lamentations as to the fate of city and its ships. In particular, Jústiz y Zayas singles out the valor of the *paysanage* (native-born civilians) "who drew their first breath in this land, and gave it their last." She contrasts them with the "hardened commanders" who "closed their ears" to all entreaty for action. The poem also sets a pattern for later patriotic images of a female Havana or Cuba resisting a male threat from the north.

> If to close the port
> they sacrificed those ships
> that was no difficult birth
> but miscarriage and mistake.
> For it left the passage open,
> that trinity poorly placed,
> and brought insult to the Port

> whose splendor feels with deep pain
> the danger of being forced.

One of the first acts of the new English governor Lord Albemarle (or "*el Milor*" as he was styled by the Havanans in one of their earliest adoptions of English words) was to invite the ladies of the aristocracy to a series of dances, "but the majority replied that they had not shed tears to then entertain themselves in diversions, and few attended." So reported a Jesuit priest in a letter to his superior in Seville, one of the few surviving views of the occupation from the Havana side. The priest added that the governor "repeated his invitation for a second night, extending the invitation and his compliments in visits to their houses, so that many attended, not being able to excuse themselves, but their displeasure could be read in their faces and the invitations ceased." In the meantime, according to popular tradition, during the first days the humbler classes took their revenge by selling the occupiers a lethal combination of bananas (previously unknown to the English) and the rough cane liquor called *aguardiente*, which made them heavily sick. *Habaneros* lampooned the British troops, who patrolled the city in their red uniform coats and black pants, by calling them *mameyes*, a Cuban fruit with bright red pulp and long black seed.

The disdain was apparently mutual in those early days. "The better sort of people," haughtily observed Joseph Gorham, a regular-duty officer from Cape Cod, "[are] courteous and civil, but seemingly indolent, fond of rich and gaudy furniture and apparel. The common people are a low, cunning, deceitful, false and thieving set, the Spanish joined indiscriminately in marriage with Negroes, mulattos, etc., which produces as bad a mongrel crew, perhaps as any on Earth." The mixing of races got a more bemused—if confused—response from Levi Redfield. He reported that the Hispanic whites were themselves "of tawny complexion," that the free white and black inhabitants "enjoy the same liberty and equality" and that "many white gentlemen, of considerable respectability among the Spaniards, are seen to walk the streets with their sweet black wenches by their sides, perhaps each leading a lusty copper colored infant *sans culotte* by the hand."

Be that as it may, the confusion surrounding the city's capitulation was the signal for numbers of enslaved Africans to escape to the countryside—fleeing their old masters or the threat of worse treatment by the occupiers, or both. The city council promptly commissioned nineteen entrepreneurs "able, of good reputation, and white," to hunt them down, along with any livestock that they had taken, for a fee of ten pesos per slave and five per mule or horse. The council specified that those to be retrieved did not include the hundred or so who had been promised freedom during the siege by then-governor Prado for taking up arms against the English, an action which Prado told the king he had taken to prevent the English from making the same promise first. In fact, some of the newly appointed slave hunters did set about capturing and selling free blacks, while other hunters were themselves taken prisoner by Spanish authorities in parts of the island outside English jurisdiction, who accused them of having collaborated with the enemy.

As time wore on, relations between English and Cubans seem to have changed. The city remained under occupation, with cannon removed from ships and batteries commanding the streets and squares, but the majority of troops from both sides boarded ships for home. Some among the elite retired to their country estates, but others who had evacuated from the city now returned, and they brought their hidden cash.

Two members of the local aristocracy—both of them sugar planters and city officials—served as lieutenant governors under Lord Albemarle. One was Sebastian de Peñalver, descended from a royal treasurer and tax collector, who had recently added a gracious arcaded gallery to provide relief from the sun outside his mansion on what was then still called the Plaza of the Swamp, terminus of the Royal Ditch. (Under the name Palacio de los Marqueses de Aguas Claras, housing the restaurant El Patio, it now looks out on the Plaza de la Catedral.) The other was Gonzalo Recio de Oquendo, great-great-great-great-grandson of an indigenous woman and Anton Recio, the "keeper of the box with three keys." Peñalver acquired the nickname *el inglesito* for his alleged subservience to Albemarle, but he was not alone in seeing what opportunities this new fleet and garrison might offer. As in times past, repeated prohibitions (from both local authorities and *el Milor*) on sales of wine or *aguardiente* to the British troops by tavern keepers or itinerant vendors testify to a practice that must have been widespread. Social barriers broke down, too. Two young women who defied their fathers and sought to elope with English soldiers were discovered hiding in empty barrels onboard departing ships, giving rise to a ditty, probably invented by Spanish sailors, that said:

> The girls of Havana
> have lost the fear of God,
> for they go off with the English
> in casks for salt cod.[2]

Cuban scholar Luisa Campuzano has observed that such couplets may have been a form of Spanish revenge on the female authors of the critical memorandum and the "Metrical Expression" for their temerity. That the blame for fraternization was unfairly placed on women, however, does not mean the fraternization wasn't real. The Jesuit (who, being of Irish origin, had his own bones to pick with the English) complained in his letter about the familiarity and courtesy offered to the English officers in many houses, including houses of some distinction, adding "I don't know where this would have led if our captivity had lasted some years more."

Some of that temptation to mix with the English must have had to do with novelty, with Havana's eternal port-town capacity to investigate and assimilate the new. More important were the economic opportunities, as the Jesuit's letter also maintains:

> Though in the beginning there were many who wanted
> to be the first to embark themselves and their goods
> back to Spain, and it seemed that many reams would be
> needed for the paperwork, I believe that after four years
> a handful of sheets would have sufficed—not owing to
> the attraction of English customs, but for the quantities
> of food, clothing, economic opportunities and other
> goods that from these countries flow.

Concretely, what happened during the British occupation was that Spanish monopolies were eliminated at a single stroke, as were the high taxes levied in Spain on goods headed for Havana. So too, at least by Albemarle's official edict, was the past practice of bribing local officials as a regular cost of doing business. Trade with England, the British West Indies, and North America was brisk. Reports from the time claim that close to a thousand commercial trading ships entered or left the port of Havana during the ten months of British control, whereas the quantity previously arriving for the purpose of trade with Cuba itself had been ten or twelve a year at most. Allowing for some exaggeration, and the fact that many ships came primarily to remove troops and captured supplies, still the change is evident.

Merchants descended on Havana from London, Liverpool, Kingston, New York, Boston, and Philadelphia. "Ourselves have great reason to rejoice," exulted the preacher Samuel Frink of Shrewsbury, Massachusetts, in a sermon of thanksgiving when news of the opening of Havana arrived. "That Englishmen should some time or other walk as freely about the city as Spaniards," he said, was an old prophecy fulfilled. "In every street, two or more warehouses have sprung up," wrote the Marqués de Jústiz y Santa Ana, husband of the poet, in a letter to the Spanish ex-governor (with whom he seems to have been on more cordial terms than the Marquesa was). His family had limited itself to buying some ceramics, he claimed, but the English had "infested us with all of their clothing and other goods." Grains, flour, wool, linen, and machinery all came in the holds of the merchant vessels.

"There was sufficient demand for everything brought to market from Europe or America," Albemarle later claimed, "the Spaniards [Havanans] having been glad to buy the goods as fast as they could, finding them much cheaper" than before. Some other testimonies disagree, claiming that Havana did not yet have sufficient purchasing power to buy everything that arrived on the boats. Lt. Governor Peñalver, among others, was involved in a scheme to re-export English goods to Veracruz. It was during the occupation, or shortly after, that Pedro José Calvo de la Puerta hired a muralist to decorate the walls of his house, a fashion that spread as the wealth of the city's aristocracy grew. The unknown artist, probably self-trained, painted colorful images of Havana—complete with aristocrats, house slaves, and English soldiers—as well as European cities and country scenes. Archeologists date the mural to the time of the occupation both from their study of the materials used and from the breadth of information to which the artist apparently had access.

In exchange for what they sold in Havana, the English and North American merchants took out cash, sugar, tobacco, and IOUs—the last of which would give them trading privileges even after the occupation came to an end. *Habaneros* voyaged to North American ports with some of these cargoes, establishing new commercial relationships that would last, and glimpsing markets that could someday be theirs to enjoy.

Historians argue as to whether there was actually a boom in sugar production during this ten-month period, or merely an image of what that boom might be. They agree, however, that the opportunity for trade with England and its possessions brought Cuban sugar planters what they most urgently needed if they were to expand production to compete with the large estates of the French and British islands which had dominated the market so far. Planters needed modern machinery, and they needed many more laborers to feed that machinery with firewood and sugar cane. The British commerce brought the machinery, but most especially and tragically, it brought slaves.

The chief merchant accompanying and supplying the English fleet was also a leading slaver, Thomas Kennion of Jamaica and Liverpool. Kennion brought in shiploads of Africans himself and also acted as authorized reseller for others in the trade. Thousands of Africans were brought in chains from Jamaica, Africa itself, and possibly the Carolinas. More entered during this brief period—and were sold at lower prices—than in the previous several years or even decade of Spanish rule. The English began to import the flood of slaves that the Spanish monopoly had been unable or afraid to introduce.

Writing thirty years later, Francisco de Arango y Parreño, the foremost Cuban economist and planter-ideologue of his day, declared the period of British domination "the true epoch of the resurrection of Havana."

Arango, an in-law of the Calvos de la Puerta and the great-grandson of yet another Spaniard who had arrived as tax collector for the King, was born two years after the occupation but wrote about it as if he had been there. "The tragic event of its surrender to the English," he declared, "gave [the city] life in two ways: the first was the considerable riches, with the great proportion of Negroes, machinery, and textiles which one year of commerce with Great Britain rained down; the second was demonstrating to our court [in Spain] the importance of this city and calling forth all its attention and care."

All its attention and care, because Havana did not remain English for long. On the worldwide chessboard of imperial conflict that reached from Manila to the Mississippi, the Cuban capital turned out to be a pawn. In December of 1762, Benjamin Franklin opined, "The taking of the Havannah is a conquest of the greatest importance and will doubtless contribute a due share of weight in procuring us a reasonable terms of peace, if John Bull does not get drunk with victory, double his fists, and bid all the world kiss his Arse." Though a faction in the British Parliament and in North America wanted to hold onto Havana, majority opinion in both places had other priorities—as did sugar planters in the British West Indies, who didn't want another English sugar island competing with them. The Treaty of Paris that ended the Seven Years' War gave Britain dominion over Canada and Florida, new navigation rights in the Caribbean, and new territories in India, Africa, and the Mediterranean. Havana went back to Spain, and with it came Louisiana (as compensation for other losses) from France.

But Spain relaxed its grip on Cuban commerce, preferring to lighten some regulations, especially on the slave trade, and to tax the increased proceeds instead. Over the next thirty-five years, 100,000 slaves entered the country, as compared to an estimated 60,000 between 1512 and 1763. In the three quarters of a century thereafter—between 1790 and 1865— something like 600,000 more Africans were brought to Cuba in chains. The sugar boom transformed the countryside and the capital, making the country a living hell for hundreds of thousands of enslaved men and women, and the city a repository for all the riches they produced. Two external events gave impetus to this transformation.

The first was the American Revolution, for as Franklin's remarks suggest, the divisions between North American colonials and England were growing even more rapidly than those between Havana and Madrid. Of the "English" who conquered Havana, Joseph Gorham of Cape Cod would fight for England and then emigrate to Canada whereas Levi Redfield of Connecticut would fight for the Thirteen Colonies and then settle down as a music teacher in Brattleboro, Vermont. Two future generals were also among the expeditionary force: Col. William Howe and Col. Israel Putnam, who thirteen years later commanded the two opposing forces at the Battle of Bunker Hill. When this new conflict came, Spain again joined France in opposing England, throwing Havana open to unrestricted trade with the Thirteen Colonies and allowing the rebel navy and privateers to make use of the port.

Though support for the rebels was tentative in Spain, it was enthusiastic in Cuba—both for commercial reasons and to wipe out the taste of the English conquest. The Havana merchant and smuggler Juan de Miralles, who had been involved in the American trade since the English occupation if not before, became Spain's secret and then official ambassador to the Continental Congress. Traveling to the Carolinas, Virginia, Philadelphia, and George Washington's headquarters in New Jersey, he promoted the export from Havana of sugar, hides, coffee, and munitions, and the import of meat, fish, lumber, flour, and rice from the colonies. Over the next decades, European wars and treaties caused Madrid to turn the legal trade between North America and Cuba on and off like a faucet, but the process now under way could not be stopped. In 1798, for a prophetic moment, total trade between Cuba and the United States exceeded that between Cuba and Spain.

Though Juan de Miralles died at Washington's headquarters in 1780, he had created the network that made possible a crucial, if forgotten, piece of Cuban aid to the American revolt: a loan of 1.8 million pesos by Havana bankers, planters, and merchants to the Spanish crown to supply the Continental Army on the eve of the Battle of Yorktown, when the troops had gone for months without pay or supplies. When the French ship that was to carry the money docked in Havana in August of 1781, not all of the promised sum had been assembled. Once more "las señoras de La Habana" played their part in Anglo-Spanish-Cuban relations, at least according to a pamphlet published soon afterward by an officer in the French fleet. *Les dames d'Havane*, he says, pawned their jewels to contribute to the loan. Finally, when Spain formally entered the war and recaptured Florida from British hands, battalions of Havana's black and mulatto militia were sent as part of an expeditionary force to capture the Bahamas under Captain-General Juan Manuel de Cagigal—son of the previous governor Cagigal, who had erected the pillar to mark the site of the famous ceiba where the city had begun. Among those who served in that expedition (accompanied by a squadron of South Carolina privateers) was a different Pepe Antonio, a woodworker by the name of José Antonio Aponte, who lived in the working-class barrios that sprang up outside Old Havana's walls. We will meet Aponte again twenty years later—at the head of an island-wide abolitionist conspiracy involving free coloreds, whites, and slaves.

Aponte's place in history leads us to the other event that would, paradoxically, make nineteenth-century Havana the capital of the richest sugar plantation economy on the globe: the slave rebellion in the French colony of St. Domingue (Haiti), the world's largest producer of sugar in the late eighteenth century. The Haitian slaves' 1791 revolt against the inhuman French yoke, and the ten years of bitter warfare that followed, destroyed that island's sugar plantations and left a vacuum that Cuban producers quickly filled.

In the two centuries that followed, relations between Havana and its neighbors to the north would go through changes that would consign the events of 1762–63 to a very distant past. Albemarle's nickname *el Milor* would vanish from the capital's vocabulary, to be replaced by *el béisbol, el yanqui, la mafia, el high-laif, el bisnes, el Ford, el sánwich*, and *el show*. The pattern of the brief period of British influence—reinforcement of Cuban identity in contrast to that of Spaniard, resisting domination by a new foreign power yet welcoming what the foreigners might have to offer—would likewise reappear in bigger and more complex ways. But one linguistic residue has persisted from the time the Redcoats appeared outside Havana's walls and across its bay. To express "when push comes to shove," a Cuban will say *"a la hora de los mameyes"*—in the hour of the mameys.

3 Paris of the Antilles

In the Plaza de Armas, midway through March of 1828, the flower of Havana's society re-celebrated the city's founding in a new era. Seventy-four years had passed since Captain-General Cagigal erected his commemorative pillar and replanted the ceiba tree. This time, the celebration featured colorful banners, bunting, lanterns, and even a hot air balloon, but its centerpiece was a work of art. For the three hundred and ninth anniversary of the settlement alongside the Bay of Carenas, Spanish authorities had appropriated 10,000 pesos (and ended up spending twice that amount) for a small Grecian temple adorned inside with murals by the French-born painter Jean-Baptiste Vermay.

The painter was himself a sign of the times. Formerly of the court of Napoleon Bonaparte, the Frenchman had transplanted himself to Havana after Napoleon's fall, by way of Germany, Italy, and the United States. As Juan Bautista Vermay, he established the city's first art school, the Academia de San Alejandro, which still exists and is still turning out world-class artists today. He established a theater, the Diorama, so called because it doubled as a gallery displaying art works in a new, back-lit form. Inside El Templete, the commemorative Grecian temple, he painted two side murals depicting the legendary first mass and first council meeting. Then he painted a central one depicting the inauguration ceremony itself

In that painting, sober dress has replaced the "birds of brilliant plumage" of earlier times. Spanish officers in black boots, skintight white leggings, black coats, and gold braid stand on a carpet laid in front of the new monument, while their wives and daughters in black dresses and white lace mantillas sit on cushions, all observing the white-robed priests officiating a memorial mass. In the background, a mixed crowd including some blacks and mulattos press forward to look—some in dark frock coats, others just a sea of faces behind a fence. Vermay's wife is accompanied by a young slave nearly as well dressed as she. This is not the rough city of the treasure fleets. It's the rich and bustling commercial center of the nineteenth-century sugar boom.

By 1828, the painter's adopted home had literally burst through its walls. Half the 130,000 inhabitants now lived in new neighborhoods outside of the old earth-and-stonework defensive barrier, into which more and more gates had been punched to make way for the flow of goods from plantations and mills in the countryside. At the gates, gangs of slaves, still mostly African born, hefted hundred-pound boxes and three-hundred pound casks of sugar and molasses, transferring them from ox-drawn wagons to smaller mule-drawn carts that could negotiate the clogged, narrow streets, muddy or dusty in accordance with the seasons. Not only sugar passed through the gates, but also cured tobacco in great pressed sheaves wrapped in cowhide, and coffee in forty-pound bags. All of it was bound for storerooms in the city and then for the holds of the thousands of ships that dropped anchor in Havana Bay every year. Through the seven gates (soon to be nine) the cart-drivers also brought fruits from the countryside and meats from the slaughterhouse to feed the city's population, and load after load of green fodder to feed the oxen, mules, and horses that pulled not only the freight carts but the passenger chaises of the upper crust.

By the 1860s, the wall would be deemed an impediment to commerce. It and the adjacent land would be subdivided and put up for sale. Those who bought the parcels had to demolish each section of the wall at their own expense, and then they could build newer, and still more imposing buildings, to live in or to rent out. These buildings featured still more stories, columns, arcades, grand wooden doors, and wrought-iron balconies. Some of them may be seen along the Paseo del Prado today.

Even without a wall, the city did not cease to be a military stronghold. After recovering Havana from the British, Madrid had invested millions in new fortifications: La Cabaña, immense and sprawling, on the ridge across the bay; Atarés, on the hill commanding the southern end of the harbor; and El Príncipe, on another hill far to the west overlooking the Royal Ditch. Spain faced a new threat, however, when its American colonies began rebelling on their own. Between 1810 and 1824, most of the Spanish Empire in the New World crumbled. In 1824, high in the Peruvian Andes, the battle of Ayacucho brought to a close a cycle of continental independence struggles that established new nations from Tierra del Fuego to the Isthmus of Panama and in Mexico as well. In the face of such reverses, Havana became the stronghold from which the Cuban countryside and Puerto Rico could be kept secure, and the lost possessions might still be recovered via expeditions then being prepared.

The Spanish garrisons in Havana totaled 20,000 to 40,000 men during much of the nineteenth century. The inscribed bronze plaque mounted on the pediment of the commemorative Templete called the city, "Most Loyal Havana, Religious and Peaceful." Captain-General Francisco Dionisio Vives and Bishop Juan José Díaz Espada presided over El Templete's inauguration. *Fidelísima, religiosa, y pacífica* was certainly their wish. Of Vives, whose name happened to mean "you live," it was said in Havana, "*Vives como Vives, y vivirás.*" Live like Vives, and you'll be living well.

Havana's importance grew economically as well as militarily. After the Haitian revolution, Cuba replaced Haiti as the world's top producer of tropical products, most importantly sugar. Cuba likewise became the importer of everything that, in its fever to produce sugar, it could not or would not produce itself—from lumber to locomotives to salted beef and cod. Cobblestones came as ballast from New England and slaves came from Africa, abducted from the Yoruba, Carabalí, Congo, Arará and other nations. The great bulk of this commerce went through Havana, whose resident Spanish officials and merchants exacted their profit tax by tax, ship by ship, and bribe by bribe.

Over the years since the English occupation, the Plaza de Armas that El Templete now faced had been transformed. In place of the humble city church rose the Palace of the Captains-General, an imposing structure made of the porous local sea-formed limestone, plastered and painted, with an entranceway of imported Italian marble. Nine archways faced the plaza to form a long shaded arcade, and rows of open windows were guarded by ironwork imported from Bilbao. At right angles to the Palace stood the military and financial headquarters, topped with a terrace and a tower a stone's throw from La Giraldilla, the insouciant *habanera* crowning the Real Fuerza, who no longer dominated the skyline quite as much as she had before. On the third side of the square, equally palatial but lighter in design, bulk, and color, stood the arcaded home and business headquarters of the Count of Santovenia, a recently ennobled Cuban-born sugar planter, whose mansion was typical of those built by the elite during these boom years.

Titles of nobility, indeed, were to be found everywhere, sold to shore up the failing Spanish treasury and to buy Cuban planters' loyalty at the same time. Some resident Spaniards derided these native-born oligarchs as "sugar nobles," as if their titles might melt. But they could not deny that the Calvos de la Puerta had become the Counts of Buenavista, or that the Peñalvers and the Recios, despite collaborating with the English, had become the Marqueses of Casa Peñalver (granted to *el inglesito's* son), the Counts of Arcos (to his nephew), and the Counts of the Royal Proclamation (to Gonzalo Recio de Oquendo himself). The mansions of such sugar planters, imperial officials, and *nouveau riche* Spanish merchants combined aristocratic luxury with the new niches in global commerce that made it possible. Built around enclosed courtyards in the style inherited from Andalusia, they used much of the ground floor space as storehouses for products destined for the ships in the harbor or recently unloaded from them, though the ground floor might also house a billiard room, library, office space, or sitting room. Atop a large marble staircase, high-ceilinged galleries provided common space and opened onto function rooms up to forty feet long and private chambers beyond. Stained glass transoms, often in the shape of half-moons called *mediopuntos* that were divided into fan-shaped windows of rainbow colors, protected the occupants from the direct rays of the sun. Halfway up, a low mezzanine housed the domestic slaves, if they did not live in smaller, darker quarters crowded into an attic or hidden toward the back of the house.

"The construction of houses in Havana is very peculiar, and one must get accustomed to them to like it," reported Danish novelist Frederika

Bremer, one of the most astute of the many foreign visitors who have left us accounts of nineteenth-century Havana. She was writing about the smaller, but still comfortable, single-story home of a British businessman and family in which she stayed during her visit of 1851. "Everything is arranged so as to produce as much air and as much circulation as possible. Long galleries, with wide semicircular arcades, open into the court (this house has them on all four sides): in these galleries the whole household may be found, all busy, and leading a sort of public life; here dinner is eaten, visits are received, the lady of the house sews surrounded by her female slaves."

Indeed, most visitors, while complaining of the heat, smells, noise, dirty streets, and lack of sidewalks, were charmed by the appearance of the old city, low to the ground compared to others of Europe or North America. Nearly all the houses and shops were painted in pastel colors of yellow, orange, green, or blue to soften the reflection of the sun which, as an American visitor said, "makes each individual building and object stand out in its clear, liquid light." The fondest such description comes from the pen of María Mercedes de Santa Cruz y Montalvo, a daughter of the sugarocracy who had left the country as a teenager, married into the French nobility, and returned to visit in 1840 as the Countess of Merlín. In her first reencounter with her birthplace, Merlín outdoes Vermay by concisely taking note of all the classes that contribute to the city and its wealth, even as she idealizes the scene:

> Here comes the city, here it is, with its balconies, awnings, and rooftops, the delightful single-story houses of the middle class, the doors wide enough to admit a carriage and the tall grated windows, but everything open, everything open, so that one can see at a glance the details of domestic life—the patio strewn with flowers, the little girl's bed with crinoline curtains tied with pink-colored bows . . . Now we reach the docks, populated by a mixed multitude of mulattos and blacks, some in white pants, white jacket, and great straw hats, others in torn short trousers and a bright colored ban-

danna tied around their heads, others still with gray felt
hats pulled down over their eyes and a red sash tied
around the ribs, all of them sweating in the heat . . . We
see an infinity of barrels, boxes, bundles, carried in wagons pulled by mules and guided negligently by a black
man in shirtsleeves. Everywhere signs that proclaim coffee, sugar, vanilla, indigo, camphor, and cacao, and the
unceasing songs and shouts of those poor blacks who
can work only to that rhythm. Everyone in motion,
stirring, no one stops. The clarity of the air lends itself
to this racket, as does the brightness of the day, something sharp, that penetrates the pores and makes one
shiver. Everything here is life, lively and fiery, like the
sun showering its rays upon our heads.

Behind the growth and animation of the city lay the spiraling production of the plantations. This production moved farther from Havana, as
the lands of the first boom wore out and turned into towns and suburbs,
but the new concentration in Matanzas province was still relatively nearby.
Havana continued to be the primary residence of the mill and plantation
owners, who left day-to-day management to overseers or relatives, and it
was still the primary port. Sugar exports had risen from 10,000 tons a year
in the 1770s to 30,000 by the turn of the century, 300,000 in 1850, and
over 700,000 by 1868. Cuba's first railroad connected Havana to the plantation zones of Bejucal and Guines in 1837 and 1838, making Havana the
first city in the Spanish-speaking world to enjoy rail transportation, and
one of only a handful on the entire globe. When Spain's first seventeen
miles of railway opened in Barcelona, a decade later, Cuba already had
twenty-two times that much. Havana was linked with the new sugar boom
lands of interior Matanzas by steel and by steam.

Equally worthy of notice is the destination of what was shipped out.
By the late 1840s, the primary consumers of Cuban exports were first
the United States, then England, and then Spain. By the end of the next
decade, the value of exports to the United States more than tripled that of

exports to Spain, and imports from the United States had surpassed those from Spain as well. The first railroads were built under Cuban owner-ship and direction, with English investment capital, and with equipment and engineering from the United States. Other technologies did not lag far behind. The first steamboat docked in 1819, just twelve years after Robert Fulton's invention made its Hudson River debut, and regular ser-vice between Havana and Matanzas began that same year. The first steam-powered sugar mill went into operation then as well.

Gas lighting arrived inside the walls in 1844. It soon extended to the outer zones. A Cape Cod tourist described his late afternoon walk spent peeking into the brilliantly lit luxury homes of El Cerro, where "flowers spread a sweet perfume through the rooms, and gas flames make each face visible, even from the street, and every detail, every adornment stand out." The upper class had begun building these neoclassical suburban vil-las, which showed more American and French than Spanish influence, in the first third of the century. They were trying to get away from the noise and dirt and disease of the old city. This migration accelerated after the cholera epidemic of 1833, which carried off some nine thousand resi-dents including Juan Bautista Vermay. The Cuban families in El Cerro (those of the Count of Santovenia among them) were joined by English, Americans, and Germans as well.

Meanwhile the working class, especially free colored people, had been building small wood-and-thatch cabins, or stucco-and-tile-roof cottages if they could afford it, closer to the walls. These barrios—Jesús María, La Salud, Guadalupe, El Horcón, San Lázaro, and Colón—sprang up in what is today Centro Habana and a part of Habana Vieja, on lots sold off by landed families including the Peñalvers and Recios, land where some of the earliest sugar cane had been grown. Late in the century, as urbanization and disease encroached on Cerro, the elite began to move again. They built new villas, with seaside vistas and breezes, on the hill sloping upward from the oceanfront between the inner suburbs and the Almendares River. This river, formerly known as La Chorrera, was rechistened more mellifluously in honor of a departed bishop (actually named Almendariz).

This new luxury district took shape in the area long called El Vedado ("prohibited") because cutting trees there had been banned in early centuries to make it harder for invaders to attack the city from the west. In 1859, a horse-drawn streetcar line was established along what is today the busy Calle Línea. The streetcar ran from the broad new Paseo del Prado outside the walls to an isolated restaurant and swimming facilities by the old Chorrera fort.[1] In 1872, a short-line railway took its place. This railway featured a contraption generally called the Cucarachita (little cockroach) or the Maquinita de Vapor (little steam engine), which combined a steam engine and passenger benches in a single car. Slowly, the development of El Vedado progressed. At the top of its slope, in the 1870s, the church, crown, and municipal government followed suit by developing a vast city of the dead, named after Columbus, although the Admiral's supposed bones continued to rest in the Cathedral downtown. (They had been evacuated from Santo Domingo to Havana in 1795—and would be evacuated again, to Spain, in 1898.) The new "Necropolis de Colón," laid out along a quadrilateral grid of streets roughly a half mile on each side, gradually filled with sumptuous family vaults and mausoleums holding the remains of the rich. The remains of the poor were assembled in common repositories there as well. The living population of the city and its suburbs, meanwhile, had reached 200,000.

In short, a new Havana emerged, less centralized and more polarized, but exaggerating two tendencies already long in evidence: it was an even richer city, and an even more cosmopolitan one. A visit to Havana's museum of urban archeology—in the restored dwelling of Juana de Carvajal and Pedro Calvo de la Puerta, where the recently rediscovered murals may also be seen—reveals what the city's middle and upper classes consumed. The collections, dug up in the recent process of rehabilitating the old city, include roof tiles from France and Italy, glass beads from Venice, Dutch gin bottles, Leipzig perfumes, English cherry toothpaste, and ivory toothbrushes. Equally telling, there is an overwhelming variety of day-to-day personal care products from the United States, such as Scott's Emulsion, Swain's Panacea, Phillips Milk of Magnesia, and a Bakelite syringe by Goodyear for cleaning out the ears. Singer sewing machines began to be imported in the 1860s, and Remington typewriters in the 1880s.

Increasingly, travel between Havana and US cities grew easier, while direct links between Cuba and Spain dwindled. New Orleans was only two days away by steamship, and New York only five. By midcentury, there was even twice-weekly steamship service to Philadelphia and twice monthly to Baltimore, in addition to service to other cities. "The civilization of Havana and Cuba in general is a mixture imported from the neighboring country," the Colombian exile entrepreneur Nicolás Tanco noted in 1853. "This mixture is one of the most surprising things here, this contrast between the Spanish civilization that is disappearing little by little, and the modern American one that irresistibly invades." Tanco himself was in Havana to arrange the importation of Chinese contract laborers for railroads and plantations, which would eventually add another strain to Havana's bubbling mix. Excavations show that there were already shops run by Chinese and Arabic merchants, and the museum collection includes Chinese porcelains and stoneware holding the preserved pits of peaches imported centuries ago.

Steamboat from the U.S. entering Havana Bay, early 19th century, between fortresses of El Morro (left background), La Cabaña (right background), and La Punta (right foreground).

At the Café Dominica at the corner of O'Reilly and Mercaderes, close by the Plaza de Armas and famed for its marble fountain, iced drinks, and fruit desserts equal to the best in Paris, the menu proudly proclaimed that English, French, and German were all spoken inside. On the other side of town, men of affairs and the intelligentsia gathered for cigars and conversation at a café on the Prado pointedly named the "Louvre." The Café Louvre also offered an elegant attached bathhouse where they might soak. Havana became an obligatory stop for tourists and businessmen bound from Europe to either North or South America, from one America to the other, or en route to California or the Far East. Modern hotels sprang up to house them—the Inglaterra (England) on the Prado next to the Café Louvre, and Telégrafo, founded in 1860 on the Calle Amistad and relocated to the corner of Prado and Neptuno in 1888.

Even the former palace of the Counts of Santovenia on the Plaza de Armas was rented in the 1860s to Col. Louis Lay of New Orleans, who turned it into the luxurious Santa Isabel Hotel. Among other illustrious guests it housed the German archeologist Hermann Schliemann, discoverer of the buried ruins of Troy. In 1880, the Catalán businessman Ventura Trotcha built a restaurant-theater in the far-off, nearly empty, bucolic Vedado. The luxurious salon featured *mediopunto* windows and wrought-iron balconies, on top of which he added, ten years later, two stories of hotel rooms and suites. Legend places a famous affair between the actress Sara Bernhardt and a Spanish bullfighter in a room on the top floor of Trotcha's hideaway.

So it was that the capital of "The Pearl of the Antilles" gained a reputation as the "Paris of the Americas" too. The ladies of the aristocracy organized philharmonic societies, importing the leading musicians, ballet dancers, and opera companies of Europe. By the 1830s and 1840s, the Opera House on the waterfront and the Tacón Theater inland offered opera, dramatic, and dance performances a minimum of four times a week; Vermay's Diorama operated under new auspices as well. Don Francisco Marty, the proprietor of the Tacón, was a horse of a different color—a Catalán ex-pirate, slave trader, and (thanks to his friendship with governor Miguel de Tacón, Vives's iron-fisted successor after whom the theater was named) monopoly owner of the city's fish market and wharves. His theater, on the other side of the Café Louvre from where the Inglaterra would be built, held upwards of two thousand spectators and was famous for its wide stage and its immense chandelier, a modern gas-lit spider imported from the United States. Visitors frequently compared the Tacón (today the Sala García Lorca) to the leading theaters of Paris or London, or even to La Scala in Milan.

The Parque Central, with Tacón Theater at left and Hotel Inglaterra at right. This postcard was mailed in 1911 (the inscription points to "my room" in the hotel), but the view appears to be earlier. The statue in right foreground is either that of Queen Isabella (removed in 1899) or the short-lived imitation of the Statue of Liberty (see Chapter 7), not the later statue of José Martí.

Havana provided enough work, audience, and remuneration that some Italian singing stars settled in this welcoming environment once they had reached the twilight of their careers. Stars in their prime, meanwhile, added Havana to the itinerary of their American tours. In 1851, P.T. Barnum brought international sensation Jenny Lind to sing in Havana after her New Orleans appearance, and Lind was still there, completing her run of performances, when her friend Frederika Bremer arrived. The "Swedish Nightingale" took the Danish writer for a drive along the length of the Paseos Prado and Tacón. As Bremer described it:

> The magnificent promenade extends for certainly upward of three English miles between broad avenues of palm and other tropical trees, beds of flowers, marble statues and fountains, the finest promenade anyone can image, to say nothing of its being under the clear heaven of Cuba. The moon was in her first quarter, and floated like a little boat above the western horizon. The entire circle of the moon appeared unusually clear.

The well-traveled Nicolás Tanco said that the promenades of Havana "can well compete with the Champs Elysees or Bois de Boulogne."

These Paseos were the showplaces of white Havana society. Parading along them in a horse-drawn *volanta* (two-wheeled carriage) was a nightly rite for the titled aristocracy, the officialdom, and anyone else who could afford it, and a weekend necessity for all who had some pretension to status in the middle class. This ritual caught visitors' attention for two reasons: the carriages themselves (which occasioned as much comment and wonder as the 1950s American cars do today) and their role in the restricted lives of white females, especially those of marriageable age, as we shall see. "A sort of large insect, with immense hind legs and a long proboscis [like] some queer kind of daddy-long-legs," Frederika Bremer said of this uniquely Cuban invention, designed to avoid getting stuck in the mud of Old Havana's streets or the potholes, ditches and rocks of the roads beyond. The *volanta* had only two wheels, but these were immense, six or seven feet in diameter, and placed behind the body of the open, single-seat carriage itself. The carriage in turn rested on two long, springy iron shafts, attached at one end to the axle housing, and at the other to the harness of the horse or mule. This made the vehicles feel "so light and springy that they would scarcely crush the legs of a fly if their wheels passed over him," said an English traveler. They were driven by a uniformed black driver in high leather boots or gaiters, a bright red jacket, and long spurs, who rode mounted on the horse. The *volantas* for hire were not ornamented, but in the case of private ones, the richer the owner, the more likely the carriage, harness, and driver to be ornamented with silver fittings, silver spurs and buckles, and gold thread, often to the value of thousands of dollars' worth. In the streets of the old city, reported Richard Henry Dana, "in most *volantas* a gentleman is reclining, cigar in mouth; while in others, is a great puff of blue or pink muslin or cambric, extending over the sides to the shafts, topped off by a fan, with signs of a face behind it."

On the Paseos, however, the women were not hidden, but on display. Visitors were struck, there, by the *habaneras'* bare heads, arms, and hands, open necklines, adornment with flowers, and readiness to flirt. "A girl whose family can afford a *volanta* would rather stop eating than fail to show off her charms," Nicolás Tanco wrote, "and the concurrence at the six p.m. promenade surprises every foreigner, the whole length of four to six miles filled by a continuous belt of carriages and spectators on foot . . . When they must stop to avoid accidents, which is often, the line of onlookers gets a chance to direct their compliments to the young ladies, which are answered with gracious smiles or the electric telegraph of the fans." The Cuban women handled these fans with such dexterity, observed the English visitor Matilda Charlotte Houstoun acerbically, "that this seems to be one of the principal employments of their lives." The evening promenade in the *volanta*, she added, "is the grand event of every day; gossip then goes on at a great rate, every passer-by is scanned and scrutinized, appointments are made, and reputations are sneered away."

The flip side of this display of white *habaneras* on the marriage market was their restriction in other public spheres. They were not seen on foot or in stores, and in very few cafés. They traveled only in their *volantas* or smaller carriages called *quitrines*, sending their slaves into shops and cafés to make purchases, or to summon clerks or waiters out to deliver housewares or fruit juices or ice cream while the carriage blocked traffic on the street. Said a South Carolina doctor, "The custom of appearing in public only in a volanta is so general that some of my fellow-boarders,

American ladies, who ventured to do their shopping on foot were greeted in their progress by the half suppressed exclamations of the astonished Habaneros, who seemed as much surprised to see a lady walk through their streets, as a Persian would be to see one unveiled in his."

LADIES ON THE PARQUE DE ISABEL II.

The promenade: Society women in volanta, coachman, mounted Spanish officer, and Cuban gentlemen on foot. In background is the statue of the symbolic Indian woman "Havana," at the inland end of the Paseo del Prado.

Mujeres públicas (public women) was a polite term for prostitutes. Decent women stayed in the private sphere. Literacy rates among Cuban women were low even in the upper classes, and females were not allowed to enroll in either of the city's universities (the more prestigious of which was a seminary, though it gave degrees in law and philosophy as well). For middle-and-upper class white women who wished to escape from these rigid formulas, especially as the women's rights movement made headway in the United States in the course of the century, the best hope was to be educated in the North as their brothers increasingly were.

Shortly after the Civil War, New York artist Samuel Hazard claimed to have been asked by a "young innocent" whether women, as well as Negro slaves, were now free in his country. When he replied that they were, she said, "It is not so here." Writer Anselmo Suárez Romero (a reformer on other issues) warned parents in 1860 not to send their daughters abroad for education for fear that they would acquire customs "diametrically opposed to those of the land of their birth." It would be, educator Carlos Saladrigas argued twenty years later, "an act against nature," doing harm to the principles "of concord and stability so essential to the defense and perpetuation of the family." Travel chronicles by Cuban female visitors to the North make frequent reference to women's greater mobility and access to the public sphere: "How often, in the midst of such gatherings, do I rue the sad and monotonous life of the girls of Cuba, always enclosed within the walls of their houses, with no more distraction than the wearisome motion of their rocking chairs." So reported a correspondent of the magazine *La Habana Elegante* who wrote under the pen name of Elga Adman.

The paradox is evident. The females who were free to move about the streets of Havana were overwhelmingly free women of color or slaves. Whether vendors, laundresses, midwives, cooks, or housewives, whether working for themselves or their owners or something of both, they went about their difficult business free of the restrictions imposed on whites. The lives of the black women and mulattas of Havana barely make it into most travel memoirs, but they figure at the center of the most famous portrait of life in the nineteenth-century capital, the one painted in loving and sometimes horrified detail by Cuban novelist Cirilo Villaverde in his classic work *Cecilia Valdés*.

One of the novel's characters, Genoveva Santa Cruz, walks every morning from her cottage outside the walls to the Plaza Vieja, where the arcades and front rooms of the mansions are rented out to dozens of Spanish immigrant shopkeepers, and where vendors of fewer resources fill the open square with their stalls selling green vegetables, fruits, root vegetables, live chickens, dead game animals, songbirds in cages, dried beans, and fresh fish from the river or sea. The makeshift shops are "all without cover or awning,"

Villaverde tells us, "nor a single respectable face; peasants and blacks, some poorly dressed and the others barely dressed at all." All the shops are filled with noise and smells and motion, below a sharp blue sky dotted with occasional passing clouds "like transparent silk or invisible angels' wings."

Genoveva takes her surname from the Santa Cruz y Montalvo family, her former owners, whose townhouse—the Palace of the Counts of Jaruco—was one of the arcaded mansions, "perhaps the haughtiest in the city," incongruously ringing the tumultuous market square (this building is today the gallery and headquarters of the arts organization Fondo de Bienes Culturales). She owes her freedom to her former fellow-slave Dolores Santa Cruz. "Dolores sold meat, sold fruit, sold everything, and Dolores bought her freedom. Then she got me out of the slave barracks, bought a shack, and I sold meats, sold sweets, sold everything for her. I worked and worked and I bought my freedom too. Now I sell meat, lard, eggs, fruit, whatever I can." She lives with her husband, the water vendor Trebusio Polanca, although, as was most common among the working class of the city, "we aren't married in the church." The day we meet her, she leaves the Plaza with a tray of pork, lard, and eggs balanced deftly on her head, and she navigates the clogged streets of Old Havana crying out, "Housewives! Won't you buy something from me today?" Her husband must follow the same itinerary, because the water vendors fill their barrels from the fountain in the middle of Plaza Vieja (from its "cloudy and greasy" spout, says the author Villaverde), and transport them through the streets in carts to sell for half a silver *real* each.

Genoveva Santa Cruz's former owners are the family of María Mercedes Santa Cruz y Montalvo, the non-fictional Countess of Merlín. In her travel memoir, Merlín describes women like Genoveva with a certain blend of envy and distaste: "Ladies are seen little in public. Only the black women parade through all the streets, with their shoulders and chests exposed, a cigar in the mouth, emitting great clouds of smoke . . . These *negras* show off, rocking their hips in the middle of street, with their kerchiefs on their heads, their bracelets, and the cigar." Frederika Bremer, without the superior air of Merlín, compares what she sees in Havana to what she has just seen in the United States: "Certain it is that one here sees negroes and mulattos much more frequently engaged in trade than there, and their wives are commonly very well, nay, even splendidly dressed. It is not unusual to see mulatto women, with flowers in their hair, walking with their families on the principal promenades in a manner which denotes freedom and prosperity."

The explanation of this paradox lies in the gender balance of Havana and in the continued growth of its precarious colored middle class. White women were in short supply, because new Spanish immigration was almost exclusively male: soldiers, sailors, officials on temporary postings, defeated royalist refugees from the continent, and increasing waves of young men who came from Spain, unaccompanied, to "do America" like the shopkeepers ringing the Plaza Vieja—to go from rags to riches as best they could. According to a detailed Havana census taken in 1861, among the white population, men outnumbered women by nearly two to one. Among free people of color, on the other hand, the ratio was approximately equal, both for mulattos and for blacks. Though male slaves vastly outnumbered female slaves in the countryside, in the city itself the numbers were probably equal as well.

The results were threefold. For the slaveowning aristocracy, white women became the symbol of exclusivity, superiority, and purity, so that their restricted sphere served, says historian Luis Martínez-Fernández "as a constant visual reminder of the separation between elite white society and the people of color they ruled." Especially, they needed to be kept at a remove from nonwhite men. On the other hand, for white men in general, colored women were either the only option or a constant temptation—as informal partners, mistresses, slaves forced into sexual services, or wives. "Necessity gives birth to mulattos," goes an old Cuban proverb, and necessity did. Finally, given the toeholds they had established in the centuries when Havana was a stopover and Spanish immigration sparser, free blacks and mulattos (or slaves doing day work) filled the working-class positions—not just street vendors but tailors, cooks, silversmiths, musicians, stevedores, decorators, and midwives—that upper-class whites found demeaning, and lower-class whites were unable or unwilling to assume.

As a result of all three factors, Havana's cosmopolitan character did not just involve the blended cultures of Spain, northern Europe, and the

United States. Havana stirred African traditions and African blood into the mix. Today, Havanans of all classes and races swallow syllables and consonants and blur the distinctions between their *r*s and *l*s and even *d*s in a way that is most reminiscent of the pronunciation Villaverde attributes to Genoveva Santa Cruz. Linguists trace this characteristic accent to the Andalusian Spanish of the original settlers as modified by the difference between the consonant sounds of West African languages and Romance ones. By the twentieth century, when any Havana family would claim a purely European ancestry, the satirical response was, "And your grandmother, where are you hiding her?"

All of this mixing of genes and cultures lies as the heart of Cirilo Villaverde's novel. *Cecilia Valdés* is Cuba's *Uncle Tom's Cabin*, *Sister Carrie*, and *Portrait of a Lady* rolled into one. It seems to traverse every plaza and barrio of the city that it celebrates, as does its heroine. Everyone in modern Havana knows Cecilia, whose story has been made into both a famous operetta and a film. They know her better in most cases than they know any actual historical figure of her era, and historians turn to the novel for its photographic descriptions of the life and customs of the time. *Cecilia Valdés* is a classic melodrama, firmly against slavery while often profoundly racist, but eloquent about the degree to which black and white Havana society coexisted, touched, and mixed. A closer look at *Cecilia* will lead us into a deeper look at Havana's mixture, mobility, and barriers of race and class.

4 Cecilia, Cabildos, and Contradance

In Villaverde's novel, we first see the heroine as an eleven- or twelve-year-old "blowing through the streets night and day," mischievously pocketing mangos, raisins, fritters, and bananas from the trays of vendors and shopkeepers. Like many people named Valdés in nineteenth century Havana, Cecilia owes her surname to the Casa de Cuna (cradle house), the orphanage at the corner of Muralla and Oficios founded by Bishop Gerónimo Valdés, which featured a revolving compartment in the front door in which mothers, fathers, or servants could deposit newborn children they did not want or could not afford. Some of these babies, like Cecilia, were the fruit of affairs between rich white businessmen and colored mistresses. Cecilia's secret father is Cándido Gamboa, whose name means pure or naive but who is actually anything but. A Spanish immigrant who started out as a building-supplies contractor and rose to the position of slave merchant, he has married into a landed Cuban family and is anxiously awaiting his title of nobility that is due to arrive any day from Madrid.

The tragedy of the novel is built around a new affair in the next generation. Cecilia grows into a dazzling young light-skinned woman, and falls in love with her half-brother Leonardo Gamboa, not knowing they are related. When Leonardo gets Cecilia pregnant, he sets her up in a rented house to keep her as his mistress, an arrangement he plans to continue after his marriage to the landed heiress selected for him. But Cecilia wants him to marry her, love her, and also allow her and especially her child to pass into white society. "He promised and he'll keep his word," she insists to her best friend, "or else I wouldn't love him the way I do."

At the same time she admits her ambitions: "Yes, it's true that I like white men better than black ones. I couldn't show my face for shame if I had *un hijo saltoatrás*" (*saltoatrás*, literally meaning "jumping backward," is slang for a child darker than its parent). Cecilia is in turn hopelessly loved by José Dolores Pimienta—a journeyman tailor, clarinetist, and composer—who has always hoped to marry her someday.

That José Dolores is a musician is no accident, for the precarious coexistence of black and white is intimately mixed with music and dance. We first see Leonardo and Cecilia's budding romance at a dance, a semi-public party in a private house. Such parties were thrown by all levels of Havana society—by some estimates fifty per night during the many saints days, holy weeks, and other festivals which gave religious cover to the revelry—in tiny homes and grand ones, in dance halls of varying reputation, in the Philharmonic Society, and even in the Teatro Tacón, where a raised dance floor could be installed in place of the orchestra seats. Most of these parties also featured gambling, especially the card game called monte. Bettors would surround long narrow gaming tables, placing bets from piles of silver and gold coins, while onlookers surrounded the bettors, their emotions riding on every card. These parties paid for themselves through the house's take from the gaming, the sale of drinks, or both. The twin passion for dancing and gambling, said Nicolás Tanco, helped account for the city's reputation as the Paris of the Americas, "a very gay city, where every man of means enjoys himself, where the people are constantly at play."

The party where we meet Leonardo and Cecilia is a *baile de cuna*, a popular fiesta in a poor district squeezed up against the city wall, "open to individuals of both sexes of the colored classes, yet not closed to those young white men who tended to honor them with their presence . . . some out of pure appreciation, others for motives not so pure." For entertainment, the party-giver has hired a seven-piece band of strings, drums, flutes, and clarinet. The band's leader and clarinetist is Cecilia's admirer José Dolores, composer of "The Candy Seller," the hit of that season's parties and the next, dedicated to Cecilia herself. Like many later hit songs such as *El manisero* (the peanut vendor), José Dolores's creation derives from the *pregones* or chants of vendors like Genoveva Santa Cruz and Trebusio Polanca.

Both the music of José Dolores's group and the "furious" dance to its beat are what Cubans of the era called *contradanza* or simply *danza*. The word is derived from the English "country dance" and came into Spanish by way of French. Originally it referred to European folk dancing, but Cuban sensibility and African rhythms gave it a new twist. The *danza cubana*, Villaverde tells us, is "such a special and far-traveled modification of the Spanish *danza* that its origin can barely be seen." Villaverde seems conflicted in his description of the *danza*: moaning and intoxicating, sad and stirring, spicy and graceful, carnal and emotional, deep and piercing, monotonous and melodious. His description of the music seems closest in spirit to North American jazz (by most accounts not yet invented, though New Orleans and Havana were closely linked by travel and trade): "The violinists tightened their bows, the flutists pierced the air with the high, sharp sounds of their instruments, the drummer's racing rhythm was an exquisite invention, and the bassist made a bow of his own body and drew the deepest notes imaginable, while the clarinet executed the most difficult and melodious variations... The clarinet cried out, 'Candy here, I'm selling candy,' while the violin and the bass repeated this in another tone, and the drums formed a clamorous chorus behind the melancholy voice of the vendor of the sweets."

What is true at the *baile de cuna* is true also at the height of native-born Cuban society—the fancy ball given on a different night at the Philharmonic, to which Leonardo arrives late after searching in vain for Cecilia at the house parties on the Hill of the Angel. "The most illustrious Cuban youth of both sexes surrendered, at least for the moment, to their favorite diversion, by the dazzling light of the crystal chandeliers [in an] intimate conversation of lovers, the caresses of souls who are mutually attracted, but whom time, space, circumstance, and custom have kept apart." In both locales, *danza* was played with European instruments, without the conga drums, gourds, rhythm sticks, cow bells, and other African borrowings or Cuban inventions that would enliven later genres. Yet the first time he notes the "moaning" character of the music, Villaverde declares that "it comes from the heart of a people enslaved."

In the end of the novel, Leonardo's selfishness, the duplicity of his and Cecilia's mutual father, Cecilia's romantic infatuation, and José Dolores's despair eventually prove the undoing of virtually everyone. Some months after the birth of his and Cecilia's daughter, Leonardo and his well-born bride-to-be Isabel Ilincheta climb the steps from the Calle Compostela to the candle-lit church of San Ángel Custodio, atop the Hill of the Angel, where they will be married as befits their class. In the soft November twilight, José Dolores Pimienta, his hat pulled low over his eyes, brushes past Leonardo. "The young man brought his hand to left side of his chest, groaned softly, tried to support himself on the arm of his bride, then fell at her feet, splashing her brilliant white silk dress with blood. Brushing his arm at the level of his chest, the knife had penetrated directly to his heart."

The plot of *Cecilia Valdés* focuses on the desire to whiten or assimilate, to rise into the Europeanized *petit bourgeoisie*. The *baile de cuna* copies Cuban high society, opening with a minuet. Another dance Cecilia attends, limited to the elite of colored society, not only features European dancing but requires European fancy dress in the form of coats and tails from the men.

In fact, real-life violinists of color like Claudio Brindis de Salas and Ulpiano Estrada, who put in cameo appearances at this fictional dance, excelled in both popular genres and classical ones. They gave lessons to the children of the aristocracy and were hired to play in church, for the dances of the Philharmonic and to serenade the *paseos*, as well as to entertain the parties of their own class. Brindis de Salas scrimped and saved to send his son, a child genius also named Claudio, to study in Paris. The junior Brindis had a distinguished career as a classical concert violinist, touring Italy (where he was hailed as "the black Paganini"), Germany, Russia, England, Venezuela, Argentina, Mexico, and Cuba. He settled in Germany, marrying into the nobility, but died finally in Buenos Aires, of tuberculosis, old and poor, in 1911.

Also named as a guest at the novel's select party is the poet Gabriel de la Concepción Valdés, better known by his pen name of Plácido. Like Cecilia, the real-life Plácido was a Valdés of the Cradle House, sent there to hide his white parentage and then reclaimed. In Plácido's case, his father was a black barber (indebted by gambling, some sources say) and his mother a Spanish dancer in the company of the Opera House. Brought up by his paternal grandfather, he later married María Gila Morales, daughter of the well-known midwife María del Pilar Poveda, who catered to Havana families rich and poor, white and black, and to some of the leading families of Matanzas as well.

Plácido worked over the years in Havana, Matanzas, and elsewhere on the island as a printer, comb-maker, silversmith, and carpenter. He also, however, managed to publish his poetry, and Villaverde called him "the most inspired poet that Cuba has seen." His sonnets, *letrillas*, and other classic forms were drawn from the Spanish romantic tradition but often adapted to Cuban nature and sometimes used to thinly disguise appeals for freedom from tyranny.

In the earliest years of the century, school teachers of color taught both white and black students in the city's small number of elementary schools. Lorenzo Melendez and Mariano Moya won a prize sponsored by a local Spanish treasury official for the teachers who could present the most outstanding students—in their case, six white children and four children of color. In this same period, Juana Pastor, a free mulatta from Jesús María, and Matías Velazco, the mulatto son of a white priest, also became highly regarded teachers of whites. From 1816 on, however, educational reformers pushed for more segregation, and by 1846 a detailed census of occupations showed no Cuban teachers of color anywhere.

In humbler but sometimes more lucrative trades, on the other hand, the 1846 records show that, in all of Cuba, free blacks and mulattos made up 99 percent of wage-earning cooks and coachmen, 75 percent of midwives, 72 percent of tailors, 69 percent of wet nurses, 63 percent of builders and masons, and 60 percent of shoemakers. They also made up 38 percent of seamstresses, 34 percent of hat makers, and 26 percent of tobacconists and cigar makers. These figures don't take slaves into account, and newspaper advertisements, for instance, reveal a common practice of selling mothers who had recently given birth to serve as wet nurses; they were generally offered "without infant" in the ads. Still, for those blacks and mulattos who did have their freedom, all these trades offered room to move up. Francisco Uribe appears in *Cecilia* as the employer of José Dolores Pimienta and tailor to Leonardo Gamboa and many others of his ilk. Uribe did in fact work at this profession, in a rented shop on Calle Muralla starting in 1833, under a sign advertising himself as "tailor of fashion." At the time of his death he owned two adjoining houses in Jesús María, with wooden walls and tile roofs, and twelve slaves, most of whom worked in his shop as washerwomen and ironers, some of them in the process of buying their freedom, to judge from papers dating from that time.

As for real-life cases embodying Cecilia's goal, examples of mistresses marrying into the oligarchy are hard to find. A more common case might be represented by a woman named Petrona Izquierdo, whose story is known through the property records of one of her sons. Born into slavery around 1835 in rural Alquízar to parents who were both Cuban-born slaves, Petrona was of a color between black and mulatta, "commonly called 'Chinese' or 'earth.' " Somehow she passed into the possession of a Don Jacinto Durán, of Casablanca, the fishing and maritime village tucked just below La Cabaña, separated from Old Havana by the narrow neck of the bay. Starting at the age of fifteen, Petrona Izquierdo had three children, each by "father unknown," each with a white godfather, and each given liberty at birth by Don Jacinto, who legally owned them. When Don Jacinto died in 1864, he left a will giving Petrona her freedom and a house in Casablanca. The will also officially recognized the last-born son, José Dolores Abraham, as his own. José Dolores inherited from his father four more houses on the same street.

Formal marriage between whites and people of color was barred by Spanish imperial laws, though there were two ways around this ban. One was to have the colored party, if light-skinned enough, declared white, often by way of a false certificate of baptism obtained through a bribe—or, occasionally, as a result of having emerged from the Cradle House with parentage unknown. The other was to petition for an exception to the law, granted only to couples involving a white man and a woman of color, and only if the white man was of equal or lower economic class. So the painter Don Simón de Jesús Barcañela appeared before city authorities in 1823, seeking permission to marry the mulatta Feliciana Pascuala Tolet y Cargnes, "whom he has made pregnant under promise." Permission was granted because Barcañela's parents were both tailors, a trade infrequent among whites. So, too, the sailor Don Manuel de León, immigrant from Canary Islands, was allowed to marry the mulatta Rafaela Pérez, with whom he had been living in Jesús María for thirty years. In the same neighborhood, the Galician Don Luis Luaces petitioned to marry the mulatta María de La Luz García, because, he said, "her parents, besides being honorable and of good behavior, own real estate which her father has pledged to make available to the petitioner for a workshop in which to roll cigars."

Cecilia Valdés is only a partial window into nineteenth-century Havana's intersection of black and white cultures. What Villaverde chose not to see was the survival of true African culture within this mix. Africa especially stayed alive in the dozens of societies called *cabildos de nación*, which don't appear in his classic portrait of nineteenth-century Havana at all. As Villaverde's fellow novelist Félix Tanco lamented in a private letter of 1837, "Who fails to see, in the movements of our boys and girls in their *contradanzas* and waltzes, an imitation of the miming carried on by the blacks in their *cabildos*? Who doesn't know that bass viol of the *danza* is the echo of [their] drums?"

The *cabildos de nación* (ethnic councils) were originally created by Spanish authorities on the model of similar societies for Africans, gypsies, and other "lower races" in Seville. The authorities' goal was social control, to be achieved by splintering African-born free laborers and urban slaves according to their native nations, languages, and localities. The *cabildo* system also created a semifeudal structure under which the "kings" or "captains" of these societies represented their members in formal dealings with the government and could be held responsible for crimes or fines. The *cabildos* however, simultaneously provided a space for traditional rituals, for mutual aid, and even for political organizing against slavery and Spanish rule.

By the nineteenth century, when the authorities were evidently worried about the cabildos proving a double-edged sword, new laws required them to be located only in the poor black neighborhoods outside of the old city's walls. The Carabalí Apapá, the Lucumí Yesa, the Congo Real, and the Congo Modongo, among many others, owned or rented houses for their *cabildos* in the *barrio* of Jesús María, to the west of the shipyard (now the central train station). Though officially limited to African-born free blacks, Havana's *cabildos* also included African-born slaves and Cuban-born blacks and mulattos, sometimes in leadership positions.

The *cabildos* collected dues, lent money at interest (often as mortgages), and collected the money or property of members who died without heirs. Like other mutual aid societies, they used their funds to pay for members' medical care or funerals. They used funds, too, to buy members, their lost children, and their spouses out of slavery. *Cabildos* also developed economic power in other ways. The Carabalí societies came to be, in effect, the hiring hall for longshore workers and foremen on Havana's docks. Many of the *cabildos'* prominent members, usually successful tradesmen, bought themselves commissions in the black or mulatto militia, which brought prestige and some degree of protection from arbitrary legal penalties such as whippings or fines. The captain of the *cabildo* of the Carabalí Ososo, Francisco Barroso, owned a funeral parlor and was first sergeant of a mulatto battalion. Dock foremen Marcelino Gamarra and Augustín Ceballos were lieutenant and sergeant in a black and mulatto battalion, respectively.

Juan Bertault and Genoveva Morejón, both brought to Cuba as slaves, had gained their freedom and saved about 1500 pesos by the time they married in Havana in 1840 or 1841. Bertault listed his occupation as upholsterer but also owned several wagons and mules, so he may have run a freight business. The couple bought a house in Jesús María at the time of their marriage and soon owned part of another building in the old city, near where the Calle de la Bomba met the wall, a block past where the fictional tailor-clarinetist and his sister lived in *Cecilia Valdés*. They bought these rooms from the captain of one of the Carabalí *cabildos*, of which Bertault became captain in turn. Around mid-century, Bertault began to flourish as a moneylender and mortgager, his fortune growing through inheritance of property left by three men and two women of the *cabildo*. By the time of Morejón's death in 1870, the couple owned seven houses, mostly in Jesús María, and a vacant lot repossessed from a Catalán shopkeeper there as well. The legal record contains a suggestion that Bertault may have mis-used his position in the *cabildo* for personal gain, but in any case his story shows the economic power that could reside there.

Cabildos also had female officials (*matronas* or "queens") who also acquired considerable power and prestige. Maria de Regla Fajardo, ex-*matrona* of the Ugri Cabildo, took advantage of a debt of 1700 pesos that this *cabildo* owed to her son. She insisted that her friend Inés de Flores be elected *matrona* upon her own death, in partial forgiveness of the loan. Shoring up their status, *cabildo* officials dressed in a style borrowed from colonial military dignitaries: starched shirts, embroidered jackets, bright sashes, silver headed canes. The *matronas*, while retaining African head scarves, wore gowns covered with Valencian silk, embroidered sashes with precious stones, and gold scepters and earrings. At the same time, the *cabildos* all preserved traditional language, religion, music, and dance. In some societies, the votes for captains and *matronas* were collected inside a *güira* or gourd that served as voting urn. The same *güira* served as a per-cussion instrument, the one still seen in Cuban bands today.

Music and dance were an integral part of all the West African and Central African religions that the slaves brought with them. They were employed to erase boundaries between the religious and secular, between worship and enjoyment, and between living beings, deities, and the dead. On Sundays and feast days, the *cabildos* were permitted to hold such events, called *toques*, for their members. Some of them also offered curi-ous onlookers the chance to watch, generally for a fee that subsidized the house, the altars and effigies within in it, and the treasury that paid for funerals, purchases of liberty, and other member needs. Frederika Bremer, once again, noted carefully what she saw:

> I found a large room, very like those of public houses among us, in which I saw these naked to the waist, wild, energetic figures and countenances, who were beating drums with energetic animation. These drums were hollowed trees stems over the opening of which was stretched a parchment skin, on which the negroes

drummed, in part with sticks and in part with their hands, with their thumbs, with their fists, with wonderful agility and skill . . . The time and measure, which sometimes varied, was exquisitely true; no one can imagine a more natural, perfect, and lively precision in that irregularly regular time.

She also saw dances by couples, not contradances but what would later be called *rumba*, stylized courtship between "ladies of various shades of color, dressed in ragged finery; men without any finery, almost without any attire at all on the upper part of the body . . . these African dances, with their peculiar wild life, at the same time so irregular and yet so rhythmical." She calls the dance an "artistic performance" and then checks herself, her racial blinders clicking in: "or shall I say a perfected natural art—they drummed as bees hum and beavers build."

Generally speaking, the ceremonies held inside the *casas de cabildo* invoked the African deities (*orishas* to the Yoruba) in their original forms. They used statues or dolls representing the Lucumí Changó and Yemayá and others, or the Carabalí Okún and Okandé. They practiced systems of foretelling the future, prescribing behavior, and influencing events through the use of shells, roots, smoke, food and drink, animals and other means. But images of the original deities were not allowed in outdoor processions (except for one day of the year), so the *cabildos* learned to cloak them in the form of Catholic saints: Changó and Okún became Santa Bárbara, Yemayá and Okandé became the Virgin of Regla, Ochún became the Virgin of Charity who would later be recognized as Cuba's patron saint. *Bailes de cuna* like the one in *Cecilia Valdés* were often thrown in honor of the host's adopted saint. This was the beginning of the long process that would lead to modern-day *santería*, a religion that mixes African and Christian traditions.

Similarly, the *cabildos* developed bilingual ways to refer to their officials and themselves. The Congo, for instance, joined the other *cabildos* in calling their officials *capataces* (overseers) in their dealings with Spanish authorities, but among themselves they called the captain a *sali*, a term of respect. As pressures for conformity mounted, the societies began adopting Christian names for themselves. So the Carabalí Iziegue y Izuama took the name Immaculate Conception, the Congo Real became the society of the Magi king Melchor, and the Carabalí Ososo became Our Lady of the Light. The fusion took place in other ways too, such that it is often hard to tell in hindsight who was fooling whom. The names for the nations were often derived from those in use among the slave traders: Lucumí for those in West Africa who mostly called themselves Yoruba, Carabalí (from the slave port of Calabar on the river of the same name) for the Ibo, Ibibio, and Ekoi, yet they each took on a life of their own. Lucumí apparently derived from a Yoruba greeting meaning "friend." A male hoop-skirted figure wearing a horned crown became known by Havana's onlookers as La Culona (big-assed woman) but this name apparently hid a Malinke and Mandingo word meaning "wise" or "educated" that described the wearer of the ritual skirt.

The most famous of all the "Negro dances" took place once a year, on the Feast of Epiphany, January 6, also known as the Day of the Magi, or El Día de Reyes, the Day of Kings. On this date only, slaves were given the day off from work. Members of the *cabildos* were allowed to parade through the streets to dance, drum, chant in their languages of origin, and openly invoke their gods whose effigies they brought out from their *cabildo* houses and bore aloft on poles. They danced in lines, in circles, and in couples. Some wore traditional masks and hoods, face paints, animal skins, and straw skirts, as well as beads, mirrors, rattles, and glitter of all sorts. Some wore Spanish fancy dress—top hats, large cravats, breast pins, swordbelts and cutlasses, cuff links, sashes, shawls, tassels, fans, ribbons, and cardboard gilt crowns—whether in emulation or in parody it was difficult to tell. (The closest U.S. comparison would be the Congo Square dances of pre-Civil War New Orleans, a tradition that later flowed into the Mardi Gras.)

From all points in the city, the celebrants converged on the Plaza de Armas, under the official pretense that they were celebrating the Three Kings, though they were honoring their own kings and queens as well. "This negro," wrote a bemused Frenchman in the mid-1850s, "who was enormously tall, and had a tolerably good-looking head, gave his hands gravely to a sort of feminine blackamoor who represented some queen or other. He walked with a deliberate majestic step, never laughed, and seemed to be reflecting deeply on the grandeur of his mission to the world." Jugglers and tumblers, meanwhile, extended their hats to onlooking whites, asking for an *aguinaldo* (tip or bonus), a practice borrowed from Catholic saints-day festivals. Costumed stilt dancers took advantage of their height to appeal for *aguinaldos* to patricians watching the spectacle from upper balconies and galleries. Once gathered in the Plazas, the *cabildos* entered into the courtyard of the captain-general's palace one by one, paying allegiance and collecting tips. "The old negro women, the most expressive or the most nervous, were the ones who most shook on high their hollow gourd rattles covered in netting, almost delirious in asking God to watch over and preserve the health of His Excellency the Governor General," read a report in a Cuban magazine toward the end of the century. This is most likely not what they were doing at all.

Indeed, accounts by Spaniards, Cuban whites, and foreign visitors all describe the Day of Kings with terms like discordant, outlandish, barbaric, dreadful, feverish, contorted, lascivious, grotesque, ridiculous, wild, savage, foolish, monstrous, and obscene. At best, a local journalist in the 1840s wrote of "the veneer of religious solemnity they give to these profane acts," but the most common adjectives were "devilish" and "diabolical." This characterization stemmed from fear of Africa and Africans, and from familiarity with Spanish festival traditions in which masked devils did play a part. White chroniclers called any costumed ritual figure in the Day of Kings processions a "*diablito*" or little devil, even though it more likely represented a god incarnate or an honored ancestor revived. The figure seen as the epitome of the *diablito* was the Abakuá *ireme*, a costumed creature known for his full mask and conical hood, checkerboard-patterned like the rest of his outfit, and his fringes and cuffs of palm fiber which, like his bells, were set in motion by the angular movements of his dance to the beat of the sacred ekué drum. However, this official or respectable discourse which saw the African influences as diabolic grew increasingly at odds with popular feelings. The Abakuá offer an early example of this change.

Popularly called *ñáñigos*, the Abakuá were not so much a separate religion as a secret society of male initiates, whose rituals probably derived from an Ekoi leopard society. First established in the Havana port barrio of Regla in the 1830s, ñáñigo societies took root among the free workers of the port cities, especially longshoremen and construction workers. Their secular functions included mutual defense and avenging of wrongs. Devils or no, on Christmas Eve of 1863, on the Calzada Ancha del Norte (now Calle San Lázaro in Centro Habana) a group of white men formed the first of many white Abakuá *ponencias* (chapters), the Akanarán Efó Muñón Ekobio Mukarará. Versions of the origins of this "reformation" vary widely, but all agree that it was work of a mulatto ñáñigo named Andrés Petit, often known as "the gentleman of color." Petit, probably a dockworker in Regla, was also an initiate of a Congo religious society and of a lay Catholic order, and the founder of a new syncretic sect of his own.

Petit either gave or sold the secret Abakuá rites (some versions say he sold them for gold to be used in buying slaves their freedom) to the whites, who were either young aristocrats in search of identity and reputation, or dock and cigar and slaughterhouse workers who labored alongside black ñáñigos, or both. Be that as it may, after some years of resistance, the Abakuá network recognized the right of white chapters to participate as equals and brothers— even as Spanish colonial authorities tried assiduously to suppress them both. This in turn opened the door to incorporation of mostly (but not exclusively) lower class whites into other religious societies and practices of African origin. Afro-Cuban religions, taken as a whole, came finally to outdistance orthodox Catholicism as the most popular religious faith in Havana and other cities. As journalist, fiction writer, and researcher Tata Quiñones, himself a declared Abakuá, argues in a recent essay, "The 'reformation' begun by Andrés Facundo Cristo de los Dolores Petit played its part in the arduous and complex process of forming the Cuban nation, by linking blacks, whites, and mulattos in a single network of beliefs, interests, and solidarity. Ñañiguismo, up to then a 'black thing,' became what it has been since: Cuban."

When the Día de Reyes celebrations were finally suppressed late in the century after the official abolition of slavery, their traditions flowed into that of the pre-Lenten Spanish carnival, which had previously been a more sedate procession of carriages and floats. Similarly, if you go today to the anniversary of a *santero's* orisha, where friends, relatives, and extended family crowd into the celebrant's home to eat, drink, dance, and pay homage to the altar of the saint, you may find yourself in the presence of a *toque de violín* in which a multiracial trio of violin, accordion, and conga drum plays a version of a Spanish sailor song in honor of Yemayá or Changó. It is one more example of the coexistence of creeds in Havana: in the crowd at this *cumpleaños de santo* may be fervent communists, black-market capitalists, or people who are a bit of both.

Something of this characteristic of coexistence and contradiction was glimpsed by the foreign visitors of the nineteenth century. They were continually surprised at how all the contending segments of Havana society lived jumbled together, how divisions of race and class were social but not strictly physical, and how, in addition, the new always existed alongside ruin and decay. Late twentieth and early twenty-first century visitors have tended to think that they are finding this for the first time, but that is not so.

"There is no 'West End' in Havana," nineteenth-century travel writers repeat over and over, implicitly comparing Havana to London with a regularity that suggests each is plagiarizing from the one before. "The stately mansion of the millionaire is often in juxtaposition with the magazine [warehouse] of *tasajo*, jerked beef, with its sign of a large slice swinging over its door . . . There is no select residential quarter of the city, the best family houses being scattered about among the business premises, and often adjoining very objectionable neighbours . . . [In the heights of Cerro] are where the aristocracy of the city reside, and where is found grandeur and squalid poverty intermingled to the greatest extent we ever beheld."

Trying to sum up the whole city, Frederica Bremer wrote that it showed:

> a great mixture of regularity and irregularity, of old and new, of the splendid and the dilapidated. Close beside the elegant arched arcade, with its gayly painted walls, stands a half-ruinous wall, the fresco paintings of which are half obliterated or have peeled off with the mortar. And this old wall is not repaired, nor the

old painting restored. All this—the countenances and
life of the colored population; the silent, wedgelike way
in which the *volantas* insinuate themselves between the
rows of houses, give to Havana a peculiar character, and
a romantic life which is unlike that of any other city
which I have seen, and especially unlike those of England and North America.

This sensation of mixture is deepened by the fact that, due to both climate and the city's peculiarities, much of life has always been lived out of
doors. In the nineteenth century, at festival times the indoor parties were
supplemented by stands set up in the street, selling drinks and all manner
of food. On the Hill of the Angel, the specialty was golden buttered corn
tortillas cooked on clay discs as the Tainos had cooked *casabe*. The area
around the church of La Merced, near where the *baile de cuna* in Cecilia
Valdés takes place, was known for its pies and sugar drops, roasted nuts,
and sweet drinks flavored with cinnamon and cloves. Outside the walls,
by the Teatro Tacón, were stands selling coffee and fruits and anything
that might be cooked, as the German visitor Edward Otto wrote. It was
pleasant, he said, to emerge from a crowded dance in the theater, "breathe
in the cool air and palms and orange trees and refresh oneself with the
coffee and fruits on sale in the plazas; everywhere were lights and fires for
boiling and roasting. It was pleasant, those thousands of men wandering
in the night."

The other side of this life in the street was the noise that came with it.
"For sleeping, I might as well have been stretched on the bass drum," complained Richard Henry Dana about a band playing outside his window, "and
the servants in the court of the hall seem to be tending at tables of quarrelling
men" who kept him up till five a.m. And then, "as the maskers go home from
their reels at this hideous hour of Sunday morning [and] the servants ceased
their noises, the cocks began to crow and the bells to chime, the trumpets
began to bray, and the cries of the streets broke in before dawn."

Some of the "thousands of men," of course, had more than eating or
sleeping on their minds. The port city had not abandoned its old trade of

Meat wagon in front of one of the many colonnaded arcades of Old Havana mansions, whose street levels were often warehouses

selling sex, only added new strata to the industry. "The priestesses of Venus," Otto claimed, "have permission to live on any street, and so, in general, they choose the best streets and rent a room next to the first house of the city . . . and cultivate the same habits as the distinguished ladies . . . peek[ing] out the bars of the high windows at nightfall, with a lit cigarette in their mouths."

Though still relying in part on rented slave women and on free women of color, the sex trade also increasingly attracted immigrants from Europe and the United States. In 1853, Otto's countrywoman Luisa Bonetti (apparently of Italian background, but born in Germany) was repeatedly arrested for "creating a public scandal." She was placed in the Casa de Recogidas, a special detention center for unmarried girls on the loose, unmarried or separated women deemed "scandalous and incorrigible," and women convicted of crimes. "Harlots" (*meretrices*), "public women," and "prostitutes" were in fact registered, taxed, and allowed to practice their trade within certain limits. Bonetti's crime seems not to have been prostitution as such but rather her public denunciations, at late hours and at the top of her lungs, of a certain Dr. Nicolás Manzini. In these tirades and her later letters of protest from the Casa de Recogidas, she charged that Manzini had encouraged her to deposit her earnings with him for safekeeping, and then kept them "for himself, his house, and luxuries that he never had before." Bonetti, who was literate and had a daughter attending a private school, was finally deported without a trial.

In the 1860s, the American Samuel Hazard professed shock at finding that "plenty of our countrywomen, in the interest of making a lot of money in their relations with rich Spaniards, come here to join this unfortunate class." Historian Louis Pérez notes that such "rich Spaniards" were not their only customers, because there were by the mid-nineteenth century already brothels "operated by North Americans principally for North Americans"—business travelers, tourists, railroad workers, and the crews of the great number of merchant ships. He cites among American prostitutes Ellen N. King of New London, who went to work in a Havana brothel after losing her job on a Cienfuegos plantation, and actress Adah Isaacs Menken, abandoned by her lover in Havana in 1853 and seeking to earn passage back to the United States. Fragmentary statistics suggest that in the 1860s and 1870s the majority of prostitutes were probably immigrants from Spain and the Canary Islands. In the 1880s and 1890s, as the economic situation deteriorated, they were joined by increasing numbers of Cuban-born women, the majority of them white.

So Havana became the Paris of the Americas in terms of high art, café society, popular entertainment, gambling, and sex. However, Paris itself in those years saw revolution and counterrevolution. So did Havana. If Cuba was the ever-faithful isle, remaining under Spanish rule long past other American colonies, it did not do so simply or enthusiastically. Alongside luxury, poverty, coexistence, and cultural fusion, Havana was also a site of rebellion, repression, and the assertion of a new Cuban nationhood. To understand, we must retrace our steps through a less exotic and more politicized nineteenth-century Havana, starting with the "Conspiracy of Aponte" in the year 1812.

5 Stirrings of Nationhood

Today, the street called Belascoaín runs through the heart of the city. It starts from the seafront Malecón, alongside the equestrian statue of Antonio Maceo and the sky-scraping Amejeiras Brothers Hospital, which looks like a bank tower because that's what it was designed to be. It traverses Centro Habana from north to south and ends at the big, busy farmers' market of Cuatro Caminos, below the old Spanish fortress of Atarés.

For most of the nineteenth century, however, Belascoaín marked the western edge of the city—marking the limit of the barrios that had sprung up outside the walls. Bordering it at the ocean end was an orphanage, along with a insane asylum, a cemetery, and further inland a bull ring—all institutions requiring distance from dwellings, a lot of space, or both. The only neighborhood on the far side of Belascoaín was called, aptly enough, Pueblo Nuevo. Sometime before the year 1811, the carpenter and woodcarver José Antonio Aponte y Ulabarra built himself a cottage in Pueblo Nuevo made of wooden planks and palm thatch. It stood on a primitive lane, the predecessor of the street that later came to be called Jesús Peregrino, a name that would obliquely memorialize Aponte himself. For Aponte would soon become a revolutionary, long before his successors Antonio Maceo or the Amejeiras brothers were born.

Aponte was a free black man who built his house thanks to a loan or a gift of 300 pesos from his mother Mariana Poveda, a free black woman likewise born in Cuba whose occupation is unknown. In this cottage Aponte lived with his wife, his youngest son Juan de Paula, and at least one stepdaughter, María Josefa Valdés. Here he maintained his workshop, which consisted of a carpenter's bench and a box of tools. More unusual was his small library—Aponte could read and he did. His collection ranged from world history to natural history, from architecture to military matters to a guide to Cuba for foreigners, from a manual on crafting letters to *Don Quijote de la Mancha* and biographies of famous men.

In 1811, Aponte was somewhere over fifty years old. He had been, as we have mentioned earlier, a corporal in Havana's black militia battalion, having served overseas during the campaigns related to the American Revolution in Florida and probably in the capture of Nassau. Official orders detailing the privileges conferred by this service hung on his wall. His father, of Yoruba origin, was a member of the prestigious secret society called the Ogboni, said to be descendants of the *orisha* Changó, and he passed this membership on to his son. José Antonio was himself the head of a small Lucumí *cabildo*, the Cabildo Changó-Teddún, of which his house-workshop was the seat. This adherence to African religion did not preclude his accepting a commission, in 1811, to carve and paint a Virgin of Guadalupe for a nearby parish church. The walls of his house bore portraits of Christian saints, and he had built an effigy on his front door or an altar within (reports differ) depicting Jesus as a pilgrim, from which the later name of his street derived. He appeared to be a model citizen (though as a black man he had no political rights), but in the same year that he carved the Virgin of Guadalupe he sent his wife and his son, an eighteen-year-old tailor, to live across the bay in Guanabacoa for their own safety. He was about to embark on a conspiracy to overthrow slavery and Spanish rule.

The plan did not arise in isolation. Napoleon's armies had invaded Spain, producing a political vacuum in the mother country that ignited independence actions all the way from the River Plate (today Argentina) to Mexico. In 1810, a wealthy white Cuban, General Luis Francisco Bassave y Cardenas, conspired with a group of fellow freemasons to overthrow the government with the help of the militias of color. The plot was discovered, and Bassave was sent to Spain for trial. Meanwhile, unfolding events in Spain gave the American colonies their first representation in the Cortes, the Spanish parliament. A Mexican delegate introduced a measure to outlaw the slave trade and gradually eliminate slavery itself.

In this climate, Aponte began spreading word that slavery might indeed be abolished—and perhaps already had been, but colonial officials and Cuban planters (both of whom vociferously opposed the Mexican resolution) had suppressed the news. He also made contact, through a Catalán merchant of republican sentiments, with Cuban-born whites who had been connected with the conspiracy of the year before. Under cover of *cabildo* meetings, he began to recruit followers, not just among the Lucumí but among most of the African ethnic groups. He made contact with important figures such as Salvador Ternero, the long-time *capataz* of a Mina society, who lived in the neighboring barrio of La Salud by the bridge where the Calle Manrique crossed the Royal Ditch. Ternero began to hold meetings in his house, too. Attendees at the meetings in La Salud and Pueblo Nuevo included shoe, furniture, charcoal, and saddle makers, oxcart drivers and porters of cane and fodder, teachers, carpenters, bell-ringers, and probably other professions. The conspirators made contact with the officers of a black Spanish regiment, raised in Santo Domingo, which happened to be returning from Central America by way of Havana. Since these officers had first-hand experience with the rebellion in Haiti, Spanish authorities were keeping them sequestered in barracks in Casablanca. Nonetheless, Aponte, Ternero, and a third ally found a pretext to talk to them, and made a request for arms and leadership to be provided once an insurrection was launched.

Throughout 1811, plans for this insurrection spread across the island. Aponte and others set up links with free blacks and slaves in Puerto Príncipe (now Camagüey) and Bayamo in the East. In meetings and by word of mouth, they discussed slavery's abolition in Haiti, and they envisioned a Cuban regime that would be free of slavery, Spain, and discrimination by race. The plan was to foment uprisings on plantations both in the East and in the environs of Havana, putting fields and mills to the torch, and setting diversionary fires in Havana's suburbs. In the confusion, the conspirators (many with first-hand knowledge from service in the militia) would seize several barracks and arms depots in the outer barrios of the city, principally the Dragoon Barracks in La Salud and the Castillo de Atarés just south of Jesús María. They would distribute to the population of color all the weapons they could seize.

Antislavery handbills started to appear, including one posted on the back wall of the captain-general's palace, where the coachmen gathered and coaches were kept. Three free black women, María de la Luz Sánchez, Patria de la Espinosa, and María de los Dolores, also held meetings and spread word of the impending rebellion to female slaves on the Trinidad plantation and mill in Guanabacoa. Secretly, a date for the uprising was set: January 5, 1811, the eve of the Day of Kings. In a coded message they alerted potential white supporters to be prepared, because "a column is about to fall" and "the hymn of celebration will be sung before the time of the mass."

When word of a conspiracy in the East leaked out to Spanish officials, the date for the uprising in the capital was postponed. After some debate, Aponte convinced his Havana allies to go forward. On March 15, three of the free blacks who had met in Aponte's house joined with slaves of the plantation Peñas Altas, in Guanabo along the coast east of Havana, to begin the revolt. They succeeded in taking the mill after a brief but bloody assault in which the owner's son was killed. They put the mill to the torch and spread out to hide or to distribute the news. An attempt to repeat the plan at the nearby plantation La Trinidad failed, however, and unbeknownst to Aponte three plotters within the walls of Old Havana (two coachmen and a shoemaker, all slaves) had been discovered and imprisoned. Then word reached the captain-general that mysterious meetings had taken place in Salvador Ternero's house, and a neighbor admitted that after the uprising in Guanabo he had been invited to join the insurrection.

A few hours later, before Aponte could raise above his house the white flag with the image of Our Lady of Remedios that was supposed to signal the time for the assault on the barracks, he and most of his network were arrested. They were soon brought to La Cabaña for interrogation. Among the evidence presented against them were African religious objects and a fleur-de-lis seal used as a countersign on documents, found in Ternero's house. In Aponte's, authorities confiscated a large scrapbook of paintings and drawings, including a map of the city and its environs, portraits of Toussaint L'Ouvertoure and George Washington, and depictions of victorious black troops and black priests.

On March 9, 1812, Aponte and his fellow conspirators were hanged from gallows erected just inside the walls, in the Plaza de Las Ursulinas at the end of Calle Sol. The captain-general ordered that their heads be cut off and displayed in "the most appropriate public places as a warning to others." José Antonio Aponte's severed head was placed inside an iron cage and hung at the border of the city near his house, right where the headquarters of the Masonic Lodges of Cuba stands today, at the busy corner of Carlos III and Belascoaín. The first attempt to end slavery and Spanish rule had failed. *Más malo que Aponte* ("more evil than Aponte") entered the vocabulary of conservative Havana, but Aponte's name lived on in its popular memory. The street where he lived took its name from the altar or effigy he had built. In *Cecilia Valdés*, when María de Regla tries to remember when she was assigned as wet nurse to the newborn Cecilia, she fixes it as "the year they sent Aponte to the hangman," which was the beginning of many troubles for her as well.

The Conspiracy of Aponte (like the contemporary slave revolts planned by Gabriel Prosser and Nat Turner in Virginia, Denmark Vesey in South Carolina, and others in Jamaica, Barbados, and Antigua) conjured up the fear among slaveowners that the history of Haiti could repeat itself. After Aponte, Spanish authorities clamped down on their nonwhite militia battalions, arresting any member who showed signs of holding meetings, teaching reading skills, or other "subversive activities" in his home. Even individual public expressions of pride were viewed with suspicion. In 1826, a mulatto painter and ex-sergeant named Pedro Cortés protested against being refused seating in a whites-only restaurant. Cortés, rebuked by a white patron for demanding a seat, declared that "the Spanish are shameless and stubborn." He was arrested and questioned, and released only after apologizing for his "extremely bad behavior that day." The restaurant in question, court records tell us, was in the Plaza del Vapor— the new indoor market, said to be one of the world's biggest, recently built outside the old walls. This was presumably the restaurant owned by Pancho Marty, the ex-pirate and soon-to-be developer of the Teatro Tacón, who decorated it with a large painting of Havana's first steamship (*vapor*) that gave the market its name.

Pedro Cortés's infraction, and all others like it, were brought before a new Military Commission established by Captain-General Vives to try cases of subversion, whether infractions by independence-minded whites or antislavery, equality-minded blacks. When Vives returned to Madrid in 1832 at the end of his nine-year Cuban tour of duty, he testified that, "The existence of free blacks and mulattos in the middle of the enslavement of their comrades is an example that will be very prejudicial some day, if effective measures are not taken in order to prevent [the slaves'] constant and natural tendency toward emancipation, in which case they may attempt by themselves or with outside help to prevail over the white population." He proposed the deportation of all free people of color, but recognized that any such attempt would produce the disease it attempted to cure, for its injustice "would awaken discontent and produce unfailingly the ruin of the country."

Vives' fear was well-founded. Many free blacks and mulattos were themselves ex-slaves or the children of slaves, and they were always subject to the racial barriers that slave society required. Even when they owned slaves themselves, they seem to have made it possible for these slaves to purchase their freedom, by paying a slight salary for domestic or business tasks, or by renting them out as a source of income for both master and slave. Plots similar to Aponte's continued to surface. Plantation slaves continued to stage isolated revolts, and far off in the mountainous interior numerous communities of runaways struggled to survive.[1]

Vives's successor, Miguel de Tacón, figures in the architectural history of Havana for his improvements of the regal *paseos* and for lending his name to the theater built by his friend Marty. He was also a law-and-order governor to the extreme. Tacón clamped down further on any hint of subversion, tightened press censorship, instituted nightly patrols to cut down on theft and assault, made some attempt to limit public gambling, and built a sinister monument to Spanish power that would last for a century, forty years longer than Spanish rule itself. At the seaward end of the Paseo del Prado, just before the Castillo de la Punta and across from where the barracks for newly imported slaves had until recently stood, he ordered the construction of an immense new jail. This yellow limestone colossus measured two hundred by nearly four hundred feet, with two stories each twenty-four feet high, and held more than two thousand inmates—political prisoners, common criminals, and those somewhere in between. These chain gangs may be thanked for the extension and leveling of the city's boulevards and the quarrying of the stone from which its new mansions were built.

One travel writer, citing a local census, claimed that there were a thousand prisoners working in chain gangs in 1841. Richard Henry Dana, walking near the jail in 1859, heard a sound like soldiers marching while banging their sabers against the paving stones, which in fact was the work gangs forming ranks. "Poor wretches!" he wrote. "Each man has an iron band riveted round his ankle, and another around his waist, and the chain is a fastened, one end into each of these bands, and dangles between them, clanking with every movement." Prisoners wore these chains working or eating or sleeping, day and night. Common prisoners in the jail were kept in wards with stone floors and no beds, according to Dana, though those who could afford to pay some of their upkeep were assigned to better-equipped "wards of distinction." The New Jail also held 1200 troops with separate pavilions for their commanders and officers. From the sea, it towered over the Castillo de la Punta, momentarily distracting shipboard arrivals from the older monuments and the striking natural setting of the bay. "Among the objects which caught my sight were the fortress where the state prisoners are kept, a second prison, and—a gallows," Frederika Bremer remarked. "But those beautiful waving palms and those verdant hills enchanted my eyes."

Beyond the verdant hills, in 1843 and 1844, a string of slave rebellions in the rich cane lands of Matanzas filled Cuba's jails with the victims of Tacón's successor, Captain-General Leopoldo O'Donnell, in what historians later called "The Ladder" or "The Year of the Lash." Reacting to the rebellions in Matanzas, O'Donnell claimed to have uncovered a vast conspiracy involving British abolitionists, free Cubans of color, members of the Cuban sugarocracy, and bloodthirsty slaves. Historians have not been able to determine the truth of this claim. Britain was by this time committed to wage labor and the suppression of the slave trade. The British consul and others held tentative talks with planters about ending the importation of new slaves, and with potential leaders among free Cubans of color as well. However, a conspiracy uniting all factions and opposing interests, such as O'Donnell claimed to have uncovered, is unlikely. Most of the evidence gathered by the Military Commissions was extracted by torture carried out in the prisons of Matanzas and Havana: specifically, by tying the suspect to a ladder, and whipping him or her until he or she confessed and implicated others, or died. O'Donnell and his allies probably took advantage of whatever conspiracy existed to teach a lesson to all potential forces for change.

As a result of the first confessions, thousands more blacks and mulattos, slave and free, were sent to be tortured on the ladder. Unknown numbers, certainly in the hundreds, died. In the capital, the brunt of the punishment fell on the free people of color, especially those with some status or some modest wealth. In fact, much of what we know about the life histories of prominent Havana free blacks and mulattos, recounted in the previous chapter, comes from the court records of La Escalera. The poet Plácido, singled out by O'Donnell as a chief conspirator, was executed by firing squad in Matanzas; his last poem was a farewell to the mother who had given him up to the Cradle House. His mother-in-law María del Pilar Poveda, in Havana, was stripped of her midwife's license and sentenced to a year's forced labor. The tailor Francisco Uribe, arrested and awaiting the ladder, committed suicide to escape that fate. The musician Claudio Brindis de Salas the elder was exiled, as were many more. In three months in the spring of 1844, seven hundred Cubans of color left the island, the majority going to Mexico, and smaller numbers to Africa, the United States, Jamaica, Brazil, and Europe. Augustín Ceballos, dock gang captain, militia sub-lieutenant, and one of the richest Havanans of color, was sent to prison in Cárdenas to waste away and die. Several more "ungrateful" dock captains were charged with involvement in the conspiracy. "Given the influence they must enjoy and have enjoyed because of their knowledge and resources," the Military Commission judged, "it is evident they were in the first ranks of the conspiracy hatched by those of their color."

Under pressure from Spanish interrogators, those tied to the ladder or threatened with execution implicated white Cuban-born aristocrats in the real or alleged plot. Jailed, held incommunicado, and interrogated many times before being sent to the firing squad, Plácido claimed (according to his interrogator) that Domingo Del Monte had attempted to recruit him into the plot. Del Monte was Havana's most prominent liberal intellectual, and its richest as well. Lawyer, arts patron, literary critic, formative promoter of Cuban literature, he had married into a mega-rich planter family and resided in the capital's grandest and newest mansion. His story is an example of the trap in which the liberal wing of the sugarocracy found itself. They aspired toward independence and even an end to slavery, but they could not lead the country to either one.

Born in Venezuela, Del Monte came to Havana with his parents as a child and entered the Seminary of San Carlos (alma mater of Leonardo Gamboa) at the age of only twelve. He moved on to the University of Havana at fifteen. In the 1820s, he became the trusted associate of a prominent but nearly blind Havana lawyer, who soon financed a voyage to the United States and Europe for this brilliant young member of his firm. On his return to Cuba he joined the prestigious Economic Society of the Country's Friends, the intellectual inner circle of the native-born planter elite, publishers of the first significant Cuban newspaper, the *Papel Periódico de La Habana*. Steeped in European culture, with a mastery of Latin, Italian, Portuguese, French, and English, Del Monte participated in the founding of several literary magazines and began to patronize and promote young Cuban writers. His position as intellectual spokesperson and cultural arbiter was solidified by his match with Rosa Aldama, to whom he proposed marriage at a Philharmonic Society fancy ball. Rosa's father, also named Domingo, was among the most prominent importers of slaves in the early years of the century, and he had invested his gains in Matanzas plantations. By 1836, a survey of wealthy Cubans ranked Domingo de Aldama y Arechaga as the twelfth richest in the land. After a stay in Matanzas, the young couple established themselves in Havana, first at a sumptuous old house in the old city, and finally, just before La Escalera, in the new "Palace of Aldama" outside the walls at the beginning of the Paseo de Tacón.

The Palacio de Aldama, which now houses the Cuban Institute of History, was actually two houses in one, linked by a colonnaded gallery which ran for an entire city block along Calle Amistad across from the military parade ground. An immense stone edifice with staircases of Italian marble and ceilings carved and painted in precious woods, the Palacio housed the senior Aldama and his unmarried children in one unit, and Domingo and Rosa in the other. Of neoclassical style, it broke with the Andalusian and baroque traditions of the old city. It embraced all that was modern, including a library for Del Monte's collection of science and literature, bedrooms facing the street rather than the courtyard, cement tiles imitating stone in the patios, and a flush toilet—something even the Spanish royal family did not have. One member of the family wrote a letter to relatives living in Paris itself, describing to them the details of this invention which they had not yet seen.

Wherever Domingo Del Monte lived in the late 1830s and early 1840s, his house formed the center of the country's intellectual life. Besides promoting literature and learning, he criticized the woeful state of education under Spanish rule. His report on the near-total lack of public primary education was suppressed by the colonial government, and his request for the establishment of a department of Humanities at the university was deemed too dangerous, and therefore denied. Politically, Del Monte argued for greater Cuban autonomy within the empire. He set about provoking a debate about the slave trade and the future of slavery itself.

The status of the slave trade requires a few words of explanation. Britain, converted to free labor by the necessities of the industrial revolution and the demands of abolitionists, outlawed the Atlantic slave trade in 1807 and abolished slavery in its Caribbean colonies in 1833–39. The United States agreed to ban the import of new slaves in 1808, and a decade later Spain agreed as well, in return for an English payoff of 10 million pesetas. However, dependent as they were on the profits from Cuba's slave-based sugar industry, neither Madrid nor its representatives made any serious attempt to enforce this ban. The governors sitting in the Palace of the Captains General usually made a practice of taking bribes to look the other way. As Pancho Marty said of his career as a slave trader, "I made my fortune buying whites and selling blacks." Britain and Spain then agreed on new enforcement measures, but these only drove the contraband trade slightly further underground. *Cecilia Valdés* features a conversation between Cándido Gamboa and the captain-general about three hundred "bundles" or "sacks of carbon" whom Gamboa is trying to sneak past the Spanish-British commission that inspects incoming ships.

In the short run, the continued importation of slaves to work the ever-expanding sugar plantations generated huge profits for the Cuban oligarchy, of which the Palace of Aldama was proof. In the longer run, however, three dangers threatened the future of this class: First, the contraband nature of the traffic raised the price of slaves while the price of sugar on the world market fell. Second, with the advent of steam-driven grinding mills (rather than those powered by oxen or by crews of slaves themselves) and other technological improvements, a more skilled and independent workforce could be more efficient than unskilled slaves who were worked to death over twenty-hour days. Third, the influx of Africans had made whites a minority in Cuba. Census figures are not completely reliable, since their implications were so politically charged, but in the island as a whole whites appear to have become a minority of the population by 1817 and remained so in 1846. In Havana itself, they were a minority of the permanent population; only the Spanish garrisons in the forts and the crews of warships tipped the balance the other way. Thus white independence-minded Cuban intellectuals feared not only a Haitian-style revolt, but also the corruption of their nation-to-be by what the "modern" scientific theories of the time construed as a biologically inferior race.

In this context, with censorship making any direct challenges to the prevailing policy illegal, and with a nascent sense of nationhood demanding a Cuban literature distinct from that inherited from Spain, Del Monte encouraged his friends and protégés to write novels depicting details of Cuban life and exposing the evils of slavery. The models for these novels included the romances of Sir Walter Scott and Alessandro Manzoni and the social realism of Honoré de Balzac. Del Monte's circle included Cirilo Villaverde, of course. The author of *Cecilia Valdés* was a doctor's son who had seen slavery up close when his father worked on a plantation in Pinar de Río, and had then been sent to Havana for education in private schools. He became a schoolteacher himself, and a journalist, but his ambition lay in literature. He published stories and short novels in magazines, and with Del Monte's support he succeeded in publishing an early version of *Cecilia Valdés* in 1839.

Another member of the circle was Félix Tanco, whose lament about the Africanization of illustrious Cuban youth, quoted in chapter 4, comes from a letter he wrote to his patron in 1837. Tanco's 1838 novel *Petronia y Rosalia* contains harsh scenes of plantation slavery and also anticipates the incest theme of Villaverde's work. During La Escalera he was fired from his job as an administrator of the postal service, and jailed. Del Monte and his group also purchased the freedom of Francisco Manzano, a runaway slave and poet, and paid him to write his memoirs. The book could not be published in Cuba, but a part of it, heavily edited and rendered more acquiescent by the novelist Francisco Suarez y Romero, was smuggled to England and translated and published there. In its earliest pages, Manzano recalls the gentle treatment and education he received as a boy from his first owner, before he was shipped off to a life of misery under successive ones. That first owner was the aged Beatriz de Jústiz y Zayas, who had retired to her Matanzas plantation many years after she had written her *décima* and memorial at the time of the English attack. Suarez y Romero wrote a novel, *Francisco*, based on Manzano's memoirs as well.

So we can see why Del Monte's circle aroused the ire of Spanish authorities and of slave traders, and also why the patrician liberal was in frequent contact with the antislavery British consul in Havana—he hoped to use British pressure to bring about a change in the policies dictated by Madrid. At the same time, we can see why, despite the testimony coerced from Plácido, Del Monte would not have been part of any insurrectionary plot. He did not favor abolition, because his wealth and that of his class was tied up in slaves. Nor did he advocate full Cuban independence, much as he criticized Spain's attempts to keep the country subservient and backward. This was the contradiction of the planter class: they wanted liberalization of trade and civil society, freed from Spanish taxation and regulation, but they needed the Spanish army to keep their human property from rising up against them. They wanted a rapid end to the introduction of new slaves onto the island and they vaguely sought some gradual withering away of the slave system itself. But they did not want to make common cause with organized groups of slaves or free blacks, or to place any weapons (physical or political) in their hands.

The Count of Santovenia, whose sugar wealth had made him owner of the mansion that faced the Palace of the Captains-General across the Plaza de Armas and of one of the first estates in Cerro as well, wrote in 1841, just before La Escalera, that slavery was an "odious system," and he called for strict punishment for slave traders and for a campaign to promote the immigration of a free white labor force. Yet he argued that "a state of freedom would be attended with greater evils than slavery itself, because all the foundations of our civil existence would be speedily overturned [and] our beautiful Cuba would return to its previous condition, uncultivated and filled with barbarians, lost at once to us and the rest of the world."

The Countess of Merlín, whose visit to Havana came a year before Santovenia's report, challenged potential abolitionists and independence advocates in a similar vein. If slaves were freed and educated, she argued, "under a constitutional regime, in a country governed by egalitarian laws, couldn't they demand to share in those same institutions? Would you give them all of your rights, all of your privileges, make them your judges, generals, and ministers, give them your daughters in marriage? They would feel themselves men like yourselves, and demand a settling of accounts."

At times, white Cubans who were frustrated with Spanish rule saw their salvation in an alliance or possible union with the United States. Del Monte, though not a supporter of annexation, invited the friendship and correspondence of U.S. diplomat Alexander Everett, a Massachusetts Democrat, former ambassador to Spain, special envoy to Cuba, and an unabashed proponent of buying or otherwise acquiring the island and annexing it to the United States. In 1842, Del Monte wrote Everett of his fear that British agents might provoke an uprising of blacks in Cuba in order to increase Britain's influence in the Caribbean. "England has decreed our ruin, and Spain does not *know* or does not *want* to know this, and the Spanish authorities on the Island do not want or do not know how to weather the tempest." He told Everett that the United States should protect its interest and that of its "lesser sister of the great Western Confederation of the Caucasian Peoples of America" by sending American warships if need be.

In the meantime, Del Monte left with his family for a visit to Philadelphia, and then to Paris, where news of his alleged involvement in La Escalera reached him. In a letter to the Paris newspaper *Le Globe*, he claimed to have met his accuser Plácido only once, when the poet sought a loan to support his literary work. Del Monte said he was opposed to the slave trade and wanted to promote free white labor, but not by "revolutionary measures." He added, "I do not want my country to have slaves and even less that these slaves be blacks, that is from such a savage branch of the human family." A year later he requested permission to return to Cuba, which was denied. In 1846, he was finally acquitted of charges of conspiracy, but he remained in Madrid, where he died in 1853.

Where Del Monte stopped short of U.S. annexation as a solution to Cuba's problems, Cirilo Villaverde apparently did not. In 1846, he joined an anti-Spanish conspiracy of a new sort. This plot was headed by Narciso López, like Del Monte a Venezuelan by birth and married into a prominent Cuban planter family, but a career Spanish military officer rather than a literary man. López planned on staging an uprising and requesting U.S. aid. However, in 1848, shortly before the uprising was to occur, the plan was discovered. López escaped to the United States, but his chief aides, Villaverde among them, did not. On the night of October 20, Villaverde was surprised in his home by a group of Spanish soldiers and police, arrested, and taken to the New Jail. Tried and convicted by the Military Commission of Havana he was sentenced to the chain gang, but he plotted an escape along with another prisoner and the gatekeeper of the jail. In April of 1849, they succeeded, spent several days hiding in a thatched-roof cottage in the outer barrios, and then fled to Florida in a small sailboat rented by Villaverde's friends.

Though he was able to return to Havana for brief periods, Villaverde lived most of the rest of his life in New York, Philadelphia, and New Jersey, making his living by teaching Spanish and writing journalism, while throwing himself into the politics of the growing Cuban exile community in the United States. He served first as secretary to Narciso López, who from his headquarters in New York and then New Orleans raised a series of invasion forces made up mostly of Americans. Two of these expeditions succeeded in reaching Cuban soil. During the second expedition, after a few victories, López was captured to the west of Havana, brought to the capital, tried for high treason, and sentenced to death. In the sandy open space between La Punta fortress and the New Jail, he was executed on the garrote, a chair fitted with an iron collar and a screw tightened to crush the spinal cord and produce instant death. Many of his American recruits perished by firing squad, shot on the slopes of the Castillo de Atarés.

After López's defeat, Villaverde kept agitating in the North, writing in favor of Cuban separation from Spain in a variety of Cuban-exile and other Spanish-language publications. He married the exile activist Emilia Casanova with whom he founded a private high school in Weehawken, New Jersey. Throughout the 1850s he continued to argue for Cuban annexation to the United States, though in later years he shifted to a pro-independence view. He finally wrote the definitive version of *Cecilia Valdés* in 1878. Spanish censorship forbade publishing the book in Cuba, so the classic novel of nineteenth-century Havana first saw print in 1882 in New York. Meanwhile, the human profile of Havana was being altered by the one policy on which Spaniards and Cuban-born whites could agree: immigration to promote the growth of a free, non-African labor force.

As early as 1845, Domingo Del Monte's brother-in-law Miguel de Aldama made arrangements to import a group of Basques whom he hoped to put to work in his fields in place of slaves. Thanks to a variety of colonization schemes involving labor contracting, indentured servitude, and subsidized transportation, by 1862 whites had again become a majority in the island's population, roughly 800,000 out of the 1.5 million total. Over the next three decades, some 500,000 more arrived, not counting several hundred thousand soldiers and officials, many of whom also stayed. The bulk of the immigrants came from Spain, especially from poorer areas (Asturias, Galicia, the Canary Islands) or areas subject to political repression themselves (Catalunya). Chinese contract laborers were included in the "white" category of the census—though they were little better than slaves themselves during the term of their indentures. About 150,000 such Chinese "*culies*" entered Cuba in the third quarter of the century and were put to work on plantations and in railroad construction.

In Havana, the new wave of Spanish immigrants, especially younger men, competed with white middle-class Cubans in the professions and the lower ranks of commerce and civil service, and they also formed, for the first time, a significant white working class. Between the census of 1846 and that of 1862, the city's white male population grew from 62,000 to 92,000. By 1862, whites—mostly born in Spain—had become a majority of the bakers, butchers, carpenters, carters, shoemakers, day laborers, and even coachmen, all trades previously dominated by Cubans of color.

Cigar rolling, the first factory-based work of any importance in Havana, surged during these years, as Cuban *puros* took the smoking rooms of the United States and Europe by storm. The Havana city directory of 1859 contains ten two-column pages devoted entirely to listings of cigar stores and brands, including not only such names as (translated) Cuban Delight, Havana Rose, and Lovely Cuban Woman's Whim, but also Británica, Crimea, Lord Wellington, Daniel Webster, Washington, Pensilvanio, and even Flor de Henry Clay. The illustrations affixed to boxes of cigars and cigarettes offered the world some of its first comic strips (with relations between white men and mulattas as a frequent theme). By the 1860s, nearly five hundred tobacco factories and workshops employed a non-slave wage-labor workforce of 13,000, about 70 percent of them white.

In 1865, cigar workers organized the country's first labor newspaper, *La Aurora*, and the next year the country's first real trade union, the Asociación de Tabaqueros de La Habana, struck against Cabanas and Carvajal cigar factory. The Asturian anarchist organizer and writer Saturnino Martínez introduced the position of Reader into the factories, a tradition maintained ever since, allowing the workers to hear news, articles, editorials, and literary works without stopping their manipulation of the tobacco leaves. The cigar rollers took up a collection to pay the Reader (often a literate member of their own ranks), and could therefore democratically choose what he read to them. Invented in Havana, this practice spread to factories in Key West, Tampa, New York, and other cities with emigrant Cuban workers.

After serving out their terms in the countryside, meanwhile, many Chinese gravitated to the capital to work in tobacco factories, as well as in construction and on the docks. They settled especially in the outlying zone to the north of La Salud, on the north bank of the old Royal Ditch, where they began to go into business as vegetable growers and street vendors. With the arrival of another wave of Chinese immigrants, the *californios* who had made some money in gold-rush era California but then fled growing discrimination and persecution there, Havana's Chinatown took shape in the area bounded by the modern streets of Galiano, Belascoaín, Reina, and Zanja (Ditch). Alongside laundries, restaurants, and small stores selling imported Chinese goods, emerged whorehouses, gambling parlors, and opium dens in this neighborhood populated largely by men. So too did traditional fraternities (similar to the African *cabildos*), Chinese political organizations with roots in the old country, and eventually newspapers and theaters. By the end of the nineteenth century, Havana's *barrio chino* could be compared only to those in San Francisco and Lima in the New World. The Chinese *charada*, an underground lottery in which bets were placed on numbers represented by different symbols, took its place alongside cards, dice, the Spanish state lottery, cockfights, and other forms of gambling on luck and skill. Ever since then, "horse" has meant "one" in Cuban slang, "butterfly" has meant "two," "corpse" has meant "nine," and so on.

Catalán merchants, meanwhile, played an ever-greater role in the city's merchant middle and upper class. "Five years of privation, and then a fortune," was said to be the motto of the Catalán immigrant. Thanks often to their links with fellow-countrymen of the previous generation, many did succeed in rising from small shopkeepers to wholesale merchants and informal bankers within one generation or two. The thirteen-year-old José Gener y Batet, for instance, stepped off a ship in Havana in 1844 at the age of thirteen and went to work for his uncle, a storekeeper in Pinar del Río. Twenty years later he was back in the capital, having acquired a position in the state apparatus. He was soon the founder and owner of an important tobacco factory and the owner of a sugar mill. Cuban planters, borrowing against the next harvest, often fell into debt to these Catalán and other Spanish merchants, who thus began to acquire more and more plantations themselves.

In this complex tapestry of classes and nationalities, old and new, Havana in the second half of the nineteenth century was not so much "the most loyal" Spanish possession, as it was divided and blowing in the wind. The new generation of Cuban-born intellectuals, hundreds of whom had studied in the United States or Europe, felt frustrated with the cautious reformism of their parents or employers. To them, being modern meant independence, democracy, and free labor, yet many were still fearful of the cataclysm that a revolt against Spain could unleash. As they were caricatured by a contemporary, "They have read Proudhon, ride in berlins [four-wheeled closed carriages], love liberty, and own slaves." They conspired in cafes, and when a revolution finally broke out in 1868, they enlisted in it. But the revolution began far from Havana, in and around the old smugglers' port of Bayamo and the cattle lands of Camagüey, in the East. It was led by planters and cattle ranchers removed from the centers of the slave-based economy. Carlos Manuel de Céspedes, Oriente sugar planter and alumnus of Havana's Seminary of San Carlos, freed his small contingent of slaves on condition that they join his rebel contingent, which they did. The rebel army's ranks were quickly swelled by masses of free mulattos and blacks, followed by rural and urban whites of many classes, and by runaway slaves. Though the civilian leadership's position on slavery was equivocal and shifting, that of the rebel army was increasingly clear.

The war was long and bloody, lasting ten hard years. It was fought largely in the eastern part of the island, but it left an indelible mark on Havana. In the person of General Antonio Maceo, a mulatto general from a farm-owning family outside Santiago de Cuba, and in the composition of its officers corps and troops, it unified white Cubans and Cubans of color behind an ideal of independence without the bloodbath that many whites had feared. The Spaniards, eager to portray the war as a racial struggle, called the rebels derogatorily by a pseudo-African term, "*mambí*." The rebels embraced it, as U.S. independence fighters had embraced the British taunt of "Yankee Doodle" a century before. Many divisions remained, however, between the rebel army, its civilian leaders, its wealthy sympathizers, and its diplomatic representatives in Havana and New York. In the end, the war changed Cuba in many ways: increasing the indebtedness of Cuban planters, provoking the gradual emancipation of the slaves, leading Cubans to adopt what would later become a new nation's anthem and flag (the flag first hoisted by Narciso López), and driving many of the rural population into cities and towns. But it did not bring independence. This "Ten Years' War" would be followed by a second independence war whose results would change the capital dramatically.

6 Revolutions and Retributions: From the Teatro Villanueva to the Maine

Throughout the Ten Years' War, Havana was a city divided. With some outstanding exceptions, it was divided between *criollos* and *peninsulares*, between those born in Cuba and those born in Spain. Pro-independence families sent their sons to the war zone, performed underground support of various kinds, or went into exile. Veterans of the black and mulatto militias (revived in the 1850s, after the fear of La Escalera had subsided) also made their way eastward to join the *mambís*. Urban Spanish vigilante groups, meanwhile, formed out of the *batallones de voluntarios del comercio*, battalions of immigrant clerks, cigar workers, and other employees recruited in the 1850s to guard against insurrections or invasions of the Narciso López sort. In 1869, the Voluntarios began recruiting Spanish deserters and veterans as well. Their task was to suppress active support for the rebellion in the cities, Havana above all.

On the night of January 21, 1869, three months after the outbreak of the war, a company of Cuban actors put on a musical comedy called *Perro huevero* in the Teatro Villanueva, a theater and dance hall located two blocks south of the New Jail. The title was taken from an old saying that a dog will go after eggs no matter how often it burns its nose in the pot. Though the play contained no political references, it did have some lines praising the physical beauty of the isle that was now in full revolt. Among the cast was a mulatto singer and actor named Jacinto Valdés, who performed under the stage name Benjamín de las Flores. According to his Spanish police file, he was an unemployed cigar roller who had turned to the theater as a means of support. He lived with Juana Relly, described as a prostitute and fortune-teller. One way or another they were members of the capital's *farandula*, its underground world where night life, criminality, and bohemia mingled together. At an opportune moment in the drama, Valdés shouted out *"Viva Carlos Manuel de Céspedes!"* in praise of the Oriente planter turned general who headed the rebellion, and he added more *vivas* for other leaders of the revolutionaries in the east. He was fined 200 pesos and warned not to repeat the subversive action, but the news of what had happened at the performance of *Perro huevero* spread.

The next night, both sides of Havana came to the Teatro Villanueva prepared. Many women in the audience came dressed in revolutionary colors, some with the single star of the rebel flag stitched into their clothes. A group of Spanish Voluntarios, meanwhile, gathered outside. At the point in the drama where one actor proclaimed, "Say it with me, or suffer your shame/Long live the land that yields sugar cane," numerous women and men in the audience chimed in. They stood and chanted the lines, and they launched blue and white ribbons, matching the stripes of the insurrectionary banner, over the crowd. The Voluntarios then burst into the theater, shooting into the audience and making arrests, paying no attention to age or gender. Over the next two days, the Voluntarios continued their reprisals, firing on patrons in the outdoor sidewalk of the Café del Louvre, a gathering point for the wealthy separatist youth, and then attacking the Palacio de Aldama. This mob was allegedly searching for an arms cache, but in reality they were punishing Miguel de Aldama, the late Del Monte's brother-in-law, for having declared sympathy with the rebel cause. In the course of three days of violence, fourteen residents of Havana were killed, sixteen wounded, and forty-five arrested. Thereafter, the Voluntarios patrolled the streets, intent on repressing any signs of disrespect toward Spain. The Aldamas went into exile, and so did Jacinto Valdés.

Since the University of Havana was a hotbed of separatist sympathy, in November the Voluntarios turned their attention that way. On orders of the governor, thirty-five medical students were arrested on suspicion of having vandalized the tomb of a Spanish journalist. Eight were put on trial by a military court, but they were acquitted. In response, a mob of Voluntarios besieged the jail, intent on retrying the students themselves. The judge of their proceedings was the Catalán immigrant José Gener y Batet, now head of a world famous tobacco firm bearing his name. The Voluntarios lined the eight students up against the wall of the jail and executed them while Spanish regular troops stood by. The rest were returned to the confines of the jail.

Havana tradition says that the eight medical students (all white, of course) did not die alone. Five members of the Abakuá secret society, all construction workers employed nearby, are said to have organized a rescue attempt and been killed in the process. One of them, as oral tradition tells it, had been a "milk brother" of the condemned student Alonso Álvarez de la Campa—his mother was wet-nurse to the condemned white student. The preeminent twentieth century historian of the colonial period, Manuel Moreno Fraginals, wrote that he had heard the story of the Abakuá rescue attempt in 1940 from a ninety-year-old Abakuá and former slave, and later from a 100-year-old who did not know the first informant. Moreno then found a name mentioned by both sources in the burial records of the city cemetery for that year. Historian Jorge Lozano cites a letter written back to Spain by Ramón López de Ayala, the Voluntario captain who commanded the firing squad, which says that "some blacks opened fire on a group of Artillery Voluntarios, killing their lieutenant. Those assaulted then charged the blacks and hacked the five authors of this aggression to bits."

In Havana during the Ten Years' War, lines of nationality cut across those of class, and vice versa. Some militant workers, like Saturnino Martínez who had introduced the Reader to the cigar factories, were also Voluntarios. On the other hand, the Spanish authorities used their wartime powers to suppress union organization and deport the organizers. They shut down *La Aurora* and temporarily banned the Readers, and then they finally clamped a lid on the Voluntarios during a carriage-drivers' strike which enjoyed some Voluntario support. More important, however, was the fact that nationality itself was always in flux. As a popular saying put it, "A Spaniard can get anything he wants in Cuba—except Spanish children." The descendants of Catalanes and Asturians and Galicians learned to speak like Cubans. Politically, the sons and daughters of many a *peninsular* declared themselves *cubanos* and *cubanas* during the

Ten Years' War, or in the uneasy interval that followed, or in the new War of Independence launched in 1895.

Spanish forces preparing to execute a Cuban prisoner by garrote in fornt of the New Jail, 1869.

The most famous example by far of this change in consciousness of nationality was the son of immigrants from Valencia and the Canary Islands. Leonor Pérez came to Havana from the Canaries with her parents, who had the good luck to win a sizeable prize in the state lottery shortly after they set foot on Cuban soil. She married Mariano Martí, who had come to the Cuban capital from Valencia as sergeant in an artillery unit, fought against Narciso López, and then retired from the army and taken a job in the police. The couple settled in a small house on Calle Paula in the old city and had a son who was baptized in the Church of the Angel in 1853 with the name of José Julián Martí. The growing family soon moved to a succession of other houses, mostly in the poorer *barrios* outside the walls, where Mariano served as a neighborhood watchman, though he was sometimes out of work. One of the briefer stays was on Calle Jesús

Peregrino itself. Though his parents were loyal to the Peninsula, the boy developed nationalist sentiments and formed a close tie with his teacher Rafael María Mendive, a poet and fervent nationalist who ran one of the very few secular schools in the city, a private school on the Prado that served the lower middle class.

During the days of the Villanueva events, José Martí, now sixteen, published the first and only issue of a short-lived literary magazine, *La Patria Libre*, printed in a small shop on the Calle Obispo near its crossing with Cuba, aptly enough. Four days later, his patron Mendive was arrested, and shortly thereafter the teenager wrote a patriotic poem in a manuscript paper secretly circulated by students. He continued to visit Mendive in the El Príncipe fortress until the teacher's deportation to Spain. Then, in October, a group of Voluntarios raided the house of his schoolmate Fermín Valdés Dominguez, behind the Tacón Theater. The Voluntarios claimed that Valdés Domínguez and friends had been mocking them from a window as they passed by in the street, returning from a military parade. In the house they found separatist propaganda and a poem by the two friends in which they challenged a third schoolmate who had enlisted in the Spanish army, calling him an apostate who had broken ranks. Valdés was arrested on the spot, and Martí two weeks later.

Valdés suffered a year's imprisonment, after which he enrolled in medical school and became one of the thirty-five arrested for profanation of the tomb (though he escaped being one of the eight who were shot). Martí was confined in the New Jail, tried and convicted of "disloyalty," and finally sentenced at the age of seventeen to six years on the chain gang. Prisoner number 113 in the "First Brigade of Whites," every day from April to August of 1870 he trudged from the New Jail to the quarries at the edge of Vedado, manacled just as R. H. Dana had described eleven years before, laboring twelve hours a day under the summer sun near what is now the Hotel Nacional.

Finally his parents prevailed upon the authorities to put him to work in a cigarette factory within the jail, then to exile him to the Isle of Pines off Cuba's southern coast, and finally to deport him to Spain where he could complete his education. He gained a law degree and in the late

1870s made his way to Central America, briefly back to Havana, and then into exile in the United States. Like Cirilo Villaverde, Martí spent more of his adult life in exile than in Havana. He lived most of his last thirteen years in New York.

Propagandist, political organizer, groundbreaking essayist, and modernist poet, José Martí would be the architect and organizer of the Cuban Revolutionary Party and the second Independence War. Around him coalesced a new notion of *Cuba Libre* "with all and for the good of all," one that promised that "the colony would not live on the republic"—that separation from Spain would also include thoroughgoing social reform. The last of the independence struggles of the Spanish colonies, the Cuban struggle was also the most radical. In the years of independence agitation, if open nationalism could not be expressed in the capital without fear of expulsion or arrest, there were other, more subtle ways in which Cuban-born Havana expressed its growing sense of nationhood. One of the most striking of these was sports.

Spaniards went to the bullfight at the *plaza de toros* on Belascoaín or the one in Regla across the bay, both of which featured exclusive boxes from which Spanish authorities would preside. Bullfights were often sponsored by the army or the Voluntarios, and nationalist-minded Havanans shunned the *plazas de toros* like the plague. Martí called bullfighting a "futile bloody spectacle" and criticized the practice of accustoming the "souls and eyes of children who will become men, and women who will become mothers" to such a thing. The Cuban alternatives were twofold, one borrowed from the Spanish heritage, and one from the United States. Cuban men had long been fanatics of the *vallas de gallos*, the cockfight pits. Beginning in the 1860s, Cubans of both sexes went to the baseball park.

"Cockfighting," the novelist Abel Prieto would observe with late twentieth-century hindsight, "took root in Cuba even before we knew we were Cuban, before we knew we were different from our fathers. Bullfighting never had a chance, because the cockfight offered a fair contest, and Cubans always prefer what's equal or even, something anyone can win. A bullfight is essentially a trap with no exit for the bull." American businessman Joseph Dimock, in Havana en route to visit his family's sugar mills in Matanzas and Cienfuegos, took the train from Regla to Guanabacoa to visit the famed cockpit there. "Those of all shades were present: white, black, lemon, and mahogany color," he noted disapprovingly. "The cockpit was a perfect pandemonium, and all were equal there—white and black, slave and free—all betting, drinking, and smoking together. It would have rejoiced the heart of the most ardent abolitionist to see the perfect familiarity between the two races." Cockfights generally took place on Sunday mornings, an indication of the lack of popular participation in the weekly masses officiated by mostly Spanish priests.

In less bloody fashion, Cubans beginning in the 1860s borrowed from the United States what they saw as a New World and democratic sport. The called it *el béisbol*, or more colloquially *la pelota*. One version of its implantation places the first game in a clearing in the still largely forested El Vedado, organized by a trio of middle-class Cuban youth returned from studying in Mobile, Alabama. The new sport took root in both Havana and Matanzas, finding equally fertile ground among dockworkers who learned it from American crews. It soon spread throughout the island and eventually, via the travels of Cuban ballplayers, to the rest of the Caribbean and Central America as well. The Havana Base Ball Club (so named, in English) was founded about 1870, while the Ten Years' War raged in the East. In 1874, Havana defeated Matanzas, 51–9, in the first recorded professional game. Ex-Fordham University and (U.S.) National Association pro Esteban Bellán held down third base for Havana. Emilio Sabourín scored eight runs. Four years later Sabourín's Liga General de Base Ball de la Isla de Cuba set up headquarters in Havana. Baseball newspapers and magazines proliferated, many of them making the opposition of baseball to bullfighting explicit. "We categorically reject the bullfight," the editors of *El Pitcher* wrote in 1888; "we will organize a crusade against the ignoble spectacle," a reporter for *El Baseball* declared. Cuban doctor Benjamín de Céspedes wrote to a baseball promoter that fans of different classes rooting for the same ballclub was "a rehearsal for democracy," nothing less.

The Almendares team's brand new stadium opened in the early 1880s across the street from the Quinta de los Molinos, the summer residence of the Captains General. The Spanish countered with a new bullring nearby. So when six thousand spectators packed the stadium to see the championship ballgame between Almendares and Habana in 1886, their statement was not only about sports. "Everyone was at baseball," a visiting Spanish poet was shocked to observe ten years later. "Men and women, old and young, masters and servants . . . I had a presentiment that Spain had died for Cuba." Episodic Spanish attempts to outlaw baseball or particular teams proved fruitless, but when war broke out anew in 1895, they immediately instituted a new ban. This time, ballplayers were among those who flocked from Havana to join the rebellion. Three members of the Almendares club's pitching staff became rebel officers. Emilio Sabourín, now player-manager of Havana, was arrested for his separatist activity and exiled to the Spanish enclave of Ceuta in Morocco. Among his fellow-prisoners was Juan Gualberto Gómez—Havana journalist, independence organizer, close ally of Martí, and former president of the Central Directorate of Societies of the Colored Race. Sabourín, wrote Gómez, loved three things equally: his family, the nation, and baseball. Sabourín died in Ceuta at the age of forty-three, two years into a twenty-year sentence. Gómez lived to return to Havana, and we will meet him again.

Another site of symbolic confrontation, far from the roar of the baseball crowd, was the city's vast new resting place for the dead in the heights above El Vedado. In the 1880s, Fermín Valdés Domínguez, returned from exile and practicing medicine, took up a public collection to build a mausoleum-monument at the Cemetery of Colón celebrating the innocence of his eight fellow students who had been executed. In November of 1889, their remains were exhumed and brought to the new memorial, in a plot purchased for 920 pesos in gold. In response, José Gener y Batet dug into his personal fortune to add fourteen Italian marble statues to his own mausoleum-chapel and future resting place, so that these figures could look down upon the column crowning the students' memorial a hundred yards away.

The 1880s also saw the first signs of organization among the city's prostitutes, who published several issues of a magazine called *La Cebolla* (the onion). *La Cebolla* did not touch the question of independence. Its pseudonymous contributors appear to have been both *peninsulares* (La

Madrileña, Lola la Sevillana) and *criollas* (La Conga, Teresa Machete). One of their goals was to present a better image of the oldest profession than the image presented in the recent exposé *La prostitución en la ciudad de La Habana* by Benjamin de Céspedes (the same who wrote about the democratic qualities of baseball), who emphasized the sordidness of the red-light underworld and particularly the victimization of children. The magazine's organizers, nonetheless, directed most of their fire at the bribes and sexual favors demanded by the Spanish officials and police. They selected as their editor a progressive Spaniard named Victorino Reinera, who later edited *El Machete*, an embattled pro-independence newspaper in Santiago de Cuba, and was deported from that city for publicizing the activities of rebel general Antonio Maceo.

The tone of *La Cebolla* was decidedly confrontational: "The ominous times of sitting still and shutting up are gone, never to return," the editorial opening the second issue declared. "Today no one sits still or shuts up, so why should we? Why should we tolerate with our silence the criminal conduct of a pack of thieves who, without cause or justification, are robbing us of what has cost us so many bumps and grinds?" Other articles complained of "the unjust fines they impose on us, because we don't want to accede to the lustful whims of some cop, or because we won't slip them the bribes they expect."

La Cebolla also echoed the universal *criollo* distaste for high Spanish taxes and restrictions on commerce: "The 'horizontals' of this capital pay more taxes to the State than are required to become [in the case of white men] voters or elected representatives. Though we contribute more than other classes to feed the treasury with the sweat of our brows, we are treated as if we were slaves, without protection of the law." The writers complained of new laws requiring them to close their windows or install lattices to block the view from the street, although in practice, one of their poems observed:

> Go ahead and peek out the window
> and stretch your arms out too.
> The soldier won't say a word
> if he gets a coin out of you.

"In what country is the industrialist banned from putting his merchandise on public view?" demanded an open letter to city's Civil Governor. "We sell our flesh—mine, as you may discover, is fresh, velvet, firm, and perfumed, a true *bocatto di cardinali*. Why should we be barred from tempting the passersby with our charms?" A profile of a leading madam praised her as a good and generous soul, a former unionist in the cigarette factories of Madrid, a "revolutionary of other days . . . who stands up before the authorities demanding justice, firm in defense of her rights." To the Municipal President of Havana, on the other hand, they pointed out, "If we are 'public women,' you are also a public man. Your life is nothing to boast about, either."

One reason for the increase in prostitution was an economic depression that hit the country and its capital in the 1880s, followed by the devastating effects in the 1890s of a new war against Spain. Conditions were especially difficult for women who had to support either children or destitute parents. According to estimates by the historian María del Carmen Barcia, in the late 1880s a room cost six to eight pesos a month, and food cost a minimum of a peso a day, while the daily pay of washerwomen, ironers, seamstresses, maids, and female cigar factory workers was only a peso or slightly more. In the last years of the century, according to the results of official surveys, at least third of the prostitutes in Havana held or had lost jobs in other trades, and half were under twenty years of age.

The depression stemmed from the lingering effects of the disruption caused by the Ten Years' War, the rapid spread of beet sugar production in Europe and cane production in Hawaii and South America, and the vagaries of U.S. tariff policies (negotiated not between Washington and Havana, but between Washington and Madrid). Cuba's share of the world sugar market dropped from 29 percent in 1868 to 11 percent twenty years later. To get under tariff barriers, cigar factory owners moved production back and forth from Havana to Key West or Tampa as needed, since the cured tobacco leaves could make the crossing in half a day or less, just as easily as the finished cigars. When the factories moved, unemployed Cuban workers followed. Cuban professionals, too, sought the jobs for which they were qualified in Mexico or the United States, jobs that were absent or dominated by Spaniards at home. About 250,000 Spaniards entered Cuba in the last third of the nineteenth century, while about 100,000 Cubans left. All these developments culminated in the second Independence War, which lasted from 1895–98.

This second war began with an uprising in Oriente and with landings on remote eastern beaches, organized in the United States and led by Martí, Maceo, and the commander-in-chief of the rebel armies in both wars, Dominican-born Máximo Gómez. Martí died in battle within six weeks of stepping on Cuban soil, but native recruits flocked to the insurgent armies. These joint forces soon extended the war to the countryside and then all over the island, including the outskirts of Havana. The insurgents' weapons were machetes, rifles, and "the torch"—they burned the cane fields of planters who did not come over to the separatist side. In response to the rebel advance, Spanish Captain-General Valeriano Weyler, pioneering a tactic later adopted by American commanders in the Philippines and Vietnam, tried to dry up sources of support for the independence armies by forcing hundreds of thousands of peasants and farmworkers off the land. This policy of "reconcentration," of driving now-jobless rural Cubans into the towns and cities, resulted in tens of thousands of deaths from starvation and disease. Between a census taken in 1887 and another taken in 1899 the country's population dropped by 60,000 (to just over one-and-a half million), the first decline in centuries. The population of greater Havana, however, grew by about 40,000 to a total of 250,000.

In Havana, the sick and hungry *reconcentrados* were crowded into wooden barracks constructed in the *fosos* or pits, steep empty holes of collapsed limestone that dotted the outer barrios. Families wandered the streets searching for aid. In Nuestra Señora de la Caridad, one of three shelters set up for children orphaned or separated from their families, 4800 boys and girls subsisted on scarce rations funded by appeals to private charity. To avoid open criticism of the policy of reconcentration, appeals from pro-Spanish organizations referred to the needs of "poor children" without specifying who they were. Agricultural production plummeted, and food prices in the city doubled. "Not only the *concentrados* lack meat," reported *La Lucha*, a paper speaking for popular

Cuban opinion. "We don't have it in Havana, because of the scandalous prices charged by the slaughterhouse. In these days we've seen people who used to weigh three hundred pounds, and now they're down to skin and bones." Prices of root vegetables and bread, the traditional foods of the poor, surged as well. *The Matter of Bread*, a comedy that debuted at the Teatro Alhambra in June of 1897, featured satirical ditties about prices: two silver *reales* for a small *ñame* (Cuban sweet potato), one for a beet or a *malanga*, and twelve *centavos* for a rotten *yuca*, "bitter and black."

At the same time, contradictorily, the capital continued its march to modernity. The New York-based Spanish-American Light and Power Company brought electric lighting to Central Park, across from the Hotel Inglaterra, in 1889. Soon its cables and lamps began to snake through the streets. A new aqueduct to replace the old Royal Ditch, whose construction began in the middle of the century, opened at last in 1893. Designed by the engineer Francisco de Albear, himself born in the Morro Castle where his father had been fort commander, the underground duct depended entirely on gravity to produce pressure. It was an engineering triumph, parts of which are still in use today. The first cinema opened in 1897, and the next year the modern La Tropical brewery and ice factory opened on the far side of the Almendares, in the municipality of Marianao.

Modernity was also marching along in the cultural sphere. Danza had become *danzón*, whose sensual rhythms and motions scandalized moralists anew. In the realm of high culture appeared *La Habana Elegante*, a fin de siecle tropical *New Yorker*, a review of poetry, high society, gossip, shopping, travel, and the arts that debuted in the 1880s. Its leading contributor, at least in retrospect, was the poet and critic Julián del Casal. Casal was particularly influenced by the French symbolists, as in his well-known verse "sleep spreads its supple mantle over all that lies in shadow, except for my thoughts awake in the stillness, bright flames of a hidden lantern, shedding light on the deep emptiness of my soul." He suffered at the hands of Cuban critics not so much for those influences as for more exotic ones, reflected in his habit of dressing in a Japanese kimono and surrounding himself with Oriental objects of all sorts, not to mention his poetic longings for the cold perfection of snow. Attacked as a bearer of unhealthy foreign contamination, and most likely homosexual, he was a forerunner of others who would suffer under those prejudices in periods to come. Yet he was part of the search for a Cuban identity distinct from Spanish sources. Fired from a job in the state bureaucracy for an article that mocked the captain-general, Casal soon published a sonnet identifying (if pessimistically) with Antonio Maceo when the ex- and future general visited the capital in 1890 to try to rally and reorganize supporters of independence there.

Maceo stayed in the Hotel Inglaterra, probably the first Cuban of color to do so. Casal visited him there, and this encounter between the farmer-soldier and the urban aesthete, the man of action and the man of letters, the revolutionary and the decadent, has become a touchstone for modern Cuban intellectuals seeking to reconcile the two. Maceo and Casal posed for a joint photograph, which has been lost, and the soldier also gave the poet a signed portrait dedicated to the "the appealing Cuban bard and intelligent young man Don Julián del Casal." For his part, Casal confessed in a letter written soon afterward that he had met only one person lately whom he had found appealing. "Whom do you think? Maceo, a beautiful man of strong constitution, sharp intelligence, and iron will. I don't know whether this affection I feel for our General is the effect of the neurosis that makes me admire those with qualities opposite to my own, but few men have made such a welcome impression on me." In another letter, which has vanished like the joint photo, Casal is alleged to have repeated an impression along the same lines, adding, "Although I am a bitter opponent of war, on hearing him talk I felt convinced that it's necessary and inevitable. Within a year, I think, we'll be in rebellion again."

It was five years, in fact, and Casal died before the new Independence War began, perishing suddenly from of an aneurysm suffered during an outburst of laughter in 1892. Juana Borrero, the most promising young contributor to *La Habana Elegante*, died in exile in 1896, of typhoid fever in Key West, where her pro-independence family took refuge during the war. Borrero's death at nineteen interrupted her poetic career just as it was taking shape—romantic, melancholy, modernist, erotic, and ethereal all at once. She is known, too, for her love letters to the poet and *Habana Elegante* contributor Carlos Pío Urbach, from whom she was separated first by family vigilance and then by the Florida Straits. "Listen," she reminds him in one of these, "I may be 'the ideal' but I'm not 'the innocent,' you know?"

Pío died in the war, in 1897. So did Maceo himself, in December of 1896, in a small skirmish near Punta Brava, about ten miles outside the capital. Many had hoped to see him enter Havana at the head of an army, but the conservative, pro-Spanish newspaper *Diario de la Marina* threw a banquet to celebrate his death. Even some who favored autonomy or independence relaxed at the disappearance of the dreaded "mulatto republic" that Maceo represented to them. On the other hand, Maceo had been kept informed of Spanish preparedness by an extensive Havana underground, one of whose members had succeeded in smuggling plans out of the captain-general's palace. The clandestine clubs of the Cuban Revolutionary Party kept up this activity, with men and women carrying messages, maintaining contacts between civilian organizers in exile and the rebel armies, raising money, sewing uniforms, and smuggling arms, ammunition, and volunteers to the battlefields. Two female leaders of the insurgency were prisoners in the Casa de Recogidas in Old Havana. These were Evangelina Cossio de Cisneros and Magdalena Peñarredonda y Doley.

Peñarredonda, born in 1846 of a Spanish father and French mother, was a movement veteran from Pinar del Río, the tobacco-growing province to the west of Havana. In the first war she had been a member of the local revolutionary club. When she and her sisters shaved their heads as a sign of solidarity with the *mambís*, they were locked in the house by their father until their hair grew back. In the 1880s, Peñarredonda lived for a period in the United States, contributing pseudonymously to *La Habana Elegante*. She was the "Elga Adman" (an anagram for "Magdalena") whom we quoted in Chapter 3 about the "sad and monotonous life of the girls of Cuba." Once back in Cuba she was the alleged recipient of Casal's second letter about Maceo as well. In the 1890s, she was elected an officer of the underground Cuban Revolutionary Party and traveled back and forth to New York to serve as liaison with Martí and other leaders. When Maceo's armies reached Pinar del Río in 1895, she became legendary as a combatant, underground organizer, and spy. Exposed and arrested in 1896, she was brought to the capital and imprisoned in the Casa de Recogidas, where she became a leader in demanding more humane conditions for political and common prisoners alike. She remained in prison until the Spanish defeat in 1898.

Evangelina Cossio, by contrast, was a teenage activist who made a dramatic escape to the North, like Cirilo Villaverde fifty years before. The beautiful daughter of a veteran revolutionary organizer from Cienfuegos, she had accompanied her father and sister to internal exile on the Isle of Pines off Havana Province's southern coast. There she organized an attempt by exiles and islanders to take the Spanish governor captive, seize arms and a boat, and join the rebel army. Cossio's plan included luring the governor, who had been pursuing her since she arrived, with a message that said, "I'll wait for you tonight in my room, but come alone." The governor was kidnapped but then rescued, and Evangelina ended up in the Casa de Recogidas, threatened with deportation to the penal colony in Morocco.

The American newspaper magnate William Randolph Hearst then entered the picture, making Cossio a cause celebre in his flagship paper, the *New York World*. A year after her arrest, she was rescued, hidden overnight somewhere in the city, and smuggled onto a New York-bound steamship the next day. According to the *World*, the escape involved a ladder, a file to cut through a barred window, and leaps from rooftop to rooftop, all under the firm hand of the paper's special correspondent sent to Havana for the purpose. Other accounts suggest that guards were bribed, or even that the Spanish found her a liability and wanted to get rid of her. In any case, Hearst used her escape to build his paper's circulation and public interest in the Cuban rebellion. In October, 1897, Hearst presented Cossio to the American public at an extravaganza in Madison Square Garden. This was the same year in which the newspaper owner reportedly cabled his artist who had complained that there was no fighting to depict in Havana, saying "You furnish the pictures, and I'll furnish the war."[1]

Three months later, mob attacks by pro-Spanish vigilantes on several Havana newspapers led U.S. Consul Fitzhugh Lee to use the excuse of breakdown of order in the capital to request sending a U.S. battleship to protect American interests there. After negotiations between Washington

U.S.S. Maine entering Havana Bay, 1898.

and Madrid, the *U.S.S. Maine* steamed between the Morro and the Punta on January 25, 1898, her "courtesy visit" balanced by the dispatch of the Spanish cruiser Vizcaya to New York. On Tuesday, February 15, at 9:40 p.m., a great explosion shook Havana. Residents rushed out of homes, theaters, and cafes, speculating that a bomb had gone off, that a powder magazine had exploded, or even that the city's natural gas tank had blown up. Then the news began to circulate, by word of mouth, that what had exploded was the *Maine*, taking 191 victims to the bottom of the bay. The sinking of the *Maine* brought the United States into the war.

7 Many Happy Returns?
U.S. Occupation and Its Aftermath

On January 1, 1899, the red and yellow flags that had proclaimed Spanish dominion over Havana for nearly four centuries came down. They came down from the Morro, from the Palace of the Captains General and soon—on the orders of Havana's mayor—from private flagpoles and balconies too. Within a month, a commentator in Havana's *El Figaro* weekly reported, the only Spanish flags were the ones flying from the masts of ships repatriating the defeated colonial army, or those hidden under the counters of Spanish merchants' shops.

By contrast, Cuban flags came out of hiding, and the capital filled with them at last. The *bandera cubana* flew from private homes, patriotic and social clubs, union halls, and the new associations of Army of Liberation veterans. Its red triangle with a single white star appeared on brooches and belt buckles, and its five blue and white stripes were sewn or embroidered onto the clothes of shoe shine boys and socialites alike. An exile recently returned from the North marveled at how, walking through the city, he heard the piano notes of the revolutionary movement's songs wafting out of houses on every street. *Cuba Libre* was triumphant everywhere in Havana—except where it mattered most. The red, white, and blue colors that fluttered in the sea breeze atop the flagpoles of the Morro, the Palace, and other seats of power were the stars and stripes of the United States. Another returning exile, the poet Bonifacio Byrne who had been supporting himself by reading aloud in the cigar factories of Tampa, described his response in a verse that every Cuban child would learn in school:

In sober mourning I returned
From a distant shore and clime,
For a glimpse of my flag I yearned
But found another in place of mine.

The Cuban war of independence did not end like the American one, with an imperial army surrendering to a rabble in arms while a band played *The World Turned Upside Down*. The war that President William McKinley asked for, in the wake of the *Maine*, was one for "the enforced pacification of Cuba," using "hostile constraint upon both the parties to the contest" to insure on the island "the security of its citizens as well as our own." U.S. ships blockaded Havana, trading cannon fire with Spanish shore batteries, but most of the fighting took place around Santiago de Cuba in the East. There the Cuban army cooperated with the American one, warily, in return for a promise from Congress that "the people of the Island of Cuba are, of right ought to be, free and independent" and that after pacification was accomplished, the United States would withdraw. In the end, beneath a towering ceiba tree at the foot of San Juan Hill, Spanish generals surrendered to American ones, but the Cuban commanders were not invited. U.S. forces in the meantime attacked the other remaining outposts of Spain's empire in America and the Pacific. Then diplomats sat down in Paris to hammer out a treaty which ceded control of Cuba, Puerto Rico, the Philippines, and Guam to the United States as "new dependencies" of various sorts.

In the Philippines, independence forces began a guerrilla struggle against the new occupiers. In Cuba, the tug-of-war over the country's future was political. The spotlight in this struggle centered on Havana, where the occupying government installed itself. A U.S. military governor replaced the captain-general. More troops came to carry out the occupation than had been sent to fight the war. American soldiers pitched their tents in the Plaza de Armas and barracked in the Castillo de La Real Fuerza, while they set about building a permanent base, Camp Columbia, on a tract of farmland in the commanding heights of Marianao. The new Cuba would be bound to the United States by "ties of singular intimacy,"

McKinley declared ominously in his State of the Union address at the end of 1899, but "how and how far is for the future to determine in the ripeness of events." No one on the island could say how long the military presence would last, or under what terms it would end.

Photo Credit: Library of Congress

U.S. troops camped in the Plaza de Armas, 1898. The Palace of the Captains-General is in the background (now the Museum of the History of the City) and the Palacio del Segundo Cabo (until recently, the Book Institute) is to its right. El Templete (commemorating the city's founding and housing the murals described in chapter 3) is not shown, but would be to the viewer's right.

In the Parque Central, across the Prado from the Hotel Inglaterra, the statue of Queen Isabel II of Spain was unceremoniously toppled from its pedestal one day in March of 1899. The weekly *El Fígaro* ran a graphic of the empty pedestal topped by a question mark and polled its mostly upscale readers for suggestions for a replacement. José Martí beat out a statue of liberty by four votes. Liberation army commander Máximo Gómez, Christopher Columbus, and an allegorical figure linking the United States, Cuba, and Spain also figured among the top nine. Antonio Maceo came in tenth. Though a committee formed to raise funds for a Martí monument, the pedestal remained empty for three years.

In the "ripeness of events," the occupation lasted three-and-a-half years and left behind an anomalous republic—an independent nation in whose affairs the United States had a constitutional right to intervene. This was, however, only one of many outcomes. The occupation changed the city's patriotism and its plumbing, its language and its layout, its commerce and its entertainment. As in the case of the British occupation, the people of Havana defended their aspirations and their culture, and they simultaneously welcomed, synthesized, or forcibly adapted to what was new.

A political split between the Cubans who had fought for independence and the army of occupation underlay everything else. From the Cuban side, the independence war had been fought for a loosely defined ideal of *Cuba Libre*, a republic, as José Martí said, "for all and for the good of all." If the first war had been initiated by planters, this one had been declared and fought by an army and an underground created, as Máximo Gómez said, from bottom up rather than the top down. The officer corps included planters (many of them ruined), but also professionals, small farmers, and workers. The officers were about 40 percent nonwhite, and the troops about 60 percent so. The series of wars that they had fought over a period of three decades represented a revolution in Cuban popular notions of race and class. "To the American at home," reported occupation veteran Lieutenant Colonel R. F. Bullard in an article called "How Cubans Differ From Us," "the negro as a social, political or even industrial equal is an affront, an offence, nothing less; to the Cuban, he is not."

The expectations of most of those who had struggled for independence included not only racial equality but land reform, an end to great extremes of wealth and poverty, and recompense for those who had sacrificed through exile, military service, displacement, or Spanish confiscation. These expectations also included a foreign and commercial policy friendly to the United States but not monopolized by it. That vision explains why, in his war message, McKinley declared it "not wise or prudent for this government to recognize at the present time the independence of the so-called Cuban Republic . . . To commit this country now to the recognition of any particular government in Cuba might subject us to embarrassing conditions of international obligation toward the organization so recognized." In what it saw as a "Spanish-American War," the United States was not fighting to turn Cuba over to the political heirs of Martí.

In fact, an American notion that the Pearl of the Antilles ought to decorate the necklace of manifest destiny can be traced back at least three quarters of a century before 1898. As a rich producer, proven market, and military outpost commanding Caribbean sea lanes, Cuba had long tempted U.S. political leaders. "I candidly confess," wrote ex-President Thomas Jefferson in 1823, "that I have ever looked on Cuba as the most interesting addition which could be made to our system of States." That same year, President-to-be John Quincy Adams echoed him in a tone of greater inevitability: "There are laws of political as well as of physical gravitation, and if an apple, severed by a tempest from its native tree, cannot choose but fall to the ground, Cuba, forcibly disjoined from its own unnatural connection with Spain, and incapable of self-support, can gravitate only towards the North American Union, which, by the same law of nature, cannot cast her off." Throughout the nineteenth century, U.S. administrations attempted to purchase Cuba from Spain, as they had bought the Louisiana Territory from the French Empire and then bought Alaska from the Russians. For Cuba they offered considerably higher sums, of 100 million dollars and up. As Adams' quote suggests, U.S. policymakers held not only that the United States was destined to control Cuba and her fruits, but that Cubans—because of their Latin and particularly their African blood—could not govern themselves.

Though Spain refused to sell, U.S.-Cuban commercial ties steadily increased, as we have described. Americans' ownership of Cuban plantations and mills also grew steadily, by purchase or by foreclosure of defaulted loans. When the Ten Years' War broke out, the Grant administration tried again to get Spain to sell the island. "All the civilized nations," Secretary of State Hamilton Fish told the Cabinet in 1869, "would be glad that we should interpose and regulate control of the island."

In the face of the new rebellion that broke out in 1895, both Grover Cleveland's Democratic administration and William McKinley's Republican one followed these same goals. At the time the *Maine* steamed into the harbor, negotiations were still under way for an armistice that would give the island semiautonomous status under Spain, or for a sale of the island to the United States. These negotiations continued after the battleship exploded and sank. When Spain would not sell, and the rebels would not agree to give up the idea of *Cuba Libre*, McKinley decided on war. There was, however, considerable sympathy for Cuban independence among the American public, and significant resistance in Congress to the creation of an American empire out of the vestiges of Spain's.

So Congress amended the war resolution. The Teller Amendment, named after Sen. Henry Teller of Colorado, stated: "The United States hereby disclaims any disposition or intention to exercise sovereignty, jurisdiction, or control over said island except for pacification thereof, and asserts its determination, when that is accomplished, to leave the government and control of the island to its people." These words may still be read on the monument to the soldiers and sailors of the *Maine* on Havana's seafront Malecón, though the American eagle that used to crown the monument was removed in 1961. Cuban representatives in the United States also demanded and received private reassurances that the U.S. withdrawal would be accompanied by the provision of funds to pay pensions to the demobilized army of independence.

In Cuba, as in the United States, support for the island's independence was not complete. Much of the country's commerce remained in the hands of Spaniards, who did not depart for home with the evacuated troops. Conservative property owners and professionals, both Spanish-born and Cuban-born, had petitioned for U.S. intervention in the last years of the war, because they too had much to fear from Martí's ideal. The McKinley and Roosevelt administrations interpreted "pacification" in the Teller Amendment to mean the creation of a government led by the propertied classes. Such a government might request continued U.S. rule, or would in any case be a hedge against radical change. The Army of Liberation was pensioned off as previously agreed, with the troops insisting on turning in their guns to local Cuban authorities, not the occupation forces—though some units refused to accept their pensions or turn in their guns until the occupation actually came to an end.

As municipal elections and then elections for a Constitutional Convention unfolded, military governor General Leonard Wood kept assuring Washington that "the Cuban people realize they are not ready for self government" and (paradoxically) that they would elect "the better class of men." He lent "the better class" his support by limiting suffrage to the best of his ability, tying the franchise to property and literacy requirements, though he was forced to make an exception for veterans of the rebel army.[1] He openly campaigned for his chosen candidates as well. However, as he reported back to Washington, most of them lost. Many of "the worst agitators and political radicals" were elected instead.

Wood cast particular private scorn on long-time journalist, organizer, and civil-rights advocate Juan Gualberto Gómez, former head of the Cuban Revolutionary Party in Havana. Gómez was one of the two nonwhites among the thirty-one elected members of the Constitutional Convention. On his official stationery bearing the letterhead "Military Governor, Island of Cuba, Havana," Wood wrote ominously to Theodore Roosevelt about certain "degenerates of the Convention, led by a little negro of the name Juan Gualberto Gómez; a man with an unsavory reputation, both morally and politically," whose purpose was "to bring forward his own race and see what he can accomplish politically to his own advantage." Before sending the letter off to Washington, Wood changed "degenerates" to "agitators." He did not change his complaint that "it is next to impossible to make them [the Cubans] believe that we have only their own interests at heart."

In November of 1900, after nearly two years of occupation, the delegates began to meet in an imposing former dance hall turned theater, often called the "coliseum of a hundred doors." Just off the Prado opposite the old Spanish military parade ground, it was originally named Teatro Irioja after its Basque developer, then Eden Concert under subsequent owners, and was finally rebaptized as Teatro Martí. The convention's members wrote a constitution very much like that of the United States, although a centralist rather than a federal one. Uniquely for Latin America, it included separation of church and state. Despite the urging of women's revolutionary clubs, the convention rejected a proposal for female suffrage, leaving this question to later legislation. But they adopted universal male suffrage, a clear change in direction from Wood's restrictive and racist rules that had governed their own election.

At the urging of Gómez and others, they twice rejected a proposed limitation on Cuban sovereignty which had been attached to a military appropriations bill in the U.S. Congress by Senator Orville H. Platt of Maine. The Platt Amendment—passed by Congress in a different mood than that of 1898—required Cuba's constitution to ratify all decisions made by the occupation government as binding obligations, to give the United States an exclusive right to build naval bases on Cuban soil, and to include a perpetual right of U.S. intervention in Cuba as needed. Article III of this Amendment stated: "That the government of Cuba consents that the United States may exercise the right to intervene for the preservation of Cuban independence, the maintenance of a government adequate for the protection of life, property, and individual liberty, and for discharging the obligations with respect to Cuba imposed by the treaty of Paris on the United States."

On March 2, 1901, 15,000 residents paraded through the streets of Havana to announce their refusal to accept the Platt Amendment. The protesters thronged through the Prado, Neptuno, Galiano, and Reina, cheered on by many more from sidewalks, balconies, and arcades. They paused outside the Teatro Martí to approve the stand taken by the delegates. After that they crowded their way through the narrow streets of Old Havana to the palace of the Captains General to present a petition to Governor Wood, condemning both the Amendment and the imperial pressure for it to be passed. The Convention soon sought modifications to the Amendment, but were told there could be none. If the Platt Amendment was not adopted verbatim, the occupation would not end. Finally they accepted it, first by a margin of one vote, and then (with four abstentions) by a margin of five.

On May 20, 1902, with the Platt Amendment embedded in the new constitution, Cuban flags at last replaced Americans ones and the occupying troops withdrew. Camp Columbia was turned over to a new Cuban army, while the incipient naval base at Guantánamo Bay remained in American hands, soon to be leased "for the time required." In preparation for the official transfer-of-powers ceremony in Havana, a zinc-and-tin statue of liberty was hurriedly shipped from the United States to fill the vacant pedestal in the Parque Central. The statue held an American shield in one arm and a torch in the other, but a hurricane that tore through Havana eighteen months later destroyed this particular vestige of the occupation. Curiously, the hurricane made landfall on October 10, the anniversary of the original Cuban declaration of independence in 1868.

Finally, in 1905, a Cuban sculptor's marble effigy of José Martí crowned the pedestal, but the first intervention under the terms of the Platt Amendment came during a disputed Cuban election only a year after that. Until the year 1959, the American political and economic presence in Havana would be a weighty and often decisive one, a source of both shame and revolt. And yet, in this cosmopolitan and always curious city, the presence of things American, and the ability to master them, would also be at times a source of pride and hope.

To begin with, at the same moment as they resisted annexation and military occupation, many residents welcomed what they initially saw as American aid in a step toward independence. Spain had been expelled "by the Cuban machete and the American cannon," as one petitioner to the military government wrote. Handbills of popular ballads from the last days of the war include one that said:

> Long live the Americans
> Who come on our part
> We ought to embrace them
> From deep in our hearts.
> Long live our flag
> Joined with that other

Which lives in the heart
Of each Cuban brother.

In the early months of the occupation it was common to see Havanans wearing both Cuban and U.S. flag pins on their lapels, or other displays of the two flags intertwined.

More profoundly, particularly for those who had lived in the North as political exiles, economic refugees, students, or some combination of all three, the United States had long served as their anti-Spain and anti-colony. Their preference for baseball over bullfights is one example, but much of what they saw during their U.S. exile gave substance to their vision of an alternative Cuban future: independent, democratic, modern, and technologically advanced. Furthermore, the occupation government, even when the honeymoon was over, was the government of reconstruction after years of war and neglect, and as such it was the only game in town. If many of the Cubans appointed to staff it had been lukewarm in their support of independence, many others had devoted their lives to that ideal. The Americanization of the capital was not only the work of Americans or annexationists.

English words, one sign of this affinity, made their way into the city's lexicon far in advance of American troops. Tobacco workers returning from Key West had christened one of the new barrios of Centro Habana, to the north of Pueblo Nuevo, Cayo Hueso—literally "bone key," but phonetically and socially an adaptation of the American place name. Cubanizations of baseball terms such as *estraik, ao,* and *jonrón* were legion. In fact, the Americanism *sport* had largely replaced *deporte* to describe activities of many kinds. If the horse track in Marianao was called the *hipódromo*—in Spanish—its daily program featured a race called the *handicap.* So when *new women* got opportunities to work for the occupation authority as *nurses, typewriters,* and occasionally *supervisors,* this only expanded an existing linguistic trend. Similarly, their male counterparts who found ways to take advantage of new opportunities in small business became *self-made men.* With the importation of new gadgets for domestic chores and entertainment—from gas ranges to light bulbs and Fuller brushes, from electric fans to gramophones to Champion bikes—the word *comfort*, usually Cubanized as *confort*, entered daily speech and also written language.

Many stores rapidly adopted English to appeal to the influx of Americans, not just soldiers and sailors but those who followed, an army of merchants, investors, tourists, craftsmen, carpetbaggers, and engineers. The long-established Crusellas family cosmetic and soap emporium on Calle Obispo in Old Havana hoisted a new sign upon its doorway declaring itself "Crusellas Store." The cachet of English also enlivened communications among Cubans themselves. In *El Reconcentrado*, a nationalist Havana paper created originally as the voice of those expelled from the countryside by the Spaniards, Crusellas announced to their Cuban customers the opening of a new lounge in which *ladies* could buy ice cream *de todos los sabores* (of all flavors), dished out by *bellas señoritas*. English brand names for new imported goods became part of the household language just as indigenous words for foods and implements had done centuries before: whether arriving home to grate *yuca* on a *guayo* or to cook up some *Quaker* (rhymed with cracker), Havana cooks first had to unlock the *yale* (pronounced "yah-lay," the lock). For breakfast, the traditional *café con leche* and buttered toast now had to compete with something called *jamanég* (ham and eggs). The word *blueplate* entered the city's gastronomic vocabulary, and even a cheap restaurant offered, bilingually, "*A comer barato. 50 cents square meal.*" A family advertisement in a provincial paper, celebrating the birthday of a lieutenant colonel in the liberation army, concluded, "*I wish you many happy returns of the day.*"

Drinking as well as eating habits mirrored this state of affairs. No one knows who invented the *Cuba libre* by mixing Cuban rum with Coca-Cola, but the daiquiri came to Havana from Santiago de Cuba, where it celebrated the coordinated landing of Cuban and U.S. troops on the beach of that same name. It was soon available in long-established bars like the Florida (later Floridita) and new ones like the New England Bar, Manhattan Bar, and Gay Broadway.

The occupation also transformed Havana physically, and many of these changes met long-delayed aspirations. Contrary to the hopes of

Cuba Libre, U.S. authorities refused to redistribute Spanish or idle private property, rural or urban, or to even to distribute desperately needed supplies or loans which could help Cuban farms and businesses revive. But they did initiate public works on a large scale and turn Spanish military sites over to Cuban institutions for civil use. Thus, many now-classic landmarks of Havana were built or begun at this time.

A plan to convert the city's rough coral oceanfront to a seawall and promenade had been kicking around colonial offices since it was first proposed in mid-century by Francisco de Albear, designer of the aqueduct. Now it became reality. Construction of the city's trademark Malecón began in 1901 and the first stretch opened a year later. Symbolically, the city began to turn its back on the Spanish fortresses and the crowded and polluted harbor, and to face the Florida Straits instead.

The new Malecón included one important American modification not foreseen by Albear: a wide boulevard, inside the promenade, for cars. The occupation years brought the automobile to Havana. The very first cars were French models, but soon came a Locomobile and its brethren from Detroit. When Henry Ford's mass production techniques gave him dominance of the auto market in the United States, his Model-T flooded Havana as well. In the rest of the Spanish-speaking world, a car that's not working has *descompuesto* (literally, "decomposed"). In Cuba, borrowing from English, it has "broken down."

Paved streets and plazas suited the bicycle as well. The environs of the Castillo de la Punta, starting place of the Malecón, had become a garbage dump in the last years of Spanish rule. This was replaced with a paved plaza, lit by electric lights and frequented by residents of every social class. The plaza became so popular with bicyclists—especially children and young women—that Mayor Perfecto Lacoste banned horse and mule-drawn carriages from nearby streets between the hours of four to eleven p.m. to avoid accidents. The French architect Charles Brun, living in the United States, was contracted to design a bandstand for the center of this area. After its construction, the municipal band played nightly concerts, as Spanish military bands had done in the Plaza de Armas—only now, even under occupation, the concerts began with the Bayamo Hymn, call to arms of the liberation movement and national anthem-to-be. The first film to be made in Cuba, a sixty-second short subject shot in 1899 called *El parque de Palatino*, depicts the comings and going of citizens in another brand-new park.

The modern campus of the University of Havana also got its start at this time. The university (under Spanish rule officially called the Royal and Pontifical University of St. Geronimo) dropped its old name and moved from its downtown quarters in a former convent to a hilltop site above Cayo Hueso, toward Vedado, an acropolis commanding a view of the city and the sea. There it occupied the buildings of the Spanish Pirotécnica, a former munitions factory and depot. "This building devoted for so many years to making elements of destruction and death," said the university's report for 1900–01, "has by the strange winds of destiny . . . become dedicated to shaping our progress, culture, and civilization."

When the Castillo de la Real Fuerza was vacated by U.S. troops moving to their new base at Camp Columbia, the city's oldest fortress became the first site of the National Archives. Among other renovations at this facility were new and modern bathrooms, with flush toilets and sinks "made in the USA," to replace the ancient Spanish pit latrines. Indeed, plumbing was a fixation of the occupation authorities. Flush toilets were almost nonexistent in colonial Havana, despite Domingo del Monte's innovation in the Palacio de Aldama, and a U.S. army survey showed that only 10 percent of houses had indoor plumbing of any sort. The occupation army's chief sanitation officer personally led a team of 120 doctors to visit the houses of the capital and impart instructions on the use of drains, garbage collection, and other measures. Sinks and toilets were imported from the United States on a grand scale and sold at modest prices. Inspectors issued orders to install and connect these new devices, often when there were as yet no supply pipes or drains for blocks around—but the pipes and sewers were usually on their way.

Sanitation measures, however, failed to stop the outbreaks of yellow fever that had been decimating the occupation troops since their first landings in Oriente and continued to do so in the capital after the fighting had stopped. Since yellow fever was thought to spread through contamination, particularly from the vomit and feces of victims, medical officers intent on plumbing and scrubbing were at a loss. The Havana doctor and epidemiologist Carlos J. Finlay, then sixty-five years old, had been proposing since the early 1880s that the fever was spread, instead, by mosquito bites. Finlay, educated in Europe, Philadelphia, and Havana, went to Washington when the United States entered the war. He used his American medical contacts to enlist in the medical corps. He continued to make his yellow fever hypothesis known, and when all other measures failed, Major Walter Reed, head of the army's Yellow Fever Commission, agreed to carry out a controlled experiment to test it.

The experiments were carried out at Camp Columbia and adjoining rented farmland, where one group of uninfected volunteers lived in a filthy cottage well-supplied with used blankets and bedclothes brought daily from a yellow fever ward, and the other lived in a scrubbed and disinfected cottage supplied with the *Aedes aegypti* mosquitoes that Finlay had bred, which had been allowed to bite infected men. Finlay's theory proved correct, and the ensuing mosquito eradication campaign effectively solved the yellow fever problem in Havana. Finlay went on to become Chief Sanitation Officer of the new Cuban government, though most of the international credit for "discovering" the cause and cure for yellow fever went to Reed.

Joining the goal of improved transport to that of sanitation, the electric streetcar replaced the old animal-traction lines. "Accustomed to seeing in Havana and Puerto Príncipe the urban streetcars drawn by horses," the exiled journalist and former Almendares baseball star Wenceslaus Gálvez had written on his arrival in Tampa during the war, "one is surprised to see here the same cars operating under their own power." Two days after the Treaty of Paris was signed, a syndicate of U.S., Canadian, and French investors bought up the horse-drawn street railway system from its mostly Spanish stockholders. The following month they incorporated the Havana Electric Railway Company, in New Jersey, and their representatives set off for Havana to begin building an electric plant. In March 1901, the first line opened, from Old Havana to Vedado. Many more followed, reaching as far as Marianao by 1903. Ridership sextupled within the first year, from 10,000 to 60,000 passengers a day. Horse droppings vanished from the streetcar rails.

All in all, says historian Louis Pérez, "Havana teemed with activity. Gangs of survey teams, construction crews, builders, and wreckers seemed to be everywhere, and at times they were." Thus the occupation and its aftermath brought to Havana the modernization many had sought, but at a steep price—very little of it was under Cuban control. The streetcars went "under their own power" but subject to U.S. ownership, as was the case with all new and expanded utilities. The majority of contractors were Americans, and so were a great many of their employees. Even the plumbers were American imports, and members of a union—Plumbers' Local 200—to which no Cubans belonged.

Some entrepreneurs came from the United States as civilians to pursue the attractions of this new frontier, while others parleyed their positions in the occupation into sizeable economic stakes. Sergeant Frank Steinhart, chief clerk of the army of occupation, rose by 1907 to the presidency of the Havana Electric Railway, Light, and Power Co., a monopoly which merged several utilities under one roof. He built himself a roof too, a mansion on the Prado to rival that of any departed Spanish count. Captain Tillinghast L. Huston arrived with the *yanqui* Corps of Engineers and became even more of a Yankee as a result. He formed contracting companies which secured commissions to dredge the city's harbor, install its new sewer lines, and build new wharves. With his profits from these ventures and others in Cuba's interior, he joined New York brewer Jake Ruppert in buying the New York Yankees in 1915—and buying Babe Ruth from the Red Sox five years after that. When Ruth in turn visited Havana, at the height of his fame, he stayed in the Hotel Plaza, which by then rivaled the Inglaterra on the other side of the Parque Central. The Plaza was founded by another officer of the occupation, Captain Walter Fletcher Smith.

A New York construction firm, Purdy & Henderson, remodeled the old colonial building that housed the Plaza, and they also built the Lonja de Comercio for importers' and exporters' offices on the Plaza de San Francisco, and the headquarters of the National Bank of Cuba and the Cuban Telephone Company (both U.S. owned firms). By the 1920s, enough of these neoclassical concrete-and-steel structures dotted the colonial landscape of the old city that a travel writer remarked that the office buildings "seem to have been bodily transported from New York."

Havana's upper and middle classes thus found themselves as junior partners to foreign capital rather than the captains of a new nation, as many had hoped. The old landowning class lost much of its land, a casualty of war, reconcentration, Spanish expropriation, and debt. Without reparations, supplies, or affordable credit to get farmers back on their feet, many (whether larger or small) had to sell out for what they could get. *Trabajar pa'l inglés*, "to work for the English," was an old expression, origin unknown, that meant to work without much hope of compensation, to invest one's effort in vain. Going to work for the Americans now offered the best chance of holding on to some of one's previous status or becoming a *new woman* or a *self-made man*. Among the plantation owners, the luckier and richer could barter their land for shares in new foreign sugar companies. Professionals with university degrees in fields such as law or engineering or architecture could go to work as employees, consultants, or representatives of American firms. Examples of the distance between the ideal of *Cuba Libre* and the role of junior partner to the Americans are provided by two veterans of the independence war, Perfecto Lacoste and José Lacret.

Lacoste, from a planter family and educated in the United States, had been head of the revolutionary underground in Havana after the arrest of Juan Gualberto Gómez. It was he who smuggled the Spanish military plans stolen from the Captains General's Palace to Antonio Maceo, who also stayed for a few days at the Lacoste family mill. Under the occupation, Lacoste became mayor of Havana (and issued the regulation banning horse-drawn carriages from the area popular with bicyclists) and then he became Secretary of Agriculture. "Nothing has been done toward the improval of our agricultural situation . . . ," he complained in 1901. He called on the military government to provide credit and other aid to farmers, but his plea fell on deaf ears. A year later, he was appealing instead for more U.S. capital and entrepreneurs. "In no foreign country will American capital and enterprise be welcomed so warmly as in Cuba," Lacoste wrote in *Opportunities in the Colonies and Cuba*, published in New York with an introduction by Leonard Wood. "The policy of the new government is to strongly encourage the influx of American capital and brains."

General José Lacret Morlot was born on a coffee plantation in Oriente, the son of Haitian-French planters. Educated in France and having lived in both Florida and New York, Lacret was a veteran of both independence wars. He had been wounded, jailed, escaped, and lived to fight again. Elected to the Constitutional Convention, he sided with Gómez in arguing successfully for universal male suffrage and in refusing to accept the Platt Amendment even on the final vote. "This for me is a day of mourning," he said when the amendment was approved, "because we have enslaved ourselves forever in grievously heavy chains." But he advertised in the English-language *Havana Post* that he had established a real estate consulting office in the capital. "Having a practical knowledge of the entire island," he offered corporations and individuals his services for "buying and selling farms and plantations, mining properties, native timber, and all kinds of leases."

As Lacret's ad indicates, rural Cuba became a land sale bonanza, another new frontier. Large companies like United Fruit and American Sugar bought ruined plantations and virgin territory. Thousands of settlers arrived too, including hundreds of North American families who set up farming communities across the main island and on the Isle of Pines, bringing their customs and Protestant religions along.

All told, by 1905 foreigners of various nations owned an estimated 60 percent of Cuba's countryside, resident Spaniards owned another 15 percent, and Cubans owned only the remaining quarter of the land. In the all-important sugar industry, U.S. individuals and corporations controlled 21 percent of production in 1905. As they expanded production on newly acquired lands, their share rose to 53 percent in 1916 and 63 percent in 1926. In the major industry carried out inside the capital itself, cigar production, American companies bought up many of the Spanish brands. The Havana Commercial Company, a holding company organized by New York bankers, acquired more than a dozen factories accounting for 161 different brands. The once-grand Palacio de Aldama, which had been converted to a cigar factory by a Spanish firm in the 1880s, now passed into the hands of "The Habana Cigar and Tobacco Factories Limited," an English concern.

For white collar jobs, potential Anglo employers were most comfortable with those most like themselves: those who spoke English and had lived in the States. The Lonja de Comercio advertised for "a young gentleman of presentable appearance and absolutely fluent in verbal translation." The telephone company sought out bilingual operators for its rapidly expanding grid. "The more progressive merchants have hired clerks who can speak English," the *New York Times* reported.

Most of all, American firms brought with them traditional American ideas about race. Occupation authorities and their successors in the private sector did not find blacks or mulattos to be of "presentable appearance," and racial integration did not fit American concepts of what was modern or progressive, since this was the heyday of scientific thinking about a hierarchy of racial types. So blacks or mulattos were not welcome as conductors on the electric streetcars. The new department stores would not hire them as saleswomen or cashiers. Even black generals, usually from peasant, working class, or slave backgrounds, did not find the same private sector opportunities that their white counterparts did. Quintín Banderas, who had been a sailor and construction worker before rising in the ranks of the *mambís*, ended up distributing advertising circulars for the Cuban-owned Crusellas soap company.

Another general, whose name has been lost, became the centerpiece of a landmark legal case when he was refused service by the American-owned Café Washington in 1899. Though discrimination in private hiring met little effective resistance, attempts to impose U.S.-style Jim Crow in the capital's cafés and restaurants proved too much of an affront to *Cuba Libre* to succeed. In the last years of the colony, once slavery was abolished, a combination of Spanish law and steady pressure from the Societies of Color had more or less established the principle of equal accommodation, at least in in Havana. So the Café Washington incident became a cause célèbre.

City authorities shut down the Café Washington until its owners promised to "obey the laws of the country and serve the public without distinctions or differences." But when the restaurant was allowed to reopen, they placed an increasingly common sign on the mirror behind the counter: "We cater to white people only." This time the owners were tried and sentenced to two months in jail, plus fines. They appealed, claiming the sign did not specifically say they wouldn't serve people of color, only that they would not "cater" to them. A long legal battle ensued, hinging on the exact translation and intent of the English phrase. In the end, the sentence was confirmed. From then on, those who wanted formal segregation turned increasingly to private clubs, though luxury hotels catering to Americans often turned nonwhite clients away with the claim that they had no rooms.

Anything that suggested African culture was even more controversial than the question of access to a restaurant or cafe. To the Cubans in charge of city government, African-derived drums and dances smacked of backwardness and barbarism. They seemed the antithesis of the modern way of life that would prove Cubans worthy of self-government, both to the Americans and to themselves. The Día de Reyes celebration and similar processions had been banned under Spanish authority when slavery ended on the ground that they conflicted with the Catholic religion and no longer served any purpose. When the Spanish flag was finally lowered, a group of Abakuá took their rituals openly into the street to celebrate. Local police promptly took them into custody and they were sentenced to a year in prison for illegal association.

A later petition by a Lucumí mutual aid society to allow their *toque de tambor* was denied by North American authorities. Finally a city council ordinance in 1900 attempted to settle the matter. It forbade "the use of African drums in any sort of assembly, whether on the public streets or inside," as well as the processions "known as *comparsas, tangos, cabildos*, and *claves*, or any other that make use of symbols, allegories, and objects which conflict with the seriousness and culture of this country's inhabitants."

However, attempts by Cuban authorities to control popular behavior in Havana were no more successful than those of Spanish or U.S. colonial authorities. In the first year of the occupation, the city government had thumbed its nose at the military government by choosing February 24 (date of the declaration of independence of 1895) for rebel army commander Máximo Gómez's triumphal entrance into the city, where he was feted in barrios rich and poor, white and black. That night there was a society ball in the Teatro Tacón and an outdoor concert across the street in the park. But a *mambí* veteran's memoir describes another celebration, still less official, by a great crowd dancing through the nearby streets to the beat of conga drums, whirling, singing satirical songs, and making barbed and earthy jokes. Such *comparsas* (street dances, usually by organized groups with practiced choreography) also made their way into the annual celebration of Carnival, which had previously been a decorous white-dominated parade of carriages and floats that occurred parallel to the Día de Reyes. *Comparsas* of blacks joined the carnivals of 1899 and 1900, dressed in mock uniforms of the Voluntarios and other repressive Spanish forces, celebrating their departure. After independence, groups from mostly black barrios like Jesús María demanded the official right to participate in Carnival. Their repertoire included songs that linked patriotism and race, celebrating the role of black and mulatto soldiers and officers in the independence wars.

Though much farther removed from its African roots, the *danzón* was also criticized as being too tropical, sensuous, and uncivilized. "The danzón, very pretty, very typical of our climate and what you will, but not an appropriate dance for a modern soiree. The intervention will bring us a government that's free and stable, and will give us new dances and habits too." So said an article on the society pages of the elite magazine *Cuba and America*. An edict from the civilizers in the city government was more explicit: *danzón* was permissible, but only if the couple held each other at arm's length, and restricted the motions of their hips. As a result, the *danzón* took on a new nationalist air and was enthusiastically performed by Havanans of all colors at celebrations of the semiofficial patriotic holidays, weddings and baptisms, in dance halls, and more. A satirical cartoon in *El Figaro* shows a caricatured black couple in which the woman insists she's obeying the new regulation, but the man pulls her close and says, to her satisfaction, that he supposes he'll have to opt for the old regime. In spite of his prejudices, the cartoonist shares his characters' bafflement at what's so modern and democratic about such puritanical rules.

A ditty from a satirical musical by Ignacio Sarachaga, author of *The Matter of Bread* described in chapter 6, contrasted the *danzón* with the two-step, the North American dance enjoying its moment of chic. The two-step was "fit for a wake," the song declared, and then it played on a rhyme setting *danzón* against *anexión*. As best it can be rendered into English, the number went:

> As long as danzón lives
> And we feel its concatenation
> No one can make us bear
> The weight of annexation

A similar contest ensued over attempts by both the occupation authorities and "modernizing" Cubans with revolutionary credentials to ban the cockfight and the lottery. Both institutions went underground, to reemerge into legality in the 1910s.

An example of how carefully the elite tried to walk a line between multiracial nationalism and "modern" scientific racism was the official commission that examined Antonio Maceo's skull. In a patriotic ceremony, the remains of Maceo and his white aide de camp Francisco Gómez (son of Máximo) were exhumed from their battlefield grave to be placed in a memorial near Santiago de Las Vegas, south of the capital. A team of three white scientists, using the "latest anthropometric techniques," examined the skeleton of the "Bronze Titan." The team's most prominent member, Luis Montané, had studied with the leading anthropologists of Paris and headed the University of Havana's Department of Anthropology and Anthropometric Exercises, founded in 1900 by the military government. The meticulously detailed report pointed out first of all that Maceo was a mulatto, and that "the crossing of white and black can create an improved group when the influence of the former predominates, but an inferior group when the two influences are equal, and especially when the black predominates." Fortunately, they concluded that while the size and shape of the general's bones matched his African heritage, his skull capacity "could be mistaken for that of the best-endowed European." Thus the mulatto hero could be celebrated for his prowess as a thinker and strategist as well as his strength and skill at arms, without challenging the notions of progress that emanated from Europe and the United States.

All in all, the American occupation period established precedents whose echoes continued throughout the twentieth century and still continue today. These trends extended beyond Havana, but in the capital—always the point of contact between the "interior" and the "foreign"—they reached their height. North American dominance was felt as a wound on Cuban pride and patriotism, but the standard of living in North American cities became the yardstick against which to measure Havana's life. Cuban culture, language, and idiosyncrasies were treasured as bulwarks of national identity, but American ones were seen as the keys to comfort and success.

8 Symbol of an Era: Alberto Yarini y Ponce de León

At dusk on November 21, 1910, a well-dressed man stepped out of his home on Calle Paula, a block from the birthplace of José Martí. His silver Nautilus wristwatch gave the time as 7:38 p.m. He was twenty-eight years old, and he lived in this house with three women in their late teens or early twenties named Elena Morales, Celia Marín, and Berthe Fontaine or Santerre, a valet called José Claro, and probably other servants whose names have not survived. It was a wintry night in Havana terms, so he was wearing a dark cashmere suit over a starched white dress shirt with six gold buttons, and underwear monogrammed top and bottom with the initials A.Y. In his pocket jingled an assortment of the more valuable coins then in circulation: a Spanish centén, a French louis, and an American double eagle. Around his waist he buckled something he didn't commonly wear, a gunbelt and a holster carrying a nickel-plated revolver with a mother-of-pearl grip, recently purchased in the United States.

A short walk brought him to the Calle San Isidro, the street that gave its name to this barrio of Old Havana near the docks. Untouched by the fever of construction in the nearby financial and commercial district, San Isidro was made up mostly of small single-story houses and quite a few hastily constructed single rooms. It was home to many stevedores, construction workers, laundresses, and other sorts of laborers, its corners replete with bars and cheap cafés. Alberto Yarini stepped into the single room at number 59 to speak to Rosa Martínez, who worked there. Then he crossed to number 60 and spoke with Elena Morales and Celia Marín.

When he returned to the street, he saw Berthe Fontaine's countryman and former employer Louis Lotot waiting for him, pistol in hand. Before Yarini could draw his own gun, he was cut down by a hail of bullets from Lotot and his confederates stationed across the street on the sidewalk and on the cracked red clay shingled roofs. Once the shooting stopped and police arrived, they found Lotot dead, shot by Yarini's friend and de facto bodyguard Pepe Bastarrechea, who carried a revolver that matched the one Yarini had not had time to fire. Yarini lay on the sidewalk, in the arms of Elena Morales, bleeding from multiple wounds. He was taken to the nearest first aid station and then to the Emergency Hospital, where he died at 10:30 p.m. The next morning, a large crowd followed his casket to the home of his parents, brother, and sister on fashionable Calle Galiano a few blocks from the seacoast and the nascent Malecón. There his body lay for another day and night, with a constant stream of visitors to pay their respects during his wake, before the funeral procession set off on the 24th.

Alerted by notices in the newspapers, masses of Havanans had already filled Galiano and the nearby cross streets. A marching band set a somber cadence for the crowd, which swelled to an estimated 10,000 mourners of all races, classes, and sexes, as four pairs of horses pulled the richly adorned funeral coach for four miles to the Cemetery of Colón. There, senator and ex-general Miguel Coyula—by most accounts one of the few officeholders of the era to live off his salary rather than graft—spoke in the name of the Conservative Party and for himself. Memorial wreaths came from relatives, political figures, the San Isidro branches of both Conservative and Liberal parties, sugar workers, well-to-do café companions, and more. Nearby, a group of ñañigos sent the dead man off with the farewell drumming and chants almost never performed for outsiders.

Alberto Yarini y Ponce de León was the third child of a family with an old Cuban pedigree. Owners of Matanzas sugar plantations in times past, now they were well-to-do professionals in the capital. His father Alberto Yarini y Ponce de León was a dentist and professor of dental surgery, his uncle a medical surgeon, his older brother a dentist and professor in the father's footsteps, and his sister a well-known amateur pianist. Until his untimely death, Alberto Yarini was one of the city's leading bon vivants—a man about town, a habitué of its dance halls, theaters, and opera, at home in both the bars of San Isidro and the posh cafés of the Acera del Louvre. Educated in the United States, he spoke fluent English and perfect Spanish and dressed almost always in a three-piece suit of pure white or somber black, topped by an elegant panama hat. He was the reputed lover of various married women of standing, the holder of a no-show job in the city government, and the president of the Conservative Party committee for San Isidro and the neighboring barrios of San Francisco and Belen. He was what in U.S. political terms of the period would have been called a ward boss, in charge of handing out favors and delivering votes. He was said to have ambitions to run for a seat in the House of Representatives, though his political friends urged him to give up his main business first, the business that made everything else possible. Yarini was the King of San Isidro, and San Isidro was the city's red-light district. Alberto Yarini y Ponce de León was famous and infamous throughout the island—then and now—as its capital's most stylish and successful pimp.

After his education in an American private school, where he had been sent to avoid the hardships of the capital in the years of the independence war, Yarini had returned to Cuba during or shortly after the U.S. occupation and taken advantage of one of the less savory artifacts the occupiers left behind. In their pursuit of hygiene, the authorities had decided to relocate the city's scattered sex industry, as much as possible, to one specified "tolerance zone." San Isidro was recommended because of its working-class character and proximity to the docks. The rows of single rooms were rented mostly to pimps, who made their nightly rounds collecting the lion's share of the take from the women working within them. Pornographic nickelodeon parlors, live sex shows, gambling houses, and low-end music bars migrated to the new red-light district, which attracted married and single Cuban men, new single immigrants, and sailors, tourists, and businessmen from abroad, especially the United States. San Isidro became famous as far away as Paris and New York. Along with the sex establishments came the requisite shooting galleries, pool halls, drug dealers, and ubiquitous stands of Chinese vendors selling the Cuban foods they had mastered—fried pork skins, sweet rolls, corn tamales, and plantain chips.

Diverse sectors profited from the industry. Landlords charged the pimps double rents, police and inspectors demanded bribes to let operations run smoothly, and unemployed men became assistants and enforcers to the pimps. Yarini roamed his kingdom, greeting everyone by name, handing out coins to children, slapping his admirers on the back. He was quiet and charming as a rule, but capable of violence when he needed to assert his authority over either women or men. In myth, journalism, and literary works, he and his legend have come to symbolize Havana in the earliest years of the Republic, and in certain ways this makes sense. Havana was the capital and showcase of a sovereign state, but the state could not be said to direct the affairs of the country, because the real levers of power lay elsewhere. Cubans who were denied center stage in the nation's economic development succeeded in the corners that were available. The nexus of political office, graft, and patronage was one of these corners, and prostitution was another. Yarini lived at the intersection of the two.

Bribery was an old tradition left over from the colony. Graft in the awarding of contracts and embezzlement in public office had taken root during the public works boom of the occupation, since the American occupiers came well-versed in the operations of late-nineteenth century big-city political machines like that of Boss Tweed in New York and the handing out of government jobs to cronies through the "spoils system." The Cuban administrations developed all of this into a fine art. Because the state apparatus offered one of the relatively few lucrative avenues of advancement for ambitious Cubans of all colors and classes, government became increasingly corrupt. The Conservative and Liberal parties drew to some extent on different constituencies; the Liberals, for instance, had a greater following among people of color and nominated Juan Gualberto Gómez for a congressional seat. The parties occasionally came into armed conflict over contested elections, twice settled by U.S. intervention. But the basis for their competition was not so much opposing programs as competing groups of loyalists who expected to be rewarded with public posts, from the cabinet member on high to the lowest lottery ticket seller on the street.

Local bosses like Yarini, called *sargentos políticos*, handed out jobs, got a troublesome relative off without a jail sentence, or found a sick one a scarce hospital bed. In return they borrowed their constituents' voting cards, to make sure the votes were cast the right way. Liberal Party leader José Miguel Gómez, president during Yarini's ascendancy and death, earned the nickname "The Shark" due to the bite he put on those seeking government contracts or jobs. But there was wisdom in the popular saying that derived from his nickname: "When the shark swims, he splashes." His successor, the Conservative Mario G. Menocal, was called "The Overseer" because he had managed a sugar mill for the Cuban-American Sugar Company of New York. On his watch, Yarini's lieutenant and avenger Pepe Bastarrechea (already kept out of jail in a deal brokered by Conservative politicians) was able to leave San Isidro behind and rise through the bureaucracy as first a lottery official, then a customs official, and finally, a port inspector. Gómez and Menocal, like their successors Alfredo Zayas and Gerardo Machado, were all white ex-officers of the Liberation Army who walked a political tightrope between enriching themselves, rewarding Cuban supporters, and cooperating with American businesses, an act often richly compensated by a seat on the company board. *El que tiene un amigo tiene un central* ("a friend is as good as a sugar mill") goes a popular Cuban saying that dates from this period. It doesn't refer to the spiritual value of friends.

Available corners of the economy also included the flesh trade, whether as entrepreneurs like Yarini or as sex workers like his prostitutes who—their position fundamentally unchanged since the days of the colony—sold their bodies to feed their families and themselves. Despite the opportunities that opened up for a minority of women in salesrooms, offices, and schools, census data from 1907 show that only about 75,000 women out of a total Cuban population over 1.5 million had legitimate paid work. Maids and washerwomen (self-employed or working in Chinese laundries) accounted for 65 percent of these female workers, followed by cigar or cigarette makers, teachers, and seamstresses. Prostitution filled the cavernous gap.

"I had long wavy hair, a good body, cinnamon skin, I was friendly, and I had a family dying of hunger," testifies Lulú, a San Isidro veteran of Yarini's time, in an oral history recorded much later by cultural historian and poet Dulcila Cañizares.

> I didn't have any brothers and my father had died of tuberculosis. All my sisters were younger and my mother was a poor woman without the strength to iron or wash. So I had to find a pimp to buy me clothes and shoes and put me to work in a room. He abused me and took almost everything I gained, but I didn't have any other way to get into the business. It wasn't easy, to go to bed and satisfy men of every size and shape—white, black, mulatto, Chinese, Spaniards, or wherever they were from, clean ones and dirty ones, ones who stank to high heaven and not just of bad tobacco and worse rum. But I had to put up with anything, or Pepe would beat me and then I had to throw my arms around his neck and tell him I loved him so much. When I could, I dropped him for another, and so on, because everyone exploited us.

Neither political corruption nor economic necessity, however, fully explains the mystique that surrounded Alberto Yarini. He is the only sex trade entrepreneur and the only *sargento político* in the city's history to be so widely remembered, so honored at his death, and so surrounded by a halo of romantic myth. It's impossible to know how much of what was said about him is exaggeration, but the fictions as much as the facts testify to the collective aspirations that gave rise to his myth. He was a Prince Valiant to a population—especially its male segment, which continued to be a majority—insulted by all sorts of unfulfilled promises, and a Prince Charming even to women who knew there were no such Princes to be found. He had a populist touch without out the pretense of superior morality, in contrast to those of his background who displayed the opposite tendencies on both counts.

Lulú, quoted above about her exploitative pimps and the squalor in which they kept her, went on to say, "Yes, I saw Yarini a lot. He was handsome and clean, going by the door of my room, where I stood waiting for customers. I would have given anything to be his woman, not just to sleep with him but so I'd be respected a little, because everyone respected him." Another, Consuelo la Charmé, recalled how she escaped from her first situation in San Isidro and found protection among women working for Yarini, whom her ex-pimp would not dare to attack. "He wasn't the type that shakes your hand and greets you because of who you are. He couldn't stand people who first wanted to know were you this or were you that. He'd just as soon talk with a black as a Chinaman, and a Chinaman as anyone else. What [his murderers] did to him is worse than I can say."

"Yarini had more women than he knew what to do with, and he dressed like a millionaire," recalled Alberto Cárdenas, who watched the funeral procession at age fourteen and went to work as a gravedigger in the cemetery the following year. "Kids my age, my friends, we envied him a lot, would have given anything to be like him. When they killed him, it was like they had killed the hero of our lives."

"He was famous for the harem he had in his house," said Federico Morales Valcárcel, the young Conservative Party organizer who gave Yarini the matched set of revolvers that didn't manage to save him from death at twenty-eight. "People in the street, in high society, in small towns and in Havana all said to themselves, 'What is it about him?' We took advantage of that popularity to gain adherents in the neighborhoods by the docks." Yarini avoided making speeches, according to Morales, but was always the perfect representative to resolve internal disputes over who should get what job. "Nobody knew how he did it, but he did. He settled these problems with *cosas de cubaneo*, with his Cuban touch."

On the afternoon before his death, according to stories collected by journalist and novelist Leonardo Padura, Yarini stopped by a broken-down house on the Calle Compostela to consult about a troublesome dream with María la Gambá, an old black woman who had been a prostitute in her youth, one of fifteen such women whom he maintained in their old age in return for their supplying him with desserts. María la Gambá gave him *arroz con leche*, Cuban rice pudding, and consulted with her spirits. She warned him that there was something like a runaway train bearing down on him.

There is one other key element in Yarini's myth, besides his alleged generosity, his way with women, and his accessibility to people of all stations. Certain key moments of his legend stood for Cuban nationalism in opposition to both North American arrogance and European immigration which threatened Cuban jobs and pride.

The confrontation with competitors that led to his death was, of course, one of these. Lotot and his confederates were French and Italians from France, Canada, and the United States, all in the business of luring young French, Belgian, and other women to Havana and putting them to work on the street. *Las francesas* (Frenchwomen, as all the European prostitutes were called) were exotic and popular with the customers of San Isidro, and were said to have introduced oral sex into the trade. Yarini had just taken the most beautiful new arrival, La Petite Berthe, away from Lotot, and he had allegedly vowed to take the rest. In the days of tension leading up to the shooting, the ballad singers in the bars of San Isidro invented a new verse that went:

> Frenchmen so lacking in honor
> You'd better leave Cuba tonight
> If you don't want Yarini
> To snuff out your miserable life.

When Yarini was ambushed instead, nationalist pride took over. New verses predicted revenge. The news of his shooting spread "as if he'd been the President of the Republic," dockworker Esteban Cárdenas later recalled. "A whole crowd of us met up in the Alameda de Paula—the pimps, and more of us who had nothing to do with that business, but we came because we were young and those were our friends and we were furious that Yarini had been shot in an ambush, not a man-to-man fight." The crowd, a typically Cuban mix of white, black, and Chinese extraction, decided to wait in ambush on the slopes below the Castillo del Principe and kill the foreign pimps as they descended the hill from Lotot's funeral. Cárdenas's family responsibilities gave him second thoughts, and he didn't go. Others did, and murdered two of Lotot's confederates. They were convicted and sent to jail, but pardoned when the Menocal administration later came in.

Another famous confrontation—one in which Yarini came out on top—had taken place two years earlier in El Cosmopolita, one of the fancy restaurants and cafés on the Prado that made up the Acera del Louvre.

Yarini, sitting and drinking and conversing with some of his political friends, overheard a man at a nearby table complaining in English to his companion about the disgraceful customs of a country where blacks mixed with whites at such a respectable place. The black man in question was General Jesús Rabí, who had, among other accomplishments, commanded Cuban troops in an attack on Spanish forces to cover the American landing at Daiquirí. Rabí was now a government inspector of mines and forests, a member of a Masonic lodge and, it was said, also an Abakuá. He was a man admired by Yarini, so the pimp and politician excused himself from his companions, walked over to the Americans, and demanded in perfect English that they show the hero some respect. When they didn't, he knocked the first man to the ground. The offender turned out to be one J. Cornell Tarler, temporary *charge d'affaires* of the American embassy, and the other man was his commercial attaché. Yarini was arrested and charged with assault, but he was acquitted with the help of his friends. The affair made the papers in Cuba and eventually those in Tampa as well. In Havana, the story of the incident passed from mouth to mouth in many different versions (some had the Americans as naval officers) but the moral was always the same: Alberto Yarini had stood up both for Cuba and for a raceless ideal.[1]

The story was rendered all the more compelling by increasing evidence that the ideal of a Cuba where race didn't matter was far removed from the facts. In 1908, a group of black and mulatto veterans who were disappointed by both the Liberal and Conservative parties had formed the autonomous Independent Party of Color to fight for an end to discrimination in general and, especially, for equal treatment of the nonwhite population with respect to access to elected office and government jobs. Two years later, the established parties outlawed the new one on the legal basis that it was racially exclusive. This prohibition led in 1912 to a brief rebellion in Oriente province and then a bloody pogrom by army troops and white vigilantes that took the lives of thousands of mulattos and blacks. Lurid tales of that rebellion in the capital's press added fuel to a fire already lit by fantastic reports of Afro-Cuban societies kidnapping and killing white children for their blood, supposedly required for the "witchcraft" of *santería* or the rites of the Abakuá. "Until the triumph of the revolution," the conservative Havana daily *El Día* fulminated in 1918 after a decade of such scares, "blacks raised white children without eating or abusing them . . . Cuba has been liberated from Spanish tutelage, legal equality and the rights of all citizens have been established, and those people have begun to drink the blood of white girls, and even to martyrize their own daughters . . . Where is progress, then, where is civilization?" The next year the same paper came out in support of lynching "in certain cases," and indeed, in a rare case in the history of Havana, a mob in Regla the next day killed José Williams, a black Jamaican immigrant accused of attempting to rape a white girl. This was the same type of mass-media hysteria that fueled lynching and the growth of the Ku Klux Klan in the United Sates in these same years.

Social organizations of color fought back against lynching and the portrayal of blacks as savages. The Club Atenas, which represented the elite of colored Havana, issued a statement signed by representatives of black organizations of all strata, in which they argued that "the history of this class [slaves, former slaves, and their descendants] is coterminous with that of this nation," and that "we have the right to be considered civilized men, not barbarians." Such social clubs continued to denounce discrimination, but after the suppression of the Independent Party of Color, blacks and mulattos did not organize politically along racial lines again.

As a result of the scandal around the shooting of Yarini, the government closed the San Isidro tolerance zone. The sex trade moved, barely underground, to other areas, especially the Centro Habana barrio of Colón. Periods of official crackdowns and unofficial bribery and toleration would continue throughout the next half century, including a crackdown in Colón in the 1940s that drove some of the business back to San

Isidro again. The role of pimps declined, according to some studies, to be replaced by madams, independent prostitutes, and protection rackets mediated by organized crime figures from both Cuba and the United States. There were no more gentlemen pimps, in any case. Opportunities for men of Alberto Yarini's class broadened as a new sugar boom fueled by World War I brought explosive growth to Havana's economy again. Before we leave San Isidro behind to look at the capital's rapid growth far beyond the precincts of the old city, however, it's worth noting that in Havana as in its sister port of New Orleans, the red-light district was linked not only to national politics but to national culture. It was a place where musicians and musical genres got their start.

When residents of war-devastated eastern Cuba migrated to Havana in the first decade of independence, they brought with them sounds the city knew and sounds that it did not. San Isidro was often the first place that the musicians among them found work. Balladeer Manuel Corona—later famous as the composer of "Mercedes," "Longina," and others of the most beautiful love songs in the repertoire of Cuban *trova*—frequented the barrio in his transition from cigar-roller to musician, during what he later called a "bohemian period that was not the most honorable of my career." He played at the bar on the corner of Egido and Merced, enjoying the generosity of the profiteers and protectors of the sex trade. Gonzalo Roig, who became the most famous composer of *boleros* and light operas (including a musical version of *Cecilia Valdés*) and a founder of the Havana Symphony, played piano to accompany the sex shows at the Zaza theater, notorious among male tourists and sailors far and wide. The legendary troubadour and composer Sindo Garay was already playing better venues, but he wrote a *bolero* dedicated to Yarini, who was often in his audience at the trendsetting Café Vista Alegre on Belascoaín:

> Don't worry, for life smiles upon you
> In your pursuit of orgies and pleasures,
> Because the poor ladies of the night
> At your feet lay all their treasures.

But in the midst of your enjoyment
Which you may think comes for free,
More sincere than women's kisses
Are these words of advice from me.

In the shadows of San Isidro grew up, also, the first Havana gay community about which any written record has survived. There were homosexual men among the prostitutes at Alberto Yarini's funeral, and openly gay Cuban men had found employment and a measure of acceptance as domestic servants doing the washing and cooking in houses of prostitution since the days of *La Cebolla*. Yarini's valet José Claro was one of them.

Rogelio Martínez, a taxi driver who frequently drove for Yarini, remembered San Isidro as "like a carnival in the morning, when the *efeminados* in their pastel-colored undershirts swept out the streetfront rooms. Passersby would yell things, and they'd answer with scandalous comments, with giggles and gestures and not getting upset. But there was one they called the Queen of Italy, as queer as they come, who could fight like a lion. Later he became a *santero* and moved to the barrio Jesús María, I happen to know."

With the clampdown on San Isidro and the spread of cinema in the 1910s, meanwhile, many of the musicians moved on to earn their bread and butter accompanying silent films in the movie palaces that sprang up all over, like the two-screen rooftop Polyteama opposite the Parque Central and others in outlying barrios throughout the city. Here the musicians provided yet another odd counterpoint in the city's eclectic mix: off-the-cuff improvisations in every Cuban musical genre to try and match the antics of Buster Keaton, Theda Bara, Clara Bow, Rudolf Valentino, or Tom Mix. At the Cine Oriente on Belascoaín, the pianist and violinist played inside a cage to protect themselves from audiences who didn't like what they made up. "You developed dexterity, speed," recalled trumpet player Lázaro Herrera of his stint at the Cine Valentino in El Cerro. "If you screwed up and didn't pay attention, you'd get run over by a train."

While the output of U.S. studios dominated Cuban movie houses, newsreel photographer Enrique Díaz Quesada, the author of *El Parque de Palatino*, succeeded in 1913 in producing the first Cuban feature film.

Entitled *Manuel García or The King of the Cuban Countryside*, it played to sold-out crowds on both screens of the Polyteama. The film itself has been lost, but its scenes of large crowds in action were said to have matched those of Eisenstein in Russia and D. W. Griffith in the United States. In content, *Manuel García* presented a myth parallel to that of Alberto Yarini. García, a legendary bandit of the late nineteenth century, appeared as a tropical Robin Hood who collaborated with the revolutionary army while he robbed from the rich and gave to the poor. In the meantime, the capital entered a new era in which the gap between rich and poor became more evident day by day.

9 Catch a Ford on the Malecón: Republican Havana's Growth and Decay

In the two decades after 1910, Cuban sugar boomed as it had a hundred years before. This time, the industry got new life from a commercial treaty which gave Cuban sugar and tobacco favorable tariff terms in the North, while increasing the island's dependency by giving U.S. food and manufactured goods equally or more favored terms in Cuba. In addition, U.S. investment fueled the opening of bigger mills and plantations further from the capital, in newly felled forests of Oriente and in the plains of Camagüey. Though many mill owners (American, Cuban, or a combination) maintained headquarters in Boston or New York as well as Havana, Havana remained a magnet for sugar wealth and the funnel for everything that Cuba imported in return. The sugar industry got its most emphatic boost from the effects of World War I, which drove wholesale prices to unprecedented levels, from 1.9 cents a pound in 1914 to 9.2 cents in 1918 and an incredible 22.5 cents in 1920. The capital lived a moment of delirium called "the Dance of the Millions" that gave rise to a new upper class and accelerated the rush to plan, pave, design, and build. By the end of the first three decades of the Republic, Havana's skyline had begun to take on its modern form.

The Malecón, completed most of the way to the Almendares in 1930, curved for nearly four miles from the docks of Old Havana past the Castillo de la Punta and along the Florida Straits to El Vedado's tree-lined boulevard, Calle G. In hurricane season or when winter cold fronts swept down from the North, waves battered the wall and splashed over onto the pedestrian promenade and the street, making the ramparts feel like the prow of a ship cruising through wind, mist, and spray. When, more often, the sea was calm and the weather clear, the Malecón became a picture-postcard place: it was sun-drenched in the daytime, romantic at sunset, the sea "a prodigy of light and color," as Federico García Lorca wrote during his 1930 stay. The Malecón has been called "the city's window"—a window where residents could escape on hot summer nights, sitting on its concrete sill.

As it marched westward in the 1910s and 1920s, this seaside drive covered what had once been the tiny bay of San Lázaro at the beginning of Cayo Hueso, which was filled in to make a park dominated by a statue of Antonio Maceo on his horse. Balconied hotels and clubs and apartment houses lined its landward side, some built around grand entrance halls and open staircases in imitation of the old aristocratic palaces, others with elevator lobbies or narrower, tile-lined flights of marble stairs. Further out, near the quarry where Martí and hundreds more had toiled on the chain gangs, car dealerships clustered around the intersection with Calle Infanta, inviting potential purchasers to take their wares for a spin along the sea. "Foot it and go!" advertised the Ford Motor Company, a slogan which gave rise to the Cubanism *fotingo*, still in use today for the venerable cars of bygone eras that dot Havana's curbs and streets. The first taxis in the city were Fords, too. For many years, the way to say "let's take a taxi" was "let's catch a Ford."

On the bluff beyond Infanta, where the Spanish shore battery of Santa Clara had traded cannon fire with American battleships and English men-o'-war, the old guns now decorated the new gardens of the elegant, fourteen-story, twin-towered Hotel Nacional, designed in Mediterranean-revival by the New York firm of McKim, Mead, and Wright and completed in 1930. From there, the Malecón embraced El Vedado, no longer an isolated suburb of rustic estates, but a riot of turrets, towers, gables, and widow's walks, steep Swiss roofs and flat Italian ones, covered with old-fashioned red clay tiles or modern poured concrete. El Vedado filled, month by month and year by year, with private mansions surrounded by fences and gardens, as well as more modest middleclass homes and apartment buildings. It also featured a scattering of tourist hotels: first the Trotcha (which expanded into two new buildings in the first decade of the Republic), then the ten-story Presidente near the seaside end of Calle G and the ten-story Palace at its upper end, and then the Nacional. Further out along the coast, where the seawall and drive did not yet reach, the Vedado Tennis Club built an imposing gingerbread clubhouse for its members who were drawn from the Cuban and resident North American elite. It looked as if the Great Gatsby might emerge from its doors.

The construction of Vedado provided a playground for Cuban-born and immigrant architects and craftsmen who offered their clients all manner of architectural display. To Havana's already eclectic architecture, they added styles from all over Europe and North America, a riot of conspicuous consumption that some architectural historians have dubbed "cockadoodlemeow." In contrast to the narrow, crowded, haphazard streets of Old Havana, with barely a sidewalk separating walls from vehicles, Vedado became a garden city, with broad, tree-lined streets and wide sidewalks in front of yards both large and small. In contrast to the old city's picturesque street names that meant avocado, light, sun, bitterness, souls, or friendship, the new district followed a mapmaker's grid where odd-numbered streets ran parallel to the seacoast, and ones denominated by even numbers or letters ran uphill from the Malecón.

At the far end of Vedado, the year 1921 brought construction of a drawbridge across the Almendares that led to the still more exclusive suburb of Miramar. This bridge, where the Fifth Avenue tunnel is today, was popularly known as El Puente de Pote after the nickname of its developer, the immigrant José López Rodríguez ("Pote" is a bean stew from his native region of Spain). Through hard work, advantageous marriage, and political friendships, the legendary Pote rose from bookstore clerk to lottery ticket printer, store owner, and publisher, and then to land speculator, sugar mill magnate, and banker in the feverish years of the boom. He bought a controlling interest in the National Bank of Cuba from J.P. Morgan, then hanged himself from the shower of his Vedado home when plummeting prices broke his bank and stripped several of his millions away. His Matanzas sugar mill, like many others in the early 1920s, soon passed into North American hands.

At the mouth of the Almendares, below the bridge, glowed a copper-roofed gazebo on the seaside estate of one of Pote's real estate rivals, engineer Carlos Miguel de Céspedes, minister of public works in the administration of President Gerardo Machado (1924–33). Céspedes was in charge of many of the great works of those years, from another modernization of the Prado to the construction of the new Capitol building on its upper reaches, from the paving of the Central Highway (the first to link all the country's provinces) to the extension of the Malecón.

These projects spread copious sums of public and private money among landowners, contractors, politicians, and real estate entrepreneurs, not the least of them the Secretary himself. Carlos Miguel had interests in Miramar, but the bulk of the land on that side of the river belonged to the González de Mendoza clan—sugar magnates, plantation owners, bankers, politicians, corporate lawyers representing U.S. firms, and the owners of the Almendares Scorpions baseball team. For his own headquarters, Céspedes decided to buy up and demolish an old honeymoon hotel on the Vedado side of the river, on the bank where fishermen built shacks to house their nets and catches, and where the first settlers had erected their short-lived village of thatched huts. Here, the Minister built his pleasure dome of house and gardens. To make amends for shunning the neighborhood which he had helped to develop, he did not call it Xanadu—or Monticello or Versailles—but simply Villa Miramar.

Behind the Villa, and linked to it by an arched bridge spanning a narrow channel, was an island in the river that the new owner named Kotsima, Japanese for the Isle of Love. There he assembled a private zoo of monkeys, flamingos, iguanas, macaws, two lions, and a bear. In a greenhouse alongside the menagerie his gardeners raised great quantities of exotic flowers. Kotsima also boasted orchids, porcelains, decorated screens, and a great bronze lion, acquired in London as the model for those cast to adorn the Prado's park-like median strip. Out in the river, the Secretary anchored his yacht *Miramar*, for fishing and cruising, and his speedboat *Cuba*, famous for the number of regattas it had won.

A bit inland from the coast, just behind the Tennis Club, was the home of a family typical of Vedado in a very different way, the Loynaz. The poet María de las Mercedes Loynaz, known all her life as Dulce María, became the only Cuban and the only woman from all the Americas to win the Premio Cervantes, the Nobel Prize of Spanish-language literature. Born in December of 1902, the year of Cuban independence, she sprang from two prominent families of the *criollo* aristocracy. Her father, General Enrique Loynaz del Castillo, fought the independence war's battles and also, in celebration of the landings of Martí and Maceo, wrote the lyrics to one of its main anthems, *El himno del invasor*. Her mother and namesake, Maria de las Mercedes Muñoz Sañudo, descended from a landowning fortune on her maternal grandparents' side. The Loynaz fortune was swallowed up by in the war. The Sañudo money, though nearly lost to Spanish authorities in an earlier period, survived. When the young General Loynaz passed a photographer's studio shortly after his arrival in Havana at the end of the war, he saw María de las Mercedes' portrait in a display of Havana's most beautiful young women. He took the photo and sought her out.

Soon after Dulce Maria's birth, the family followed high society westward from a house on the Prado to one in Centro Habana, a few blocks from Galiano at the corner of San Rafael and Amistad. General Loynaz went out on the front balcony to make speeches to cheering crowds of the Liberal Party, but the children's life was protected, as if to keep them purer than their times. They did not go to school, even to a private one, but received their education from tutors. They were visited only by carefully selected offspring of their father's comrades-in-arms. They grew up indoors, surrounded by antique vases, marble statues, paintings and portraits, and a library full of books. At her mother's urging, however, Dulce María enrolled in the university to study law, and on her own account she fought for and won the right to go unaccompanied to her classes and exams.

When Dulce María was in her teens, her mother divorced the General because of his frequent and public extramarital affairs. Hers was one of the earliest divorces to be granted in Cuba under a new republican law. This first Cuban divorce law had to overcome objections from both the Catholic hierarchy and William Jennings Bryan, then U.S. Secretary of State, but Cuban legislators (regardless of their varying attitudes toward other rights for women) saw it as an emblem of the separation of church and state. Soon after the divorce, grandparents and mother and children moved to Vedado, where Dulce María would live for the next seventy years.

They bought one of the oldest houses in the district, a *casa-finca* on Calle Línea with tiled walls, tinted glass, exuberant plantings, an inner courtyard, and extensive grounds. The property bordered that of the Tennis Club, extending nearly to the coral seacoast where the Malecón had not yet arrived. "The house stood in middle of a leafy garden," the poet recalled later, "filled with begonias, jasmines, rare lilac-hued dahlias, honeysuckles, vines of blue and white and red, and sturdy trees; everywhere were comfortable benches, antique marbles, fountains with brightly colored fish, and white peacocks—never before seen in Cuba—who admired their reflections in the pools." In the late 1920s and 1930s Dulce María and her three siblings—all poets—turned this retreat into a salon. Every Thursday at five o'clock, amateur and professional literati of many schools and tendencies assembled to read from the classics and their own latest works. The salon took place in a large blue-grey room with the signs of the zodiac and silver stars painted onto the ceiling in addition to a quote in Italian, borrowed from a princess, "Maybe yes, maybe no." After a disastrous hurricane blew down the nearest telephone pole in 1926, the house on Línea had no phone because none of the brothers or sisters bothered to get the pole replaced. For a time they even banished electricity from their salon, lighting the room with antique candelabras instead. Regardless—or attracted by the eccentricity—literary guests found their way to this retreat.

When Federico García Lorca visited Havana in 1930, he came not just on Thursdays but every afternoon to play the piano, drink whiskey and soda, and read from his work. His favorite Loynaz was not Dulce María but Flor, the youngest sister, whose rebellion mirrored her namesake, the black revolutionary general Flor Crombet. In Flor's new Fiat, Lorca accompanied her and her brother Carlos Manuel to El Templete, not the memorial temple but a sailors' bar. When the General protested Flor's unconventional habits (she shaved her head, for instance, to proclaim that men should find her attractive for more than her looks and locks) she replied, "In these times it's very hard to live a moral life. It's even harder to seem to."

What her sister did in public, Dulce María Loynaz did in her verse. "In my poems I'm free," she wrote. "I walk on water . . . on waves unfolded out of waves and other waves." In these poems, which range from unrhymed classical Spanish meters to long declamatory prose poems and short ones like Zen parables, she often put herself in the position of women observed (or observing) from unique angles. Her verse speaks for Lazarus's betrothed when, returning from the dead, Lazarus demands that she pick up right where things left off—and for the pregnant Virgin Mary when another expectant villager wants to gossip about ambitions for their sons. It speaks for a woman visiting Egypt (as Loynaz did, traveling with her mother and sister, without male accompaniment) who falls in love with the famous mummified king.

At the same time, much of Loynaz's poetry invokes Cuba, and especially her corner of it, El Vedado, because her central metaphors evoke the river and the sea. One of her poems to the Almendares describes how it "drinks in the sun at daybreak, wraps its lover's arm around the city's waist, rises in the spiral winds of the Cuban hurricane." Her long, untitled prose poem beginning "Island of mine" likens Cuba's shape to "the antenna of America," "a fine gold iguana," and "the drawn bow an invisible archer wields from the shadows, aimed at our heart."

Thanks to her father's position, Loynaz's poems began appearing in Cuban newspapers and magazines when she was still a teenager, but she did not pursue publication herself. "Out of a mixture of shyness and pride," she explained later, "a bad combination for the game of life." When her first collection was published in 1938 at the urging of literary friends, it attracted little notice, failing even to be included in the "new books" display at El Encanto, the department store catering to Havana's elite. Stung by this indifference, she vowed to never publish again and to destroy the rest of her writing before her death.

That this did not happen was due in part to the recognition she soon gained from prominent female contemporaries in South America, such as the Uruguayan poet Juana de Ibarbarou who, after Loynaz's visit there, called her "the greatest woman in America." But it was due mostly to one of those juxtapositions of opposites always close at hand in Havana: in her mid-forties, the reclusive and aristocratic daughter of the *mambí* general married a social butterfly, a Spaniard, and a model of the self-made man.

Pablo Álvarez de Cañas arrived in the port of Havana as a struggling immigrant from the Canary Islands at the tail end of 1918. To the impoverished regions of Spain, Cuba was still a powerful magnet, and Havana exercised the strongest pull. Between 1902 and 1934, more than a million immigrants entered the country, three quarters of them from Spain. As in the colonial period, they were predominantly young men seeking to "*hacer América*" (to "do America"). That America was now independent did not dampen their ardor, so a new wave of Spaniards became Cuban, adding to the capital's genetic mix and somewhat bleaching its skin. This white immigration was promoted by the Chamber of Commerce (still largely dominated by Spanish-born merchants) and by the government of the Republic through generous laws. The Centro Gallego, the social club and mutual aid association of the most successful Galician immigrants, hired Purdy & Henderson to build a sumptuous headquarters that literally surrounded the Teatro Tacón. Inside this new structure, they rebaptized the historic auditorium the "Teatro Nacional."

Álvarez de Cañas was part of this flood. He worked over the years as a bookkeeper and salesman for a variety of firms in the capital and for their branches or mills in the interior, while cultivating his social ties to high society at every turn. He first proposed marriage to Dulce María Loynaz when she was only eighteen, two years after his arrival, but the romance and proposal were quashed by her mother out of hand. In the early 1930s, Álvarez de Cañas landed a job with Senator Alfredo Hornedo, yet another of the dubiously self-made millionaire politicians and real estate moguls of the era. Thanks to his friendship with President Machado, Hornedo had won a monopoly status for his Mercado Único meat and produce market (today Mercado Cuatro Caminos). To defend this and other interests, he founded the newspaper *El País* and was looking for ways to boost its circulation. Álvarez de Cañas depended on ghost writers to pen the actual copy, using his connections and his incisive eye to make *El País*'s society page the most popular in Havana, read by both the elite and those who wished they were.

Showered with gifts and services by merchants, professionals, and plutocrats anxious to see their names in the paper, the columnist soon had his own fortune—and he finally married Dulce María Loynaz (now divorced from her first husband, a Loynaz cousin) in 1946. The fabled recluse of Línea and 14th became the hostess of a new colonnaded mansion at the corner of 19th and E, her husband's companion at social events, and the author of "The Event of the Week," one of the columns that appeared under his name. Her new husband was a born promoter who was to become chief publicist for Cuban tobacco in the United States though he neither spoke English nor smoked. His picture soon filled U.S. dailies as he presented boxes of cigars and cigarettes to Gary Cooper, Clark Gable, Bette Davis, and other stars. In similar fashion, he began to get Loynaz's work published in Spain. A triumphant reading at the Ateneo of Madrid in 1947 established her international reputation, though she remained better known in Havana for her role as hostess and her eccentricity than for her literary work. For her part, she continued to credit the former family salon: "[Nothing] would have been possible without the house," she wrote later. "The repose of its gardens that shut out the loud hum of the city, the atmosphere where every object showed off not its price but the art and skill of the hand that had created it. [That was] my attempt to revive in Cuba a salon in the style of 19th century—a refuge for the aristocracy of the spirit."

If the Loynaz salon in Vedado represented one extreme of Havana culture and society, the other extreme was an equally emblematic living space, the *solar*. *Solar* in conventional Spanish means land or building lot, and by extension it means both noble lineage and mansion house. Thus the mansions of Old Havana were originally called *solares*. When their owners left, poor people and new immigrants moved in, but the old name stuck.

On Calle Tacón across from the ancient Castillo de la Real Fuerza, for instance, the eighteenth-century house of the ex-slave Juana de Carvajal, enlarged and upgraded by the Calvos de la Puerta as we have seen, had passed in the later nineteenth century into the hands of the Catalán businessman Salvador Samá, recently named Marqués of Marianao. Samá, who partnered with a British company in the development of the first

Dulce María Loynaz in her house at 19th & E in El Vedado. Portrait on wall is Loynaz in the 1920s or 1930s. Photo was taken many years later, when the poet lived in seclusion well after the revolution of 1959 (see chapter 13).

Photo Credit: Biblioteca Nacional José Martí

railroad to Marianao, lived on his suburban estate, while renting out the Old Havana building piecemeal. His descendants, absentee landlords in Barcelona, continued the practice, and by the twentieth century it had become a tenement made up of single rooms rented out to the poor.

In similar fashion, the descendants of the Counts of Bayona, whose ancestral mansion faced the Cathedral, sold a fifty-year lease to a real estate entrepreneur with rights to transform it as he saw fit. The old palace began to resemble Swiss cheese, its nooks rented out to poor families, generally black, who hung their laundry from the balconies where the countesses had once sat to watch the *volantas* pass by. The same destiny awaited many of the grand colonnaded villas of Cerro, when their residents either lost their fortunes to American or Spanish creditors, or prospered and moved on to the chic neighborhoods of the moment, Vedado and Miramar.

Thus *solar*, in Havana, came to have a new meaning entirely opposite to what it had meant before. A *solar* was now a tenement, called elsewhere a *ciudadela* or *cuartería*, a place where many families crowded into a single room each. All the residents did their washing and cooking and bathing in common facilities in the courtyard, sharing a single cookstove and tap. When independence came, there were already more than two thousand *solares* of one sort or another, housing over a third of the city's population. During the Republic, the process continued apace, as the city's population swelled not only with immigrants from abroad, but also with immigrants from the Cuban countryside. To poor Cubans in the interior, Havana was the place to go in search of work.

When times were good, with large purchases and high prices for sugar in the United States, the capital offered the possibility of advancement. When they were bad, when U.S. imports or prices plummeted, the capital offered the possibility of survival. Small farming families who had lost their homes and scant fields to landlords or bankers sought jobs in Havana to stave off the threat of death from malnutrition or disease. So did the landless canefield and mill workers who fled the "dead season" of unemployment between harvests. As domestics or delivery men or dockworkers, they had a better chance of feeding their families and themselves. They also worked as secretaries or shoeshine boys, sellers of lottery tickets,

entertainers, electricians, elevator repairmen, as employees of cigar factories, and inside whorehouses.

Poor families who rented from the new managers or owners of old
mansions often added makeshift rooms themselves, narrowing the courtyards down into passageways. It's common today to walk into a decayed
colonial palace or *casa-finca* and find a wall running smack into the middle of a colored-glass *mediopunto*, or a spider web of do-it-yourself electrical wiring in the entranceway where the coachmen used to wait for the
commands of the master or mistress.

To a higher stratum in the interior, the hilltop campus of the university—symbolized by the marble statue of Alma Mater at the top of the
majestic entrance stairway of a eighty-eight steps—was a magnet drawing
young men and a few women from provincial towns and cities in search
of both professional careers and cosmopolitan sophistication: "At the end
of the journey he will see the university, the stadium, the theaters," imagi-
nes a provincial tailor's son in novelist Alejo Carpentier's *The Chase*. "Then
he will stroll into a café and order a martini. At last he will know how it
tastes, that mixture they serve with an olive at the bottom of the glass."
Many such students lived in new or converted rooming houses, but the
tailor's son in the novel goes to live in a turret in a sort of *solar*, subletting
his room from an old black woman who had been his wetnurse long ago
and had in the meantime come to the city and worked for the family that
then abandoned the house. The statue of Alma Mater was herself a similar
symbol of the city's mixed heritage (and of the city fathers' ambivalence).
The sculptor crafted her body after that of a mulatta model, and her face
after a statue from ancient Greece.

As pressures and opportunities grew, landlords and speculators built
new *cuarterías* or *solares*—even in Vedado, where they were hidden behind
neoclassical facades, but especially in Cayo Hueso, Pueblo Nuevo, and
other old barrios of Centro Habana, the former neighborhoods "outside
the walls." Such *solares* took on names like El África, El California, or even
El Ataúd (coffin). Makeshift squatter settlements also sprang up on empty
lots, growing into shanty towns with equally eloquent names: Las Yaguas
(palm thatch), Llega y Pon (squat and build), La Timba (guava paste, a

traditional food of the poor), and Cocosólo (coconut-and-that's-all). If the poet Dulce María Loynaz has served to exemplify the Cuban culture that took root in the salon, the musician Luciano "Chano" Pozo González may do the same for that of the solar—all the more so because, like most paths in Havana, the paths of their twin stories will nearly cross. Chano Pozo was born in a solar called Pan con Timba on the outskirts of Vedado. After his mother died, the family moved to El África, at the border of Pueblo Nuevo and Cayo Hueso, close to where his father shined shoes on the corner of Zanja and Belascoaín.

"El África was a hell of a place," recalled Herminio Sánchez, a long-time resident of this *barrio*, trying to describe Chano Pozo's roots. "At night the courtyard was lit with one single bulb, and the clotheslines full of wash made it even darker than that. Something like two hundred people lived there, all of them black. The police didn't go in there. And if they did, or anybody came after you, the place had five exits. That was the beauty of it. You could go in on one side, and come out anyplace else." Short but strong, and with a temper, Chano got in his share of fights, petty thievery, and trouble with the police. He was sent to reform school in the countryside, where he learned to read and write. He got back to Havana in the early 1930s, in the depth of the Great Depression which caused both sugar prices and U.S. purchases to plummet, and went to live in El Ataúd, in the barrio of Colón. Pozo shined shoes like his father, sold newspapers, and did whatever else he could to survive. Then he went to work for senator Alfredo Hornedo, at about the same time as Dulce María Loynaz's future husband did.

Exactly what Chano Pozo did for Alfredo Hornedo is not clear. He may have started out selling *El País* on the street, but oral history says he was also a bodyguard or enforcer. In any case, Hornedo supported him, and he became a habitué of the magnate's home on Carlos III, a modern castle (now the Casa de Cultura of Centro Habana) with a massive first story, two recessed levels above, and a terrace with two-story watchtower. Whatever the reform school graduate might have done for the politician-businessman-publisher with his fists, what made Chano Pozo's career was what he could do with his open hands and a goatskin stretched across a wooden tube. For all its privations and cruelties, the culture of the *solar* was also the culture of the *rumba*. At the center of *rumba* was the drum.

From various parts of Africa, the slaves had brought knowledge of sacred hollow-log drums, played with the hands rather than with sticks, and tuned by tempering the skins over a fire. They made and played these drums in the *cabildos*, and their descendants continued the tradition in all of the Afro-Cuban religions and secret societies—despite near-constant prohibitions by Spanish, U.S., and Cuban authorities on the public use of anything resembling African drums. Over time, among the black working class of both Matanzas and Havana, these sacred drums gave rise to the modern conga drum or *tumbadora*. And they gave rise to *rumba*, a Cuban creation, the secular music of the *solar*.

Rumba was a lively, flexible, improvisational music of congas, *clave* sticks, and voices, danced by soloists or by couples, in one of its most popular forms as a pantomime of flirtation and sex. In the courtyard of the *solar, rumberos* improvised lyrics that displayed their knowledge of African languages or that dealt with gossip, politics, neighborhood characters, romance, sex, and work.[1] When there was no drum—or to avoid trouble with the police—the *tumbadores* played wooden crates instead, creating the famous "box *rumba*," the *rumba de cajón*. At carnival time, the *congas* and the *rumba* came out of the *solares* and into the street as *comparsas*, performed in conga lines and featuring brief, repeated, catchy lyrics. Even these constantly went in and out of legality—and, when officially illegal, in and out of control.

In the 1920s and the 1930s, however, a new generation of nationalist artists and intellectuals, both black and white, began taking a new look at Afro-Cuban influences and incorporating them in fields such as anthropology, literature, and the visual and musical arts. Nicolás Guillén, who had newly arrived in the capital from Camagüey, began introducing Afro-Cuban rhythms and colloquial urban working-class language into his poetry, in a similar fashion to what Langston Hughes (soon to be Guillén's friend) was doing with the blues in New York. Havana poet and journalist José Z. Tallet had already published a poem called "La Rumba" that tried to capture the rumba's music, its lyrics, and the presence of the Afro-Cuban deities. Composers of avant-garde orchestral music such as

Alejandro García Caturla, Amadeo Roldán, and Gilberto Valdés added elements of *rumba* and other grassroots Cuban genres to their works. García Caturla wrote an orchestral piece called *La rumba* (1933) attempting to capture its essence, and in the late 1930s Valdés finally brought the African drums themselves into a symphonic orchestra.

In pop and dance music, meanwhile, the *son* invaded Havana from Oriente, and like *contradanza* and *danzón* before, it was first considerd black before being considered Cuban. In the process, it picked up the influence of *rumba*. Miguel Matamoros brought his trio from Santiago to sweep the capital off its feet with "*Son de la loma*," while Ignacio Piñeiro and the Sexteto Habanero converted the choruses of the wooden-box *rumbas* into classics like "*Échale salsita*" and immortalized picaresque Havana characters such as Papá Montero in their songs. In the musical melting pot of Havana, where instrumentation was always on the move, not only the sextets and septets of *son* suddenly wanted to add the forbidden *tumbadora*, but so too did Cuban jazzbands and interpreters of other genres as well. Changing tourist tastes began to demand more openly Afro-Cuban music as part of the package of sun, rum, and sensuality that brought Americans to Cuba during Prohibition and after. By the same token, *rumba* rhythms and sanitized lyrics were adapted for groups featuring brass, piano, and strings. Chano Pozo—self-taught *conga* drummer, composer, dancer, singer, choreographer, itinerant newspaper vendor, shoe shiner, and bodyguard—found himself in demand.

In the late 1930s, Pozo performed and composed with the neighborhood groups that prepared *comparsas* for Carnival: El Barracón (slave barracks) of Pueblo Nuevo, El Alacrán (the scorpion) of Cerro, La Jardinera of Jesús María, and La Sultana of Colón. The diva Rita Montaner brought him into the standout group Los Dandies de Belén, in Old Havana, for which he coauthored the prize-winning carnival song of the same name. He was also in demand by musical groups performing in private parties, beachfront bandstands, and musical theaters. His compositions—though not yet his too black skin—were featured in revues at tourist hotels and recordings by the groups that played there. In 1938, he debuted on the grand stage as *conga* player in works by Obdulio Morales and Gilberto

Valdés at the Teatro Martí and the open-air Amphitheater of Havana by the neck of the bay.

Finally, in the 1940s, Pozo played and danced in the Afro-Cuban ballet extravaganza Congo Pantera at the new open-air Tropicana night club, which also featured his own evocation of life in the *solar*, the song *"Parampampín."* His songs were recorded by top Cuban artists including Arsenio Rodríguez, the blind *tres* guitarist, bandleader, and composer, and by Cuban musicians working in the United States. Both mainstream Cuban audiences and North American devotees of "Latin" music found themselves singing and dancing to his numbers with onomatopoetic titles and lyrics such as "Blen, Blen, Blen," and *lengua* (African-derived) ones like "Ariñañara" and "Guagüina yerabo." He found a new patron in the tobacco heir and radio mogul Amado Trinidad, for whom he guarded the door of the Radio Cadena Azul's studios on the Prado and led the house band Conjunto Azul. When he was shot in the stomach by a music publisher's bodyguard in a dispute over royalties, Trinidad and Senator Hornedo got him the best possible medical care.

Once in the money, Chano Pozo became one of the best dressed men in Havana. One hot, sweaty day in the 1940s in the *solar* El Ataúd, according to musicologist Jesús Blanco, Pozo covered his bed with five and ten peso bills and declared that the amount which stuck to him was his budget for the day. Stores and tailors vied for him to wear their latest suits and jewelry. In carnival *comparsas* he appeared in white dress clothes, immaculately attired from top hat to tails. "He drove a Cadillac and wore Chanel #5," recalled Litico Rodríguez, ex-dancer and comic actor. "He and [pianist, composer, and singer] Bola de Nieve were the only black men who could shop in El Encanto, the most expensive and chic department store at the time." But Chano Pozo continued to live in *solares*, drink in neighborhood bars, buy marijuana and cocaine from the dealers in the notorious Parque Trillo and elsewhere, and join in whatever *rumba* was at hand. In the 1930s, he joined an Abakuá chapter in Cayo Hueso, though rumor had it that he was expelled, finally, for incorporating its sacred songs into recordings for Cadena Azul. He was about to take on a patron *orisha* in the rites of *santería* when he got an invitation to work in the United States.

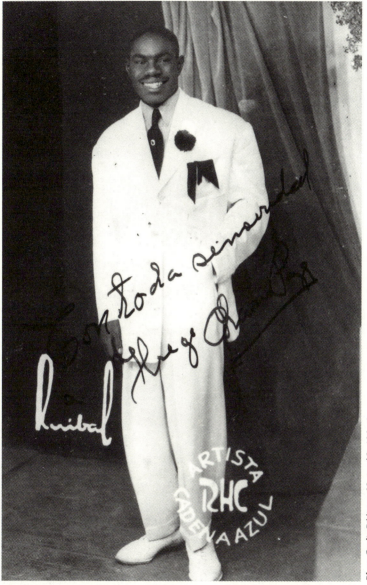

Chano Pozo, autographed publicity photo from radio network Cadena Azul.

In 1946, Pozo set out for New York, center of the recording industry and therefore a beacon for Cuban musicians. He boarded ship along with a new red Cadillac convertible he bought with the advance money. In New York he recorded a few pure percussion rumbas as well as a variety of popular tunes—including "El Pin Pin," his celebration of the defeat of fascism with the addictive refrain *pin pin, cayó Berlín, pon pon, cayó Japón* ("pin pin, Berlin fell; pon pon, so did Japan")—and performed in nightclubs and theaters specializing in Latin music. Then he was introduced to Dizzy Gillespie, who was looking for a "tom tom player" ("I didn't know it was called a conga") to add a new dimension to bebop music. And that, said Gillespie, "is when the Latin innovation in [U.S.] jazz began." Afro-Cuban bebop was the result, with Pozo playing his rumba rhythms alongside Gillespie's trumpet in Carnegie Hall in 1947, the same year that Dulce María Loynaz read to a packed house at the Ateneo de Madrid. With Gillespie he recorded the classics "Cubana Be," "Cubana Bop," and "Manteca," touring Europe, the West Coast, and the American South.

Life in the United States, however, was no more free of trouble than Havana, and it brought its own dangers. Pozo left the southern tour when his drum was stolen in North Carolina, and decided not to return because of the discrimination he ran into there. Then, on the cold northern night of December 3, 1948, he was standing in the Rio Café and Lounge on 112th St. in Manhattan's Spanish Harlem, playing his own hit "Manteca" on the juke box, when an ex-sharpshooter World War II veteran from Puerto Rico (Cuban born in some versions of the story) pulled out a revolver and killed him with a single shot. A bad drug deal, a debt, an insult, an assassination paid for out of envy, a punishment for his failure to *hacerse santo* with the *orisha* Changó—theories abounded, but whatever the cause, Chano Pozo returned to Havana a corpse, leaving his compositions and the future of AfroCuban jazz behind. All in all, says Leonardo Padura, "Chano Pozo was the underside of Havana of his era, and he was also Havana itself: mistreated and joyful, boisterous and suffering . . . able to express with his hands a way of life, a way of understanding the world."

Dulce María Loynaz and Chano Pozo represent the extremes and the unexpected intersections of Havana's society and culture in all the decades between the Dance of the Millions and World War II. The majority of Havana lived between the extremes, neither in the tree-shaded mansions of Vedado nor in the crowded *solares* downtown—working, looking for work, striving to survive or get ahead. Therefore we need to briefly sketch the city's physical growth during this period, and introduce some ordinary families, not famous but equally representative, whom we can follow during these years and the ones that will follow.

From the coming of independence to the mid-1940s, metropolitan Havana's population quadrupled, from about 250,000 to a million inhabitants, fourfold growth in a little more than forty years. To house the increase, the city expanded, growing both larger and taller. As the city of the rich spread to the west along the seacoast, that of the working and lower middle class expanded everywhere else, especially along the streetcar lines, the old roads to surrounding villages, and the ferry routes across the bay.

Across the Almendares but inland from Miramar, the old outlying settlement of Marianao spread eastward to the banks of the Almendares and westward to La Lisa. Its living links to the city's core strengthened with the opening and expansion of entertainment centers such as the Oriental Park racetrack (owned by the Cuban-American Jockey Club) and the beer gardens opened by the Tropical Brewery to promote its brew. The Jardines de la Tropical, designed by Catalán architects in the spirit of Gaudí, featured riverside pavilions that blended Moorish cupolas and mosaics with tropical jungle motifs, linked by sinuous paths that snaked through royal palms and other trees. In the 1930s and 1940s, the Jardines de la Tropical became one of a limited number of social venues where almost all segments of Havana society met.

To the south of the city working-class *barrios* like Lawton, Diezmero, Arroyo Apollo, and Mantilla grew up, as did middle-class ones like Santos Suarez and the euphoniously Spanglish Vibora Park. Along the main roads heading south and southeast, neighborhoods like El Calvario, Párraga, and San Miguel de Padrón likewise became part of what was known as La Gran Habana, while the old villages of Guanabacoa, Regla, and Casablanca across the bay were tightly connected to the economic, social, and cultural life of the city through tiny passenger ferries that crossed the water at all hours of the day and night.

In the meantime, the old city grew vertically to match the horizontal sprawl. Though Havana remained a low-rise city in comparison to many, apartment houses of three, four, five, and sometimes more stories replaced the one-and two-story structures of many older neighborhoods. In Centro Habana, a new shopping district grew up along the streets of Galiano, Neptuno, and San Rafael. Its signature venue was El Encanto (where Dulce María Loynaz was angry that her book was not put on sale, and Chano Pozo finally became able to shop) at the corner of San Rafael and Galiano. Along these streets and others, an endless procession of columns and arcades provided shade for shoppers while supporting multiple stories of apartments above. If Centro Habana lacked the space and capital that made Vedado an architect's paradise, a walk through its streets still reveals myriad decorative touches in cement and iron, wood and glass, plaster and tile, mica and marble dust, in styles ranging from beaux art to Italian renaissance to art deco and art nouveaux. All of this brought work to craftsmen and artists, while the stores and shoppers brought business to the milliners and seamstresses of the district, which like Old Havana housed a population that was mixed in every way.

Early in the century, for instance, the sisters Cecilia and Virginia Larrinaga, dressmakers and hatmakers with roots most likely in Oriente, set up shop on the Calle San Rafael and rented an apartment upstairs. They made women's clothes and hats to order, and they saved their money to offer the best future they could to their nephew Luis, whose father worked nearby as a cook. The Larrinaga sisters were mulattas, and while they wanted to send Luis abroad for high school, they feared the racial prejudice he would meet in the United States, so they managed to send him to France. When he returned, he went to work for the weekly newsmagazine *Bohemia* as a French translator, but since the pay was by piecework and there was less demand for French than for English, he worked mostly as a chauffeur for the publisher of the magazine. After Luis married, he and his family moved frequently from apartment to apartment around Centro Habana, along the borders of Cayo Hueso, in accord with what they could afford in the face of ever-rising rents. His son Carlos remembers the devastating hurricane of 1926 (the same one that deprived the Loynaz of their telephone service) blowing down the wall of the *solar* across the street and leaving its many inhabitants exposed. Carlos in turn went to work at the Victor Adding Machine Company on Galiano, a Cuban-owned franchise of the American company, where he repaired adding machines and typewriters, Remingtons and Underwoods above all.

Meanwhile, Pablo González Palacios had come to Havana from Santa Clara in 1914 and begun to do what the Chinese most recently had pioneered, as the free blacks of the treasure port had done centuries before. He sold fried meat patties and corn tamales from a cart, first on the southern edge of Miramar, and then alongside the private clubs and the public beach in the nearby Playa de Marianao, where he became known as "Pablo el Cumbanchero" after a popular dance. With his savings, he bought a lot in one of the most affordable of the new working-class suburbs, called Buenavista, recently laid out on former farmland south and east of Camp Columbia.

Buenavista was first subdivided into lots by a U.S. speculator named Joseph Barlow in 1906 and 1907, the years of the second U.S. occupation when American troops again occupied the Camp. In the early teens, the developers received formal authorization for building and paving, on a plan of small lots and narrow streets with set back sidewalks. It was a sort of mini-Vedado for the working class. About 1920, Pablo el Cumbanchero bought a lot in Buenavista, hired local carpenters to build him a house, and set up stone ovens in the patio to bake bread and sweets to add to his wares. Buenavista was then mostly empty, and up the hill was still an open grassland called "*el parque de los chivos* (goats)" where locals pastured their animals. In the patio behind the house he grew fruit trees—a mango tree, a banana, an anón. But Buenavista soon gained a reputation as a barrio both hardworking and tough.

"I love Buenavista," recalls his granddaughter Raquel Cañizares who still lives in that house on what is today Calle 64 of the municipality of Playa, "and I was a protected child, too, but it has always been a *barrio caliente*, a hot place, and I remember how they used to go to the park to rob people and steal the goats." Buenavista even became famous for a gang of female thieves, Las Villalobas, who would sometimes assault the customers in local stores. Like many popular neighborhoods, it was also memorialized in songs such as "Buena Vista en Guagancó," by Arsenio Rodriguez and "Social Club de Buenavista" by the bassist and mambo innovator Orestes "Cachao" López.

There was indeed a Social Club of Buenavista, one of many societies of "recreation and instruction." Distant descendants of the old *cabildos*, these private societies were created by and for Havana's working- and middle-class population of color whose access to other venues was limited by discrimination and high prices. Founded by Julio Dueñas on Avenida 31 about six blocks from the house of Pablo el Cumbanchero, the Buenavista club had no house band (the internationally famous Havana oldies band of the 1990s was an amalgam put together by the U.S. guitarist Ry Cooder), but it did welcome prominent black and mulatto musicians who performed for public dances as well as private parties to celebrate weddings and *quinces*, the parties held to celebrate girls turning fifteen.

Besides hosting the dances which nurtured musicians and musical innovation, these clubs sponsored other forms of recreation (such as athletic teams and domino competitions) as well as offering classes in English, skilled trades, and domestic arts. The societies thus provided Havanans of color with a measure of support in the economic competition to stay afloat in Havana, which was severe in spite of the economic growth. Raquel Cañizares and her family were also members of the Club Ameno, another society based in Marianao, which in December of 1946 rented the clubhouse of the Oriental Park horse track for a New Year's dance. That was where she met Luis Larrinaga's son Carlos for the first time. They married in 1949, uniting the Centro Habana family with the Buenavista one. They lived for two years (and had their first two children) in two rented rooms on San Rafael in Centro Habana. Then Carlos bought a used 1948 Lincoln in which to commute to his job at Victor Adding Machine, and they moved back to Buenavista for good.

Still more strands of ethnicity and culture wove their way into popular neighborhoods of Havana. In the mid-1930s, the Cañizares and their Buenavista neighbors began to be visited by a peddler whom they referred to as *el polaco*. Literally a *polaco* is a Pole, but in the city's terminology it had come to denote anyone from Eastern Europe and, by extension, any Jew. The peddler in question, Alberto Motola, was the son of Sephardic Jews from Turkey who had emigrated to New York at the outbreak of World War I. His family soon heard of opportunities in Cuba, and after a spell in the cities of the interior, they settled in the capital. Jews made their way to Havana by other routes as well. Composer Moisés Simons, who turned the chants of black peanut vendors into the popular hit "El manisero," came from a family of Basque Jews who reached Havana in the nineteenth century.

By the time the Motolas arrived, Jews had established a foothold in the textile and clothing businesses along Sol and Luz and Muralla streets in Old Havana. The Sephardim, whose ancestors had been expelled from Spain the same year Columbus set sail for the new world, established a synagogue on the ironically named corner of Luz and Inquisidor. Alberto went to work by the age of ten, first running errands for a Greek shoemaker, and then sweeping floors and delivering messages for a clothing wholesaler on Muralla. In 1936, he began taking the streetcar out to Buenavista to peddle clothes and fabrics on time payments, door to door. Eight years later he married Maria Roffe, whose parents had made the same journey from Turkey to New York to Havana, and this couple in turn moved from downtown to an increasingly crowded Buenavista, where they rented an apartment and a tiny store a few blocks from the Cañizares house. Alberto too now commuted to the city center, in his case to buy wholesale from his contacts there. For this he depended on the streetcars and delivery trucks, until finally, in the early 1950s, he bought an old Model-T.

The Motolas, the Larrinaga-Cañizares, and their neighborhood of Buenavista provide a glimpse of some often-hidden dimensions of Havana during these decades, which go unmentioned in histories of architecture, entertainment, and the culture of either salon or *solar*. There is still something else to be considered, however. The residents of the city did not act only as individuals or members of families, but sometimes as masses of citizens in the political sphere. As we did with the nineteenth century, we need to refocus on the period we have just covered with a different eye. The political centerpiece of those years in Havana, which left its mark on the city forever after, was what is known as the Revolution of 1933.

10 The Battle of Havana, 1933–35

Juan Criollo, the protagonist of Carlos Loveira's 1927 novel of the same name, described the Cuba of the early years of the century this way:

> [It's] a soccer ball covered with ants, to which an unknown player has given a tremendous kick, sending it spinning through space without the ants having the slightest idea where they came from or where they're going or why. That doesn't stop the little animals from clinging to the surface or from killing each other so as to keep holding on to the ball and their dreams.

Juan Criollo is a novel foremost about Havana, the story of a boy who lives by his wits, who climbs from a miserable shack on the undeveloped seacoast into the realm of politics as the city grows along with him. Loveira had been a teenage exile in New York, an officer in the army of independence, and then a translator for the U.S. occupation force. "At first, just knowing English was enough to change you overnight into the representative of some official or firm," he said later. "But soon, even the cobblestones started speaking English," so he had to look for other work. He found it on the railroads as a brakeman, baggage handler, engineer of a sugar mill locomotive, and eventually machinist. Finally he became a journalist, government bureaucrat, and prominent novelist. But in his railroad period, he was a founder of the Cuban League of Railroad Employees, and he remained attached to union and socialist sympathies in the years that followed. *Generals and Doctors* (1920), his other best-known novel along with *Juan Criollo*, ends with a workers' general strike against the pervasive corruption and inequality which defined that era.

Loveira knew what he was talking about. In 1933, a general strike that began among the capital's bus drivers toppled a government and unleashed the only Cuban revolution truly made in Havana. Years before that, manual workers and their unions, in and out of the capital, were among the first to emerge from the political passivity that followed the frustration of the hopes of 1898.

Even during the first U.S. occupation, the notion of founding socialist or workers' political parties had emerged within the trade unions of Havana. Proponents included old activists of Martí's Cuban Revolutionary Party, such as Carlos Baliño and Diego Vicente Tejera, both connected to international socialist organizations. Among the strongholds of union organizing were the city's cigar factories, whose workers built on the militancy that had made their unions in exile a base of support for the independence movement in Tampa, New York City, and Key West. In the expansive open rooms of the Gener, Partagás, H. Uppmann, and other factories, the old tradition of the *Lector*, or Reader, continued. This designated employee declaimed the news and editorials of the daily press and chapter after chapter of famous literary works. As a result, the cigar workers, like the typographers in the newspapers and publishing houses, were generally well-informed and in possession of a level of culture beyond their formal education. The papers they "read" through the voice of the reader included workers' publications of a socialist bent.

Strikes for higher wages or better conditions emerged along with the founding of the Republic, bringing frequent street clashes between unionists and police. In 1907, during the second U.S. occupation, seven thousand tobacco workers in factories belonging to the Henry Clay/Bock & Company trust walked out and stayed out for more than six months, until the company agreed to pay them in U.S. dollars (rather than the less valuable Spanish and French currency also in circulation in the city). Shortly afterward, railroad workers striking against United Railways (which was also American-owned) had to confront a group of

Photo Credit: Library of Congress

Havana cigar factory, early 20th century

fifty strikebreakers brought directly from the United States to maintain train service between Havana and surrounding towns. Masons, carpenters, lithographers, and teamsters also walked out in spite of warnings from U.S. provisional governor Charles Magoon, known in popular songs as the Hothead for his impulsive personality. In January of 1908, while houses along the coast from the Castillo de la Punta to the mouth of the Almendares were flooded by a storm surge from the ocean, the cigar rollers of the Romeo & Juliet factory struck in protest against impending layoffs. Havana sewage system workers likewise struck against the Huston Contracting Company (whose profits helped Tillinghast Huston buy the Yankees, as noted earlier), and construction workers walked out on the Cuban Engineering Company.

Soon after this wave of strikes, the Hothead departed along with his Army of Pacification, leaving the restive city in the hands of its Cuban officials. In 1914, a National Workers Congress assembled in the capital, with 1200 union delegates from all parts of the country. The mid-1920s saw the formation of the National Workers Confederation of Cuba

(Spanish initials CNOC) led by Alfredo López, a typographer by trade. López was an anarchist who believed in trade union unity and political dialogue, and who had gained a strong reputation for incorruptibility in a country where money bought anything. With the founding of the CNOC, general strikes on a national level began to occur.

In the 1910s and especially the 1920s, this nascent labor movement was joined by movements in other sectors, as Cuban politics and intellectual life emerged from the torpor that had set in when the promise of full independence and thoroughgoing reform was blocked by the American occupation. Pent up demands for national sovereignty, cultural independence, social justice, and an end to corrupt government reemerged in overlapping national organizations of labor, war veterans, students, women, professionals, and small business owners. In 1919, while the government prohibited the flying of red flags in demonstrations, the movie *The Harvest in Six Acts, or The Blood of Sugar* debuted in the Payret Cinema on the Prado across from the site where the new Capitol building was going up. Expressions of social unrest came to form part of the city's life. The many new reform groups won some important victories in the late 1910s and early 1920s, most notably tariff protection for local industry, wage increases for unionized sectors of the workforce, reform of the university, and some small steps toward gender equality.

Women's groups fought for access to education and jobs, changes in family law, and the vote. As early as 1913, Magdalena Peñarredonda, the independence fighter and organizer of fellow prisoners in the Casa de Recogidas in 1896–98, published an article entitled "Feminism in Cuba" in which, among other things, she called on women to boycott stores that did not hire female employees. The following year, the new divorce law was passed. At the first National Women's Congress, held in Havana in the Teatro Nacional (formerly Tacón) in 1923, the more radical delegates challenged the sexual double standard as they called for equal rights for illegitimate children and unwed mothers, and for jobs and respectability for former prostitutes. One legal victory for the women's movement was the repeal of the colonial-era law that legitimized a husband's murder of an adulterous wife. Among the Cuban feminists or proto-feminists of the early 1920s were Dulce María Borrero, sister of the late poet Juana, and Mariblanca Sabás Alomá, a journalist and one of two female members of the Grupo Minorista, Havana's new cultural avant garde.

They called themselves Minoristas (the minority) because they saw themselves as bearers of a national ideal of freedom, independence, renewal, and social progress in the midst of the pervasive atmosphere of decadence and corruption which had categorized the first two decades of the Republic. Meeting in weekly *tertulias* (salons or talk sessions), the Minoristas founded new magazines and lecture series, forming a Cuban point of contact with a wide variety of modernist, antiimperialist, and socialist schools of thought abroad.

Among the Minoristas were the writers José Z. Tallet and Nicolás Guillén (not a founder, but a participant), and the composer Alejandro García Caturla, whose incorporations of Afro-Cuban popular culture into Cuban poetry and classical music we have already described. The group also promoted several soon-to-be famous painters who did the same for the visual arts. Alejo Carpentier, a prominent Minorista, began his literary career exploring African roots, and noted that, among the avant garde composers of his circle, "Those who already knew the score of *The Rite of Spring* began to notice, justifiably, that in Regla, on the other side of the bay, there were rhythms as complex and interesting as those created by Stravinsky."

Guillén's body of work would make him a leading poet in the years stretching into the 1970s, and Carpentier would become the most important Cuban novelist of the century and a leading chronicler of Havana's architecture, history, and music. Other Minoristas became political leaders as well as influential intellectuals. These included the poet Rubén Martínez Villena and the essayist Juan Marinello (both later to join the Communist Party) and the brilliant polemecist Jorge Mañach (liberal and anticommunist, who would later write the best political biography of José Martí).

Denouncing government corruption and U.S. domination, the Minoristas and their fellow travelers allied themselves with the political wing of the Cuban intellectual renewal, which was based at the hilltop campus of the University of Havana. In 1923, while students in Argentina and other Latin American countries were demanding and proclaiming the reform of higher education, the new Cuban University Students' Federation forcibly occupied the campus's buildings and plazas, demanding removal of anachronistic and corrupt professors, modernization of curriculum and textbooks, free higher education, and autonomy from the government.

One of the main leaders of this action was Julio Antonio Mella—who was at one and the same time a rowing champion in the university regattas, a disciple of the union leader Alfredo López, and an organizer of the independent José Martí Popular University. Mella was among the small group who assembled in 1925 in a building on the Calle Calzada in Vedado (on the site where the Hubert de Blanck theater now stands) to found the Cuban Communist Party. The party's initial base was a small group of Central European immigrants and other Cuban workers, some veterans of the Cuban Revolutionary Party, and some former anarchists. Mella himself was soon expelled by the new party's leadership, who saw him as too much of a free spirit. In the late 1920s and the 1930s, the communists became increasingly influential in the union movement and among middle-class intellectuals, as both of these sectors fought repression by the state.

In the late 1920s, the winds of change blowing through Havana ran up against the dual barriers of the Great Depression and the dictatorship of Gerardo Machado, president from 1925 to 1933. Machado was, like his predecessor Menocal, a former Liberation Army officer who entered politics and managed a U.S.-owned sugar mill before reaching the presidency. He was first elected president as a reformer but then solidified his grip on power and wealth through increasingly brutal methods, including murder and torture of opponents, chief among them radical students and unionists.

As the 1930s dawned, the blow of the Great Depression shook the island. In Cuba, just as in the United States, unemployment soared and wages dropped. The poor subsisted on a diet of "corn and *boniatos*" (Cuban sweet potatoes) and "water with brown sugar"—and these popular expressions were not far from the literal truth. Alberto Motola's Jewish immigrant father, for instance, brought home only forty-five cents a day to feed nine children, on soup fortified with bread and a little cheese. It was in that context that Alberto went to work at the age of ten. As the Machado dictatorship met growing protests with intensified repression, many members of Havana's political opposition and its intellectual avant garde were driven underground or into exile.

Julio Antonio Mella, one of the earliest to denounce Machado, was expelled from the university and arrested. He went on a hunger strike in jail, and finally into exile in Mexico after his release. In 1929, he was shot dead by agents of Machado's political police. His image as a light-skinned mulatto Adonis was immortalized in a portrait by Tina Modotti, the photographer and professional revolutionary who moved in the same Mexican circles as Frida Kahlo and Diego Rivera. In Cuba, union leaders including CNOC founder Alfredo López and the Abakuá and communist Aracelio Iglesias (leader of the stevedores on Havana's docks) were tortured and thrown into the sea from Navy ships by Machado's assassins, who sowed terror on the capital's streets.

The Student Federation founded by Mella, now converted into the underground University Student Directorate, gave birth to a labyrinth of clandestine groups who proposed to fight terror with terror by way of armed attacks against politicians and others associated with the government. The most audacious act of this underground resistance was directed against the dictator himself. The plan was to assassinate one of Machado's key lieutenants, Senate President Clemente Vázquez Bello, and then blow up the entire top echelon of the government including the dictator when they assembled at the Colón Cemetery to pay their last respects. For weeks, the revolutionaries toiled literally underground, digging a long tunnel from a house on Calle Zapata to the Vázquez Bello family tomb. A group armed with machine guns ambushed Vázquez Bello on the street as planned, while confederates placed enough explosives under the tomb to convert it into a gigantic land mine. Then the Vázquez Bello family decided at the last minute to bury Clemente in Santa Clara, their home town. The plan failed, bringing on a new wave of government repression. It was later immortalized in fictionalized form in John Huston's film *We Were Strangers* (1949), a surprisingly sympathetic portrayal of revolution just before the McCarthy era came to Hollywood.

Demanding an end to Machado's rule and relief from the desperate economic straits of the Depression, a defiant public grassroots opposition emerged alongside the armed underground. The government found itself besieged by protests, strikes, and assassinations on all sides. During this time, Flor Loynaz joined the University Student Directorate and drove her Fiat in one of these violent demonstrations. For years afterward its bullet-scarred chassis, hidden in the family garage, bore testimony to the lengths to which even such patrician rebels were driven by the times. Luis Larrinaga, chauffeur and translator, had joined the Communist Party, influenced both by the gravity of the Cuban crisis and the political ideas he had picked up in France. He too participated in the uprising against Machado, as did thousands more. Finally in 1933 a work stoppage by Havana's bus drivers turned into a general strike that paralyzed the city. Clashes between strikers and Machado's police had the capital teetering on the brink of civil war.

On the morning of August 12, 1933, the orchestra of competing sounds to which Havanans had been accustomed since time immemorial suddenly changed into a chorus chanting in unison one and the same phrase: Machado is gone! Streetcars and trucks overflowing with exultant young people circled through the city in a triumphal march, seeking out those who had collaborated with the dictatorship, breaking into mansions in a gesture of anarchic reprisal for everything stolen during the preceding years. The strike that brought down Machado had been called by the CNOC and seconded by the university students, the communists, the paramilitary organization ABC, and other groups fighting against the dictatorship. But none of these revolutionary organizations could control the populace of Havana. In the streets, crowds seized and executed agents of the feared political police of the dictator, popularly known as La Porra (the blackjack). They sacked the luxurious Villa Miramar at the mouth of the Almendares, carrying off many of the treasures that Machado's Minister of Public Works had amassed. In Buenavista, the looting was more practical. Raquel Cañizares has never forgotten how at the age of six she watched two diminutive women, her neighbors from down the block, staggering under the weight of a great sack of rice.

Machado and his closest collaborators, including the head of La Porra and the owner of the Villa Miramar, had already escaped into exile. In most cases, they went to the United States. From that distance they observed the

Photo Credit: Biblioteca Nacional José Martí

In a well-known image from the Revolution of 1933, jubilant Havanans on the Prado celebrate an army corporal who has just changed sides and shot a notorious member of Machado's secret police.

events that spread throughout the country over the next twenty months. If the struggle against Machado had ended, the Revolution of 1933 had just begun. It had started in the streets of Havana, and there it would be fought to the end.

In the middle of the cacophony on that first day of celebration, the city's radio stations announced the formation of a provisional government led by sixty-two-year-old Dr. Carlos Manuel de Céspedes Quesada and General Alberto Herrera Franchi. Céspedes was a lawyer, former ambassador to Washington, and most importantly the son and namesake of the man who had proclaimed independence from Spain sixty-five years before. Herrera was the head of the armed forces under the regime that had just collapsed. But the people of Havana were fed up with "generals and doctors." Even many rank-and-file police and soldiers refused to follow orders from these figures from the old regimes, and soon the revolutionary organizations (armed and unarmed) named their own government, whose short life would leave a deep imprint on Cuban history. The new president was a physiology professor at the University of Havana, Ramón Grau San Martín, and his minister of justice and armed forces was a young graduate of the college of pharmacy and ex-pharmaceutical salesman, Antonio Guiteras Holmes, born in Bala Cynwyd, Pennsylvania of a Cuban father and Irish mother. Citing Martí's dictum that the colony should not be allowed to live on in the republic, the government adopted the slogan "Cuba for the Cubans" and sought, as Grau put it, "to liquidate the colonial structure that has survived in Cuba since independence." This was the first government in the history of the Republic to take office without the approval of the United States—which, in fact, withheld recognition for as long as the government survived.

The people of Havana, according to a phrase popular in Cuba, "threw themselves into the street." Teachers, longshoremen, cigar rollers, students, and feminists flooded the city's public spaces in perpetual demonstrations carrying all sort of banners and demands: eight-hour work days, female suffrage, laws to protect Cuban-born workers against low-wage immigrants, subsidized breakfasts in the elementary schools, raises for the public employees, and more. The Government of the Hundred Days (as it would be known in retrospect) would proclaim many laws, including price controls, mandatory collective bargaining, and eventually the first nationalizations in Cuban history, which affected the telephone and electric companies as well as a few sugar mills belonging to American corporations. It also declared the Platt Amendment null and void. In spite of these audacious policies, much of Havana wanted more. The accumulated effects of the Depression, together with seven years of tyranny, censorship, and repression, had them feeling that they could not take any more of that. They erupted into demands for still more sweeping change, which overwhelmed the capacities of this new government, the most radical government Cuba had ever seen.

This wave of demands was so intense that it whipped through the armed forces themselves. A few weeks after the fall of Machado, the soldiers and sergeants of Camp Columbia, under the influence of the leaders of the University Student Directorate, had mutinied against the officer corps and ousted the high command of the army, made up of sons of the upper class. This so-called Revolution of September 4, led by sergeants Pablo Rodríguez and Mario Hernández, took possession of the headquarters of the general staff. Also part of this movement, lurking in the background, was a stenography sergeant who spoke some English. He was a native of the small town of Banes on the eastern end of the island, the illegitimate son of a laundress of mixed blood. His name was Fulgencio Batista y Zaldívar. Sergeant Batista soon demonstrated his capacity for leadership, negotiating with the civilian revolutionaries behind the backs of his colleagues to make himself head of the army, from which position he gave the formal coup de grace to the deposed high command.

Instead of going into exile, however, the ex-chiefs of the armed forces decided to take refuge in the luxurious Hotel Nacional, barely three years old. Convinced that the U.S. embassy would support them, and armed to the teeth, they held out for several days against a siege mounted by the mutinous troops who—together with civilians from the revolutionary organizations—surrounded the magnificent hotel and fired their artillery at its Mediterranean revival facade. In the first days of the Battle of the Hotel Nacional, members of the army's skilled sharpshooter corps practiced their marksmanship against the soldiers from the advantageous position of the fifth floor balconies. Finally, suffering from hunger and thirst as the supply lines to their luxurious rat trap were cut and their ammunition ran out, the aristocratic officials put up a white flag. Some were shot immediately in the hotel's gardens, while others were tried and sent to the Model Prison on the Isle of Pines. The first potential counter-revolution, mounted by the remnants of the power structure that sustained Machado, had been crushed.

The capacity of now-Colonel Batista to find solutions to problems had caught the attention of the U.S. ambassador in Havana, Benjamin Sumner Welles. At Welles' request, the *U.S.S. Wyoming* and other warships had been dispatched to the Cuban capital and were anchored expectantly in the bay with marines on board—a reminder to one and all that, as far as the U.S. government was concerned, the Platt Amendment was still in effect. Welles invited Batista to sit down and talk in his office, which over-looked the Plaza de Armas in the solid building of North American archi-tecture that now houses Old Havana's public library and was then the embassy of the United States. The two discovered they had some things in common. Nonetheless, the ambassador decided that emergency measures were needed. He telegraphed Washington to say that neither the govern-ment nor the revolutionary organizations nor the right wing were capable of controlling the crowds that had taken over the streets.

The first great confrontation involving these crowds took place on September 29, when Julio Antonio Mella's ashes, brought back from Mexico, were carried in a funeral procession down Calle Reina toward the new Parque de la Fraternidad (the old Spanish parade grounds) at the head of the Prado between the Palacio de Aldama and the Teatro Martí. Rubén Martínez Villena, one of the moving spirits of the former Grupo Minorista and at that moment leader of the Communist Party, addressed the assassinated revolutionary in a voice nearly extinguished by tuberculosis: "Here you are, yes, not in this heap of ashes but in the immense demonstration of the people that accompanies you." A few moments later, mounted police under Batista's orders received a com-mand to break up the demonstration. When they attacked with gunshots and clubs as the police of Machado had done, hundreds of demonstra-tors sought refuge in the doorways and behind the columns of the former mansion of the Aldamas. Along Calle Reina, the dead included old men, women, and children. The communists, the unions, and some of the general population blamed the government for this violence, weakening its popular support.

Events like this were not the only factors which kept Havana in a state of permanent turbulence and expectation. On the other side of the political spectrum, a new right, also armed, was restless to act. The clandestine organization ABC placed bombs on street corners and organized assassinations. Explosions could be heard in the capital day and night. Inspired by the paramilitary structure of Mussolini's blackshirts, and created originally as a group of shock troops to destroy the power of the Machado dictatorship, the green shirts of the ABC had joined the Céspedes-Herrera government and had then been left out of the government that replaced it. They now made war against the Government of the Hundred Days, the communists, the unions, the student movement, and the new generation of the army.

This new counterrevolution attracted support within the air force and some discontented sections of the army. In early November, a convergence of the fascist-leaning ABC, the surviving old guard of the military leadership, and some in the lower ranks who felt they had missed their chance on September 4 staged an uprising that turned parts of the city into a battlefield. This battle began with the bombing of Camp Columbia by air force mutineers, followed by an unsuccessful attack on this base by police and the ABC. As had been the case with the former officers in the Hotel Nacional, the commanders of this rebellion believed they would receive decisive aid from the United States. The *Wyoming*, still anchored in the harbor, went into battle alert and brandished its cannons, which were pointed at the Presidential Palace. By the time the rebels discovered that the U.S. ambassador was supporting the loyal sector of the army under Batista, it was too late. Commanded from the Castillo de La Punta by Guiteras (still the minister of justice and the armed forces), loyal forces cornered the dissidents in Atarés castle, south of Old Havana. Forced to surrender after a prolonged mortar and cannon barrage, the mutinous officers were sent before a firing squad. The new counterrevolution found itself leaderless, for now.

In the midst of this theater of war which unfolded on top of the daily life of the city, newspapers and radio transmitted reports and rumors of unexpected events. Guiteras visited the navy units, which had all remained loyal to the government, and handed each officer a copy of *Ten Days That Shook the World*, John Reed's chronicle of the Russian Revolution of 1917. The radical American journalist Carleton Beals interviewed Guiteras, calling him the "John Brown of Cuba" in a series of articles published in mid-September in the United States. Meanwhile, the cigar makers' union went on strike, paralyzing the most important factories of the capital. From the eastern provinces arrived news that councils of workers, peasants, and soldiers had taken over several sugar mills. While the U.S. government refused to recognize the administration of President Grau San Martin, its ambassador announced that Cuban officers would be welcome to train at West Point.

After a conversation with Guiteras at Camp Columbia on November 15, and frustrated in all attempts to tame or coopt him, Ambassador Welles wrote secretly to President Franklin Roosevelt that Guiteras was the most dangerous enemy of the United States in the Cuban government. A plot to depose him, with the participation of sugar mill owners, Welles, and Colonel Batista, got under way. Now there was a counterrevolutionary conspiracy that brought together the interests of the old regime, the United States and the military wing of the revolution itself. Welles returned to Washington, replaced by the experienced diplomat Jefferson Caffery, who was entrusted with the mission of overseeing a coup.

By the time Caffery arrived, the situation had become more polarized still. The American companies that controlled telephone and electricity service had refused to comply with government price controls that lowered their rates to levels the bulk of the population could afford. At Guiteras's urging, these utilities were nationalized in response. To resolve the uprisings on at the eastern sugar mills, two of those were nationalized as well. As if to symbolize a break with the past, one of them was the Chaparra, which former president Menocal had overseen for the Cuban-American Sugar Company.

With its ability to govern weakened by disobedience on all sides, internal dissension, and the ever-rising popular demands for more radical measures, the government of the Hundred Days found itself alone between the left and the right. It proved an easy target for a coup d'etat. Relieved not to have to land the marines, Ambassador Caffery announced to his government that democratic forces had replaced Grau San Martín and Guiteras with the ex-colonel Carlos Mendieta, who represented the interests of the sugar mill owners and was a friend of the United States. Among this new government's first measures was the return of nationalized properties to their American owners. The government's true strongman was not Mendieta, but the head of the army, the ex-sergeant from Banes, Fulgencio Batista. His pending tasks were the elimination of the revolutionary leaders and the restoration of social peace.

For a time, the Havana of the Caffery-Batista-Mendieta government remained a beehive of insurgency, street confrontations, and uncertainty. The jail in the Príncipe Castle, perched on the heights at the far end of the university campus, filled with students and unionists once again. The repression of the workers' and students' organizations grew worse as the new police commander, Batista's friend and ally José Eleuterio Pedraza, boasted that he would meet any threatened strike with "*palmachristi* and rubber." Every resident of Havana knew the meaning of this cryptic term. *Palmachristi* was a laxative, a home remedy made of castor oil, which in sufficient doses could do away with anyone's intestines. Rubber meant the blackjack. Both ingredients of Pedraza's formula were applied to the prisoners in police stations under his command.

With the leftists under government attack, and encouraged by the rise of Mussolini and the earliest signs of Hitler's ascension in Europe, Cuba's indigenous fascist forces felt more daring. On the morning of June 17, 1934, more than fifty thousand adherents of the ABC, wearing their bright green shirts, covered the surface of the Paseo del Prado from the Parque Central to the Malecón. But among the crowds of onlookers milling beneath the columns of the buildings were squads of two separate opposition groups, the communist party and a secret organization created by Guiteras among his old and new followers, known then as TNT. In the midst of the speeches and slogans of the ABC, the communist and Guiteras squads, each acting on their own, attacked with gunfire and sticks, catching the green shirts unawares, causing several deaths, and scattering the crowd. In its first attempt at public rather than clandestine action, Cuban fascism was severely shaken.

In this convulsive context, while the hopes for change that had been raised by Machado's fall faded into smoke, new armed groups of self-declared revolutionaries multiplied. Their names flashed through the head-lines—Brigade of the Dawn, ORCA, Liberation Army—as they carried out attacks on the most notorious police officers and on U.S. businesses, land-owners, and spokesmen for the establishment. The multimillionaire sugar baron Eutimio Falla Bonet paid 300,000 pesos ransom to free himself from a revolutionary commando group. Pepín Rivero, publisher of the daily paper *Diario de la Marina* and dean of the conservative Cuban press, escaped as if by a miracle from an assassination attempt in the middle of the street.

With the advantage of a new system of "emergency tribunals" cre-ated to send elements considered subversive directly to the Castillo del Príncipe, Colonel Batista launched an offensive which militarily occu-pied the University of Havana and dissolved all the unions in one stroke. At the same time, to protect himself against any possible "friendly fire," he ordered the assassination of his old colleagues, the surviving leaders of the sergeants' revolt. Without unity or coordination, and above all overtaken by the popular desperation in Havana and the rest of Cuba, the organizations in opposition found themselves caught between the withering fire of the Batista regime from above and an explosion from below. In a desperate and largely spontaneous general strike in March of 1935, workers attempted to create a new crisis like that which had precipitated Machado's fall in August of 1933. But this time the establish-ment had consolidated itself and was prepared to confront opposition at every turn. For several days Pedraza's police forces distributed the prom-ised *palmachristi* and rubber, while hunting down revolutionary groups in the streets of Havana and sowing terror among the population. Luis Larrinaga was one of many who suffered imprisonment during this time.

On May 8, 1935, in what would be the last act of this tragedy, the former Minister of Justice Antonio Guiteras and his closest collaborators gathered at a small military outpost called El Morrillo, on the Matanzas coast between Havana and the Varadero beach resort. Among them was the Venezuelan Carlos Aponte, a former colonel in the guerrilla army of Augusto César Sandino in Nicaragua that had kept the U.S. marines at bay for years. They planned to leave for Mexico by boat, and there undertake military training so as to return to the island's mountains to begin a guerrilla war at home. But they were surrounded by the army and killed. With the death of Guiteras and the triumph of Batista—who would control Cuban politics for the next nine years—the epilogue to the Revolution of '33 came to an end.

Three months later, the American warships finally departed from Havana Bay. Many Cubans who had seen their revolutionary dreams broken also took ship, via New York, for Spain. There they joined with other Latin Americans and not a few North Americans to defend the Spanish Republic against Franco and his allies. In proportion to their country's population, the Cubans in the International Brigades made up the largest share of the foreign fighters defending the Spanish Republic and rose highest in its ranks. Among them were leading writers like Pablo de la Torriente Brau, journalist and veteran of the Havana student movement and underground, who died fighting the fascist advance toward Madrid.

The most conspicuous of the North American writers who covered the Spanish war soon installed himself in Havana to chronicle it in fiction. In a room in the Hotel Ambos Mundos in Old Havana, Ernest Hemingway wrote *For Whom the Bell Tolls*. He would then stay in Havana, to write and to fish in the Gulf Stream, and he would still be there, together with the rest of the city, when history returned to its roots twenty-five years after the battles of 1933. This time the crowds would not be shouting about the departure of Machado. "Batista is gone!" they would exult instead.

11 Radio Days

Habaneros of the 1940s and early 1950s lived with their ears glued to the radio. Cuba ranked first among all Latin American countries in per capita radio ownership, and its capital city was largely responsible for this figure. In playwright Virgilio Piñera's classic drama about this period, *Aire Frío*, a working-class household that can't afford an electric fan in the summer heat nonetheless owns a radio. The radio is practically a member of the family, its voice heard throughout the play.

Havana boasted thirty-four stations, twice as many as Buenos Aires. Listeners could choose among a vast array of programs. For news junkies, the all-news, all-the-time Radio Reloj then as now reported bulletins punctuated by the sound of a ticking clock and the announcement of the time, minute by minute, day and night. Elsewhere on the dial, the Marine Corps Hymn introduced the evening news show sponsored by General Motors, which reported on events from the halls of Montezuma to the shores of Tripoli and beyond. Listeners devoted to adventure serials hung on the episodes of *Tarzán* (pronounced tar-SAHN), played by the famous actor Enrique Santiesteban, whose face would become as familiar as his voice in the Cuban cinema of the next fifty years.

Lovers of true-crime shows tuned in to the dramatic, macabre, and daily recreation of bloody events, narrated by the popular singer Joseíto Fernández and introduced by a catchy country-style melody of Fernández's own composition. This tune, *La Guantanamera*, would later be adopted by Pete Seeger and spread throughout the world attached to the verses of another well-known Cuban, José Martí.[1] Naturally, during baseball season, the feats of the professional teams competing for the championship were delivered play-by-play. Three of these four teams represented metropolitan Havana. Fans could hear detailed descriptions of the hitting prowess and basepath speed of Marianao Tigers star Orestes Miñoso, or the catches of Havana Lions outfielder Edmundo Amorós, both of whom would become familiar to U.S. listeners (if anglicized as Minnie Minoso and Sandy Amoros) when the Major League color bar finally came down. Miñoso became a frequent guest of honor at the societies of color, including both the upper-crust Club Atenas and the more popular Buena Vista Social Club. The Almendares Scorpions games were broadcast from La Tropical stadium, their home park, built by beer magnate Julio Blanco Herrera above his brewery and beer gardens. The Lions' new Gran Stadium de La Habana in Cerro, seating 30,000 fans, opened in 1946.

Housewives at home and cigar-rollers in the great factories of Partagás and H. Uppman cried with equal ardor over the tragic events of the soap opera, *The Right to Be Born*, by Félix B. Caignet. Playing throughout Latin America, it became the model for the later radio and television *novelas* produced and aired in Mexico, Colombia, and Brazil. Musical shows featured the young composers and singers of the new music called *feeling* (Cubanized into *filin*), a form of the traditional bolero influenced by the sounds of cool jazz. *Filin*'s leading promoters included a station known by its broadcast frequency, 1010 or Mil Diez. This was the voice of Cuba's reconstituted and legalized communist party, the Partido Socialista Popular.

One of the most popular programs on Cuban radio at the very beginning of the decade, however, was neither fiction nor music nor sports, but live transmission of the debates over a new Constitution to replace the one adopted in 1902. Fulgencio Batista, once he had established himself as Cuba's ultimate behind-the-scenes authority and put a definitive end to the revolutionary currents of 1933–35, displayed his usual capacity for maneuver. In the late 1930s, he entered into a populist and fence-mending phase. Unions took advantage of the opening to regroup into a new confederation. Likewise, the outbreak of World War II in Europe, which was followed by *habaneros* with the same intensity they awarded to the championship baseball series, had brought a new pluralism to the political scene. Exiles including the Hundred Days president Grau returned from their exile in Mexico and the United States. As elsewhere in the world, the left enjoyed a summer of legality that preceded the Cold War, and under the politics of the Popular Front the communist parties themselves were more inclined to cooperate with former enemies than to compete with them. For all these reasons, the delegates elected to the constituent assembly—itself a delayed effect of the sweeping away of the old regime—brought all of Cuba's ideological currents into their deliberations in the Capitol building on the Prado, which only on the outside was a carbon copy of the one in Washington D.C.

Held in a semicircular chamber adorned with precious Cuban hardwoods, the sessions of this constituent assembly went out live and unmediated over the radio to the country at large. At one extreme were figures like the Italo-Cuban Orestes Ferrara, ex-colonel of the independence struggle, able orator, former cabinet minister and ambassador to Washington under the government of Machado, and leading conservative political figure. Enriched through all possible mechanisms of the political apparatus of the Republic, Ferrara had built a Tuscan palace alongside the walls of the University of Havana, commanding a panoramic view of the old city below. At the other end of the spectrum, Salvador García Agüero, black and communist, pressed for a guarantee of workers' rights alongside his party's leader Blas Roca, a shoemaker by trade. In between, an array of old Conservatives and Liberals were surrounded by more youthful figures who had emerged from the revolution of 1933 and now took their inspiration from such varied currents as European social democracy, Latin American populism, Italian fascism, and the New Deal.

This radiogenic assembly debated and finally approved one of the most advanced constitutions of its time, including such progressive measures as an agrarian reform, the final guarantee of votes for women and their right to hold office, and a percentage of the Gross National Product to be devoted exclusively to public schools. It was the first Cuban constitution free of the Platt Amendment, which Franklin Roosevelt, as part of his "Good Neighbor Policy" of avoiding direct military interventions in Latin America, had allowed to lapse after the fall of the Hundred Days government in 1934.

Not just radio but also railroads brought Havana and the rest of the country the presidential election campaign of 1940, a campaign of whistlestop tours that pitted Grau against Batista, now retired from his post as army commander and seeking the official presidential chair. By the end of the campaign, their smiling faces had been pasted on every street and wall of Havana and the interior. Grau was backed by a center-left coalition grouped around his new party, the Auténticos; Batista, by the Socialist Democratic Coalition, a strange conglomeration of conservatives and communists. Batista won. Four years later, in a peaceful, electoral transfer of power, he was succeeded by Grau San Martín, who returned to office as the embodiment of the hopes of '33.

In 1944 Havana was also shaken by a hurricane, the worst since 1926, which dumped great quantities of rain onto the city. Residents stocked up on candles and cans of guava paste and chocolate as was their custom, but the storm flooded low-lying neighborhoods. The water overflowed front steps and doorways, pouring into homes. Juan Valdés, an eight-year-old child of a single mother, watched the blocked sewers turn his street into a lake at the corner of Manrique and Salud in a Chinatown that had become as Cuban as it was Chinese. Though Juan didn't know it yet, the winds and rain had already destroyed the *solar* in Old Havana, just off the Plaza de la Catedral, where he, his mother, and his older brother had lived a few years before. Now the boys of his new block observed a group of grownups trying to clear a clogged drain, laughing at the fears expressed by older onlookers that the current could sweep one of them into the sewer.

But hurricanes were not the only threats to the tranquility of the citizens. The political renewal marked by the new constitution did not bring any new security to the lives of residents. Many of the provisions of the Constitution of 1940 remained merely words on paper, without any legislation or enforcement to put them into effect. In Havana, it could not be said that order and social peace reigned. On the contrary, the 1940s and the early 1950s turned out to be an era dominated by organized robbery, murder, violence, and administrative greed and neglect. The settling of scores among competing factions and gangs was the daily bread of the capital, and so was corruption in the halls of state.

From jobs and sinecures in government ministries to positions of leadership in the University of Havana, access to public employment and influence fell into the hands of mafias, often armed to the teeth. The various gangs were made up of ex-revolutionaries, hit men employed by political chieftains, or pure and simple bandits, all of them manipulated or tolerated by government. Student leaders carried revolvers as if they were fountain pens. Their armed factions, in the ever-present borrowing from the language of the northern neighbor, were called *bonches*, a species of Wild Bunch. The gangster films starring Edward G. Robinson and Paul Muni, which showed in Havana's movie houses, found their analogue in the city's public life. Gang battles, in addition to the standard baseball games and constitutional assemblies, came to be broadcast live. A sampling of headlines from the era yields many like these: "While attempting to rob the cash box of the District Court of Guanabacoa, the mayor of that town was gunned down by an Army detachment." "Professor Ramiro Valdés Daussa shot dead by members of the university Bunch." "Student event gives rise to incident; deaths and injuries result." "Well-known concert composer Alejandro García Caturla murdered in full view on the street." "Leaving the apartment building Metropolitana, Dr. Modesto Maidique, ex-senator from Camagüey, shot dead."

In January of 1948, an army officer assassinated the leader of the sugar workers' union, the largest workers' organization in the country, in full daylight in a railroad station, in front of witnesses—and he got off. The coffin of Jesús Menéndez, the murdered leader, snaked through the streets of Havana, followed by a multitude. His assassination inspired the "Elegy to Jesús Menéndez," one of the major poems of Nicolás Guillén. Not only worker and student leaders or ex-underground-revolutionaries and political figures fell victim to this fratricidal settling of accounts. Presidential security guards, ex-officials of the secret police, civilians, and military officers alike were assassinated on the street or in their offices; the murders were attributed to political vendettas and quarrels over spoils among the factions and gangs.

The most spectacular case of political gang violence was known as "The Events of Orfila." On the afternoon of September 15, 1947, members of the National Police led by Major Mario Salabarría surrounded the residence of a rival police captain named Antonio Morín Dopico, head of the police force in the municipality of Marianao. The attackers laid siege with machine gun fire for almost three hours straight and received answering fire in return. This battle between opposing factions took place six blocks up Calle 64 from the house of Raquel Cañizares, just outside Buenavista in a more prosperous district commonly called Orfila, after a store on the corner of Avenida 31. Radio Reloj reporter Germán Pinelli (later to become one of the most popular television icons of the 1950s), who was present from the start, positioned himself as close as possible and narrated the firefight as if it were a ball game, giving a minute-by-minute account over the background of his station's signature ticking clock.

The residents of Havana listened, horrified, to the moment in the bloody spectacle when the attackers, after swearing to respect the life of Morín's wife Aurora Solar if she would leave the house, shot her down as she walked out waving a white sheet. Only at the end of the carnage, when the massacre was over, did a detachment of the constitutional army appear from nearby Camp Columbia, driving tanks and tossing tear gas grenades.

Hand in hand with gangsterism, government corruption matched any of the true crime stories on Joseíto Fernández's show. Though run-of-the-mill embezzlement by the "kleptocracy" had ceased to be news in Havana, the case of José Manuel Alemán was an exception, a story out of *Arabian Nights*. Alemán was Minister of Education in the Grau government that took office in 1944, and he was the most spectacular practitioner of *la botella*—the bottle, a universal Cuban term for a no-show job in the government apparatus. In the Ministry of Education in the 1940s, an estimated 13,000 jobholders appeared only to collect their pay—if they appeared at all, because many *botelleros* were phantoms whose invented names covered the direct embezzlement of funds. José Manuel Alemán's rolls of *botelleros* swelled to such proportions that he was said to keep a soap opera writer on retainer to invent the necessary mass of ghost names. In his moment he was the richest man in Cuba, wealthier than any sugar baron, piling up real estate within the borders of the national territory and colonizing South Florida as well. He bought the Miami sports stadium in the name of his son, and apartment buildings along Biscayne Boulevard in the name of his wife, while for himself he acquired Cape Florida, a palace that had once beloned to Al Capone. Alemán's gifts to friends ranged from Cadillacs to night clubs, and on one occasion, to a very special friend, he gave the Marianao baseball club worth half a million dollars at the time.

On the afternoon of October 10, 1948—the eightieth anniversary of the outbreak of the Cuban independence struggle—Minister Alemán led a fleet of trucks from his offices through the narrow streets of Old Havana to the Treasury of the Republic at the corner of Obispo and Cuba, where they had a mission to fulfill. Alemán's men, with himself at their head, entered that edifice through the doors of its Wall Street façade and passed through the Art Deco interior to the vaults, where they withdrew funds variously estimated from $50,000,000 to $174,250,000. They loaded these stacks of bills into the trucks, and then drove to a chartered aircraft. The Minister, his followers, and the money all took off for Miami, where they passed through customs without any difficulty. The only thing that kept Alemán from living happily ever after was his death from natural causes, which came seventeen months after his great feat of embezzlement.

Grau's Auténtico successor Carlos Prío took office with pledges to respect citizens' lives and the public treasury, but matters did not improve. The official two-year investigation into the details and the guilty parties in the Alemán case pointed at President Grau himself. On the eve of the judicial process, however, the five thousand pages of inquiries and evidence disappeared as if by magic from the office where they were held. Neither Alemán nor Grau was ever formally charged. Grau would die of old age in 1969 in a very different Havana, where he became a relic of the old order, still ensconced in his mansion on Fifth Avenue in Miramar, which he called "The Shack." After his death, the estate became a home for children with no parents able to care for them.

Despite all the corruption and violence, Havana went about its business, still noisy and vibrant—if increasingly cynical. With the coming of World War II, sugar crops and export revenues finally regained the levels of the pre-Depression years, proving the thesis once propounded by Orestes Ferrara that the country had a "vulture economy." In Havana, as was always the case, the number of people employed in commerce, transport, and public or private services dwarfed those in manufacturing, since most consumer and industrial goods were imported from the United States. On this precarious foundation, the city hummed to the rhythm of retail trade much as it had in the days of the Spanish fleet.

Every few blocks, there was a corner store, a butcher shop, a bar, and a pushcart or two of root crops and vegetables, joined by a laundry, a stand that took barely-clandestine bets on the numbers, a small *botica* or pharmacy, and stands selling tiny hamburgers called *fritas* or small cups of oysters in cocktail sauce. A twenty-centavo *frita* accompanied by a three-cent glass of cold pressed sugar cane juice could quickly kill the hunger of those without time or money to lunch on anything else. The oyster stands were surrounded by groups of men, who attributed sexual stimulant properties to this dish. The *botica* owner was happy to save his customers the cost of a doctor by recommending Cuajaní Jordán elixir with ephedrine to combat a cold, or Scott's Emulsion as a general pick-me-up.

All these establishments created a dense network of immediate goods and services within a radius of one or two hundred yards, or less in the poorer and more populous barrios. The web that connected all these elements was a buzz generally called *la bulla*, the city's commotion and its noise. Vendors took to the street early in the morning with their chants that had been passed down through the generations, offering tamales or snowcones, peanuts or mangos, sour-sweet mamoncillos or coconut-filled caramels. They offered door-to-door service, ranging from sharpening knives to tightening bedsprings, fixing irons or sweeping ceilings free of the city's grit and soot. They hawked newspapers by calling out the headlines, or they proclaimed their willingness to shine shoes.

These hawkers' chants had long since made their way into popular music, so that Rita Montaner's piercing voice singing, "Housewife, don't go to bed without eating a peanut cone," was as famous in Paris, London, and New York as it was in Havana, where it echoed through the city on radios and *victrolas*, as jukeboxes were universally called. Every bar had its community *victrola*, ready to play the tunes that customers chose. From early in the day they filled the air with the *boleros*, *guarachas*, and *sones* that radio disc jockeys and word of mouth had made into hits. The voice of Roberto Faz made whole barrios vibrate as he crooned. His double entendres were equal to those of Montaner, "I tighten springs, children's cradles or old folks beds, I tighten springs" or "Some are hot and some are not, the tamales that Olga sells."

At the center of this web was always the corner store or bodega, humming with the murmur of news and gossip while news or music played on the radio. The bodega was open before the neighborhood residents set off for work, and housewives and other clients showed up early to get what they needed. This market supplied the basic foods of the working–class Cuban diet—rice, beans, butter, corn meal, sugar, coffee—as well as nonperishables such as canned sweets and conserves. Most buyers depended on a popular system of credit, the *fiado*, which allowed them to acquire the so-called *factura* (literally a bill, but figuratively the weekly or monthly market basket of basic goods) and then make good on their debt when payday came at the end of the month.

The bodega-keeper, whether Spanish, Cuban, or Chinese, offered not only credit and supplies but also the use of his telephone, and he served as barman to customers who stopped by to drink "the morning" or "the evening"—the shot of aguardiente or cheap rum taken on the way to or from work. Sometimes the bodega itself was the place to play one's daily number, at the same counter that dispensed Lucky Strikes, Peter's Chocolate Bars, and Hershey's Kisses, which represented Cuban sugar making its way from the Hershey mill east of the capital north to Pennsylvania, and then back again. This diversity of functions meant that movement in and out of the bodega door was constant, and the murmur emanating from it spread from the corner down the street. In districts like Vedado, the bodega was also where the housewives and the servants of the block rubbed elbows and chatted across class barriers.

Alberto Motola never acquired a *bodeguero's* license, but he did prosper in Buenavista. He expanded his store to reach the nearest corner, adding glass display windows, broadening his stock beyond kitchenware and fabrics to clothing, hardware, housewares, school uniforms, and books. By the end of the decade, he managed to buy the building he had previously rented, with an apartment upstairs for his family, by way of a mortgage from the branch of an American bank. He rented another storefront, across the street next to the local café, and set up a bargain shop where he sold out-of-season clothes and leftover goods. Surprisingly or not, he also joined the Popular Socialist Party, enrolling in courses offered by an affiliated social organization about both politics and commerce, from which he graduated with a certificate in bookkeeping.

Small businesses like Motola's were not exempt from the reigning corruption. His Old Havana suppliers on the Calle Muralla arranged to import clothes and fabrics without paying even the reduced tariffs levied on U.S. consumer goods. "A ship would come from the U.S. carrying refrigerators," his son Daniel later recalled, "and inside they'd be stuffed with clothes that weren't declared to customs. The extra profit on the clothes paid for the refrigerators, almost." Local merchants had to pay off the local police in return for protection, because the police in barrios like Buenavista had ties with both merchants and thieves. "My mother had been working late decorating the shop windows," Daniel also recalled, "and had two dolls from a famous factory, that cost forty pesos each, which was the top of the top, there was nothing more expensive. When the store closed for the night, the police chief came by with his wife, and they saw the doll and wanted it, so they took it. There were other kinds of bribes to pay, but my mother was particularly bitter about this one."

The distinctive character that the webs of small stores gave to each neighborhood masked a deeper instability. Havanans both new and old were constantly forced to move when they failed to keep up with rising rents. Juan Valdés's mother and her two sons—white and poor—moved frequently throughout the 1940s and the early 1950s, from one room to another in *solares* and *cuarterías* from Old Havana to Chinatown to Casablanca, La Vibora, and Luyanó. This cycle ran from the day they arrived with their bundles of belongings and paid a month in advance, to the day they couldn't pay any more, had used up their security deposit, and had twenty-four to forty-eight hours to move to another and always transitory home. In Juan's childhood memory, that constant movement was marked by the changing faces of the other boys who spun their tops in the doorways of the various *solares*. At the home he remembers best, the one at the corner of Manrique and Salud where he witnessed the hurricane, the web of stores included an agency with a moving truck, another staple of the time.

The radio offered something for such families too. To the vast numbers of working- and middle-class Havanans who dreamed of escaping from the spiraling rents of the ever-more-crowded capital, the Crusellas soap company offered prizes inside its popular bars of Jabón Candado laundry soap, which wives, daughters, grandmother, and housemaids all over the city used to launder clothes in washboard sinks. Along with the company's radio jingles about the purity and endurance of its soap, Crusellas advertised that the lucky buyers of certain bars of Jabón Candado would find a small plastic capsule embedded in the middle of the soap. Inside that capsule would be a slip of paper announcing what gift the customer had won. The top prizes were houses or apartments. There were two of these "*casas de Jabón Candado*" on 41st Avenue near Buenavista, halfway between the Tropical Stadium and the block where the Events of Orfila had taken place. They're still standing today, identifiable by the padlock logo (*candado* means padlock) pressed into the plaster, just as it was stamped into the bars of soap.

When Juan Valdés contracted tuberculosis, a common enough ailment in the crowded neighborhoods where he lived, he began a series of stays in hospitals and boarding schools for poor children in need of medical treatment, arranged through relatives with the necessary low-level political connections to get him in. But at the age of fourteen, much like Alberto Motola a generation before him, he went to work. His first job was in a Centro Habana laundry called El Buen Gusto (good taste), for twenty-five pesos a month. His morning walk of twenty blocks took him through the barrio of Colón, a dense area of six square blocks made up almost entirely of brothels, relatively peaceful at that hour because the employees were not soliciting customers at their doors. He recalls

Photo Credit: Nancy Falk

"Casa de Jabón Candado," Avenida 41 and Calle 58, a few blocks from Buenavista. These houses were given as prizes to lucky buyers of Jabón Candado brand soap—the padlock design that decorates the house was the soap brand's logo. The second story was added later by the owners, probably post-1959.

something hypnotic about the whole walk, "because in Havana you went walking and melodies accompanied you, from victrola to victrola, a new one each time you crossed a street, each playing a new song, and varying from neighborhood to neighborhood according to class and taste, though with a certain repetition of the hits."

A few years later, still in his teens, Valdés got a new job near the old one, joining his brother Tony in the Indochina department store. The store, the property of a Jewish Cuban named Max N. Lichy, was called the Indochina to make the store seem exotic, not because of the war for independence underway in that far-off land. It was on San Rafael near Galiano, in the busy retail district close to the legendary El Encanto. El Encanto was joined in the early 1950s by two modern, sophisticated department stores, Flogar and Fin de Siglo. Some called this intersection "The Sinners' Corner" in honor of both the expensive purchases and the extra-marital flirtations that inevitably took place there. On the fourth corner of Galiano and San Rafael stood one of the capital's several Woolworths—known in the language of the city as the Tencén (ten-cent).

For those who couldn't afford to do their shopping in such bastions of style and taste, window shopping was a cheap and addictive form of entertainment for Havanans of all classes and colors. The culture of decorative shop windows reached its maximum expression at El Encanto, which was famous for dressing mannequins in a dozen gleaming windows in its own designers' versions of the latest styles from the runways of Paris and New York. At the beginning of September, when the sun still fell with full summer force on the polished granite sidewalks of the shopping district and the people of Havana sought refuge in the central air conditioning of these retail palaces, an annual announcement that "It's Autumn in El Encanto" accompanied the mounting of a new seasonal display.

When Juan Valdés got a job as floor cleaner, elevator operator, and window display assistant in the Indochina, that meant a salary of sixty pesos a month as compared to the twenty-five he'd been making in the laundry, or the legal minimum of forty-five. It meant, too, working in an establishment that complied with the legal eight-hour day. Every month he gave half of his salary to his mother, with whom he still lived, and had the rest for his personal use. He dreamed of a MacGregor brand shirt he had seen in window of Fin de Siglo, an emblem of distinction, elegance, and style that he could wear on Sundays, freshly pressed at the Chinese laundry, with pride. A MacGregor cost fifteen pesos, half of his monthly budget, so he availed himself of another institution of the era, a charge account. Some of the big stores issued their own charge cards, like their North American cousins, and others cooperated in an arrangement that offered a credit of fifty pesos, payable over a period of five months and good in several different stores.

Thus the two poles of credit and commercial advertising drove the popular imagination, in a consumer market which was highly stratified yet

Calle San Rafael, in the Centro Habana shopping district, with polished granite sidewalks, late 1940s or early 1950s.

among the most sophisticated of Latin America and the Caribbean at the time. Cuba had one of the highest per capita incomes in Latin America, and the distribution of this income was skewed toward Havana. But the cost of living in Havana rivaled that of U.S. cities where average incomes were several times greater. In addition, 55 percent of the total national labor force worked less than thirty weeks a year. Though the dead season in the countryside accounted for much of this high percentage, unemployment threatened wage workers and professionals in the capital, too. Economically, residents of Havana lived with uncertainty. This increased public anger at the evident pilfering of the public treasury even more.

It was no aberration, therefore, when the ageless Caballero de París, who had made himself a popular institution as he walked the streets of the capital for the past thirty years, decided to write in large letters on the wall of a prominent building, "Long Live King Dr. Carlos Prío Socarrás"—a protest against the impossibility of holding the president accountable in any way. Arrested and brought before a judge for this act of disrespect, the Caballero was sentenced to confinement in the mental hospital of Mazorra, on the city's southern outskirts. This action against one of the city's treasured characters brought an outcry from the public and press, and the president himself decided to make amends.

Acting under presidential decree, Havana's chief of police Cornelio Rojas took custody of the Caballero and brought him to a clothing shop where he could be fitted out in a decent suit and tie. Then he delivered his prisoner to the Presidential Palace for a personal interview with Prío Socarrás. The content of their conversation was not reported (though the press in general attributed to the president an affinity for nightlife and bohemia)—only that the Caballero left the palace, recovered his cape *a la* the Three Musketeers, his rope belt and pencils, his mysterious bundles, and went back to the city's sidewalks, where he declaimed speeches such as this: "I assure thee all that, God be Praised, the worthy Minister of Public Works restoreth to our metropolitan capital its ancient sense of beauty and loveliness. See thee not those potholes that so resemble miniature valleys, that in traversing them we enjoy the exquisite sensation of treading in the footsteps left behind by prehistoric animals of the remotest and most distant times?"

Anger at corruption also found an outlet on the radio. Attacking the rampant corruption tolerated and promoted by the Auténtico administrations, a new breakaway opposition party called the Ortodoxos adopted the slogan "morals over money," gaining instant popular support. The chief communications medium of its charismatic leader, Havana Senator Eddy Chibás, was his radio hour. From the studios of station CMQ, he denounced cases of public embezzlement and the abuses of the Cuban Electric Company (which was, despite its name, owned and head-quartered in the United States). Exposing more than twenty individual cases of high corruption, Chibás' weekly broadcasts made him a danger-ous magnet for popular discontent, and therefore a likely candidate for president in the elections scheduled for 1952. He was a growing threat to the powers-that-were: political parties, sugar barons, government officials, the established press, and even the radio networks themselves.

Among the many who listened regularly to this program were Carlos Larrinaga and Raquel Cañizares, now married and living in the old Buenavista house that Raquel's grandfather had built. Carlos knew Chibás personally, because the Café Las Villas, on Galiano near the show-room and repair shop of Victor Adding Machine Company, was a regu-lar haunt for both. While not Ortodoxos, Carlos and Raquel respected Chibás's political agenda and his radio show.

In typical stormy style, Chibás one Sunday afternoon denounced Minister of Education Aureliano Sánchez Arango, the successor to the infamous Alemán, for having diverted school breakfast funds to buy real estate in Guatemala. But Arango mounted a spirited defense, question-ing the basis of the charges and enlisting the support of powerful groups including the owners of Chibás's own platform, Radio CMQ. Research by Chibás's associates failed to turn up definitive proof.

Put on the defensive by the acid attacks from Sánchez Arango and his followers, and seeking to keep the morale of his movement alive, Chibás came to the studio on Sunday, August 5, 1951 with something dramatic in mind. He broadcast his most famous speech, the most dramatic appeal to the public conscience made during the years of the Republic. "People of Cuba," he concluded, "this is my last clarion call!" Then, with the radio microphone still open, he shot himself in the chest. His motives have never been completely established (some say he meant only to wound himself), but he lingered for a week in critical condition before dying. His funeral ceremonies lasted for another three days—the largest popular funeral to date in a city that had known many spectacular ones.

Although Chibás's death was a blow to his new party, some of the younger Ortodoxos who came of age in the shadow of his leadership played important roles during the tragic days surrounding his death. One of them, whose statements over the radio during Chibás's deathbed days first made him known outside the university, would later be the subject of a good deal of talk. As a law student he had been involved in one of the campus *bonches* but had lately taken another path: he was running as an Ortodoxo congressional candidate in the elections scheduled for the following year. Fidel Castro was his name.

12 City Lights: The Fabulous Fifties

When public works czar Carlos Miguel de Céspedes's sumptuous Villa Miramar was sacked in the rioting that followed the fall of Machado in 1933, among the treasures that disappeared was, appropriately enough, a painting that depicted the fall of Rome's Iberian city of Numancia to the Visigothic hordes. Some years later, after Céspedes had returned from his brief exile in the United States, he found the missing canvas quite by chance. He spotted it on a wall in the Hotel Sevilla-Biltmore, just off the Prado, property of one Amleto Battisti, an Italian immigrant by way of Uruguay. The ex-official demanded his painting back, and the hotel owner complied.

That story was first reported in *Bohemia*, the popular magazine for which Luis Larrinaga worked. The Sevilla-Biltmore also figures in a fictional story, which is perhaps better known. In Graham Greene's *Our Man in Havana*, an unassuming British vacuum cleaner salesman named Wormold is summoned to an appointment in the magnificent though slightly tattered Sevilla of the 1950s, in room number 510. Wormold has lived in Havana for fifteen years, Greene tells us, long enough to watch the boys who had once charged a nickel to guard his car grow up into men offering him taxis and girls. He declines these offers, even though he walks with a limp through a city that seems to "turn out human beauty on a conveyor belt." When he gets to the Sevilla, at eleven in the evening, he takes refuge in the darkened, air-conditioned bar, which he finds to be full of American tourists nursing their drinks. Then he goes upstairs to meet his fate, which is to be inducted into his country's secret service as a spy.

Our Man in Havana is set in the Havana that has lodged in the nostalgic American imagination ever since: a city of bright lights and dark corners, glamour and grit and gambling, outdoor music and secret conspiracy, high rollers and traveling salesmen, strategic position and sensual allure. Or as Greene put it in a note about the impressions that caused him to set his novel there, "this extraordinary city where every vice was permissible and every trade possible." That Havana did exist, alongside others. The Hotel Sevilla may serve as an entry point.

The Sevilla was famous for its courtyard café where mambo king Damaso Pérez Prado held sway, and for its illuminated Roof Garden where Cuban and American elites had long held their luncheons and balls. It was also famous for its casino, just upstairs from the cafeteria, where silver roulette balls danced in spinning wheels and blackjack dealers held sway. Like a growing number of Havana's tourist hotels, it was controlled by the mafia. Amleto Battisti surely felt no chagrin about being caught in possession of a purloined painting, because he was the founder of one of the leading crime families of the capital. His silent partners in the Sevilla's gaming room included Santo Trafficante, Jr. and Meyer Lansky, both of them increasingly present in Havana as American mafia interests and investments grew.

Gambling was no U.S. export to Cuba, of course. Cards and dice had been favored pastimes of all classes in the port city since the days of the Spanish garrisons and fleets, with bets on cockfights joining soon after. The state lottery became a major national institution under the colonial administration and then, after a brief hiatus, under the republican one. Tens of thousands of itinerant ticket vendors represented the lowest rung of political patronage. The *bolita*, the extralegal numbers racket, emerged first in the Barrio Chino and then spread throughout the city under the aegis of various syndicates, of which Battisti's was a major one. The capital's pattern of comings and goings, the contrast of immense inherited riches with immigrants or freedmen starting from nothing, its folklore of chance meetings and striking coincidences, its rituals of divination drawn from *santería* and spiritism—something in Havana's soul fed its addiction to games of chance.

Guiding themselves by the symbols of the Chinese *charada*, residents
of Havana who dreamed of a horse ran out to bet on the number one
in the weekly national lottery or any of the underground games which
took bets and paid out pots every day. Those who passed a nun on the
street hurried to bet on five, those who had just caught a fish along the
Malecón bet on ten, those who were visited by a spider bet on thirty-five,
while those on whom a butterfly magically alighted were sure that the
winning number would be two. Those who passed by a funeral cortege
crossed themselves or didn't, but either way they bet on number eight.
To drum up more business, some numbers racket bankers would offer a
hint for the players to interpret—such as announcing that the winning
number would be linked with "an animal that walks on the roof without
breaking the tiles." Customers hurried to bet on four, which the charada
represented as a cat. The swindle became apparent when the winning bet
drawn was the elephant, number nine.

Besides these games of chance played in barrios of every class, and the
cockfight which was most common on the outskirts of the city, Havana
also boasted the Oriental Park horse track in Marianao, where Carlos
Larrinaga and Raquel Cañizares had met at the Club Ameno dance.
Oriental Park was joined in the 1950s by a dog track on the traffic circle by Marianao's beach district, across from the imposing Havana Yacht
Club. At these posh locations where victory depended on the feet of thor-
oughbreds or the paws of greyhounds, the prevailing bets were not the
centavos, *medios* (nickels), *reales* (dimes), and or *pesetas* (twenty cents) of
the lotteries, but Cuban pesos, pegged to the dollar at the rate of one
to one. So the U.S. mafia did not arrive in Havana to implant a new
vice. Rather, it promoted a particular new style of gaming—luxury casino
gambling dominated by blackjack and roulette. This was an evolution,
one more instance of the meeting of "interior" and "exterior" in Havana.

American organized crime families had founded their fortunes, in
part, on the traffic in Cuban rum during Prohibition. After the demise
of Prohibition, they returned to Havana in the late 1930s and 1940s
as advisers and investors in casino gambling, working with whoever was
in power at the time. In 1946, the Hotel Nacional had been the site

of a famous mafia conclave convened by Meyer Lansky's boss and boy-hood friend Lucky Luciano. At this conclave, the major chieftains met in safety, entertained by Frank Sinatra among other headliners, to plan their postwar rackets and the division of the spoils in the United States and abroad. This was the conference at which the execution of Buggsy Siegel was decreed. Fulgencio Batista had originally brought Lansky to Cuba in 1938 to reorganize and professionalize gaming rooms in the Oriental Park clubhouse and the nearby Gran Casino Nacional. When Batista returned to power in the 1950s, therefore, the stage was set for a new drama with Lansky in the leading role.

Batista, like Eddy Chibás, had declared himself a candidate to suc-ceed Carlos Prío in the presidential elections scheduled for November of 1952. But his prospects were not encouraging, even after Chibás's suicide. In that chaotic climate he decided to seize the moment. On Monday, March 10, Havana woke up to the news that the retired general and ex-president had taken power in a coup d'etat. The coup began in Camp Columbia, seat of the army general staff and site of the coup that Batista had helped lead nineteen years before. Within forty minutes, the general and fifteen other plotters took control of the main military bases in the capital. The remaining major bases, in Santiago de Cuba and Santa Clara, were soon in their hands as well. Without making any effort to resist the coup, President Prío abandoned the Presidential Palace. He boarded a plane for Miami with his family. Batista declared himself president in law and in fact.

The surgical efficiency of the coup—which occasioned no deaths—was not so much a testimony to its planning as a symptom of the coun-try's political state. The Spanish language *Reader's Digest*, widely read in Havana, described the coup in its Latin American edition a few months later as a "model revolution" carried out in a "lush, passionate, and fickle country" by a figure endowed with "the softness, swiftness, and daring of a panther." The magazine added that "Cubans are too disillusioned by a long succession of corrupt, inefficient governments—even though duly elected—to care for anything more than a hard hand at the helm." Asked about Communism—the issue of the day—Batista declared, "I'm a friend of the United States and the United Nations. Besides, I won't stand for any foolishness." The governments in power in Washington, London, and other Western capitals immediately recognized Batista's dubious claim to the presidential chair. Dwight Eisenhower's reasoning presumably reflected what Franklin Roosevelt had once remarked about the Nicaraguan dictator Anastasio Somoza, "He may be a son of a bitch; but he's *our* son of a bitch."

Once restored to power, Batista decided to take the business of gambling more seriously than ever before. It became the centerpiece of his ambitious program to put Havana firmly in the center of the American tourist map and to collect a personal share of the gaming industry's profits in return for assuring its security and safety. He put his old associate Lansky on the state payroll as an official adviser, and offered licenses and matching funds to anyone who would invest. "Havana will become the Monte Carlo of the Caribbean," he declared.

The center of this Monte Carlo was to be El Vedado. It was no longer "barred" as its name meant literally, but rather no-holds-barred, and increasingly it took shape as the city's new downtown. Meyer Lansky's personal project, the twenty-one-story seaside Hotel Riviera, opened in 1957 on the site of a former sports arena at the foot of Paseo along the Malecón. The world's largest hotel-casino complex outside Nevada, the first hotel in Havana with central air conditioning, the Riviera was topped by a giant neon-script logo visible from both directions along the length of the Malecón. Though it cost an extravagant 18 million dollars to build, its gambling operation alone produced a net profit of 3 million dollars in the first year.

On the other side of Vedado, toward Centro Habana, a glittering new gambling, entertainment, hotel, and retail complex took shape in the area called La Rampa, where Calle 23 plunged down a steep slope from the heights near the university to the stretch of the Malecón between the Ambar Motors showroom and the gardens of the Hotel Nacional. Meyer Lansky took over management of the Montmartre Club, just off 23rd, and made it the venue of choice for the most serious gamblers with the most money to put at risk. He set up another casino in the Nacional, which he entrusted to the capable hands of his brother Jake. On Calle

21, his associate Santo Trafficante, Jr., controlled the casino and the Salón Rojo nightclub in his own new skyscraper hotel, the Capri. Trafficante, heir to the numbers racket and other enterprises built by his father among the Italian- and Cuban-American communities of Tampa, was the mafioso who knew Havana best. He also ran the Sans-Souci nightclub and casino in Marianao, while he and Lansky shared interests in the gaming rooms at the Comodoro in Miramar, the Deauville along the Malecón in Centro Habana, and Amleto Battisti's Sevilla Biltmore downtown. The third of the towering new hotel-casino-nightclub complexes, the Havana Hilton, opened at the top of La Rampa in 1958.

High-end gambling was not the only manifestation of the mafia or of Havana's renewed role as a tourist magnet drawing Americans eager to see and to do what they could not see and do at home. American and Cuban gangsters used Havana as a way station for heroin smuggling to the United States, and facilitated increased domestic sales of heroin and marijuana as well. Drugs went by such street names as *manteca* (lard, as in the Chano Pozo number), *maní* (peanuts), or *taladro* (drill, for a joint). More visibly, prostitution flourished even more than in the past. No longer Paris but not yet quite Monte Carlo, Havana was increasingly called the Brothel of the Caribbean. Unlike during the times of Yarini, the sex industry of the 1950s was not contained within a single red-light district or tolerance zone, but rather distributed throughout the city in zones differentiated by class.

The sons of the Havana bourgeoisie, the moneyed tourists, and the mafia aristocracy rubbed shoulders in the elaborately decked out entrance rooms of the exclusive Casa Marina, located on the street of the same name, near Maceo Park along the Malecón. In this luxury bordello, just blocks from El Vedado, the services of the most exclusive Cuban and foreign prostitutes were sold. Their prices, differentiated by specialty, were equivalent to what many of the city's white collar workers earned in a month. There were also private live spectacles in Vedado palaces. Frank Ragano, Trafficante's lawyer, recalls in his memoir going to one such luxury residence redesigned as a series of stage sets where visitors could preview the actors and choose which ones they wanted to watch having sex with whom.

The middle-class and white-collar patrons, like the tourists of average means, went to the Calle Pajarito, south of Carlos III. These discreet brothels—known in Havana slang as *bayús*—were administered by madams under strict rules set up to maintain hygienic conditions. Their employees worked in rooms with individual baths and charged prices on the order of three pesos and up. A rung further down was one of the most famous red-light districts, the old barrio of Colón through which Juan Valdés walked to work, densely packed into a few square blocks between the commercial districts along Galiano and the Prado. Here the sex business spilled out onto the streets, the bars, and the corners, where the prostitutes hawked themselves to factory workers, American sailors, employees of bodegas and laundries, and other men for a two-peso price. On a smaller scale, the sexual market of the Barrio Chino competed with that of Colón. Some of the prostitutes from each of these districts also performed as showgirls and actresses in the productions at the Shanghai Theater, the famous mecca of Havana pornography on Zanja, the street that covered the route of the old Royal Ditch. The Shanghai's live shows competed with those offered by certain bars of the Playa de Marianao, immortalized in the film *Godfather II* and the novel *Three Trapped Tigers* by Guillermo Cabrera Infante. Finally, in the lowest echelon of Havana's sex market, the streetwalkers of the Avenida del Puerto served sailors for one peso or a few pesetas—usually without beds, often in doorways or between trucks or underneath boxcars on the rail line. They were still called *fleteras* (rented boats) as they had been centuries before.

As in the past, the sex industry was a way of life for thousands of women, most of whom stayed in it for many years. Tomás Fernández Robaina quotes a sex worker about her life during this era:

> Not all of us were always *fleteras*, or always worked in bars, or *bayús* or the better houses. Many of us passed through all these classes, or some of them. Everywhere, we had to pay bribes. The madams and landladies had to pay a quota every week to the Secret Police, the Bureau of Investigation, and the local police captain,

and besides that each had to pay the cop on the beat a half peso or box of American cigarettes, because they wouldn't accept Cuban ones, and a full peso on Saturdays, or else they'd take us to jail. If we made some money, we'd run out and buy jewelry, bracelets or gold rings, though people never understood why. It was practical. If you got sick, or had a family problem and needed money, you could run to the pawn shop and take care of it that way. It wasn't just to show off. In other circles, people put money in the bank. Buying jewelry to pawn was what we did.

North American tourism, shipping, and naval "courtesy calls" all added to this business. "My fellow countrymen reeled through the streets," Arthur Schlesinger, Jr., later recalled of a visit to Havana in the 1950s, "picking up fourteen-year-old Cuban girls and tossing coins to make men scramble in the gutter." Says one of Fernández Robaina's informants, "We were always glad to see the U.S. fleet come into the bay for one of their 'good will' visits, and we lived in such a world of our own that we thought it was funny when they went charging into decent houses by mistake. On the other hand we weren't fools. We knew what they were like, and we tried to take them for whatever we could."

High or low rollers in search of sex or drugs were not the only market for services that were illegal or unsafe to buy at home. Though abortion was nominally prohibited in Catholic Cuba, abortion clinics catering chiefly to American middle and upperclass women were also a growth industry. This business too involved investment by organized crime and the promise of political officials to look the other way in return for a share of the revenue under the table.

At the same time, of course, Havana continued to attract U.S. businesses of a legal sort. In the 1950s, the Cuban capital developed its most sizeable colony of resident Americans (some of Cuban ancestry), many married to Cubans and living their lives on both sides of the Florida Straits. A look at the annual Anglo-American Directories of Havana for the years of the mid to late 1950s reveals several thousand such residents, living alongside members of the Cuban elite in places like the new thirty-two story FOCSA condominium tower near the Capri and the Nacional, or the Riomar and Rosita de Hornedo apartment buildings developed by Alfredo Hornedo at the mouth of the Almendares on the Miramar side.

One Nelson Alfred Anderson, for instance, president of a firm selling electrical, mechanical, and industrial goods, lived in the FOCSA, had his office nearby in the Radiocentro building on La Rampa, and belonged to the Havana-Biltmore Yacht Club and Havana Country Club. Cuban-run with English names, these private preserves had also given birth to suburbs similarly called "Biltmore" and "Country Club." His neighbor Pastor Lagueruela, listed as a lawyer and industrialist, lived with his U.S.-born wife Rae Casas and their son Andy in one of the FOCSA's two twenty-ninth-floor penthouses; their club was the Miramar Yacht. Dr. Twyla Snell, who lived on the fourth floor, taught English at the University of Havana and at the private bilingual Ruston Academy in the neighborhood of Country Club Park, which enrolled both Cuban pupils and North American ones. The school's director, James Baker, is also listed as a member of the Havana-Biltmore and the American Club.

In general, the marriage (literal and otherwise) of the descendants of the old landowning aristocracy and the new rich who owed their wealth to speculation in real estate, hotels, and casinos characterized the elegant venues of Havana in the 1940s and 1950s. Old wealth and new socialized in the top-rung clubs known as the Big Five: Havana Yacht, Vedado Tennis, Havana Biltmore, Miramar Yacht, and Casino Español. Sunday afternoon gatherings in these private enclaves for croquet, tennis, golf, swimming, boating, smoking, drinking, and gambling were the focus of the capital's Cuban and North American elites. The clubs' patriarchs were men like Juan Gelats, owner of one of the largest banks relying on Cuban capital; Néstor González de Mendoza, real estate magnate, congressman, and banker; Laureano Falla Gutiérrez and Manuel Aspuru, sugar millionaires; and the brewery owner Julio Blanco Herrera, also owner of the Tropical baseball stadium named after his beer. Their membership included not only temporary Havana residents who maintained their U.S. citizenship, but Cubanized ones such as the textile magnates James and Burke Hedges, or the contractor Frederick Snare, president of the Cuban Country Club. The case of Burke Hedges is illustrative of the social relations among industrialists from the two shores. His properties included an apartment in Manhattan, several factories including a rayon plant (and accompanying house) in Matanzas, and a two-century-old hacienda in the other direction from Havana, in Pinar del Río to the west. This Yemayá estate—named after the goddess of the sea and protector of family love in the Lucumí pantheon—was famed for its private landing strip and yacht anchorage, a pool and cabañas for guests, barracks for the many servants, and a monumental bar carved out of Cuba's ancient precious woods like the decorations of El Escorial palace in Spain. The Hedges' adoption of Cuban citizenship brought them several advantages. They were exempt from U.S. taxation on the one hand, and rewarded by General Batista on the other. Thanks to his friendship with the general, Burke Hedges was able to unload his rayon plant in a sale to the government when it did not flourish as he had hoped. He became director of the Cuban Association of Manufacturers, a member of the presidential advisory council and, in the last months of Batista's reign, Cuban ambassador to Brazil.

Outside of the upper crust, U.S. influence was primarily cultural rather than person-to-person. In the 1950s, the impact of American culture grew stronger than ever before. Only the well-heeled could go see Eartha Kitt in the show at the Nacional, Nat King Cole in the Tropicana cabaret, George Raft greeting guests in the Capri's Salón Rojo, or Ginger Rogers in the Copa Room of the Riviera on its inaugural night. Almost everyone, however, could put together the price of admission to see American films premiere in La Rampa cinema, halfway up the glamorous slope of 23rd, or the Warner cinema in the Radiocentro complex at the top of the hill. Radiocentro, an updated version of Radio City Music Hall, also housed CMQ's new studios for both radio and TV. In the mind of most Havana residents, the United States was still identified with efficiency in business organization, modern technology, gadgets for the home, and a faster pace of life. Juan Valdés and his brother Tony Irízar were both habitués of La Rampa, where their employer, Max Lichy, had coincidentally opened a new branch of his Indochina department store. In 1957, Juan was dazzled when the Cine La Rampa installed a stereophonic sound system to premiere *Around the World in Eighty Days* in the new technology of Todd-AO. The next year Radiocentro premiered another American invention, showing *This is Cinerama* on its specially equipped screen. Tony, like much of Havana, was a devotee of Hollywood musicals, knew the songs of Bing Crosby, Doris Day, and Frank Sinatra by heart, and could describe perfectly the steps of Cyd Charisse and Fred Astaire in each shot of *High Society*. He regularly read the magazine *Show*, which published the lyrics of songs on the U.S. hit parade.

Television, meanwhile, had gone on the air in Havana in 1950. It was the second city in Latin America to offer the new medium, thanks to the efforts of the Cuban radio entrepreneur Gaspar Pumarejo in collaboration with RCA. Pumarejo brought color TV from the United States in 1958, making Cuba the second country in the world to present color on the small screen. Tony Irízar, counting on a knowledge of major league baseball which rivaled his knowledge of American music and cinema, auditioned for *El Show de los 64,000 Pesos*, directed by Pumarejo himself on his Channel 2. In a city where three out of every five male inhabitants were experts in the abstruse science of baseball trivia, Tony got lucky and made it onto the popular quiz program, modeled after *The $64,000 Question* in the United States. For several weeks he showed off his mastery of the bases once stolen by Lou Gehrig, the hits currently racked up by Bob Skinner, and the way the last game of 1955 World Series between the Brooklyn Dodgers and the New York Yankees was decided by the fielding of the Cuban Edmundo Amorós who doubled Gil McDougald off first base. Then he prudently retired from the program with the sum of $4000 pesos. Having been a wage worker since the age of eleven, he quit the Indochina and invested the money in his own shop, a photography studio which he hoped he could keep afloat.

Havana was an easy place for North Americans to live or visit precisely because of the implantation of customs and consumption styles characteristic of the northern middle class. *Habaneros* who could afford it drank Coca-Cola, Pepsi, Orange Crush, and Ginger Ale, dressed to the nines in MacGregor and Arrow shirts, washed their clothes with Fab and Tide as well as Jabón Cándado, ate canned peaches from Del Monte and Libby, brushed with Colgate (pronounced col-*ga*-tay), washed themselves with Camay or what they called Pal-mo-lee-vay, wore U.S. Keds, rubbed Mum and Arrid in their armpits, rode Niagara bikes, and of course drove Oldsmobiles, DeSotos, Studebakers, and Fords. In Havana it was possible to get through the day reading one of the many English papers, breakfasting on Kellogg's Corn Flakes with hot cakes and maple syrup, and listening to American radio without needing to resort to short wave. Besides the easily available Miami stations, two Havana stations played North American music exclusively. One of them, Radio Kramer, got a new shipment every week of the latest records of American rock and roll.

This coexistence of *yanqui* and Cuban culture left a singular imprint on the identity of Havana. At Christmas time, Alberto Motola filled the sidewalk outside his Buenavista variety store with Christmas trees imported from Canada, and the shelves inside with glass balls, plastic icicles, and other ornaments from Jesus to Santa Claus. Alongside the trees on the sidewalk were stands full of cheap toys and more expensive ones, including great numbers of baseballs and baseball bats, destined for the neighborhood children on the Día de Reyes, when the ancestors of many residents used to parade through Old Havana to the Plaza de Armas in full African dress.

Similarly Tony Irízar, when he was not arguing over the artistic merits of Bob Fosse versus Ginger Rogers with the other employees of the Indochina, devoted himself to working out his own choreography, not of Hollywood musicals but of *casino*, the sophisticated Havana dance style that was the rage in the 1950s and is still dominant among the young dancers of the city today. When he got off work he would rush across the river to the Tropical Brewery's Salón Rosado, an extension of its old beer garden into a new space beside its stadium on Avenida 41. The Salón Rosado was a world apart from the tourist cabarets and exclusive clubs, or even from the societies of the white and colored middle class. It was the mecca of *casino* for the masses of Havana. Its clientele were predominantly black and mulatto but far from exclusively so. It was the place where local bands underwent their trial by fire. There the Conjunto Casino, one of the major dance bands of the 1950s, wowed the dancers with the hits of moment, from the most heartrending *bolero* to the most frenetic *guaracha*, behind the extraordinary and versatile voice of its leader and lead vocalist Roberto Faz.

For thousands and thousands of Havana residents, the Spanish, African, and North American cultures flowed together into one syncretic identity as never before. This explains why the culture of the North was generally not rejected even by the groups with the most nationalist consciousness, including those who were most determinedly on the left. Anti-imperialist sentiment could run parallel to the inclinations and tastes of Cuban popular culture, and Cuban popular culture had been linked to that of the United States for a long time.

Furthermore, personal contacts with Americans were not always of the sort Arthur Schlesinger recalled. "For the immense majority of the population," Juan Valdés remembers, "an American was a tourist. Tourism was an activity which existed in the country and was accepted, the way we accept the Italian tourists today. After all, the gringos of that time were no more uninteresting than the Italians who visit us en masse now. The majority of the Americans came to blow off steam and to drink rum. The one who was drinking rum was accompanied by Cubans who were happy to be around him, because the gringo paid for the bottle. Only, when those three Marines climbed on the statue of Martí in the Parque Central and pissed on it, everything was different. Then everybody said they were sons of bitches, and hated them."

That last incident, famously caught by a local photographer, illustrated the other side of the eternal Cuban love-hate relationship with Americans and the United States. Darker-skinned Cubans had to contend with the more strident racism of the neighboring culture as well. When Carlos Larrinaga and his white Cuban boss went to Chicago for a two-month training course at Victor Adding Machine headquarters, his boss unthinkingly reserved them both rooms at a middle-rung commercial hotel. When they arrived, Carlos was refused admittance, and told to go stay at a colored hotel instead. In Havana itself, the more a private club or luxury commercial establishment catered to the U.S. tourist trade, the more likely it was to discriminate against Cubans of color. Even Batista was refused entrance to the Havana Yacht Club because his ancestry was mixed.

Architecture followed U.S. trends too, particularly those associated with the "urban renewal" of American cities in the 1950s. Besides the skyscraper hotels, a slum clearance project made way for construction of the Plaza Cívica, a vast but automobilized and sterile new seat of government offices and monuments between Vedado and Cerro—far different from the green space envisioned there in plans drawn up by French consultants in the 1920s but never realized. The historical and architectural value of the old city, meanwhile, counted for little with investors intent only on the new. The colonial heritage continued to deteriorate under the combined assault of sun, sea air, storms, and time. Visitors noticed, as they had in other times, that one of the most striking characteristics of Havana was its decay.

In 1953, twenty-seven-year-old Allen Ginsberg, unknown and drunk on cheap rum and Coca-Cola in the Havana Club bar that used to face the Plaza de la Catedral, saw that plaza as "weatherbeaten tropical antiquity, as if rock decayed . . . blunt cornucopias and horns of conquest made of stone . . . a great, dumb, rotting church." Similarly Graham Greene depicted what he called "the ruins" of Havana: "The pink, grey, yellow pillars of what had once been the aristocratic quarter were eroded like rocks; an ancient coat of arms, smudged and featureless, was set over the doorway of a shabby hotel, and the shutters of a night club were varnished in bright crude colors to protect them from the wet and salt of the sea. In the west the steel skyscrapers of the new town rose higher than lighthouses into the clear February sky."

In one of those skyscrapers, a gala New Year's Eve celebration was underway on December 31, 1958, bringing the year that *Our Man in Havana* was published to a close. In the Copa Room of the Riviera, the sons and daughters of sugar and real estate magnate families like the Suárez Rivas, the González de Mendoza, the Lobos, and the Gómez-Menas danced in the company of the sons and daughters of the Cuban political elite and the American organized crime families. They all looked forward to a modern Havana, a city of greater luxury and brighter lights.

Among the plans in the works for the Cuban capital of the 1960s was an artificial island to be built in the curve of the Malecón, straightening the graceful seaside drive and hiding its baroque and sea-battered architecture behind a complex of newer hotels, casinos, and high-rise apartment blocks, Miami-izing the 450-year-old city as never before.

Old Havana, for its part, was to be populated by a new wave of modern buildings. A sample already constructed was the ugly utilitarian steel-and-glass box of offices that filled the square block behind the Palace of the Captains General, where the Royal and Pontifical University of San Geronimo de La Habana had been founded two centuries before. For its roof, nothing less than a helicopter terminal was planned. Another urban renewal plan called for bulldozing a strip through the heart of Old Havana to make way for a new, broad avenue built for automotive traffic to link the Capitol and the port. This project would have demolished the pattern of narrow streets and short blocks designed by the planners of the earliest eras to provide cooling shade for high-ceilinged houses of the old city, converting it to an open field for modern commercial investment and development. But most of these plans never left the drawing board, because a different transformation intervened, a transformation unimaginable to those present in the Copa Room of the Riviera that New Year's Eve.

13 Havana in Revolution

Just a week later, on January 8, 1959, an army of bearded rebels entered the other end of the Malecón from the Hotel Riviera. They were packed into trucks, armored cars, civilian autos, and vehicles of every other type. The image of Fidel Castro and fellow *comandante* Camilo Cienfuegos mounted on a tank, followed by smiling young long-haired guerrillas and passing through crowds of cheering Havanans, circled the world within a few hours. Though this was clearly the opening of a new chapter in the city's history, few could foresee how different it would be. To understand the change, we need to go back to the first months of 1952.

Three days after the Batista coup, the junior partner of a law firm called Aspiazu-Resende-Castro presented a formal accusation that Batista had violated the Constitution of 1940, and requested a prison sentence for the usurper, but Fidel Castro neither expected nor received a positive response from the courts. Soon after, some University of Havana students organized the first anti-Batista *tánganas*, a Cuban term meaning a heated argument, now more specifically referring to spontaneous political actions in which a series of speakers shouted speeches or slogans from improvised platforms on the stairs and benches in the central plaza of the school. One of these *tánganas* led to a demonstration that descended the broad neo-classical stairway from that plaza, below the statue of Alma Mater, scene of many other demonstrations in the Machado era and since. The demonstration proceeded downhill toward Centro Habana, but at the corner of Infanta and San Lázaro the police opened fire. By coincidence, the first student victim of the dictatorship shared the surname of "El Hombre," as Batista had styled himself in his electoral campaigns. Rubén Batista's funeral became the first popular repudiation of the regime.

January of 1953, ten months after the coup, marked the hundredth anniversary of the birth of José Martí, "The Apostle," who by then was treated with the kind of secular religious devotion that name implies. The new government attempted to capitalize on the birthday with a lavish official celebration, but on the night of January 27, on the eve of that commemoration, a procession of students, youth, and other citizens preempted it. Carrying improvised torches, they avoided the fatal stairway, marching down the Avenida Universidad toward the Fragua Martiana, a memorial containing relics of the Apostle on the site where he had toiled in the quarries as a teenage prisoner of the Spanish crown.

Within the crowd spilling down the hillside, one group of 200, mostly young men, formed itself into military style ranks and squadrons. These were a section of the group within the Ortodoxo youth, organized by Castro and Abel Santamaría, who were beginning to prepare for an armed action against the dictatorship at a time and place not yet known. Santamaría, a twenty-seven-year-old bookkeeper at the local Pontiac dealership who had previously been an office worker for one of the Hedges family's textile firms, was more typical of the membership of this group than was Fidel. Son of a sugar mill carpenter in the interior province of Las Villas, Santamaría had come to Havana in search of education, advancement, and a wider world. He was belatedly putting himself through high school while reading widely in politics, history, and other spheres. Castro by contrast was the son of an Oriente sugar planter, a self-made Spanish immigrant who had flourished by selling cane to the large U.S.-owned mills, to the point where he could send his son to Havana for a Jesuit high school education and then a university law degree.

After participating in the demonstration, this group henceforth assembled only in small subgroups in sites spread out through the city such as the apartment of Abel and his sister Haydée on the corner of 25th and O, a block from La Rampa and the roulette tables of the Montmartre. Six months later, 165 of them, including both Santamarías, reassembled far from Havana in a small farmhouse on the outskirts of Santiago de

Cuba. There they boarded a caravan of innocent-looking Oldsmobiles and Chevies and proceeded to attack the Moncada garrison, the country's most important army base after Columbia. The failed attack, which cost the lives of many including Abel Santamaría, was seen as an act of madness by many sectors opposed to the dictatorship, including the communists. After a week of fierce repression, including torture and assassination of many of those captured during the attack itself, the dictatorship put Castro, his brother Raúl, and the remaining leaders on trial. They were sentenced to long prison terms on the Isle of Pines, off the south coast of Cuba, opposite the area that the first founders of Havana had abandoned to the mosquitoes four centuries before.

Two years later, in a gesture designed to demonstrate his moderation and generosity and to establish democratic credentials for his regime, General Batista decreed an amnesty for all political prisoners. Castro and his colleagues returned to Havana where, taking advantage of a pause in press censorship, they declared that they would continue to fight. After a few months they left for Mexico, leaving behind a new underground political organization, the 26th of July Movement, named for the date of the Moncada attack. By December of 1956, when the group (including new recruits such as Ernesto "Che" Guevara) left Mexico on board a yacht purchased from a Texan who had named it *Granma* after his grandmother, the 26th of July Movement could count on some degree of resources and organization for clandestine struggle in the cities, particularly Santiago and Havana.

The 26th of July was not the only organization to attempt to dislodge the dictatorship by any means possible. Three months after the landing of the *Granma* ("more of a sinking," as Guevara later wrote), the University Students' Federation (known by its Spanish initials FEU) assaulted the Presidential Palace. José Antonio Echeverría, the architecture student and FEU president who led the action, was a well-known figure in his own right. Nicknamed Manzanita (Apple) for his round face and rosy cheeks, he had been arrested many times at the head of student demonstrations, and publicly beaten by the police. A short time before the attack on the Palace, a group under his leadership sneaked a banner into the stands of the Grand Stadium in Cerro during a nationally televised playoff game. Eternal rivals Havana and Almendares were competing for the championship, and the Lions, under a new agreement incorporating the Cuban leagues into the farm system of stateside organized baseball, pinned their hopes on St. Louis Cardinals veteran hurler Wilmer "Vinegar Bend" Mizell, who was positioning himself for a comeback by playing winter ball. At the right moment, the students unfurled their slogan "Down With the Dictatorship" in the outfield. The banner stayed in place for the few minutes it took police to charge onto the field from their choice seats and rush across the diamond with truncheons at the ready, to administer punishment in full public view.

The action at the Palace was much more ambitious, an attempt to behead the regime by executing the dictator, on the assumption that none of his military or civilian subordinates would have the skill or prestige needed to reorganize the ranks of the dictatorship, much less gain the respect of the citizenry who were fed up with the Batista government. They almost succeeded. The group of attackers drove a truck with the emblem of the *Fast Delivery* service up to the front door of the Palace and poured out. Armed with submachine guns, they overcame Batista's personal guards and reached his private office on the second floor. But Batista had managed to escape through a back door they did not know about, reaching the top floor of the Palace where the bulk of his guards had the advantage of better cover and heavier arms. The survivors among the attacking group had to retreat under a rain of machine gun fire.

While this was going on, Echeverría and a smaller group assembled on La Rampa, where they took over the offices of Radio Reloj in the Radiocentro complex opposite the construction site of the Hilton Hotel. Echeverría's sharp, high-pitched voice, honed in the university *tánganas*, went out over the airwaves, declaring: "People of Cuba, the tyrant Batista has met justice in his own lair. The University Student Federation, in the name of the people, has come to settle accounts." A few seconds later, Radio Reloj went dead, interrupted in its central transmission tower while residents of Havana listened, electrified. Echeverría then tried to reach the university on foot, but police opened fire from a patrol car and left him mortally wounded on the sidewalk below its walls. The Apple was one of many to fall on the afternoon of the attack on the Presidential Palace and during the days and nights of retribution that followed.

To avenge the attack, Batista unleashed a wave of terror that reached far beyond the FEU. That same night of March 13, Dr. Pelayo Cuervo Navarro, former leader of the Ortodoxo party, was taken from his home by eight armed men. Cuervo's offense was that he had denounced the abuses of the Cuban Telephone Company, hikes in the rates of the electric company in violation of public utility laws, and the government's complicity in both. He was transported to the shores of the Laguito, an ornamental lake in the exclusive Country Club district, and riddled with bullets. The message to the "legal" opposition was clear: regardless of ideology or social position, no one opposed to the regime should feel safe. Many other political figures received warning visits that night from the SIM (Military Intelligence Service), the most feared of the regime's political police.

The FEU, however, suffered the most. Esteban Ventura Novo, chief of one of the Havana police divisions, discovered that several leaders of the attack were hidden in an apartment near the Fragua Martiana. Ventura's men stormed the apartment and killed the young revolutionaries Fructuoso Rodríguez, Joe Westbrook, José Machado, and Juan Pedro Carbó Serviat. Their bloody corpses were dragged down the stairs of the apartment building to the street, in full view of terrified neighbors.

That night, nocturnal Havana ceased—for many—to be the dazzling world it had been up till then. The underground networks of 26th of July, the FEU (now renamed March 13 Revolutionary Directorate), and to some extent the communists' Popular Socialist Party counterattacked the repressive organs of the dictatorship on their home ground. Colonel Blanco Rico, head of the SIM, was killed by a Directorate commando squad in Meyer Lansky's Montmartre cabaret. The 26th of July proclaimed a new slogan, "0-3-C," which meant "No Buying, No Movies, No Cabaret" (*Zero Compra, Zero Cine, Zero Cabaret*). Revolutionary graffiti and leaflets exhorted citizens to boycott stores and entertainment venues as a way to highlight the society's political ills and to mobilize the discontent of merchants and entrepreneurs. Homemade bombs called *petardos* were placed in streets, parks, and other public spaces to dissuade the populace from going out at night and to make the security forces feel that the city did not belong to them. One memorable night, 100 *petardos* went off in different locations around Havana. *Habaneros* could not tell which explosions were the traditional nine o'clock firing of the cannon in the Cabaña fortress, and which were detonations of another sort.

For most of his nearly seven years of dictatorial rule, Batista governed through a suspension of Constitutional guarantees and with iron censorship of the press. U.S. journalists who managed to reach the Sierra Maestra and interview Fidel Castro's rebels had their notes and film taken away by the army. News of the rebellion was available only from Radio Rebelde, the clandestine Voice of the Sierra, where the *Granma* expeditionaries had been reinforced by volunteers from the cities and, especially, by landless peasants and smallholders recruited in the mountains. Gluing their ears to radios turned down to minimum volume, so that they could not be overheard a few feet away, Havana listeners tuned in at night to the Radio Rebelde announcers, making out the course of the battles in the Sierra over the constant hiss of the shortwave.

Juan Valdés, while part of an aboveground group trying to bring the employees of the Indochina department store into the commercial workers' union under the protection of the country's labor laws, was also working in the anti-Batista underground. So was his brother Tony, who had been a member of the 26th of July Movement since 1954 (unbeknownst, of course, to those who watched him field baseball questions on TV). Alberto Motola and María Roffe were quietly selling 26th of July bonds to their Buenavista neighbors and customers, to raise funds for the rebellion. Buenavista was a barrio divided, since many low-level army officers lived at the end of the neighborhood closest to Camp Columbia, but as Raquel Cañizares remembers, "there were all types here—there always are—but there were many of us opposed to Batista, the young people especially. Young people always want change, and Carlos had his ideas that came from his father, too."

The closer the end of the dictatorship, the more intense the actions in the cities grew. A general strike called for April 9, 1958 was supposed to provide a final urban push needed to topple the regime, by combining shutdowns of all workplaces with daylight armed actions. Though the rebels gained control of some provincial cities, especially Cienfuegos, for a few hours, in Havana the concentrated power of the army and police was too great. The strike failed, as did any possibility that the revolution might be carried out in the capital as it had been in 1933. Juan Valdés and Tony Irízar were identified as conspirators in the general strike, possibly fingered by the owners of the Indochina. Juan was fired under a new Batista law removing labor law protections from subversives, and both brothers were jailed. Daniel Motola remembers watching his parents burn the clandestine 26th of July bonds before they could be found by the police. From then on, rebel strategy turned chiefly to the Sierra, to a war of attrition against the army on ground friendlier to the guerrillas and unfamiliar to the regime. That summer, an exasperated Batista launched an offensive of 20,000 men attempting to occupy the Sierra and root out the rebels. Their defeat by a much smaller guerrilla force marked the beginning of the end.

Between blackouts produced by sabotage of electric installations, explosions of *petardos* and nighttime shooting, *habaneros* heard over Radio Rebelde how the guerrilla war had spread beyond the Sierra Maestra in columns led by rebel commanders Che Guevara and Camilo Cienfuegos. The climax was the rebels' December siege of Santa Clara, the major city of the central region. Not many went out to enjoy Havana's legendary night life that tense New Year's Eve. Even the party at the well-guarded Copa Room of the Riviera received some two-hundred last-minute cancellations of reservations by phone. Just about midnight, Batista returned to Camp Columbia for the last time, to board a military aircraft that whisked him, his family, and his closest associates to Santo Domingo. Havana awoke on New Year's Day to a state of delirium comparable only to August 12, 1933 when Machado fell.

In a city always filled with noise, the citizens outdid themselves. Cars full of 26th of July and Revolutionary Directorate militia, now openly carrying weapons and wearing the armbands of their organizations, drove in all directions as they tried to capture remaining Batista henchmen. The crowds did not repeat the lynchings and sacking of mansions that had occurred in 1933,

Celebrating the fall of Batista, January 1, 1959.

though they did direct their violence at parking meters and slot machines, both of which were believed to have directly fed Batista's pockets. The doors of the Castillo del Príncipe opened to let hundreds of political prisoners out. The rebel army column led by Camilo Cienfuegos soon arrived from Santa Clara, entering Camp Columbia by the same gate, number 4, through which Batista and his confederates had entered in the predawn hours of March 10, 1952. Cienfuegos, the son of a Spanish anarchist tailor, was the most prominent of the rebel commanders to hail originally from Havana. As a teenager he had participated and been wounded in early anti-Batista protests, then gone into exile in the United States where he worked as a waiter and dishwasher in New York. A few days after entering Camp Columbia, in a symbolic gesture to signify a break with the past, he personally took a sledgehammer to the wall that anchored gate number 4.

Che Guevara, in turn, arrived and set up his characteristically spartan headquarters in the fortress of La Cabaña, where the British gun emplacements had fired on the Morro 200 years before. On January 8, Fidel Castro and the main force of the Rebel Army arrived in a triumphal parade, passing through the city to cheers of jubilant crowds. Castro made his first postvictory speech in Havana at Camp Columbia to a gathering that numbered in the hundreds of thousands. "The tyranny has been overthrown," Castro said that night, "The happiness is tremendous, but nonetheless much remains to be done. Perhaps all that lies ahead will be more difficult." He had already made clear—speaking from Santiago on his way to Havana—that there would be no transitional governments or negotiations. The old armed forces had to surrender and be dissolved, and the old order would perish.

What would replace the old order was not yet clear. Whatever it was, Castro implied, would fulfill the hopes for social reform, national pride, and independence from foreign influence that had been frustrated in 1898 and in 1933. In the middle of his speech, two doves landed on the rostrum before him, and one on his right shoulder. The Catholics thought immediately of the Holy Ghost, and the *santeros* of the *orisha* associated with mental strength, Obatalá. Castro turned for a moment toward Camilo Cienfuegos and asked, "How'm I doing, Camilo?" Camilo smiled, and the crowd, charmed, burst into applause.

Outside the circles closest to Batista, enthusiasm for Castro and the bearded rebels was near universal in a jubilant Havana. Interviewed by the popular magazine *Carteles* as he strolled down Calle Maloja in Central Havana, the Caballero de París dropped his antique speaking style and declared, "I like the *barbudos*. Those boys are fine with me. My subjects are pleased to have them among us. But the issue of the beards should not be overlooked, because, just between us, they stole that idea. They're taking advantage of my popularity among the people of this town by imitating me."

Not everything was luminous in those initial glory days. Clouds appeared over the sky of Havana. The first dark cloud blew in from the United States, which the rebels viewed suspiciously due to Washington's support of Batista, to whom the Eisenhower administration had supplied weapons until March of 1958. After cutting off the sale of arms, U.S. envoys had tried to convince the general to abdicate in favor of a successor who could take the steam out of the revolution and prevent it from coming to power.

"Never in any Latin American land has popular antagonism toward this country been more bitter than it is now in Cuba," reported U.S. journalist Carleton Beals, who had been covering the Caribbean and Central America since the 1930s. The Cuban press fiercely criticized U.S. ambassador Earl E. T. Smith for his past involvement in the granting of nickel mining concessions to Bethlehem Steel, the shady agreements with the U.S.-owned Cuban Telephone Company that which Pelayo Cuervo had denounced, and the ambassador's support for elections that Batista had stagemanaged in 1958. During the guerrilla war, Smith had denounced Castro in no uncertain terms, and had praised top Army figures even after the cut-off of arms sales.

The fundamental differences between the revolutionary government and the United States would hinge on agrarian reform and measures to undercut the traditional dominance of American companies—and, later, on Soviet ties and the fear of "other Cubas in the hemisphere." But the dominant theme in the first months of 1959 was the punishment of Batista officials judged guilty of violence against civilians. Starting on January 1, revolutionary tribunals organized by the Rebel Army had began to sentence army officers, policemen, and members of paramilitary groups in summary trials which led—if the accused were found guilty of killing unarmed civilians—to the firing squad. The Cuban press now reported the grisly details of murder, torture, and rape which they had been unable to report before. In profusely illustrated editions of more than a million copies, mass circulation magazines such as *Bohemia* and *Carteles* recounted the deaths of an estimated 20,000 victims at the hands of Batista's repression. They also listed the names of their killers, many of whom were now out of reach of the tribunals, having escaped to the United States or the Dominican Republic in the wee hours of New Year's Day.

While many Cubans found the trials and executions proof of the return of law and justice after long years of terror, they were counterproductive for the revolution's image abroad. "Spilling across Fidel Castro's Cuba," *Life* magazine reported, "an ugly tide of blood vengeance last week put a curious strain on relations between the liberated island's people and their friendly U.S. neighbors." The trials of Fulgencio Batista's "unlucky henchmen" lacked the necessary legal guarantees for the defendants, U.S. observers found, and were held before hostile crowds. Yet, as *Life* also reported, "Castro's support could not be doubted. Everywhere Cubans assembled to cheer him—and the executioners. 'There is hardly a family which has not felt the brutality of the Batista police,' cabled [Life's] correspondent. 'After seven years of rage, Cubans are now going to make the sadists pay.' "

One of the most controversial images to be reproduced around the world was a sequence of snapshot images of the firing-squad execution of Colonel Cornelio Rojas, the same officer who had brought the Caballero de París to appear before President Prío ten years before. Under Batista, Rojas had become police chief of Santa Clara, where he had been responsible for numerous deaths and tortures which he carried out himself with instruments specially invented by an auto-dealer friend. Nonetheless, the photographic sequence of his execution, as an old man in civilian dress, did not communicate any of the well-known sadism of the man. The volley of the bullets striking his head threw his hat several yards into the air, while his body shook from the impact of the blast.

The most famous of the public trials was that of army colonel Jesús Sosa Blanco, transmitted live on TV from the Sports Palace. Sosa was accused of causing the deaths of more than thirty peasants in the Sierra Maestra. The main witnesses were the survivors of the Argote family, the majority of whose thirteen members had been killed on his orders. Every Cuban with access to a television set saw Señora Argote point out Colonel Sosa as the man guilty of the deaths of her parents and brothers, in a type of confrontation between the rural poor and the symbols of traditional authority that had never gone out over the airwaves before. Sosa Blanco lifted his hands and smiled, declaring, "I'm in the Roman circus, just like Jesus Christ." The colonel's statement and the photos of the angry crowd were circulated the next day by the AP and UPI wire services, as a proof that a spirit of vendetta dominated the revolutionary courts.

The prosecution of the killers of Dr. Pelayo Cuervo was typical in a different respect. The defendants were seven policemen (said to have also been involved in other, similar abuses and deaths), a sergeant from the Bureau of Investigation who was shown to have fired the six fatal shots, the ex-police chief of Havana, and the former chief of the SIM. The prosecutor demanded capital punishment for the killer and the seven participating policemen, and twenty years imprisonment for the two superior officers, Hernando Hernández and Carlos Cantillo. A private prosecutor, a well-known lawyer hired by Cuervo's widow, asked for the death penalty for Batista and two other superior officers as well. The tribunal's response was the death penalty for three of the police and long prison terms for the other four. Cantillo was sentenced to fifteen years in jail, and Hernández was absolved. The fact was, however, that neither Cantillo, nor Hernández, nor the sergeant who pulled the trigger stood at any risk. Like Batista, they were well out of reach, walking the streets of Miami or other cities abroad.

Beyond the trials, Castro converted the new medium of television into a nightly window into every home so equipped, a window that often remained open into the wee hours of the morning. On the small screen, he educated, chided, exhorted, explained, answered his enemies, and made decisions on the spot. On one occasion, while Castro was criticizing Francisco Franco's government's policy toward the Cuban revolution, the Spanish ambassador, the Marqués of Bellisca, burst into the studio to challenge him in the man-ner of a duel. Castro's idea of mobilizing voluntary teachers from the capital in order to begin reducing illiteracy in the mountains first appeared during a TV appearance, and before the program ended there were students sign-ing up. At midnight, the *comandante* might turn up for a milkshake in the kitchen of the Havana Hilton—renamed Habana Libre—where the tempo-rary headquarters of the rebel army had been set up, or he might drop into a crowded and inexpensive Chinese restaurant on the grittier Calle Infanta for a meal. In the Grand Stadium of Cerro, a team of Barbudos played exhibi-tion games before the professional matchups, sometimes with Fidel on the mound and Camilo Cienfuegos behind the plate.

If much of this was theater, it was theater mixed with substantive measures. Some of the government's early reform actions had direct and popular effects in Havana, like the institution of price controls that drastically lowered rents and electricity and telephone rates, or the abo-lition of private beaches and the end to racial discrimination in any venue open to the public as well as in private clubs. Casino gambling was quickly banned—though implementation was delayed for some months after croupiers, dealers, and other employers protested that they would be left without work. Renegotiation of labor contracts raised dis-posable income for many in the capital, in a variety of trades. But the agrarian reform, which broke up the large rural estates and guaranteed a minimum of land to any peasant, sharecropper, or squatter already working it, was a fundamental break with the past. It found echoes in the capital very soon.

To celebrate the 26th of July of 1959, poor peasants who had received land under the new law were invited to the city as honored guests, and Castro asked *habaneros* to express their respect by lodging these new land-owners in their homes. The response to the slogan, "Open your home to a *campesino*" meant that half a million peasants, in their country clothes and straw hats, arrived in a dazzling city which received them with open arms. Those who couldn't find space in private homes were lodged on cots in the Hall of Mirrors, the Presidential Palace's main gala reception room. To be a *guajiro* (hick) in the capital suddenly lost its pejorative connotation, and became instead a kind of badge of citizenship, as normal as the bearded rebels with crosses, *santería* beads, and other amulets round their necks who scattered cigar ashes on the thick carpets of the Havana Libre before tumbling onto the nearest armchairs and sofas to sleep.

For the youth, especially, Havana in revolution meant new adventures and a redefinition of style. When they enrolled in the voluntary teachers' movements, and then in the "army" of the 1960–61 literacy campaign, they left behind electricity, air-conditioned movies, parental authority, and the pleasures of urban life to go to places reachable only on the back of a mule. Without pay, they taught reading and writing while relying on their own abilities and the support of people whose like they had never met before. For those remaining in the city or returning to it, wearing uniforms suddenly went from anathema to chic. Parading in militia outfit, carrying a gun, marching, and standing guard became the thing to do.

Juan Valdés, who had now finished three years of high school by attending at night, went to Oriente as a literacy teacher. He was followed two years later by Carlos and Raquel Larrinaga's first-born son Pablo, the namesake of his great-grandfather the tamale vendor. Over the objections of his fearful grandparents, but with the support of Carlos and Raquel who had both (as contemporary language had it) "incorporated themselves" into the revolution by taking up posts in new neighborhood organizations, Pablo went off with schoolmates at the age of twelve to help harvest coffee on lands redistributed by the agrarian reform. In inspiring youth to go to the countryside or join the militia, the revolution ruptured tradition in another way. It included girls in these mobilizations as well as boys. Particularly for girls of the white middle class, this was a radical break from the old attitudes of the capital. The writer Mirta Yáñez later described this rupture in her story "All Us Blacks Drink Coffee" (the title taken from a song popularized by Rita Montaner), in which a middle-class white teenager goes to pick coffee in spite of her mother's dismay: "And who knows, your mother demands in a powerless rage, if out there you won't go so crazy as to fall in love with a Negro. And you know what it means to be a nice white girl, as white as the paper daisy that your mother crushes nervously between her hands in your birthday photograph, its yellow heart overflowing with innocence . . . How times change."

As the story indicates, the honeymoon between all of Havana and the triumphant revolution did not last very long. Antagonistic economic, social, and political interests emerged, and the first signs of a political opposition and a hostile emigration started to appear. Batista allies and business partners like the Hedges brothers departed first, as they lost their properties to the new Department for the Recovery of Stolen Goods. The owners of the Indochina also left, accused of having informed on the underground, and their department store was confiscated under a new law that governed property left behind. Then the cross-class alliance that had temporarily accepted Castro's leadership against Batista began to break down over the radicalism of the reform program, and the increasing hostility between the new government and the United States. The interests affected by the agrarian reform included large cattle ranches and sugar mills with extensive landholdings, many of them owned by American concerns such as the King Ranch or United Fruit, and others by the upper crust of the Cuban bourgeoisie. Owners, executives, and stockholders of the casino hotels and the U.S.-based utility companies saw their power and income threatened, and many in the upper class were unnerved by the loss of the privileged physical spaces they had exclusively enjoyed until then. The moderate anti-Batista figures who had made up Castro's first cabinet saw that real power lay with the Rebel Army, and so, over one or another issue, they began to resign.

Within the first few months, by late spring of 1959, the State Department and CIA had decided that it was "impossible to carry on friendly relations with Castro government" and that it was necessary to "devise means to help bring about his overthrow and replacement by a government friendly to the United States." One by one the mansions of Biltmore and Country Club and many in Miramar and Vedado began to empty out, as their residents emigrated for what they thought would be a temporary stay in Florida or New York until things got back to normal again. In turn, the affected sectors of the professional class who had traditionally gone to American-affiliated private schools and worked for the Americans or the Cuban upper crust began to take sides one way or the other. The conflict between the revolution and an emerging counterrevolution began to fill more and more public space.

At night, the ghostly silhouettes of airplanes without running lights flew over the city and strafed certain buildings, or dropped fire bombs on outlying fields of sugar cane. These planes took off from airfields in Florida, flown by pilots from Batista's air force or by ex-rebels who opposed the direction taken by the revolution since its triumph. Nighttime explosions began to be heard in Havana, summoning echoes of the struggle just concluded against Batista. Those ensconced in Miami publicly announced their crusade against Fidel Castro, and boasted that they had the support of the United States. Of the various assassination plots later revealed by the Senate Select Committee on Intelligence hearings in 1975, one involved the CIA's top directorate, two mafia figures recommended by a former FBI agent, an ex-official of Grau San Martín's cabinet now organizing anti-Castro forces in Miami who was suggested by former Havana mafia boss Trafficante, and poison pills supplied by this chain of command to an agent working in the cafeteria of the Habana Libre. By some accounts, the cafeteria worker had the pills in his hand and was ready to introduce them into Castro's milkshake, but at the last minute he lost his nerve or changed his mind.

In this history of Havana, we will not rehearse the four-year-long series of back and forth, tit-for-tat Cuban and American government actions—economic reforms, economic sanctions, nationalizations, subversion, repression, new sanctions and threats, new nationalizations, and new aggressions—that marked the breakdown and then final rupture of all trade, transportation, and diplomatic relations between Cuba and the United States. One end result was the Cuban adoption of a Soviet alliance, a Marxist-Leninist ideology, and a state socialist system in which all major industry, commercial establishments, media outlets, and entertainment venues came into the hands of a state that defined itself as representing the poor, the patriotic, and the revolutionary against the conservative, the American, and the rich. Another was the exodus, during the years

1959–62, of some 200,000 Cubans out of the six million population, primarily from Havana and including the bulk of the elite.

Those who stayed got to keep their homes, cars, furs, art works, and bank accounts, and they often lived off these for many years, as islands in the sea of change around them. One of them was ex-president Ramón Grau San Martín, who continued to live in his Miramar home as we have mentioned above. Another was Dulce María Loynaz. In a philosophical prose poem written many years before, she had compared physical pain to a civil war in which the body, always taken for granted and obedient, suddenly rebels against the mind, seeking compensation for its losses and defending its rights. "It never demanded anything," the mind complains wonderingly about the body. "Now it comes . . . shouting its name in the silence of my nights . . . the simple, angry beggar who used to sleep every night outside my door."

After the actual revolution of those previously taken for granted, Loynaz withdrew more and more behind the pillars of the house in which she and Pablo Álvarez de Cañas had entertained at the Vedado corner of 19th and E. The rejection was mutual, as the cultural figures of the revolution had little use for her Catholicism or her intimate and personal style of verse. But she was too Cuban, too nationalist, and too *habanera* to leave. "Keep giving birth to me always," another equally prescient poem had asked of her island, "and pluck away my attempts to leave you, one by one." Her sister Flor, in similar fashion, remained ensconced in her estate in La Coronela, on the city's western outskirts, where the revolutionary 1930 Fiat was still hidden in her garage. She was accompanied by a collection of thirty pet dogs.

Dulce María's husband, on the other hand, left his adopted island behind. His employer Hornedo had gone and there was no more *El País* nor any other society pages. Pablo Álvarez de Cañas went to the United States for eye surgery and then took up residence in his native Spain. He returned to Cuba only much later, in the 1970s, old and sick.

Still others of the family, however, "incorporated themselves." Dulce María's younger half brother and his wife, both doctors, were among the half of Cuba's physicians who did not join the exodus to

Miami but rather stayed to build the new state-run health system. "They didn't become Party members or Marxist-Leninists or anything like it," recalls their daughter Verónica, "but they were humanists and Cubans and they threw themselves into the public health work that the revolution undertook."

In the course of these transition years, from 1959 to 1962, Havana faced two moments of high drama, known in Cuba by the name of a beach and a month—Playa Girón and the October Crisis—and known in the United States as the Bay of the Pigs and the Cuban Missile Crisis.

On April 13, 1961, a phosphorus bomb set the historic and national-ized El Encanto on fire, burning the department store to the ground and causing the death of one employee. Two days later, B-26 bombers bearing Cuban air force insignia attacked the military airports of San Antonio de los Baños, to the south of the capital, and Ciudad Libertad (formerly Camp Columbia) in the city itself. Raquel Cañizares and Carlos Larrinaga were on a train to Camagüey at the time, when word spread of the attack. "You can't imagine our panic, as close as it was to where we lived, and our children back there with my godmother and cousins. When we got to Camagüey we got hold of a phone, and called. They told us it was terrible, that they could hear the explosions, that they hid under the bed. But they were okay."

The next day, from a podium at the busy commercial intersection of 23rd and 12th, a block from the Cemetery of Colón, Fidel Castro spoke at a memorial for the seven who were not so lucky, who died in the raids. He announced that the planes had not been flown by defecting Cuban pilots but by members of an invasion force based in Nicaragua, trained and supplied by the CIA, for an invasion that might come any day. Paraphrasing the Gettysburg Address, he referred to a revolution "of the humble, by the humble, and for the humble." But pointedly depart-ing from such antecedents, for the first time he used the word "socialist" to describe the revolution he asked his listeners to defend.

The invasion came that night, at two beaches along the Bay of Pigs on the southern shore of Matanzas, about three hours from the capital by road. "After you make the landing," one of the CIA trainers had said in a morale-boosting speech to the expeditionaries, "all you have to do is drive your trucks to the Central Highway, stick out your arms for a left turn, and head for the capital, because the *habaneros* will be waiting for you with open arms."

In fact, thousands of Havana militia members—some already trained and some newly signed up—piled into hastily conscripted trucks and city buses to go and fight against these expeditionaries. What had been chic had become real, and militia from Havana (as well as Cienfuegos, Santa Clara, and small towns closer to the main battlefront at the beach called Girón) fought, bled, and died in the sixty-six hours of combat which resulted in the defeat of the invasion force before it could secure a beachhead as planned. U.S. strategists relying on information from their traditional Cuban allies, mostly in exile, had vastly underestimated the support that the Cuban government could count on, especially against an operation evidently sponsored by a foreign power. Any potential for an internal rising was neutralized by a wave of preventive detentions and arrests, most of them temporary, whose effect was to strengthen the new regime. The nearly 1200 survivors of the invading force did arrive in Havana—but as prisoners. In another round of trials broadcast on TV and radio late into the night, they were sentenced to prison terms ranging from fifteen to thirty years—or, as an alternative, wholesale ransom by their sponsors for food and medicine to the tune of $5000 apiece.

After the Bay of Pigs, Havana once again became the sort of fortified garrison that it had been in its early centuries of pirate attacks and inter-imperial wars. On the horizon, instead of the sails of British and Dutch privateers, the watchful destroyer *U.S.S. Oxford* became a familiar and permanent sight. The gardens of the Hotel Nacional reverted to their original use as trenches, sandbags, and the antiaircraft guns popularly known as *cuatro bocas* (four mouths) appeared. It was the same elsewhere along the seafront as the population awaited a new invasion that might include a fullscale air attack on the capital. Military radar receivers swivelled day and night on top of the Habana Libre, Riviera, and FOCSA, while on the Puerto Rican islet of Vieques, U.S. Marines trained in landing exercises against an imaginary regime presided over by a dictator called Ortsac, a name which could be read backwards with ease.

Among those most severely affected by the atmosphere of polarization leading up to and following the Bay of Pigs invasion were some of the youth just a bit younger than those in the militia and the Literacy Campaign. Worried parents put 14,000 unaccompanied children onto planes at the Havana airport for delivery to the uncertain mercies of churches, foster families, orphanages, relatives, and special camps in the United States. What became known as "Operation Peter Pan" was concocted by the CIA, the Catholic Church, and Cuban and U.S. citizens active in the underground opposition to Castro. One of its founders was James Baker, headmaster of Ruston Academy, the private school that had served Havana's American residents and their associates among its Cuban upper- and upper-middle class. Urging the proposal for a children's exodus on authorities in Washington, Baker argued that, "As the programs for turning more and more children into Communist robots are accelerated, we become more than ever eager to try to save more children." Washington empowered Monseigneur Bryan Walsh, a Catholic welfare agency official in Miami, to use clandestine channels to issue special U.S. immigration visa waivers to any and all Cuban children between the ages of six and sixteen. Evidence of the new social fault lines running through Havana is provided by one of the operatives in the Peter Pan network: María Teresa Cuervo, daughter-in-law of the murdered Pelayo Cuervo, who used her position at an Old Havana travel agency to make reservations for children brought to her by Catholic priests in lay clothing.

The generally white and well-to-do parents who sent their children out of the country were motivated by real fears (as in the Mirta Yáñez story) that they were losing the hearts and minds of their children to the new ideals of the radicalized revolution, and by the prospect that the government would soon close the private and parochial schools that they had always counted on. These parents were also stampeded into panic, however, by false rumors spread through underground leaflets and telephone campaigns and shortwave broadcasts on the CIA-operated Radio Swan. Chief among these rumors was that a new law was about to transfer *patria potestad* (legal authority over children) from parents to the state, which would send them off to Russia for years of indoctrination and return them as "materialist monsters" beyond their parents' control.

Most parents who entrusted their children to Peter Pan expected the separation to be temporary, until the government fell or they too were able to emigrate and join their children in the United States. But the government did not fall, and air traffic to and from Miami ceased permanently in October, 1962. Many of the children ended up separated from their parents for years, and some forever. The parents' worst fears had been realized, but in an unexpected way.

The catalyst to the end of air service was, of course, the Cuban government's acceptance of Soviet short and intermediate range missiles to be stationed at various points throughout the island, which from the Cuban point of view would serve as a deterrent to any further invasion attempts. Between October 22 and November 20 of 1962, Havana lived in a state of high alert, as its horizon filled with numerous and threatening U.S. naval vessels. Children continued going to school, theaters kept showing films, the cafeterias on La Rampa stayed open until the wee hours as usual, but teachers, service workers, and bus drivers alike went about their business in blue and green militia uniforms. The radio broadcast a steady stream of patriotic songs, both new and old. Trenches and antiaircraft emplacements multiplied from the sandy beaches east of the capital to the coral reefs on the west while the city braced for the invasion that many of John F. Kennedy's advisors were urging him to order.

When Kennedy and Nikita Khrushchev instead agreed on a Soviet withdrawal of the missiles in return for an unwritten U.S. promise not to invade Cuba in the future and the removal of U.S. missiles from Turkey, Havana breathed a sigh of relief. But many felt let down by the way the Soviets had left Cuba out of the negotiations and failed to openly declare the results. Their mixed sentiments were reflected in a new rhyming tune that Havana high school students sang and danced in their conga lines: *Nikita, mariquita, lo que se da no se quita.* Nikita, you sissy, giving should be for keeps.

When the Bay of Pigs prisoners finally left their Havana prisons in late December of 1962, in return for 53 million dollars worth of baby food and medicine, they were feted in Miami's Orange Bowl by John and Jackie Kennedy, with the First Lady greeting them in Spanish and the president promising that their flag would soon "fly over a free Havana." The main weapon of U.S. policy was implemented in February 1962: a complete economic embargo that banned not only trade with the United States but also trade with Western Europe and Latin America insofar as this could be enforced. Over the next year, the number of Western ships docking in Havana and other ports dropped from 352 to 59, and the capital's remaining commercial air links dwindled to three: Mexico City, Prague, and Madrid.

The city once preferred by American corporations for testing their latest consumer goods had lost its borrowed glitz. The Sears & Roebucks, the new Studebakers and DeSotos, the Chesterfields and Salems preferred by many smokers over their traditional brands, the premieres of the films of Marilyn Monroe and Marlon Brando, all vanished. More important to the economy, the managers and technicians who had overseen everything from electricity generation to beer bottling were gone too, as were the inputs and spare parts that had always been just a day away.

Yet, despite these shortages and dislocations, Havana would remain the capital of the triumphant revolutionaries through the terms of eight more U.S. presidents after Eisenhower and Kennedy, through five decades which would involve great breaks with the past and great continuities too. JFK's Orange Bowl speech was broadcast and reprinted in Cuban state media as the year 1962 ended, but this did not dampen New Year's Eve festivities in Havana. The residents of the capital imbibed great quantities of beer and rum and danced until dawn.

14 Revolution with Pachanga: Havana Transfigured

Last Saturday I couldn't get a seat at the Tropicana. After a long wait I got a chance to applaud the most extraordinary choreographic spectacle: The Agrarian Reform, a sumptuous, dynamic, and inspiring ballet that's an excellent example of revolutionary theater . . . Let visitors to Havana go to the beaches, let them enter the stores, stroll the streets, loiter in the cafés . . . They will feel they have landed in a transfigured city.

(Alejo Carpentier, "A Jubilant Havana," July 1959)

In his journalistic portrait of the changes in his city, the fifty-four-year-old novelist Carpentier marveled at much that he saw: toy stores awash in dolls of bearded guerrillas, exhibitions of tractors and other farm implements multiplying throughout the sophisticated capital, vendors of tamales and *fritas* displaying signs that said, "Eat what Cuba grows." This was not the city of American postcards and films, of Hemingway, Graham Greene, and Guillermo Cabrera Infante, of bright lights and carefree people, the bongo player Ricky Ricardo of *I Love Lucy* or the crafty, smiling mulatto gambler with a wisecrack always on his tongue. This city was undergoing a profound transformation, not just in its superficial appearance but deep inside.

The wave stirred up by the revolution—including its wave of discontents—inundated everything. Throughout the country, the thick soup of Cuban nationalism boiled over. Into the old simmering ingredients of Spanish sausage, African root vegetables, and Chinese or Arabic spices profusely sprinkled with American cocktails, new liquids now dripped. The peculiar ideology of "creole communism" blended idealism and personal sacrifice, volunteerism and collectivity, exaltation of the figures of the worker and the guerrilla, a spartan style and a radical ethic of doing away with the old and inventing the new. It affected every class and race, and every barrio of the capital. Still in love with its new heroes and new slogans, Havana did not stop dancing and enjoying with every pore. "This is Revolution with *pachanga* (raucous partying)," said many Latin American radicals visiting the city in the early 1960s said. Yet the city submitted to the nation's long-deferred dream, for which many of its residents had fought in 1895, in 1933, and in the struggle against Batista and against U.S. domination.

In a space of barely four years, Havana was abandoned by its elite and invaded by the poor people of the countryside. Its enclaves of middle-class comfort, its glamorous theaters and concert halls, and its towering hotels all opened their doors much wider than had ever been imagined before. Its connections with the North were abruptly cut, and Cuba was more and more isolated from the South as well. The city had to create new and unexpected supply lines from the remote East, whose strange languages had to be learned in a rush. The most cosmopolitan and culturally diverse city of the region, born as the crossroads of the New World and accustomed for centuries to international commerce and familiarity with strangers, Havana now underwent another test of survival.

First and foremost, the experience of the revolution made the citizens of Havana conscious as never before that they inhabited the privileged capital of an island whose countryside had long teemed with poverty, hunger, curable diseases, illiteracy, and neglect. When the Rebel Army marched into Havana in 1959, four out of every five of its soldiers—recruited largely in the mountains of the east—did not know how to read or write. The same was true of nearly one out of every three Cubans throughout the country. Yet the illiteracy rate in the capital was only one out of eleven. The cities of the interior, not just the remote countryside, suffered from such imbalances too. The only three television stations on the island were based in the capital. Havana had 123 movie theaters, while no other city had more than five. Commitment to rectify this disparity, together with ideological radicalism and the politics of state socialist centralism, meant that the victorious revolution would pour more resources and energy into the interior than into the capital. Thus, the hundreds of thousands who assembled in the Plaza de la Revolución—many of them with experience as militiamen and women, literacy teachers, voluntary cane cutters and coffee pickers, administrators of sugar mills, or those who simply considered themselves revolutionaries—applauded economic policies that prioritized the construction of roads, hospitals, utilities, and schools in the mountains instead of the capital.

Parallel to this movement, the resources of the capital were redirected internally from the rich to the working class and the poor. The exclusive private yacht and beach clubs of Miramar and Playa Marianao were thrown open to the public for admission fees of fifty cents, or turned over to labor unions for their members' use. The Country Club became the site of a new, free-of-charge National Arts College—an innovative red-brick design of beehives with sinuous paths and corridors, some of them later invaded by the jungle of vegetation along the narrow Río Quibú. Alfredo Hornedo's mansion on Carlos III became Centro Habana's Casa de Cultura, where aspiring writers could join workshops and the modern equivalents of Chano Pozo played not for patrons but for those who would have previously gathered in the courtyards of El África or El Ataúd. The Grand Stadium became the Latinoamericano, where all ties to U.S. professional baseball were cut.

The Habana Libre, when it ceased to be a makeshift Rebel Army headquarters, became a crossroads for international revolutionaries and radical activists of many stripes. Its rooms and night clubs and swimming pool, like those of the Riviera and the Nacional and the Capri, also became a playground for Havana honeymooners of all classes and races, for Cubans from the countryside attending political events in the capital, and for young dating couples who could save up twenty pesos for decaying luxury, privacy, and a bed. The nearby FOCSA apartment building, thirty-two stories of luxury condominiums and top-floor restaurant/observation point, became a dormitory for students from the interior who came to study in the capital. The older estate across the street—a mansion house and carriage house, with steep, green-tiled roofs that seemed to belong in Switzerland—became an elementary school. Many abandoned or confiscated apartments went to Rebel Army soldiers and their families, who stayed in Havana to fill new or old government posts. So did great homes newly subdivided into apartments or single rooms. The old and crumbling Loynaz estate on Calle Línea, where the salons of the 1920s and 1930s had taken place, was partitioned by new residents, adapted, and partitioned again. The same fate befell the house of General Enrique Loynaz in suburban Lawton, after the aged general went to live in the seaside town of Santa Fé.

Other classic buildings became museums of what was gone. The Presidential Palace turned into the Museum of the Revolution, in fact a museum of all of Cuban history from the revolutionary point of view. The politician Orestes Ferrara's Tuscan mansion alongside the wall of the university became the Napoleonic Museum, housing the departed Ferrara's imperial French art collection and the collection of émigré sugar magnate Julio Lobo (equally obsessed with Bonaparte) who owned, among many other treasures, a lock of the emperor's hair. The Palacio de Aldama, rescued from its fate as a tobacco factory, was restored to become the home of the Historical Institute. The mansion and gardens of sugar heiress María Luisa Gomez-Mena, the Countess of Revilla-Camargo—famed for parties with 100-pound gold candelabras, 5000 dozen gladioli, and 500 pheasants flown in from the United States—became the Museum of Decorative Arts.

When the Literacy Campaign ended, Juan Valdés, at the age of twenty-three, was offered a job as manager of a newly nationalized sugar mill in the central province of Las Villas. Though self-taught in philosophy and mathematics, he still lacked a high school diploma and he knew nothing of sugar or agriculture. But like thousands of others whose political militance or trade union activism qualified them to take the place of former owners and administrators, he threw himself into this work. In his few free weekends, especially between harvests, he returned to Havana. There he walked in his muddy Russian boots and olive green military pants past the famous corner of Galiano and San Rafael, where El Encanto had burned to the ground. In the windows of the Indochina, Poljot and Raketa wrist watches from Moscow, ugly but cheap, had replaced the glamorous Swiss timepieces of a few years before. To the west, in the Barrio Chino where Valdés had spent part of his youth, the photo of Chiang Kai-shek had come down from the Casino Chung Wah, the offices of the Kuomintang had been closed along with the pornographic cinemas, and a militia brigade had been named after the fallen Cuban revolutionary José Wong.

In the other direction, in the barrio of Colón through which Juan had once walked to work at the laundry, the brothels had gradually been shut down, their employees enrolled in school or retrained for other jobs. "I wasn't one of those who rushed out with an armband on January 1 to pretend I'd been a Fidelista all the time," a former prostitute named Violeta recalled. "After the triumph, at first we were happy as clams, because everybody in the city felt safe and had money and came out to enjoy the new times, and we didn't have to pay any more bribes to cops or mafias of any kind. I was making more money than ever before. Then the rumors started to spread: that they were going to round us up, move us someplace else, put us in jail. We thought it would be one more crackdown like with other politicians before. The first shock was the urban reform. It was radical, it made us the owners of our rooms. Then they rounded up the pimps, who had to shut up shop for good, and many of them left the island, and others went to jail or went to work. It was hard for us to adjust, some more than others, because we never thought that way of life would end—much less considered whether we could have had a role in contributing to the change. But many of us, when we saw it was really different from the past, then we joined up. And there was one of us, Cuca, whose boyfriend had been in it, always running from the police who accused him of distributing leaflets or setting bombs. He went to the Sierra, and six months later Cuca disappeared. Afterward she was one of those coming to us and telling us we ought to give up that work."

Despite all the changes, *la bulla* continued apace. Radios and televisions blared with broadcasts of all sorts of ceremonies, assemblies, and new soap operas featuring stories of patriotic struggle alongside the latest hits of Roberto Faz and Beny Moré. The resonant Cuban dance music now shared airtime with militia marches and songs. Fidel Castro reported on a recent trip to the USSR, or Minister of Industry Che Guevara detailed ambitious plans. This background competed with truckloads of students performing Carnival congas that insulted the president of the United States, or riding floats in whose three-story towers young dancers wiggled to the beat of rumbas dedicated to construction workers. Cars with loudspeakers announced assemblies in the "Red Plaza of La Vibora" or dances in the Parque Central and Prado, where the city's most famous bands played deep into the night for free.

In the meantime, new lines of division opened, with the city's patchwork of religious beliefs as the terrain of one such split. Havana's Catholic clergy were mostly Spanish-born and conservative. Their initial coolness to the revolutionary ideology, and their outright opposition once it took a Marxist-Leninist form, rapidly divided the political terrain into camps of believers and nonbelievers. Eduardo Boza Masvidal, the parish priest of the church of La Caridad across from the Valdés family's temporary Chinatown home, had become auxiliary bishop of Havana. He wrote passionate homilies against the government, excoriating its atheistic communism, its catering to foreign interests (the Russians), and its disrespect for private property (including the nationalization of private schools, particularly Catholic ones).

However, in Cuba the Church hierarchy did not have the following it could count on in many other parts of Latin America. For a population of over a million, there had been only 232 priests in Havana in 1953, and most of them had taught in the private schools attended by the children of the white middle and upper class. Though a majority of Cubans declared themselves Catholic, mid-1950s surveys by the Church itself showed that only 11 to 18 percent of the country's population regularly attended mass. Another 6 percent of the population were members of Protestant churches, most of which sought an accommodation with the revolution. But the great majority of Cubans believed in God and/or gods "after their fashion," practicing grassroots religion that mixed various proportions of Catholic, spiritist, and African rites. The atheism newly embraced by the leaders of the revolution drew on utopian sentiments embedded in each of these faiths, on the belief that a better world could be formed.

Bishop Boza Masvidal was among 130 priests expelled from the country as counterrevolutionaries five months after the Bay of Pigs. The catalyst for this move was a combination of religious procession and political demonstration that he convoked outside the church of La Caridad. The conflict between the Catholic Church and the new state played a major role in the departure of thousands of the capital's middle-class children in Operation Peter Pan, and practicing Catholic adults also left the country in much higher numbers than nonpracticing ones. A survey of Havana parishes taken in the late 1960s estimated that 50 to 70 percent of their members left the island in the decade after the revolution came to power. Churches of all faiths continued to operate, but among the hundreds of thousands of believers of one sort or another who stayed in the capital, the majority let go of their religion, kept it quiet, or something of each.

Those most accustomed to such an uneasy balance, of course, were the practitioners of Afro-Cuban religions, whose predecessors had spent centuries balancing conflicting traditions and public versus private display. Pragmatic and polytheistic, the African elements emphasized personal faith and daily conduct above catechism and had no official hierarchy or institutions to defend. The rebel troops had entered Havana wearing not just crosses but the beads of *santería*. For many believers in the "people's faith"—blacks and whites living in those barrios that had once been Havana outside the walls—the top leaders of the revolution were illuminated and protected by the *orishas* of the Yoruba pantheon. Otherwise, it would have been inconceivable that they should escape from death and the designs of their powerful enemies. Among Fidel Castro's popular nicknames was "El Caballo," the horse, a reference not only to his stamina but to the Chinese *charada*, in which the horse represented Number One. There were those who felt he had been bathed in the virtues of the Three Warriors of *santería*—the strength and battle spirit of Changó, the tenacity and will of the blacksmith Oggún, and the ability and vision of Elegguá, lord of the roads and opener of doors. It was well known that some of his closest collaborators, like René Vallejo, his personal doctor, and Celia Sánchez, his closest aide, were hidden believers who consulted with distinguished *babalawos*. The layer of official atheism brought the unwieldy word *oscurantistas* (obscurantists) into daily vocabulary to describe religious practitioners of all sorts, and it frowned heavily upon the *toques de tambor* celebrated in the courtyards and rooftops of the city or the annual San Lázaro's Eve procession to the outlying chapel of El Rincón in honor of Babalú Ayé. Underneath, however, the old beliefs not only maintained themselves but functioned as a social glue.

What the revolutionary ideology did not tolerate as religion, it celebrated as culture, giving Afro-Cuban traditions an official nod they had never received before. Audiences crowded into what had previously been the Tacón Theater and then the National, now renamed in honor of Federico García Lorca, to see the dancers of National Folklore Ensemble perform the traditional dances invoking Yoruba *orishas*. They packed the former Rodi movie theater in Vedado, renamed Julio Antonio Mella, to see the Modern Dance Ensemble interpret the Afro-Cuban poems of Nicolás Guillén dedicated to Sensemayá, the snake of the Mayombe rite. His poems were converted into subjects of much praised ballets and films.

More dramatically than religion, the private commerce that had sunk its roots deeply into the street life of Havana visibly withered away. Before leaving for the countryside as a teacher and then a mill administrator, Juan Valdés had won back his job at the Indochina, where he briefly became part of the management team of the nationalized store. Supermarket chains, which had time for only a brief appearance in Havana of the late 1950s and the early 1960s, were nationalized too. The change in the city's economic life also swept away local businesses the size of Alberto Motola's, which had lately added an appliance store, Motola Electric. Motola, already elected president of his local Committee for the Defense of the Revolution, cooperated with the new state employees sent to "intervene" his three linked stores, but when he continued to assist them in straightening out accounts and procedures, this was too much for the ideology to handle. " 'How can it be that this capitalist, this bourgeois, is working with you?' his son recalls the intervenors' superiors telling them. 'Kick him out!' He may have been president of the CDR, but Cuba is like that. Many contradictory things coexist." María Roffe, on the books as an employee, was immediately given employment at another store, as the new laws required. Alberto finally got a job as a warehouse supervisor in another newly nationalized Buenavista commercial establishment not far from his home.

Unlike Alberto and María, the majority of Havana's Jewish population, including most of the Motolas and Roffes, left Old Havana, Vedado, and other neighborhoods to seek their fortunes in Miami or New York. The Arab stores on Montserrate, Bernaza, and Monte in the old city also closed their doors. But the smallest retail outfits were unaffected by the nationalizations of the early 1960s. The hand laundries and snack counters, many small bodegas and fruit stands, and the hundreds of varied carts and holes in the wall hung on, especially those in the hands of Chinese-descended merchants. Then, in 1968, a final wave of socialist radicalism known as the "Revolutionary Offensive" wiped out these last residues of the private urban economy, which would not reappear for another thirty-five years. The sole and honorable exceptions were the aged Fords and Plymouths whose proprietors made up the National Association of Revolutionary Taxi Drivers and continued to ply their trade. The Chinese entrepreneurs left little by little, especially for New York, where they opened Chinese-Cuban restaurants whose menus had egg rolls and Manchurian soup alongside demitasse cups of sweet dark coffee and specials like Cuban black beans with ground beef.

By then, the city's economic life had radically changed. The nationalizations of foreign businesses brought a patriotic sense of settling accounts, and a feeling among workers that they were in control of the factories at last. These new state enterprises tried to reproduce the rationalized efficiency of private monopolies. The big Crusellas and Sabatés soap and perfume factories, the paper and cardboard plants along the Avenida de Puentes Grandes, and the Antillana de Acero steel plant (formerly American Steel) in the southeastern suburb of El Cotorro had all been subsumed into large state corporations affiliated with the new Ministry of Industries. Former small firms were now grouped together along product and service lines and known as consolidated enterprises or, commonly speaking, *consolidados*. Victor Adding Machines became part of one of these, and Carlos Larrinaga was transferred to the new *consolidado* in Old Havana. From 1968 on, the tiny private workshops that made faucet washers or pressure cooker gaskets and storefronts that sold thread and fountain pen ink were dissolved in great conglomerates too—with acronyms that verged on the bizarre.

For example, the hundreds of retail sellers of cigars and cigarettes known as Romeo y Julieta, Partagás, Bauzá, or Hoyo de Monterrey, had been subsumed in a company called ECODICTAFOS, whose hermetic Spanish initials meant Consolidated Distribution Enterprise of Cigarettes, Cigars, and Matches. The monopoly wholesaler of old beverage brands such as Tropical and Hatuey beers and Coca-Cola was now in the hands of ECODICEMARAM (Consolidated Enterprise Distributing Beers, Maltas, Soft Drinks, and Mineral Waters). The entity in charge of distributing many products formerly available in stands and storefronts (buttons, brushes, barrettes, combs, mops, detergents, and hundreds of small useful objects) answered to the improbable title of ECODOQUINLIM. Although the majority of the streets and places in the city were still known by the same names as always, mostly as old as the Spanish colony, the commercial establishments were draped in these new, Orwellian names. So the shoe shop *La complaciente* ("at your service") became Unit 023-4577 of ECORERCARCU (Consolidated Repair Enterprise of Shoes and Leather Articles). Centralized decision-making, combined with centralized supply, the mushrooming of administrative regulations, and the growing effect of the U.S. economic embargo, kept the new businesses from running with the expected efficiency. When the customers of United 023-4577 of ECORERCARCU did not feel it was "at their service," they were often dismayed to be told, "those are our instructions," or "that service is not foreseen in the Ministry's regulations," or simply "we're all out of that."

On the edges of this state economy, small gray markets of semilegal private activity continued to exist. Alberto Motola, once he retired from his warehouse job and from another job in the Sports Ministry as a judge of marlin fishing contests, found that he could not sit home idle, and that business was in his blood. He went to an undeveloped green area near the coast below Buenavista and beyond Miramar, known as Monte Barreto, and made an arrangement with a longtime squatter who had built himself a shack there. Together, Alberto, María and the squatter grew tomatoes, cucumbers, and other vegetables to eat and to sell. Later he got in the business of recycling wholesale-sized cans of lard and jam from bakeries. Though these activities were sometimes questioned by the police, his standing in the community and—he claimed—his ties to old Popular Socialist Party leaders always prevailed.[1] Many other families bartered rationed goods that exceeded their needs, or odd lots of hardware brought home from the workplace, all of which took the place of the vendors and small shops that had just about vanished from the city's streets. One other form of commerce that neither revolutionary morality nor state enforcement eliminated was grassroots gambling. The casinos, the mafia, and the National Lottery were gone, but *la bolita* (the numbers game) survived, as did *la valla* (the cockpit) in rural areas and on Havana's outskirts.

An issue weighing much more heavily on the minds of residents of the capital was putting a decent roof over their heads. Within the limits of its orientation toward the countryside, the revolutionary government attempted to do something about this. The original urban reform and later legislation eliminated the problem of prices, reduced rent to a maximum 10 percent of income and gave rights of perpetual occupancy and inheritance to many citizens. Throughout the formerly middle and upper-class barrios of the city, housemaids and cooks and gardeners often went from being live-in servants to owners of the places where they had worked. More difficult to tackle, however, was the problem of supply. In spite of the exodus of the elite, the growing migration to the capital, combined with a baby boom of 1960–65, increased the population of the city to a million and a half.

A slum clearance plan eradicated more than thirty squatter settlements and other unhealthy barrios of Havana, including Las Yaguas, The Cave of Smoke, and Llega y Pon, whose residents moved to new projects. These projects were originally financed through an imaginative system which made use of the profits of the century-old National Lottery. The later political decision to shut down all types of gambling, along with the increasing centralization of the state, and a desire to discourage immigration from the interior to Havana, all meant that these building projects began to decline after 1963–64.

The decision to reduce housing construction, together with the growth in employment, education, public health, and social services in the rest of the country, was highly effective in reducing the Cuban capital's rate of growth. Today's Havana has barely twice the number of inhabitants as in 1959, an exceptional case in a region which produced megalopolises like Mexico City, Sao Paolo, Caracas, and Buenos Aires during the same period of time.

Nonetheless, the decline in the construction of new houses contributed to decay in the traditional centers of the city and later to the creation of new makeshift settlements like El Romerillo near the Playa de Marianao, El Fanguito alongside the Almendares below the heights of Vedado, or La Güinera in the southeastern district of San Miguel de Padrón. The nationalization of the small shops in 1968 converted many storefronts into improvised living spaces that housed those most in need while accelerating the deterioration of the buildings and the decay of the cityscape. Most of the old *solares,* if they were not leveled, gradually got individual plumbing and cooking and lighting facilities. But the resulting mazes of gas, electric, and water lines were like spider webs, and the buildings' structural deterioration was often not addressed. By the end of the century, more than half of the buildings in Cuba characterized as being in substandard condition were concentrated in the capital.

During the 1960s, nonetheless, whatever the problems in housing, the overall living standards, work and educational opportunities, public health services, and cultural life of Havana grew tremendously. There were more schools, colleges, daycare centers, clinics, theaters, museums, libraries, and bookstores than ever before. Not only rent but prices of basic food (a market basket of rationed goods), public transit, concerts of all sorts, books, a ballet in the García Lorca, and an occasional dinner in a luxury restaurant or night at the Tropicana or in the Hotel Capri were within the reach of almost everyone. Even the poorest Havanans could attend a decisive game in the baseball finals at the Latinoamericano, send their children to study trumpet or violin, or get psychiatric or dental attention or a heart operation, or receive funeral services—all completely for free.

Juan Valdés climbed the ladder of the sugar industry to the point of becoming director of agriculture for the whole province of Las Villas. He finally returned to Havana as the national vice minister in charge of agricultural labor, but his true vocation still lay in ideas and books. He was a friend of every used book dealer in the capital and spent a good deal of his salary on works of history, philosophy, and social science. Eventually he got the chance to study sociology in the university, left his post in the Ministry of Agriculture, and fulfilled his dream of becoming a professor of philosophy himself. His children, named Elena and Alejandro out of his admiration for classical Greek culture (after Helen of Troy and Alexander the Great), took swimming lessons in the pool of a state sports academy in Miramar. Divorced some years before, he married a young doctor, recently graduated from medical school. The white philosophy professor and mulatta doctor lived with the aunt who had raised her, in the crowded, racially mixed, prerevolutionary workers' housing development of Pogolotti in Marianao.

The Motolas, meanwhile, had paid for their middle son, León, to attend junior and senior high school at the private Candler College in the years before its nationalization, but their youngest son Daniel went to the same school, now part of the state system, for free. Both went on to get university degrees. Isaac, the oldest son, became a bus and truck mechanic, as he had determined to be when he sneaked off from school to the bus yard at the age of twelve. He studied mechanics in nearby Ciudad Libertad, the educational complex that had been Camp Columbia. That was where he met his future wife, who came from the provinces to study biology at the teacher's college there.

Verónica Loynaz went every day from her parents house in Lawton, near where the Loynaz family arms could still be seen on the crumbling former home of the general, to the high school of La Vibora (a former convent school), where she mixed with all classes and races. General Loynaz's granddaughter regularly visited her aunts Flor and Dulce María in their secluded retreats, and she also joined the Communist Youth. She went on to the university to study law. When she was criticized by fellow students there for her "bourgeois" speech and reluctance to curse, she declared in a Youth meeting that revolutionaries did not have to abandon the manners they had been brought up with, which were part of who they were.

In the cultural sphere, the reverberant Havana that had once been the Paris of the Caribbean again filled with illustrious visitors and cutting-edge international cultural events in the 1960s. The city received intellectuals and entertainers ranging from Jean Paul Sartre to Gabriel Garcia Márquez (who worked in the Cuban news agency Prensa Latina), Graham Greene (who came back to see what had changed), Julio Cortázar, the French film and stage star Gerard Philipe, Gina Lollobrigida, Mario Vargas Llosa, Carlos Fuentes, and Josephine Baker. Allen Ginsberg returned in 1968, no longer unknown, at the invitation of a Cuban-based publishing house to judge a poetry contest, though his advocacy of homosexuality and marijuana got him expelled after a few days.

The most famous French modern art exhibit, the Salon de Mai, was held on La Rampa that same year, and ordinary Havana was astonished to see Warhol's soup cans for the first time, in addition to the smashed cars of César Baldaccini, and original paintings by Picasso, Braque, Jackson Pollock, and Vasarely. Art even found its way onto La Rampa's sidewalks, which were repaved to include colorful mosaics by the Cuban artists Wifredo Lam, Amelia Peláez, Mariano Rodríguez, and René Portocarrero. At the top of the hill, also in 1968, the Habana Libre hosted more than five hundred artists, philosophers, and writers from seventy countries at the legendary Cultural Congress of Havana. From Belgium, Maurice Béjart's Twentieth Century Ballet showed thousands of delighted spectators a whole new way of imagining dance. In the meantime classical romantic ballet provided the name for Coppelia, the new, modernistic ice-cream palace and park built catty-corner from the Habana Libre. Coppelia had more flavors than Howard Johnsons, the *habaneros* who knew the northern chain proudly proclaimed.

The hundreds of thousands of readers who visited bookstores also discovered American literature, translated and distributed in the 1960s more than ever before or after. For under three pesos, they could buy the novels of Dos Passos and Steinbeck, the stories of Hemingway and Faulkner, science fiction of Asimov and Bradbury. Theaters put on works of Leroi Jones, Edward Albee, Arthur Miller, and Eugene O'Neill. Certain radical U.S. political figures, such as Malcolm X, Angela Davis, Martin Luther King, Jr., and the leaders of the Black Panther Party received widespread exposure and were seen as heroes in the city and beyond.

Popular Cuban music stayed as dynamic as ever, with a proliferation of new groups, genres, and dance styles. The Mozambique emerged in the mid-1960s, developed by Pello el Afrokán and his band led by a phalanx of drums and trumpets at the head of the floats and conga lines of university students groups in the annual Havana carnival. The Mozambique caught on for its new dance steps, reminiscent of the traditions of rumba and danced en masse rather than in couples, as well its catchy lyrics and the volume of its great chorus of drums. Even Fidel Castro, known for being among the minority of Cubans who did not dance, was said to have invented a Mozambique lyric about voluntary cane cutting, which could be attacked with the same infectious "crazy pleasure" as dance.

Another famous dance band, Los Van Van, took its name from the mobilization around the 1970 sugar harvest, whose slogan was *los diez millones van* ("we'll make 10 million tons"). Los Van Van recovered the tradition of the *charangas*, the big dance bands of the 1940s and 1950s, which had incorporated the wind instruments of jazz groups into the previous sextets and septets of *son*. They added their own rhythms including those of rock and roll. The complex choreographies and steps invented by the dancers at the Salon Rosado of La Tropical served as inspiration for bandleader Juan Formell. His electric bass, which went almost unnoticed on the far left end of the big band, set the beat for the dancers whose improvisations he carefully observed. Van Van was an instant success among the youth, and their lyrics introduced new slang and mythical characters into popular speech.

Where Havana gave birth to something almost completely new, however, was in a medium in which up till now the city had produced very little—film.

As consumers, the capital's residents in the 1960s had a shrinking number of cinemas but a broader access to world cinematography. In 1960, more than 200 of the 380 films shown in the capital were still American, but later years brought not only numerous Soviet and Eastern European films, previously almost unknown, but those of Japan, Italy, France, England, Spain, and Latin America. Tony Irízar, still an incurable moviephile, now haunted the first-run cinemas to feast on the images of Roman Polanski's Warsaw, Pasolini and Antonioni and Fellini's Rome, the Paris of Truffaut, Resnais, and Godard, Milos Jancsó's Budapest, and Milos Forman's Prague. Yet Hollywood films never disappeared, trade embargo or no. By 1980, there were as many U.S. films shown, by hook or by crook, as British and Italian ones.

For almost the first time since the early productions of Enrique Díaz Quesada, Cubans now got into the act as significant producers of cinema too. What had been made in Havana in the interim had been mostly melodramas and musicals produced by short-lived and poorly funded movie studios doing their best to imitate either Hollywood or Mexico. The first cultural institution created by the revolutionary government, in March of 1959, was the Cuban Institute of Cinematographic Art and Industry (ICAIC), established on one floor of the Atlantic office building at the busy Vedado intersection of 23rd and 12th. When the building was nationalized two years later, ICAIC got the whole thing. The film institute excelled first at politically innovative, fast-cutting, and intellectually challenging newsreels and documentaries in the style pioneered by Santiago Álvarez. Álvarez, born in Old Havana in 1919, had worked in Pennsylvania and New York in the late 1930s and early 1940s as a coal miner and dishwasher, and returned to Havana where he studied philosophy and joined the Popular Socialist Party and then the anti-Batista underground.

Other ICAIC directors, influenced particularly by the Italian New Wave, made feature films on a wide variety of Cuban themes (rural, urban, contemporary, and historical) which soon began to win awards at European festivals in both the East and West. Some of the most notable features focused on the life of Havana and the complexities of its transformation. Tomás Gutierrez Alea's *Memories of Underdevelopment* (1968) sympathetically portrayed the alienation of a member of the old bourgeoisie on the eve of the Missile Crisis. Staying but not belonging, he observes the city as a spectator, through the telescope set up in the spacious living room of his high rise Vedado apartment. Alea returned to this theme again in *The Survivors* (1978), the story of an aristocratic family that tries to maintain the *ancien régime* within a compound of their own. *The Survivors* was shot at Flor Loynaz's suburban estate, where she still lived. It starred Germán Pinelli, the radio newsman who had narrated the events of Orfila and gone on to be a prominent television host.

In the meantime, however, the *pachanga*—as well as the epic drama of the early years of the revolution—was coming to an end.

15 Russian Meat, Miami Butterflies, and Other Unexpected Adventures

Havana's cultural effervescence went into decline toward the late 1960s as the Cuban attempt to invent an experimental socialism different from that of the Soviet Union entered a critical phase. Che Guevara's death among a group of Cuban guerrillas in Bolivia, the accumulated effects of the U.S. embargo and international isolation, and the Revolutionary Offensive of 1968 all contributed to chilling the old atmosphere of cultural diversity. The margins between what was considered to be within the revolution and what was seen as antagonistic toward it grew more rigid, and the syndrome of seeing Cuba as besieged fortress made prohibitions multiply. Homosexuality and religion were already viewed as stains left over from the capitalist past, and their practitioners as people who had to be reeducated through work and the study of "scientific atheism." Now the hunt for such deviation (especially in the previously more tolerant spheres of culture and education) became more intense. Unorthodox strains of Marxism, potentially critical of the Soviet model, also found themselves hemmed in.

The philosophy department at the University of Havana, of which Juan Valdés was a member, published a journal of Marxist theory called *Pensamiento Crítico* (Critical Thinking), which published articles from Europe, North America, and Latin America, including Cuba. The young professors who had founded the journal, convinced they were carrying out a task of the revolution, were surprised to learn that they had been criticized by Raúl Castro, Fidel's brother and Minister of Defense, for circulating the ideas of writers critical of Soviet Marxism and for exposing their students to this influence. *Pensamiento Crítico* was closed in 1972 and the philosophy department was reorganized as the department for the teaching of Marxism-Leninism. Juan had to return to his post in the Ministry of Agriculture, and his other colleagues also moved to other jobs for the duration of the 1970s.

Prohibition of contacts with emigrants grew more rigid, as did strictures on rock music and even jazz, because these supposedly represented imperialist culture—as did miniskirts on women, long hair on men, and beards that did not sprout during the guerrilla struggle itself. A puritanism alien to Cuban culture took over radio stations and schools, periodicals, and political discourse.

At approximately the same time, the attempt to produce 10 million tons of sugar in 1970 led hundreds of thousands of Havanans to cane-cutting camps. The streets lost their old nocturnal vibration, while generalized shortages affecting the whole country left their mark on Havana as well. The accumulated costs of U.S. hostility and the unprecedented effort required by superambitious economic plans led to a virtual paralysis of the economy. Unlike the later crisis of the 1990s, when dollar stores and a thriving black market would constitute an escape valve for some, the severe shortages at the end of the 1960s simply distributed nothing among all. When the 10-million-ton goal was not reached in 1970, the government recognized the need for a change. It could not keep asking the people to sacrifice while the stores remained empty and a long wait in line was required to eat in a restaurant or buy food beyond the ration or an appliance as humble as an electric fan. The revolution could not maintain the extreme egalitarianism that meant the salary of pizza parlor employee and a cardiovascular surgeon bought almost the same in the market, if there was anything to buy. Castro made a speech accepting responsibility for the 10-million-ton debacle and offering to resign. The multitude assembled for the speech did not take up the offer, and government policy thereafter changed course.

To provide more consumer goods while maintaining the vital supply of petroleum and arms, the government made a new arrangement with the USSR and the socialist bloc. Among the main characteristics of the new period would be the implantation of a much more strictly Soviet model in the economic system, government organization, national constitution, Cuban Communist Party, armed forces, and communications media. A futuristic new Soviet embassy (half modernist skyscraper, half medieval watchtower, and popularly dubbed "the robot") would eventually come to tower over Miramar, dwarfing the nearby Jesús de Miramar cathedral that had formerly served the capital's well-to-do. Well before that, Marxism-Leninism came to be taught in state schools in the same rote form that the catechism and the Bible had been taught in parochial schools before. This new bargain took its toll on consciousness and culture, but the flip side was that living standards grew steadily throughout the next twenty years.

An example of problems and solutions in the realm of housing is the case of Teresita Roca, who in 1970 got on the bus from Santiago de Cuba with her four children to escape from an alcoholic husband and start a new life. For a week, the five of them stayed with her sister, who had come to the capital long before the revolution to work as a housemaid. Then they slipped into a former storefront on a main thoroughfare in Marianao, while Roca got a job in a daycare center nearby.

"We lived in a room right on the main sidewalk," Teresita recalls. "It was an illegal residence but the law also said we couldn't be thrown out. That was the story of those places—each time the housing agency talked someone out of there or found them a new place, somebody else slipped in before they could close it up or tear it down. We were just one in that series, and we lived there for almost two years. I felt happy just to have a roof over my head, even though the ceiling was falling down, and it leaked in the rain."

After two years, the state housing agency finally found the Roca family an apartment on Calle Montserrate at the edge of Old Havana, in a former hotel with an intriguing history. The Hotel Montserrat was "one of the most modern and luxurious hotels of Havana, containing eighty splendid rooms with all the comforts including telephones and private baths," an advertisement a year after its opening had claimed. The site had once been occupied by a Carabalí *cabildo*, the Isuamo Isiegue de Oro, which later became a mutual aid society for people of color. It was bought by Spaniards toward the end of the colony, and in 1924 a Spanish-born investor opened the new hotel, a five story steel-and-concrete edifice with an open-cage wrought-iron elevator, balconies shaded by awnings that faced the bustling street, and a penthouse apartment on top.

By the time of its nationalization, the Montserrat had become a residential hotel, and the only old residents still left when Teresita Roca arrived were a pair of French women, probably former prostitutes, who had remained in Havana. The rest of her neighbors were a mix of Cuban whites, blacks, and mulattos including a flower arranger, a steelworker, a sculptor, a ship captain, a bartender, a policeman, a dining hall worker, and a novelist. "When I was still in Santiago, I dreamed of a balcony," Teresita recalls. "So I figured this was that vision, come true." Blacks, practitioners of *santería*, and descendants of slaves, the Rocas had in a certain sense come home. Teresita set about subdividing the bathroom to make a tiny kitchen and bath, and expanding the living space by doing what tens of thousands of Havana families in tight quarters had done: building a *barbacoa* or loft. Teresita Roca went to work in the personnel office of an electric plant, and later sewed and crafted wigs and candles in her home. Her children all went to boarding school for either junior high or high school, relieving the crowding somewhat.

The exact etymology of *barbacoa* is lost in conflicting claims and legends, but it is the same as barbecue, and the coinage referred either to its being built on a rack of crossbeams like a cooking grill, or to the fact that this arrangement made the room so hot. Though the practice in Havana must date back to the late nineteenth century (because regulations prohibiting it were adopted at that time), the great flourishing of the *barbacoa* came after the revolution. Families who found themselves the new owners of high-ceilinged houses or apartments did not feel the need to ask anyone's permission. They invented. A stroll down many streets of older neighborhoods revealed new ceilings and floors, visible through open shutters that had once sat high on single-story walls.

Despite the Soviet influence within Cuban ideology and political culture, some of these critical issues were addressed by filmmakers.

Sara Gómez's *De cierta manera* (*One Way or Another*, 1974–77) looked at working-class Afro-Cuban culture, including its machismo, through the contrasting eyes of a white schoolteacher in an area slated for slum clearance and the black factory worker with whom she becomes involved. Throughout this story, the film intersperses documentary footage of the actual demolition of the El África *solar* in the barrio of Cayo Hueso (childhood home of Chano Pozo and a cradle of both crime and *rumba*) for replacement by a new housing project.

The relative abandonment of the housing stock during the 1960s was replaced by a new initiative in the early 1970s. This program attempted to decentralize the city by building bedroom communities on the east side of the bay (Alamar and Bahía) and the west side of town (San Agustín). The new concrete five-story apartment buildings—modeled after those of East European capitals like Moscow, East Berlin, and Sofia—were an escape valve for the pressure created by the lack of homes. They made use of a labor force of voluntary workers known as microbrigades, who built their own housing under the supervision of the universal state-sponsored unions. In a latter-day transfiguration of the Jabón Candado soapbar lottery, microbrigade-built two and three-bedroom apartments were distributed to union members by workplace assemblies on a mixed basis of participation, credentials, and need.

This novel incorporation of rank-and-file Havanans into housing construction succeeded in resolving some of the needs, but it brought new problems in its wake. Microbrigades turned out to be costly in terms of time and materials. Under the pressure to deliver the houses to those anxious to get out of their cramped spaces in the old neighborhoods, the brigades cut corners. The design—foreign to the architecture of Havana and to proposals developed by Cuban architects of the time—was not very good, either functionally or aesthetically. Alamar, for instance, became a sprawl of hundreds of nearly identical rectangular five-story concrete walkups spread out between a highway and the sea. The *cinco plantas* (five stories), as the design became universally known, had low ceilings by Havana standards, weak electrical and plumbing connections, leaks in the walls, and doors and windows with little resistance to hot sun and tropical storms. When the designs were increased beyond five stories, the buildings needed elevators, which generally could not withstand the number of residents they had to carry. Finally, many residents of the *cinco plantas* added makeshift extra rooms, and they closed in common spaces or used them as garages or patios in which to grow bananas. They sat on the stairways to play dominos and drink rum as they were accustomed to doing on the sidewalks and in the courtyards of older neighborhoods. Some began to call the microbrigade buildings "vertical solars."

In the area of food supply, imports of cattle feed and powdered milk gave birth to a sophisticated Cuban cheese industry, which put its products within the reach of all. Waiting lines for ice cream cones or three-scoop platters at Coppelia, which had become a fact of life in the early 1970s, dwindled to fifteen minutes or so. The shelves of the capital's stores filled with consumer products from Eastern Europe including canned meats and new televisions from Moscow, wines and fruit preserves and canned vegetables from Bulgaria, blenders from East Germany, and more. Many of these goods were sold in a so-called parallel market at elevated but not astronomical prices. The best-supplied of all the parallel market stores, where shoppers went to stock up for special occasions, was located in a spacious building in Centro Habana across from the old site of the Plaza del Vapor. Its official name was Supermercado Centro, but most people still called it by its old name, Sears.

Though only a minority of the capital's residents had the opportunity to buy a private car, the number of cars multiplied thanks to purchases by state companies and some designated categories of managers, professionals, and outstanding workers. Alongside the pre-1959 products of Detroit circulated more and more Russian Volgas and Ladas, Czech Tatras, and Yugoslavian Yugos. By the 1980s, rush hour traffic jams returned to Havana. They were called *tranque*, the word for what happens in Cuban dominoes when the game gets blocked. Day trips from Havana to Varadero beach by bus, complete with lunch and cabaña at a hotel, were cheap and easy to book.

At the Czech Culture Center on La Rampa, meanwhile, anyone could buy hand-blown glassware from Bohemia, pick up recordings of

Photo Credit: Greg Cluster

Alamar housing project residents playing basketball

the Prague Symphony playing Mozart, or enjoy imported Pilsen beer in glazed ceramic mugs. Across the street, where the Montmartre cabaret had been, the Restaurant Moscú offered the chance to try out a Russian soup, a *salianska* or *borscht* washed down with a cup of Ararat cognac or Stolichnaya vodka. Textiles were abundant, diverse, and cheap at Havana dry goods stores thanks to imports of natural and synthetic fibers from Eastern Europe. They combined with old Singer sewing machines and sewing skills to produce a variety of clothing styles and colors that surprised visitors expecting a population dressed in army fatigues or like Chairman Mao. When Carlos Larrinaga traveled to Germany for a training course in the late 1970s, he brought back the finished outfit his daughter Santa would premiere at the traditional party that celebrated her turning fifteen.

The close encounter with the East left other marks in the city's culture beyond the culinary ones. The teaching of Eastern European languages, along with Vietnamese and Chinese, had been initiated in the 1960s, but now it turned into a whole branch of education. Free language academies operated in every neighborhood, offering classes in many tongues by day or by night. Daniel Motola, after starting at the University of Havana in pure mathematics, decided he was not a mathematician but a linguist, and switched to Russian, which became his career. His mother— a Fidelista because of Castro's support for education rather than his ideology—told him this was a mistake, because Cuba was ninety miles from the United States and one way or another English would once again become the language to know. Meanwhile, her son León became one of tens of thousands of Cubans to study in the Eastern Bloc, spending six years in Warsaw becoming a specialist in physics and an electrical engineer before returning to work for a good salary at the ministry of armed forces. Those who went to northern Russia returned from long cold winters with memories of friendly and extroverted dormitory mates who insisted that they sit down to breakfasts of sardines, black bread, sausage, and vodka. Many brought back shoes and scarves they had bought in the immense department stores around Red Square in Moscow. More than a few also returned with a spouse from Warsaw or Leningrad or Prague.

A quarter century later, one of Havana's angry young men of the generation born in the 1980s, the writer José Manuel Sánchez, known by his pen name Yoss and for his punk/heavy-metal attire, would sum up the effect of the Russian cartoons, household goods, and rock groups that permeated his childhood: "Russian culture was a muted but constant influence in many areas of daily life, a contradictory symbol of both modernity and ugliness, poor quality yet great durability, an ambivalence that for decades shaped Cuban attitudes toward everything Russian, and that underlies our calling them 'bowling balls.'" *Bolos*, bowling balls, was indeed the slang term Cubans coined to describe the Russian advisors and technicians who lived among them, especially in the capital. They lived alongside Cuban residents in the FOCSA in Vedado as well as in Alfredo Hornedo's last two developments, the former Rosita de Hornedo and Riomar apartment complexes on the Miramar seafront, both renamed Sierra Maestra after the scene of the guerrilla struggle.

Bolos remains in the Havana idiom of those who lived through that period, and so do a very few words of Russian, out of many that were popular when enthusiasm for things Russian was at its height. An old automatic rifle used by the local militia is called a *pepechá* to this day, the summary of an academic dissertation in the University of Havana is still a *referat*, and many who studied in Kiev or Baku still call sausage *kalvasá* or say *smetana* for cream.

Foreign influence in those 1970s and early 1980s cannot be reduced, either, to Soviet Russia or the countries of the East. Cuban participation in wars in Angola and Ethiopia, the Sandinista revolution in Nicaragua, and the official friendships with Algeria and South Yemen all opened paths to and from a variety of global locales. Beyond the thousands that fought in the battle of Cuito Cuanavale against the troops of the South African apartheid regime, many more doctors, teachers, and sports instructors traveled to many parts of sub-Saharan Africa, Algeria, Yemen, Iraq, and Iran, as well as to Managua and Granada closer to home. From the early 1970s onward, the medical schools of Cuba and especially Havana produced an ever greater supply of doctors, who came to constitute an exportable surplus, ambassadors of a significant part of the country's foreign relations effort.

At the same time, thousands of foreign students came to study at the University of Havana, which took in Palestinians, Ethiopians, and Afghans, as well as Ukrainians and Vietnamese. So *habaneros* of those years—and not only those of the middle class—came into contact with more new cultures than ever before. House-seeking immigrants from Oriente like Teresita Roca were dubbed *palestinos* by the longer-time residents of the capital, who saw them as uprooted and homeless like the Palestinians whom they met.

Nor was the study of English completely neglected. Tony Irízar, who had once practiced the words to "Somewhere Over the Rainbow" on his way to and from the movies, became an English professor after earlier stints as an agrarian reform official, security officer, and principal of a junior high. Teresita Roca's daughter Gloria and the Larrinagas' son Carlitos became professors of English as well. "We had no money for me even to buy an alarm clock," Gloria remembers, "but I figured out how to tell the time before dawn by the position of the stars against the nearby buildings. So I could get up, do everything I had to do, and catch the bus to my college class."

In 1978, another group of Spanish-speaking strangers appeared on the streets of Havana. They were the opposite of the *bolos* in a certain sense—they were culturally Cuban yet they were distinct from those who lived there now. These were Cuban-Americans from Miami, invited back in a sudden thaw.

Since the early 1960s, Cubans who left for the United States had been condemned in official discourse as traitors, excoriated as *gusanos* (maggots or worms). Popular language had picked up the term as a synonym for those disaffected from the revolution, *gusanos* even if they lived in Regla, Vedado, or Marianao. On the other hand, family loyalty ran deep, and many in Havana kept up with their Miami relatives in spite of prohibitions (just as many of their opposite numbers swallowed pressures from the most rightwing Miami groups to cut all ties with "Communists" left behind). This contradiction torpedoed what would have been Carlos Larrinaga's first trip abroad since Chicago, a training course in Italy in the late 1960s, because the local CDR president denounced him for lending his phone to a neighbor to receive phone calls from her ex-husband in Miami. The implication was that he, despite his and Raquel's own service as officers of the CDR, would seek political asylum while in the capitalist West.

In 1978, however, this picture abruptly changed. Among the causes were the stabilization of the economy, the recovery of commercial ties with most Western countries other than the United States, and a certain temporary detente with the Carter administration (which for two years allowed U.S. residents to travel legally to Cuba for the first time since 1962). In this context, the Cuban government began a dialogue with a portion of the Florida émigré community. Those who had left were henceforth not *gusanos* but "the Cuban community abroad." They could board special charter flights to Havana's José Martí International Airport to see family and revisit old homes and haunts. Or, as the street humor of Havana described this sudden turnaround, "the worms have metamorphosed into butterflies now." Almost 100,000 butterflies came in the first year, in a spirit of reconciliation and with suitcases packed full of American consumer goods.

These visits, however, were soon overshadowed by the pent-up desire of a minority on the Havana shore to make the hop the other way, and permanently. In the spring of 1980, ten thousand of them crammed into the grounds of Peruvian embassy on Fifth Avenue in Miramar, seeking asylum not in Peru but in the United States. This chapter in the drama of migration to the north led to an organized exodus of 125,000 Cubans, some 80 percent of them from Havana. By an accord reached between the two governments, for a period of five months those who wanted to make the trip could board small craft from Miami which were allowed to land in the minor port of Mariel to the west of Havana, where the British had sheltered some of their ships while waiting to fight their way into Havana Bay in 1762. Those who left through Mariel ran the spectrum of the society—white and black, employed and unemployed, with all levels of jobs and education, including about 10 percent who were released from jails.

In some cases their departure was no surprise, as was the case with the writer who lived across the hall from Teresita Roca. Gay, censored, and forced to publish the majority of his work by smuggling the manuscripts abroad, Reynaldo Arenas had been jailed, released, and in search of a way to leave the country for years. In the meantime, he lived in the Hotel Montserrat, thanks to a thousand peso bribe to the official resident of the room, where Arenas too built a barbacoa and a terrace in the back. In *Before Night Falls*, his phantasmagoric first-person novel written in the United States, Arenas describes the Montserrat as "a real jungle on the far side of the law," a den of feuding families, witches, sex slaves, and thieves. Or, according to Teresita Roca's less sensational version, "We got along fine with him, we helped him, but later everybody got fed up with what he wrote about us that wasn't true."

The friends and families of some who made their way to Mariel, however, were completely surprised by their decision to emigrate. Isaac and Nirma Motola, the mechanic and the biology teacher, announced suddenly that they were going to join Nirma's relatives in Florida. The rest of the family had never heard them express this degree of disaffection, but two days later they were gone.

Though Alberto Motola later went to visit Isaac, and even put in some time selling shoes with him at a Miami flea market, in general Mariel set the clock of family reconciliation back many years. The official classification for those who left this time was neither *gusanos* nor *mariposas*, but *escoria*, the scum that floats to the top. Upon their arrival in Miami, they were received as *marielitos*. Both terms were derogatory. In Havana they were labeled criminals, and repudiated in public marches, sometimes by mobs outside the homes they were leaving. In South Florida, white and upper-class Cubans considered them inferior, because among them were too many blacks and people who didn't speak English.

Family visits to Havana were severely reduced—until the 1990s— while visits in the other direction, such as Alberto Motola's, continued on a limited scale. In a curious footnote, the CDR president who had nixed Carlos Larrinaga's trip to Italy in the 1960s went on a family visit to Miami in the 1980s and decided to stay. "Behind every extremist there's an opportunist," goes another piece of Havana street wisdom, chosen by Raquel Cañizares to explain this event.

Those who fit in neither category went on with their lives in Havana, but the theme of family reunion did not disappear. In the 1985 film *Lejanía* (Distance) by Jesús Díaz, a mother who had left her teenage son behind returns for a visit ten years later. Her attempt to revive the relationship runs up against the toll taken by distance and the lack of a shared life. The young man does connect, however, with the female cousin who has also come to visit, as their shared memories form a bridge across the cultural and geographic divide.

Other Cuban films of the 1980s also touched on sensitive spots. No female directors took the place of Sara Gómez, who died young. However, Tomás Gutiérrez Alea's *Hasta cierto punto* (Up To a Point, 1983) reprised the themes of class and gender with the story of a single mother who breaks barriers by going to work on Havana's docks, and the male filmmaker, working on a documentary, who falls in love with her. Pastor Vega's *Portrait of Teresa* (1979), begins and ends with still shots of its title character, a Havana textile worker. One shot is of her on the Malecón and the other is of her at the corner of San Rafael and Galiano, where a band is performing in the park where El Encanto once stood. Vega wanted to make a "problem" film and so surveyed a number of psychologists about the most prevalent dilemmas facing their patients. *Teresa* examined the "double shift" and double standard faced by the women of the capital: plunged into paid work and cultural activity but at the same time confronted with all their old household duties; given economic freedom by employment and divorce laws but subject to the sexual double standard of old.

Cuban films, along with simultaneous work in Brazil, Argentina, Bolivia, and Mexico, kick-started the birth of a new film aesthetic throughout Latin America, whose products were (and continue to be) showcased at Havana's annual Festival of New Latin American Cinema. Begun in 1979, the Festival projected its entries on screens throughout the barrios of Havana, and after the cinemas closed its participants and audiences partied all night in the Hotel Nacional.

The socialism of some abundance, which counted on the Cuban-Soviet alliance as its central pillar, began to falter in about 1985. Bureaucracy and overcentralization took their toll. The prolonged economic growth began to stagnate, and despite equal educational opportunity it grew more difficult to rise on the social scale. It was evident, for instance, that few youth, blacks, or women were getting into positions of power, and that religious believers were discriminated against for such posts. People complained that less and less could be settled in the meetings of local assemblies, while the number of bureaucrats multiplied. The mass media reflections of daily reality were boring and unreal. In the second half of the 1980s, trade union meetings, student meetings, and meetings of professionals and intellectuals discussed these problems. These were called "the process of rectification of errors and negative tendencies," or simply Rectification.

Among the problems discussed in the Rectification assemblies were absenteeism and lateness at work, shrinking productivity in factories, the inefficiency of the city's buses, the critical housing situation and lack of stable water supply in many barrios, and the lack of entertainment venues for young people. Another theme was all the red tape that had to be negotiated by the citizens as they bounced from one office to another, which popular language called exactly that, *peloteo*, being tossed around like a ball. In this context, a certain air of renewal suffused the press, especially the radio, which reported some of these heated assemblies. What began as a discussion of the causes of economic slowdown ended up being a debate about the role of the bureaucracy and party officials in all the organs of government, about rigidities of ideology and political mistakes.

Where this would have led if the economic base had remained intact is impossible to say. Once again, as many times before, the economies of the capital and the nation were about to be affected by events taking place somewhere far away. In the late 1980s, through the ten thousand kilometers of intense traffic and communication that linked and separated Moscow and Havana, the echoes of *glasnost* and *perestroika* could be felt. In Soviet publications such as *Sputnik* and *Moscow News* and *Literary Gazette* on sale in Spanish versions at the newsstands of Havana, a discourse which questioned the socialist system from top to bottom left Cuban readers astounded.

In August of 1989, *Sputnik* and *Moscow News* were removed from sale, but that summer the populace was busy dealing with yet another shock. General Arnaldo Ochoa, hero of the wars in Africa and one-time commander of the Western Army in charge of the defense of Havana, was put on trial along with other high officials of the armed forces and the Ministry of the Interior, accused of corruption. The public trial electrified the TV viewers of the capital and the island. At the end of the trial, Ochoa and others convicted of drug dealing and personal enrichment were sentenced to death. A few months later, the announcement of the demolition of the Berlin Wall closed this year full of surprises. Consequences now lay ahead that, like those following the triumph of the bearded rebels in 1959, almost no one accustomed to the Havana of the past three decades could guess.

16 The Blackout: Havana in the "Special Period" and Beyond

In part of a former mansion just off the Plaza de Armas, the gallery of the artist Pedro Pablo Oliva displays his paintings, among the most sought-after in Cuban art today. Oliva comes from the generation that studied in the 1960s in the National Art School, the fantastic complex of brick beehives and sinuous paths designed by Ricardo Porro on the former golf course of the Havana Country Club. Unlike the majority of students from the provinces who came to study in the capital, Oliva returned after graduation to his native Pinar del Río, a hundred miles to the west, where he went on creating his distinctive works. The human and animal figures in his canvases float in the air or recline in large armchairs, sofas, or beds, apparently sleeping, with peaceful expressions on their face. Unlike the art of his contemporaries, his work does not usually feature explicit ideological challenges, irony, or commentary on other works of art. Knowledgeable viewers are surprised, therefore, to discover "The Great Blackout" (*El gran apagón*), an enormous canvas that fills an entire wall of his gallery. In this painting, numerous creatures—children, grandparents, cats, youths, birds—are curled up in a sort of tunnel lit only by a few candles and kerosene lamps. The painting is swathed in darkness and shadow except for the feeble glow that illuminates the inhabitants of the space. Among them, not particularly standing out, appear the serene faces of José Martí and Fidel Castro. Both of them seem to be asleep.

The fall of the Berlin Wall in the autumn of 1989 and the breakup of the Soviet Union in the summer of 1991 were, for Cubans, the entrance into a tunnel, a prolonged *apagón*. Unlike residents of Warsaw or Prague

Photo Credit: Oscar Llanes

Pedro Pablo Oliva, "The Big Blackout" (1994). Oil on canvas. 290 x 520 cm.

or Budapest, the *habaneros* never had Red Army tanks patrolling their avenues or squares. So for them, the breakup of the Soviet bloc was not a moment of independence, a thrill of freedom or renewal. Rather, its effect was devastating. It brought an economic depression—not only a lack of light and electricity, but a simultaneous shortage of nearly everything else.

The demise of its special trade and aid agreements with Eastern Europe cost Cuba 80 percent of its import-export trade, brought an end to cheap oil and stable sugar prices, and cost the economy its main source of loans. As had happened with the loss of U.S. trade thirty years earlier, spare parts for machinery and inputs for agriculture and industry disappeared. Sixty percent of Cuban factories shut down or were forced to produce at bare minimum capacity. Electricity generation plummeted, as did supplies of food. "The revolution has only three problems," a typically ironic joke in the capital had it: "breakfast, lunch, and dinner." Most households in Havana had cooked on gas stoves or kerosene ones, supplemented by electric hot plates. Even when there was food to cook, now all three of these sources of energy might fail. Planned blackouts, by neighborhood, were instituted to share the electricity shortage equally. Unplanned ones added to the burden. Residents of the capital began to speak of *alumbrones*—brief periods when the lights went on. Those responsible for cooking, usually the women, often had to wait at home for the moment during the day that gas or electricity would come on. Those responsible for finding some food to cook, frequently the men, might be out scouring markets, legal ones or those underground.

By Latin American standards, no one was malnourished or starving in the Cuban capital, though the daily intake of vitamins and protein fell drastically. Havanans' anxiety about what they would eat and when grew. For those still working, lunchrooms at their jobs continued to serve a free basic meal, often just rice and beans—except that when there was no fuel, and both lunchroom and workplace shut down at midday. Schools, hospitals, clinics, and other essential services all kept functioning, if only on a shoestring. Many other facilities did not. Coppelia stayed open, but going for ice cream became an activity that took an entire afternoon or evening, with lines often four hours long. The government called the wartime-like austerity a "Special Period in Time of Peace." The euphemism stuck, and "Special Period" became the name of this crisis time.

Verónica Loynaz was living in Miramar in a large house surrounded by fruit trees and vines of blue bellflowers entwined in the fence. Unlike her aunt Flor, she did not live with thirty dogs, but rather with her husband, two small sons, two aging parents, three aunts, two dogs, and a few cats. She worked at a research center that studied European affairs, where she enjoyed a professional's salary that through the 1980s had guaranteed a comfortable life in socialist Havana's terms.

When the crisis broke out, what she could buy with her ration book suddenly shrank. The vegetable oil, soap, and detergent she was accustomed to getting at the state-run corner bodega nearly disappeared, as did the chicken and eggs. In the capital's ever-evolving slang, eggs were known for a time as *americanos* "because no one knows when they are coming or how many they will be." The monthly ration of beef became a mixture of ground-beef and soy powder of dubious flavor. The liter-a-day ration of milk still supplied to her younger son (as to all children seven or below) would not stretch to allow everyone in the household the morning *café con leche* to which all Cubans were accustomed. Off-ration sales of milk and other dairy products in Cuban pesos came to an end. There was no wheat flour, and the bread ration shrank to one small roll per person per day. The parallel market located around the corner from the bodega shut down. There were no more Bulgarian canned vegetables, Russian canned meats, German sausages, or Hungarian wines and sweets.

Although she was among the lucky ones who still had work, Verónica had to get there every morning by bike or on foot, because the city's bus service was decimated by lack of gas and spare parts. Hundreds of thousands of Chinese bicycles, distributed through workplaces, practically replaced cars on the streets. The Flying Pigeon, Forever, and Phoenix brands took the place of Ladas and old Chevies and Fords. Though these bikes were sturdy—the Flying Pigeon was said to have been used by Chinese peasants to bring harvests to market and by the Vietnamese to transport ammunition on the Ho Chi Minh Trail—they were heavy and limited to one gear. La Gran Habana had reached a total of 2 million inhabitants, spread out over an area of 280 square miles, a lowslung city with only a few tall buildings outside of El Vedado. For many thousands, the Special Period meant a bicycle trip of five to fifteen miles every morning and afternoon.

José Ramón Rojas, a cousin of the younger Larrinagas, worked as personnel specialist at the Pedagogical University in Ciudad Libertad. His job had formerly involved a bus commute from home to office, followed by many trips in a Ministry of Education car from his office to the Ministry in Old Havana, other offices, schools, teachers' residences, and student dorms. All of that now had to be done by bike. Throughout the city, three and even four people, parents and children, could be seen perched on handle bars, cargo racks, and makeshift extra seats of a single bicycle. At night, in blacked out zones devoid of the usual sound of radios, TVs, or record players, the ghostly sound of whizzing tires was punctuated by hisses of breath to warn other cyclists, or the tinkling of old-fashioned spring-action bells. Between the biking and the reduced diet, Havana became a city of citizens who ranged from slender to skinny. Very few looked like their photos from only a few years before.

In spite of being a committed member of the Communist Party, Verónica Loynaz found herself with no alternative but to buy food on the mushrooming black market. There one could find beans or eggs or vegetables brought privately from the countryside, as well as powdered milk and cheese and other commodities stolen from the hard-currency stores in tourist hotels or those maintained for diplomats. In relation to salaries, prices were high in the black market and astronomical in the dollar stores. The black market value of the Cuban peso dropped to 150 per dollar. Verónica's and her husband's salaries plus her parents' pensions equaled less than seven dollars a month.[1] Taking advantage of the yard surrounding the house in Miramar, she decided to create her own subsistence economy on the side.

This generation of Loynaz harvested the fruit from the trees of their garden to supplement their diets. Luckily, their plantain trees yielded *platanos burros*, a banana variety that could be eaten either raw or cooked. Above all, however, they devoted their yard to raising chickens, rabbits, and piglets. They acquired the animals from friends who went to the countryside to buy them from farmers, or sometimes from government stores in the city that offered them for this purpose. Thousands of families did likewise, using porches and makeshift window-boxes if they didn't have yards, so that the conflict between treating these animals as pets or as food became a staple of Havana humor and literature in the 1990s. One joke—or true story—told of the parents who named their chickens Breakfast, Lunch, and Dinner so the children would not lose sight of the problems they were intended to solve. *La Manteca* ("Lard"), a popular theater piece, revolved around a family raising a clandestine pig inside their apartment, an animal none could bring themselves to kill.

Over every extra duty that the economic crisis brought to the households of Havana hung the threat of the *apagón*, whether scheduled or unforeseen. After finishing her daily work as a researcher, Verónica Loynaz hurried home to face her domestic tasks before night fell. She had to see whether anything new had come in at the bodega, take care of the animals, invent a supper menu out of whatever was at hand, and urge the children to do their homework while daylight lasted—all before a blackout hit. On weekends, she went to the countryside in search of feed or fodder for the animals, and melted cakes of soap to serve in place of detergent in her washing machine, ready for the hours when there was electricity to make it run. She picked bellflowers from the vine to marinate for the week's vegetable salads. And finally, when they could, she and her husband went out to visit a pair of lucky friends who lived beside a maternity hospital, which meant that their current never shut off. In March of 1993, Havana was hit with yet another calamity, a vast and unruly winter hurricane later dubbed the "Storm of the Century" which drove the sea over the seawall, flooding inland for up to five blocks. This catastrophe flooded the home of the lucky friends who lived next to the maternity hospital. While helping them rescue their furniture and television set, Verónica decided it was time to change her life.

The next day she went to see a friend of her father's who worked in the import-export firm CIMEX, one of the state corporations newly created to earn foreign exchange for the public treasury. She decided to leave the research work which she had always enjoyed so much, and submerge herself in learning business, so she could earn a part of her salary in the hard currency which was becoming essential to daily life. She went to work for CIMEX in the commercialization of such Cuban products as commemorative and antique coins. To deal with the crisis, the government legalized possession of dollars by Cuban citizens, and made them the legal tender in an ever-broadening network of stores no longer limited to tourists and diplomats. On the import side of CIMEX, Loynaz worked on the acquisition of clothing and shoes to sell in these dollar-only outlets, *el shopping* as they soon became known.[2] CIMEX flourished as Cuba slowly went about reinserting itself into the capitalist world market. Today, the offices of CIMEX occupy the former Rosita de Hornedo (later Sierra Maestra) apartment-hotel on the Miramar seafront, which has recovered from the inroads of the Storm of the Century. In the meantime, as Cuban economic policy made room for more foreign companies and joint ventures, Verónica went to work for the Havana branch of an Indian home appliance firm.

The foreign business sector, however, was unknown territory for most of the city's residents. Among *habaneros* of color, the feeling was common that in this sector old patterns of racial discrimination had again reared their head. The foreigners that most of Havana saw were the growing influx of Italian, Spanish, German, and Canadian tourists, as the government promoted tourism as a quick source of foreign exchange. These tourists increasingly monopolized the few nightlife venues that were able to stay open. The Turquino Bar of the Habana Libre, the new Salsa Palace recently opened in the Riviera, the disco in the Comodoro and the emblematic Tropicana cabaret became exclusive sites for visitors with dollars. So what Havanans began to call "apartheid tourism" made these years of lean cows especially bitter.

Unlike the depression of the 1930s, this one took place in a city where all of the people had grown used to having access to these particular playgrounds—to not having to stop "at the door of a *dancing* or a bar/or at the desk of a hotel" as the triumphal verses of Nicolás Guillén's poem "Tengo" proclaimed from the pages of schoolbooks, a poem that practically everyone had learned by heart. The Malecón, the eternal nighttime porch of the Havana coast, now literally filled with people who brought portable radios, guitars, and bottles of homemade rum in search of recreation in a city battered by crisis and disillusion. The nicknames of the Cuban-style moonshine testified to its kick—*Chispa de Tren* (Train Spark) or *Saltapatrás* (Jump Back).

More than half of Havana had not experienced any earlier time to which the Special Period could be compared. The majority hadn't been born or couldn't remember the scarcities of the first years of the American embargo or the 1970 harvest, nor the inspiring hurricane of revolutionary ideas that had raged alongside this time of hardship. Many fewer could remember the ills of the decades before 1959. Those who did remember often believed that this last decade of the twentieth century was the worst they had ever known, and they felt the wind blowing in a completely new direction. The restoration of capitalism in Eastern Europe not only shook the daily economy of Cubans, but also shocked their way of thinking. On August 5, 1994, hundreds of them poured into the streets near the Malecón in Centro Habana, from the Prado to the Parque Maceo, in the first tumultuous demonstration of popular discontent in Havana in twenty-five years.

Although the initial motivation for this gathering was a rumor that a ship would arrive to take on passengers for a new version of the Mariel boatlift, the anxiety of the groups in the street overflowed into disorder, violence, and vandalism. They broke the windows of a dollar store and chanted slogans including "Down with Fidel." Castro himself, about to turn sixty-eight years old, promptly appeared on the same streets, walking down Calle San Lázaro toward the heart of the disturbances. Those who had silently watched the angry demonstrators a few moments before now welcomed Castro with applause and *vivas*, testimony to the volatile mixed emotions with which many in the city confronted these years of crisis, paralysis, and change.

This demonstration ended without significant effects on political stability, but it was clear that the city was teetering on an edge. A few days later, the government announced the opening of new farmers' markets, long requested at workplace assemblies and neighborhood meetings, where small farmers, cooperatives, and state farms could bring fruits, vegetables, and pork from the countryside to sell at prices regulated by supply and demand.[3] While very expensive by Cuban standards, these *agromercados* were significantly cheaper, more accessible, and less morally compromising than the black market. Together with other measures they quickly boosted the purchasing power of the Cuban peso, which soon traded for the dollar (in new legal state exchange booths) at the rate of twenty or twenty-five to one. More unexpectedly, the doors to northward migration were thrown open, without any kind of control.

Along the thirty miles of coral shores, inlets, river mouths and sandy beaches of greater Havana, emigrants launched every imaginable sort of boat and raft. This time, unlike the Mariel exodus of 1980, those who wanted to try their luck in the United States did not need a boat to come from Florida to fetch them nor a predetermined place to meet. An even greater difference between this and all other emigrations since 1959 was the attitude toward those who left displayed by those who stayed behind.

In Pogolotti, a few doors down from the home of Juan Valdés and his wife Daisy—where the CDR headquarters of the block were located—an entire family set to work building a raft in their own house. Laboring night and day, fastening pine boards to tractor inner tubes, they fashioned a craft which took up all of their modest living room. They made oars out of baseball bats and mops, and a sail out of an old sheet, and found a way around a moment of crisis when it seemed they wouldn't be able to fit the raft through the door. Then they carried it to the coastline accompanied by young and old neighbors of the barrio, all offering advice about the voyage or helping to convey the saints from the altar that the mother of the family had maintained in the back room of the house. Particular care was paid to Yemayá, goddess of the sea, and Eleguá, opener of doors and roads. The raft was launched, loaded down by the number of passengers and the weight of provisions they'd put together for the perilous trip. It promptly sank. After rescuing the saints, the family and its supporters returned to Pogolotti and got busy building a new boat.

This scene was repeated up and down the coast, from Mariel to Cojímar where the British had landed and Hemingway fished, to the beaches of Guanabo where tourists watched Cuban families send off their relatives among a mixture of cheers, tears, and entreaties not to risk their lives. "It was a kind of hysteria you had to see to believe," reported a resident of Calle 60 at the edge of Buenavista who watched the parade of rafts on trucks, carts, and shoulders proceed down hill past her house toward the coast. "It was shocking to me, but it showed how people wanted to do something, anything, anything at all."

Things did not go exactly as planned. Facing an unprecedented numbers of rafters, the U.S. Coast Guard did not do what it had done with the scattering of rafters or boaters who had taken this plunge and eluded Cuban patrols over the past thirty-five years. Instead of bringing these migrants to Miami and granting them resident status, U.S. authorities sent them to the naval base in Guantánamo and interned them in a tent city under the searing sun of Cuba's southern and easternmost part.[4] There they waited almost a year, 35,000 of them, the great majority from Havana, until the two governments could agree on what to do. When they finally got to Florida, this wave of Cubans would not be called exiles, or freedom fighters, or *marielitos*, but just *balseros* (rafters), a plain unvarnished fact.

After that summer of 1994, the doorway from Havana to Miami closed again from both sides. Thereafter, by official agreement, the only migrants to be accepted would be those who traveled on the 20,000 annual visas that the United States agreed to give, for which the residents of Havana could enter a lottery or apply in long lines that formed outside the United States Interests Section on the Malecón. Those who launched themselves into the sea knew that if they were intercepted by either U.S. or Cuban coast guard patrols, they would be brought back. But paradoxically, the *balseros* of 1994 (along with those who had left through Mariel fourteen years earlier) continued to be a presence in the life of Havana, much more so than those who left in the 1960s and 1970s and cut their ties. Fifty or a hundred dollars sent or brought each month by relatives and friends living abroad began to signify, for many families without other income in dollars, a way to keep their heads above water. Soon the total of such remittances sent by Western Union or carried by visitors reached a total of 800 million dollars throughout the island. The majority of these funds came to rest in Havana, in its widening network of dollar stores and currency changing stands. A CADECA (currency stand) went up outside every new farmers' market, so the remittances could be changed into Cuban pesos to buy vegetables and meat. Though corner bodegas continued to distribute minimum rations of certain staple foods, the dollar stores became the main source of other basics like cooking oil, pasta, canned goods, dairy products, and soap.

In the second half of the 1990s and first years of the new century, the injection of hard currency from tourism, remittances, and new exports, and the continued growth of farmers' markets of various types, provided an escape valve from the reigning tension. Slowly, *habaneros* gained back some of their lost weight. Blackouts, the symbols of the worst years of the crisis, decreased but did not go away. The twenty-centavo "camels," officially called Metrobuses and denominated with routes running from M1 through M6, took the edge off the transportation crisis. Along the same routes, for those who could afford a quicker and less exhausting alternative, state-regulated private taxis began to ply, mostly Detroit products of the 1950s. Because they cost ten pesos, they went by the popular name

"M-10." Private cars, tourist rental cars, and state or company cars gradually began reclaiming the streets from bicycles, though the bikes in no way disappeared. Meanwhile, other novelties began changing the physical face of the city, always in contradictory form.

To the west of the Almendares, where urban planners of past periods had called for preservation of a coastal strip that would truly let residents *mirar al mar*, new hotels grew up to house new waves of tourists, clashing with the ambience and blocking the view. The grassy, wooded Monte Barreto, where Alberto Motola had gardened in the 1970s, disappeared under an anonymous office-park-style hotel built in a joint venture with the French chain Novotel. Walking along still-elegant Fifth Avenue, with its green median and leafy trees, one came to not only the ex-Soviet (now Russian) embassy and the nearby towers of the 1980s-built Hotels Tritón and Neptuno with a whiff of the microbrigade about them, but also to the new Hotel Panorama which appeared to have been flown in from Cancún, and a square, undistinguished office block hopefully called the Miramar Trade Center, built to house foreign firms.

In spite of these eruptions of contemporary bad taste, the drive to convert Miramar into an international commercial district also brought benefits to the old buildings of the neighborhood. Hotels such as the Copacabana and the Comodoro were renovated, and many of the mansions along First, Third, and Fifth avenues were restored and rented to foreign firms such as Castrol, whose logo figured prominently in front of one of them, or new Cuban state corporations like CIMEX. A much larger wave of restoration swept through the older parts of city—along the Prado and especially in Old Havana, the former walled city between the Prado and the bay.

Around the Parque Central, the revival of tourism brought the resurrection of tattered monuments like the hotels Inglaterra, Plaza, and Sevilla. The nineteenth-century Telégrafo rose literally from its ashes on the corner of Prado and Neptuno. The restoration of the Centro Gallego, Centro Asturiano, Capitolio, and other nearby buildings brought some of the old splendor back to this former showpiece area, which had been abandoned by both the capitalist development of the 1950s and the socialist priorities of the decades after. Tourists followed, drawn away from Vedado by the architecture, atmosphere, proximity of the colonial quarter, and the animation of city life. In the "hot corner" of the park, to the south side of the statue of Martí, Cuban men of all descriptions gathered as they always had to argue about baseball. They disputed the make-up of the Cuban national team which they patriotically supported, or the merits of famous players of the past, or developments in the U.S. major leagues which they continued to follow from afar—including the key games won by El Duque Hernández and other Cuban stars.

In Old Havana, the pace of restoration and improvement in the late 1990s and early 2000s seemed to quicken month by month. The priority granted to tourism brought unprecedented resources and authority to the office of the Historian of the City, in charge of preserving the nearly five centuries of national heritage and putting it on display. Through drive, creativity, and ability to gain the trust of the predominantly working-class residents of this historic district, the office and its director, Eusebio Leal, managed to win direct control over the redevelopment of the old city. Above all, the Historian won the authority to tax tourist and commercial development and directly reinvest a share of the profits into both historical reconstruction and improvement of the water and gas supply and other imperatives or enhancements of daily life.

The Historian's office gradually restored the Plaza Vieja, where the old mansions had long deteriorated into overcrowded apartment buildings and *solares*, putting part of the space to new uses to serve both tourism and the city's artistic and cultural life. The Palace of the Counts of Jaruco, which we have mentioned before as the colonial home of the family of the Countess of Merlín and ex-owners of the fictional food vendor Genoveva de Santa Cruz, was restored and given to an arts organization for its exhibit rooms and office. The ground floors of other buildings on the onetime market square became galleries and even a microbrewery. On the rooftop of a renovated apartment building, a *camara oscura* periscope was installed, allowing guided "tours" of the old city and the bay as seen from above. Unlike in New York's SoHo or the historic districts of Paris, however, these improvements did not price out the old residents. The renovated apartments on the upper floors of most of the buildings on the

Plaza Vieja and nearby streets were returned to former residents, who had meanwhile been housed in temporary units nearby—though, to be sure, to reduce density other former residents were given apartments in outlying districts such as Alamar. The *camara oscura*, like almost all historic monuments, museums, concerts, and other attractions in the old city, charged tourists and residents differentially. It admitted Cubans for one peso and foreigners for one dollar apiece.

In the Plaza de Armas, the former palace of the Counts of Santovenia became the Hotel Santa Isabel once again, a luxury tourist spot as it had been in the nineteenth century under the management of Colonel Lay of New Orleans. But the office building that had once housed the U.S. Embassy, now restored from its deterioration, became home to a new

Photo Credit: Greg Cluster

Plaza Vieja, Old Havana, after restoration. At back left is the Fondo de Bienes Culturales art center and gallery, formerly the Palace of the Counts of Jaruco (see Chapter 3). The restored buildings also house an elementary school (note the uniformed Cuban school children), a hard-currency microbrewery and café (back right), and a rooftop cámara oscura for viewing Old Havana as a whole.

neighborhood library on the ground floor and Cuba's Museum of Natural History on the floors above. The former home of the freedwoman Juana Carvajal, which had deteriorated from *solar* to uninhabitable ruin by the 1980s, was meticulously restored to its eighteenth-century appearance, its murals carefully uncovered from beneath successive layers of plaster and paint. It now serves as the city's archeological museum, displaying the artifacts dug up in the course of the efforts to rescue Old Havana from neglect. Elementary school classrooms in the barrio have also been distributed among its many old and new museums, so that the heritage can be built into their curricula.

Other resurrections brought by the renewal of tourism and a dollar economy were not as positive as these. The ghost of Havana as the city of sin, temptation, and pleasure-for-hire rose from the coffin where it had been resting for a third of a century. Alongside retired Canadian or German couples and groups of adventurous backpacking youth, the planes touching down in José Martí International Airport began to unload single men and women, above all from Spain, Italy, and Mexico, who came not only for sun and sea but also for the smiling and seductive mulattas and mulattos who appeared in advertisements and postcards in the foreground of beaches and cabarets.

In search of the necessary dollars to get through the month, and also looking for bridges to emigration, hundreds of young Cuban women and men began to circulate in the tourist area, working as part-time or full-time sexual companions. The majority were well educated, many of them with professions and jobs. The city's hotels, discos, and beaches became centers of this new prostitution, which the language of the street baptized as *jineterismo*. To *jinetear* (derived from the word for horseman or jockey) previously meant to bust ass in pursuit of something, and had therefore been identified with hustlers who changed money or acted as informal concierges for the relatively scarce foreign visitors. Now it came to mean selling one's ass to tourists. The image of Havana as a destination for sexual tourism, reproduced in the tales of travelers, gave the *jineteras* and *jineteros* a mythic status reflected in films, novels, and even salsa songs that circulated on the world market. Havana resident and leading crime novelist Daniel Chavarría, a Uruguayan exile whose pre-Special Period books had featured Cuban spies and grassroots characters outwitting agents of the CIA, tells how in the late 1990s he invented *jineteras* as his new heroines to meet the expectations of foreign publishers (though his new characters, like his old ones, usually turned the tables on the foreigners at the end).

In its sex industry, as in its dependence on remittances, Havana came to inhabit not so much a "Special Period" as the real world of late twentieth-century Latin American capitals, from Santo Domingo to Buenos Aires to Bogotá. It did not, however, return full-blown to the era of Graham Greene or *Godfather II*, either in the size of this industry or in its place in the city's social life. Many of the young *jineteros* of both sexes were not looked down upon in the barrios where they and their families lived. Their contribution to the domestic economy, especially in families that had no aunt or uncle or son or daughter abroad, could be decisive in the attempt to make ends meet every month. In more than a few cases, the *jineteros/as* ended up maintaining lasting and long-distance relationships that their families could look upon as a sort of engagement—and sometimes it was. The embassies of Spain, Italy, Mexico, and other countries processed more and more marriages between foreigners (generally middle aged) and their younger Cuban partners, who eventually emigrated and came to form parts of families regarded as respectable in their new homes.

Emigration in the 1990s and 2000s was not limited to *balseros*, U.S. visa lottery winners, and *jineteras* or *jineteros*. Many professionals sought or found work in Europe or South America, teaching courses or designing computer systems or training athletes or using whatever skills the Cuban education system had given them. Some went temporarily, on short-term contracts. Others went for good.

Daniel Motola went to Bolivia on a temporary contract, negotiated by the Ministry of Education, to teach educational methods at a provincial university. In the meantime, his mother's prediction was proven right, as he and hundreds of other professors of Russian retrained to teach English—newly revalued as the language of international commerce, tourism, and academic exchange. Teresita Roca's daughter Gloria married an American colleague who had been invited as a visiting professor in the university English department where she taught, and she went to the United States to teach Spanish and study for a Ph.D. Others who had studied languages found jobs on both sides of the Atlantic. Of two brothers who had been undergraduates in Gloria's department, one went to Spain to work in tourism and then as an English teacher, while the other set to work at home learning Italian, which allowed him to specialize in freelance translation of bureaucratic documents for the binational marriage boom.

One profession that figured heavily in emigration and work abroad was music. Sergio Larrinaga, Carlos and Raquel's third son, left for Europe in 1995 to follow the market for Cuban music, pursuing his career as a percussionist in Italy and Holland. He was far from the only Cuban musician in search of hard-currency employment. The renewal and dollarization of the Havana music market had begun in 1994 with the inauguration of the Palacio de la Salsa in the Hotel Riviera and other dance venues like La Cecilia near the Playa de Marianao and Papa's in the modernized yacht basin formerly called Barlovento, now rebaptized as Marina Hemingway. The best bands in the country rotated through these stages, especially Los Van Van (still adapting and going strong a quarter century after the 1970 harvest), NG La Banda, the always provocative Charanga Habanera, and the groups headed by Adalberto Álvarez, Isaac Delgado, and Paulito F.G. At the tables and on the dance floors of the clubs, a new breed of clients joined the tourists and the few fortunate Cubans there. These were minor league talent scouts seeking acts for bars in Amsterdam or Hamburg, and major league recording executives intent on investing in the juicy and undercapitalized Cuban music business and building its international appeal. Suddenly, the musicians in top bands began to earn dollars and drive Audis around Havana, inaugurating a new style of life which was equally vilified and admired.

The most famous case of the resurrection of Cuban music in the world market was the Buena Vista Social Club. The Social Club phenomenon was the result of a careful merchandising operation which made use of the formidable talents of old smiling musicians who smoked big cigars, drank rum, and played acoustic instruments. The Cuban music of the 1920s and 1930s, already familiar to North American and European ears, thus made a new appearance as a natural product uncontaminated by technology and splendid in its simplicity. In the concert film that followed the initial success of the album, these engaging musicians appeared against the background of a dirty but imposing city, unpainted and enchanting, whose beautiful buildings and residents shined in the midst of physical decay just as the aged musicians did. Above all, the film and the music evoked the magical images of Graham Greene and Ernest Hemingway, buried in the memory of the West. The popularity of Buena Vista Social Club spread like wildfire and opened a new path in Cuban music.

For their own part, Havanans without dollars, who were the majority, kept going to the Salon Rosado of the Tropical, where the famous bands often played in between their more lucrative engagements and international tours. At La Tropical, a new kind of music was taking shape. This was *la timba*, an updated evolution of *son*. Extending the experience of salsa, *la timba* added new elements of musical fusion, sprinkled extremely rapid rhythms into the mix and led the dancers to show off their abilities with abrupt, fluid, sensual moves not easily accessible to European tourists. *Timba*, Los Van Van's Juan Formell explained in one interview, "is any Cuban rhythm, then mixed with Afro-Urban American styles—funk, jazz, soul, blues, rap, anything that jives the hips."

Timba brought different subjects and languages into the mix as well as new rhythms and steps. Invocations of the gods of Afro-Cuban religions, which had practically vanished from Cuban popular music, reappeared in the new lyrics. Changó, Orula, and Yemayá were acclaimed from the leading stages, their names chanted by thousands of excited dancers. In a song called *¿Y qué tu quieres que te den?* ("What do you want them to give to you?") the lead vocalist of Adalberto's band sang rap-style lyrics that spread from mouth to mouth, asking the "packed house" of the dance hall not to hold back, but to make their requests of Elegguá (who "opens the roads, and that's the truth") and other *orishas*. The packed house always repeated along with the singer: *And what do you want him to give to you?*

Outside the dance hall, of course, asking and waiting were not enough. Cuban *orishas* also helped those who helped themselves.

Economic reforms that accompanied dollarization and farmers' markets also legalized small-scale self-employment in a variety of trades. Following this reversal of the "revolutionary offensive" of 1968, many in Havana set up shop as auto mechanics, carpenters, manicurists, or plumbers. Pablo Larrinaga, an office machine mechanic like his father, began to repair essential home appliances in his free time, from electric fans to rice cookers. Fast food stands like that of his great-grandfather repopulated the streets of the city, offering homemade sweets and drinks and fritters and sandwiches. More new services flourished with government licenses or without them: baking birthday cakes to order, teaching private classes of English or Italian, selling crafts, gardening, cleaning houses, catering weddings (with photos, dresses, video, food, and drink) and renting rooms and houses to tourists along with food or city tours or classes in Cuban dance. Approximately a quarter of the workers who had previously worked for the state now lived on an income from this type of work.

Clandestine restaurants in private homes had emerged in the early 1990s and were legalized soon after. Their popular name, *paladares*, came from that of a fast food chain established by the villainess of a popular Brazilian soap opera to which most of Cuba's TV viewers were addicted for entertainment and escape. *Paladares* sprang up in the living rooms of elegant houses and in garages and bedrooms of more modest ones. One, the famous Juana la Cubana in Vedado, served its fried pork, fried fish, fried plantains, rice, and beans in the single room of an apartment-with-*barbacoa* in which the beds were folded up against the wall during business hours. *Paladares*, however, remained subject to strict inspection as to the sources of their ingredients, some of which were available or affordable only on the black market. So they inhabited a gray area much like the *casabe* vendors of the sixteenth century who had to establish where they got their yuca from.

Luchando (struggling) is the universal term for this process of finding some way to make a necessary buck. Not everyone could set up a *paladar* or had a saleable skill. Thus some dedicated themselves to *bísnes*, to buying and selling things obtained legitimately like cigarettes or sugar from their ration or things stolen from the warehouses of the state. All told, the ingenious residents of the city came up with hundreds of such activities—illegal, semilegal, or quite legal but not quite by-the-book. Exaggerated descriptions popped up in the fiction published in Cuba in the late 1990s and 2000s just as the clandestine pigs had nosed their way into the plays and films of the years shortly before.

In Leonardo Padura's *The Novel of My Life* (2002), one character describes his friend's business this way: "He makes rum in his own house, and has a machine to seal the caps the same as in the factory. Then, with two or three contacts he has, they sell this rotgut rum in the dollar stores and he takes the same number of bottles of good rum and sells it himself at a lower price. So his confederates in the store never get caught stealing, because there aren't any bottles missing, and he's always got steady customers. He told me that soon, he's going to start making Coca-Cola too." In Mylene Fernández's *Other Answered Prayers* (2003), the heroine's neighbor invents the expedient of renting spots on her balcony to foreign tourists, who can enjoy Havana's glorious sunsets for a dollar a pop. Besides stretching the hostess's budget, the practice helps out the visitors who "prefer enjoying the Havana of their dreams without having to actually rub elbows there." Low-level corruption has of course accompanied all these activities, as inspectors and functionaries of various sorts are bribed with money or services to look the other way.

Equally important, however, is the fact that most of these forms of extra-legal activity also support the safety net (or high-wire act) of free or very inexpensive state services that continue to function despite the crisis. In any family, someone's racket may allow someone else to dedicate herself or himself to a job in a hospital or clinic or theater, and the same individual often works in both spheres. The teacher who coaches would-be emigrants in English for dollars also teaches in a high school or college with equal care. The electrician who moonlights installing cables for pirate internet access also keeps the low-rent apartment building's collective water pump working. The bus driver who sells gas on the black market also drives the crowded metropolitan bus, under very difficult conditions, every day.

One way or another, and thanks also to other economic policies and events that lie outside the scope of this history of the city, the crisis in its original form began to fade. The dual currency remained an inescapable fact of life, but after 2004, U.S. dollars no longer circulated. Instead, the hard-currency sector now used a new, separate Cuban "convertible peso" that could be acquired with U.S. or Canadian dollars, Euros, British pounds, etc. In popular speech it was usually referred to by its acronym, CUC, pronounced "kook." By hook, crook, or CUC, most *habaneros* gained back the weight they had lost, and the sea of bikes in the streets ebbed, so that Havana in peak commuting hours no longer seemed so much like Hanoi (which was itself evolving into a city of motorbikes). A light grew visible at the end of the long, dark tunnel, but everyone emerged into a very different place than the one they had left a decade before. What protection the tunnel had offered them had been distributed unequally. Some now had children abroad, while others had retired from old jobs and taken new ones. A good many had better salaries, sometimes double what they were making before, and some (such as doctors, teachers, sports instructors, and artists) now counted on regular stints working in other countries of either the First or Third World, with modest hard-currency salaries to subsidize their Havana lives. Another obvious fact was that Havana had more old people and fewer young ones than ever before, thanks to the combination of continued health services, insecurity about the future, and reduced births.

Racially, as in every other way, the effects of the ten-year tunnel were mixed. Some neighborhoods with the highest concentration of black population, like Old Havana, breathed a certain optimism exhaled by the restored buildings and the prosperity that tourism brought. In others, like Cerro or La Lisa (beyond Marianao), the shortage of employment and housing, exacerbated by a surge of immigrants from the eastern provinces seeking the opportunities of the capital, could be felt in the streets. With relatively fewer relatives abroad and less presence in the well-paid posts in tourist hotels administered by foreign firms, black Havanans—whose ancestors had lived in the capital since the days of the free Africans of the sixteenth century—did not so much try to escape the city as to find new niches which would permit them to advance.

All told, Havana emerged from the tunnel into a twilight zone, something that was no longer the Special Period but as yet had no name. On the one hand, it was a city in the grip of disillusion and abandonment. On the other, it was animated by a drive for reconstruction which sought to offer jobs and social protection to young and old, black and white. In the midst of such contradictions, as had been true ever since the appearance of Francis Drake's fleet outside the mouth of the bay, the population continued to unite and cooperate in the face of any external threat.

In the late summer of 2005, an enormous hurricane called Wilma moved steadily toward Havana, its size and strength presenting a threat almost like an impending nuclear attack. As the hurricane approached from the east, the *habaneros* boarded up windows, took shelter in the more solid houses of their neighbors, bought great quantities of bread and crackers, warehoused potable water, and teamed up to push Chevies or Ladas awaiting repair or gas to safety. They lit candles to Yemayá Olokkún, the patroness of storm-tossed waters, and to St. Christopher after whom San Cristóbal de La Habana had been named. They sat religiously in front of the television to watch the weather report which showed satellite images of the monstrous hurricane blowing toward the bay where the treasure fleets had taken shelter.

Miraculously, Wilma skirted the southern shore of Cuba. Havana got drenched but avoided a direct hit. The hurricane then hovered over the Yucatán peninsula 120 miles to the west, and finally followed the Gulf Stream toward Florida, leaving Havana behind. That night Juan Valdés, the Larrinaga-Cañizares, Daniel Motola, Verónica Loynaz, and all those who lived some distance from the sea went to bed relieved to escape hundred-plus mile an hour gusts, glad that the rain had subsided. But in the predawn hours the sea rose and began to pour over its wall and into the city, from the rocky coast of Miramar to the Bay of Carenas itself. Salt water penetrated block after block of streets and houses in Vedado and Centro Habana, especially between the Hotel Riviera and the Parque Maceo, land stolen from the sea a century before. The flood destroyed walls within the massive and newly restored Castillo de la Punta, the fort that had defended the mouth of the bay during the taking of Havana by the English in 1762. When day dawned, a Monday, the coastline had moved. The only vehicles cruising up and down the Calle Calzada, where the gardens of the Loynaz de Castillo had looked toward the coast in the 1920s and 1930s, were lifeboats rescuing the residents of flooded homes. A few days later, the sea decided to retreat as suddenly as it had advanced. The neighborhoods all along the Malecón seemed to have emerged from a shipwreck. The flood had dragged huge boulders five hundred yards inland to the Calle Línea, beyond Calzada—along with boards, planks, tree branches, lampposts, and even six-packs of beer which the sea had plucked from the expensive stores and cafés bordering the Malecón. The ornamental plants, the bushes, and the grass along sidewalks and in the yards of the houses had changed color. There was no electricity, and government crews were supplying free canned goods, pasta, and powdered milk to all the families of the inundated zone.

Even in the midst of the flood, however, the families who lived in the water-soaked houses had come out at first light to witness the spectacle of the sea breaking noisily over the seawall. They stood watching with their eternal curiosity, joking with those who came from other parts of the city to observe the taking of the Malecón by the sea. Then it was time to come back to life, to clean up the ruins, to set up the domino table on some dry sidewalk or corner while the sea went back where it belonged. Time, as a smiling mulatto said as he watched the sea retreat, "to go on *luchando*," to continue the struggle the way that residents of the port city had always done.

Epilogue (2006–2017)

A dozen years after Hurricane Wilma, a walk down one of the city's oldest streets offers ample testimony as to how the city's residents continue *luchando* in new times. To walk down Calle Obispo in Old Havana today, from one end to the other, is like taking a trip through the economic and social changes sweeping the city and the island.

Although its name, which means "bishop," pays tribute to the prelates Jerónimo de Lara and Morell de Santa Cruz (the latter was taken prisoner by the British during their occupation of Havana in 1762), Obispo functioned from the seventeenth century to the mid-twentieth as the city's most important commercial artery. Traces of that history are everywhere, from the imposing bank buildings that once belonged to the North American Trust Company, the Banco Gelats, and the Banco Gomez-Mena to the storefronts with such names as Johnson Drugs, Western Union, and Woolworth still visible on their facades. Near the bottom of Obispo, close to the Plaza de Armas and the port, is the Hotel Ambos Mundos where Hemingway began writing *For Whom the Bell Tolls*. After a long commercial decadence that began with the revolutionary changes of the 1960s, the decades of the 2000s and 2010s have breathed new life into this axis of Old Havana. The new winds stem in part from a political fact of these decades, the transition from the Fidel Castro presidency to that of the first vice-president, Raúl.

Obispo is now a pedestrians-only street, closed to automotive traffic. To a walker recently arrived from other parts of Havana, of the island, or abroad, the first impression is likely to be the intensity and vibrancy of the crowd. The narrow street and sidewalks have recovered their old hum of movement and commerce after the blackout of the Special Period. What is newest along this old Havana street, however, is its diversity. Anyone wanting to learn about the social and economic changes underway, to see with their own eyes how the different social groups are coexisting and interacting, to see both public and private economies, official Cuba and social Cuba, islanders and foreigners, the most varied kinds of markets and the two official currencies that still circulate in the country, the spectrum of religions and skin colors, the clothing and the culture that are superimposed in the city of Havana, should go right to this street and take notes.

We could begin our virtual visit to the Calle Obispo almost anywhere. Since our visit is in the form of a book, we will begin with bookstores. Consider the two bookstores that face each other at the very first intersection, where Obispo crosses Calle Bernaza. Are they state-owned, or private? Why, if you look through their windows on opposite sides of the street, do you see such different prices? Are they selling their volumes in Cuban pesos (CUP) or hard-currency ones (CUC)? How can you guess the quality of their titles, or the income levels of their customers?

The contrast between these two bookstores—La Moderna Poesía and Ateneo Cervantes—is not unique. Although Obispo seems like an ordinary street, it is also a hall of mirrors like those in old amusement parks, offering visitors images and representations that are almost always wrong. The incongruence is multiplied because there are bookstores all up and down the street. Some are state-run, doing business in pesos, others state-run in hard currency, others private, almost always in CUC. Some have ample space, plate glass windows, shelves of brilliantly varnished wood, internal stairways and balconies. Others occupy the entryway of a multi-family apartment building or a narrow living room piled high with used books, including many that were previously sold in the more elegant stores, but are now offered at higher prices in the makeshift ones. In this curious hall of mirrors, the works of the best literature, still smelling of new ink, may cost ten times less than the most ordinary used ones. To guess what is going on, especially for a foreign visitor, is a feat.

The picture is further complicated by coffee shops and lunch counters of all sizes and for all budgets, eat-in or take-out; restaurants whose employees solicit passersby, menus in hand; five star hotels in former sugar-baron mansions alongside small apartments converted into pensions that rent modest rooms to foreign tourists by the night or week, or to Cubans for a few hours at a time; state-run stores that sell designer-label eyeglasses and clothing, next to tiny private stalls where a smiling young woman offers caps bearing the *I* of the Havana *Industriales* baseball team or the logo of the Spanish soccer squad Real Madrid, Che Guevara t-shirts or olive-drab berets with his red star. You can buy dresses and vests knitted from packing twine, and plastic bearded guerrilla figures, all piled together on makeshift shelves.

Along Obispo we will also find an outdoor artisans' market, where members of the Association of Artistic Artisans of Cuba sell their adornments for the home and body. We will find numerous barber shops and hair salons, most but not all of them private, offering sophisticated treatments and cuts, not particularly cheap. But also in this urban landscape are mechanics, electricians, carpenters, shoemakers, and cell phone repair and unlocking wizards, all offering service in either of the two currencies at prevailing rates of exchange. Obispo even has a pet store, where upper-class dogs and cats can be bathed, trimmed, combed, and brushed.

And, of course, the neoclassical bank buildings still stand, many of them in the complex near the Plaza de Armas once called the "Cuban Wall Street," most of them housing Cuban state banks and financial offices as they have for the past sixty years. Elsewhere, a second floor balcony has a hand-lettered sign attached, *se vende este apartmento,* apartment for sale, and an inquiry to a museum doorman across the street yields the alleged asking price of $160,000, and an offer to introduce you to the owner.

***

By the end of this brief epilogue, we hope to have provided some lenses through which to see more clearly what's being reflected in the hall of mirrors. For the moment, let's leave Obispo for an airplane en route from the province of Holguín to Havana in July of 2006, nine months after Hurricane Wilma. On this flight, Fidel Castro suddenly fell ill. The suddenness was surprising, but his replacement (at first provisional, later permanent) as President was not. He was succeeded, as spelled out in the constitution and in many previously announced plans and procedures, by his younger brother Raúl, then seventy-five years old.

Physically, Raúl Castro was unlike Fidel, one of whose many unofficial nicknames was "El Caballo," a reference both to his athletic stature and proclivities and to the fact that in the Chinese *charada,* the underground numbers game, the horse was the symbol for the number one. At 5'5", Raúl more resembled his Cuban mother than his Galician-born father. He was not a charismatic orator nor had he mastered the ability to improvise long speeches, and he had never been an athlete. On the other hand, in private conversation he was more typically Cuban, enjoying jokes, dancing, and having a drink, none of which were true of his older brother. In the armed rebellion of the 1950s, though an effective guerrilla commander, Raúl had stood out particularly as the head of a *de facto* state, directing departments of education, health, justice, agrarian reform, security, and a small air force within the territories seized from the Batista regime. During the Special Period of the 1990s, it was widely rumored in Havana that Raúl was the one to convince his brother of the need to re-open private farmers' markets to lure food to the capital and other cities. It was expected that his leadership might tilt further in that direction in the new conditions of the twenty-first century.

One of the first such new steps was a public recognition that the private sector constituted a legitimate part of the socialist system. With that came an increase in the number of licenses granted to small private businesses. Although legislation authorizing a list of sole-proprietor occupations had been adopted more than a decade before, the fifteen district administrations within the capital had established a ceiling for each, so that the number of barbers, manicurists, shoemakers, pizza bakers, or tropical fish breeders in each district could not exceed a certain limit. Licenses for taxis and for renting out rooms were frozen throughout the city, and *paladares* could not serve more than twelve diners at a time. The new winds brought by the Raúl Castro administration began dissolving this ceiling bit by bit, especially once Fidel's retirement became permanent and the National Assembly recognized Raúl as the new president and Fidel's replacement in all of his positions (concluding, in 2011, with that of Secretary of the Communist Party). By the most recent count, of Havana's total employed workforce of 785,000 people, 136,659 are employed in the private sector.

With the expansion of private taxi service, the look of the city's streets changed. The number of old U.S. cars circulating through Havana seemed to multiply overnight. The advantage of these Chevrolets, Studebakers, Fords, and Plymouths compared to the more abundant Ladas, Moskviches, and Polish Fiats was their capacity to hold six or more passengers while traveling along popular fixed routes. Thus the enterprising new taxi drivers from such working-class districts as La Lisa or San Miguel de Padrón went off to the small towns and the cities of the interior in search of these old behemoths that could be put to work in the more promising Havana market. *Habaneros*, always ready to invent new words for new phenomena, didn't call them Fords or Chevies or Old American Cars, but *almendrones*, a word derived from a type of large coconut-palm-dwelling cockroach whose shape bore a striking resemblance to the output of Detroit's auto plants in the 1940s.

One of the many customers for these *almendrón* drivers was Juan Valdés, still living in the neighborhood of Pogolotti and now employed as a historian by the Institute of Cuban History, housed in Domingo del Monte's former mansion where Centro Habana met Habana Vieja. Though he mostly worked at home, when he needed to go to a meeting at the Institute, Juan could climb into a 1952 Ford station wagon with an extra seat installed in the cargo area and a diesel engine from some Mercedes or Hyundai under the hood to save on fuel costs. That vehicle would take him all the way downtown along with nine other passengers—all the while emitting the sounds and smoke of a motorcycle—for ten Cuban domestic pesos. The price was twenty-five times the cost of a city bus, but only one-twenty-fifth the cost of a taxi charging in CUC.

Juan continued to live in the same working class barrio where he had been since the 1970s. When his old friends teased him by asking what he was doing stuck in this down-and-out neighborhood instead of moving to the house he'd inherited from his mother in historically more upscale La Vibora, he would answer that he liked it because its residents (*la negrada*, the black-skinned ones, in his habitual ironic tone) maintained a high sense of solidarity with mutual aid as the norm, and on hot nights the Valdés family could sleep more securely with their front door open than anywhere else in town. Juan—the only blue-eyed, white-skinned resident of the block—and Daisy, the cinnamon-skinned doctor, had instead gone about repairing and improving their old wooden house at the end of the street, inherited from the aunt who had brought Daisy up, president of the local CDR until she was afflicted by Alzheimer's at the end of her life. After so much repairing, and so many years living in the neighborhood, Juan couldn't ever feel more at home anywhere else.

The Valdés family also illustrated another trend of the '90s that accelerated in the 2000s, the number of Havanans living, working, or traveling abroad. Thus Juan's oldest daughter Elena, the one named for Helen of Troy, was living closer to Greece than to Cuba, employed by a Swiss hotel chain. She had been married first to a Swiss citizen and then to a Cuban from the eastern part of the island whom she had met on a visit home to Havana and had taken back to far-off Bern. The younger daughter, Karen, had followed in her mother's footsteps, graduated from medical school, and then done her two years of obligatory social service in far-off Guantánamo province in a town where the majority of her patients could trace their descent back, in part, to the Tainos who had lived there when Columbus arrived. Every time he visited either of his daughters, Juan experienced the distance between the civilizations and cultures, as if they lived on different planets and he were jumping from one orbit to another. His older brother Tony still taught English, and now worked a second job for a British publishing house specializing in dictionaries. This gave him the ability to travel abroad frequently. The same was true for Juan's son Alejandro, a natural guitarist who had taught himself to play, picking up the flamenco sounds of Paco de Lucía by ear, and who now performed as an accompanist to well-known Cuban singers on international tours.

In contrast, most of Juan's professional travel outside the island stemmed from invitations by leftwing academic friends in Spain or Mexico to give talks in public institutions that paid only the price of his ticket and maybe some living expenses on a per diem basis. When he would return from several weeks in Seville or Mexico City, Daisy, who worked long hours of rotating shifts as a specialist in one of the city's best pediatric intensive care units, asked him smilingly why his other Cuban academic friends brought back foreign salaries sufficient for several months' shopping in hard-currency stores, or at least boxes holding flat-screen TVs and DVD burners, while he returned with suitcases full of books and maybe a small wad of Euros in his pocket.

In Buenavista—not so far from Pogolotti—the next generation of the Motola family also had one sibling in Havana and one abroad. Daniel Motola's daughter Patricia, having completed her master's degree in Cuban cultural studies with a thesis on the image of Havana in the works of the mid-20th century writer José Lezama Lima, was teaching at her alma mater, the University of Havana, while pursuing her doctorate. Her brother Daniel, Jr., who had returned to his paternal family's religious roots and become very involved in the city's Jewish community center and synagogue, emigrated first to Israel and then to Miami, where he worked for a chain of shoe stores owned by his relatives who had left in the Mariel boatlift. Patricia, firmly rooted in Havana, had later become active in the Jewish community as well.

The other Buenavista family we have followed, the Larrinagas, nearly all remained in Cuba. Carlitos, the English teacher, continued to live and work on the Isle of Pines off the southern coast; his daughter went to Havana for college and stayed there to work as a psychologist for patients at a cardiology hospital, while his son, who likewise studied in Havana, returned to the Isle of Pines as a lawyer employed by the government. Their uncle Sergio, whom we last saw in the 1990s as a percussionist in Italy and Holland, returned to Havana after a divorce from his Italian wife, and was trying to decide whether to pursue another European career or not. Carlitos's sister, Santa, an accountant, shifted from working for a series of state-owned businesses to a new job, still somewhat precarious, in a private, foreign-capital firm.

In 2013, the issue of international travel, migration, and employment was affected by another major public policy reform that has altered the life and plans of many in Havana and will continue to do so in the future. Previously—for reasons dating back to the upheavals of the early 1960s—Cubans wishing to travel abroad had needed to present a letter of invitation from a foreign individual or institution, to obtain a Cuban government exit permit, and then return to the island within eleven months or less, also paying significant fees. Otherwise, they were legally judged to have lost their status as permanent Cuban residents, which meant they lost access to medical care and other social services, and their homes and other property could be confiscated. On January 16, 2013, in a long-promised but much-delayed reform, the exit permit requirement was scrapped and the others were considerably loosened. As far as Cuban law was concerned, all that was needed to travel abroad was a valid Cuban passport. Cubans outside the country retained their official residency as long as they kept these passports up to date; the passports, in turn, could be renewed every two years, an unlimited number of times, for a fee of 20 CUC each.

In practical terms, this meant that anyone, including doctors and other professionals, could legally leave the country, live somewhere else, work abroad as long as they wanted, marry or divorce or start a business or acquire legal residency or citizenship in another country (including the United States), and return to their native land as often as they wanted—all without jeopardizing any of their property or their rights as citizens. In addition, those previously classified as permanent emigrants could apply for repatriation. International migration, which had been a one-way street ever since the departure of much of Havana's upper classes in the early '60s, suddenly became circular. It is still too soon to calculate the change in the outflow, because who is a temporary emigrant and who is permanent cannot be distinguished for at least two years. But it is noteworthy that the number of formerly "permanent" emigrants who repatriated to the island rose to 12,000 in 2015 and 14,000 the following year. Many brought funds with them to invest. Meanwhile, the total of remittances sent by Cubans living abroad reached an estimated $3 billion per year. In all these ways, in Havana particularly, a new type of dual nationality has begun to emerge, and a much larger number of people are part of the economic life of the capital regardless of how many months of the year they spend there. Some of the effects on Havana's economic and social life will be evident in what follows in this epilogue.

***

One area of significant change is housing. Though visiting journalists persist in pointing to Havana's ruins (as they have in every century), anyone who knows the city well can see the increased pace of repair and construction of homes. We have mentioned the Valdes' improvement of the cottage in Pogolotti. Sergio and Santa Larrinaga, meanwhile, moved into the downstairs and upstairs apartments of a concrete-block house the family built in part of the yard surrounding the old wooden house constructed by their grandfather Pablo el Cumbanchero in the 1920s, though they had to cut down a number of old mango and banana trees to make room. Patricia Motola sold her late mother's small house in the Santos Suarez district (adjoining La Vibora), and, along with her new husband, a playwright, put some of the money into fixing up the old Motola family apartment above the former corner store. All this testifies to public policy and economic changes transforming the look and feel of the city.

By the early 2000s, the housing problems discussed in Chapters 14 and 15 had intensified. The longstanding policy of redressing past grievances by prioritizing investment in the countryside over that in the capital, the lack of housing units adequate to Havana's population, plus the scarcity of construction materials aggravated by the economic crisis, altogether created a perfect storm. Many *habaneros* who left the country cited, among the causes of their decision, that they were not going to be able to fulfil the dream of having a home of their own.

As a result, in 2010 the trade union microbrigades that had been organized since the 1970s as a means to lessen the enormous housing deficit were replaced by a commitment to aid families in building or repairing their own units. Expanded, non-rationed sale of construction materials at accessible prices and the legalization of private construction crews had an impact throughout the city, including in its less advantaged neighborhoods. Eighty percent of loans awarded by Cuban state banks went to households applying for funds to repair and build houses. After 2011, families classified as poor became eligible for grants rather than loans.

At the same time, the continued growth in tourism and in local private businesses offered a new way to finance home improvements. Some Havanans began to build or fix up extra rooms or units to rent to small entrepreneurs and travelers from other provinces, as well as to international tourists who could not find rooms in the city's overbooked hotels or who wanted cheaper accommodation or a better entry point into Cuban daily life. Between 2012 and 2016, the number of such private hostels doubled, to 10,482 rooms in Havana (out of approximately 22,000 throughout the island, totaling one third of the total number of rooms available for rent). Renting of rooms thus began to rival the operation of private restaurants, coffee shops, and takeout counters, whose numbers in the capital remained at about 8200.

The parallel innovation in housing policy was the 2011 legalization of buying and selling homes. Thus, a recently married couple who could scrape together 10,000 CUC, whether from savings or via loans or contributions from relatives abroad, could buy an apartment in one of Havana's lower income neighborhoods. Perhaps the seller would be an elderly woman who didn't want to keep living on the top floor of a five-story walkup and was able to move in with someone else. Or perhaps it was a family who were emigrating and needed to take some dollars with them to get something of a head start. Buying or renting an apartment became a new option for many who lacked a home. Experts calculate that since 2011, 110,000 properties in Havana have been bought and sold.

This new situation revived a phenomenon extinguished by the urban reform law of 1959: a housing market. That market attracted buyers of many sorts, even from outside Havana. Among those who had left the country, some began to think that their dream of owning a home could be fulfilled more quickly in Havana than in Hialeah, after all. This has been one of the causes of the trend toward repatriation. Other homebuyers had similar notions, but were pursuing less of a dream and more of profitable investment. Thus an elderly woman who owned a seven-room mansion in El Vedado could sell it to a Milanese businessman married to a Cuban, who would legally speaking be the owner (since property ownership by non-Cubans remains illegal). The Italian, a visionary real estate pioneer in the new Havana, imagined a luxury urban inn for visitors who could pay $200 a night, excited to spend it in the bedrooms of the vanished Cuban upper class, attended by uniformed staff.

Besides such foreign investors and the Cuban emigrants who began to return, Cubans from other provinces, if their incomes permitted, came to the capital with plans to buy homes in Alamar and other less coveted zones. This flow of buyers and sellers has brought new demographics to Havana's neighborhoods and reconnected them with other parts of the country.

The simultaneous effects of all of these factors—diverse alternatives for repair, more available resources, buying and selling of property, growth of the private sector, and new and old patterns of migration—has brought about a notable renewal of city's housing stock. The pace of restoration is evident throughout the city, from the more refined blocks of Vedado or Miramar, to parts of Old Havana or Centro, La Vibora, or the much-maligned San Miguel de Padrón, where new plaster, paint, tiles, and windows have restored ancestral buildings to some of their former splendor. Even in the post-revolutionary squatter settlements of El Romerillo or La Güinera, wooden shacks with precarious tile coverings have been replaced by concrete-block walls and Fibrocem roofs that can withstand at least a medium-intensity hurricane.

All told, in the period from 2011 to 2016, the actors of this new sector devoted to construction, restoration, and real-estate dealings have produced 10,000 new units, while state enterprises have produced less than a third of that.

None of this has been sufficient, however, to stem the accumulated effects of deterioration in areas neglected for more than half a century. The ruins are also a reality. Alongside construction and restoration, collapses continue and other buildings become uninhabitable. In 2017, according to official sources, nearly 34,000 families who had lost their houses or feared for their safety were residing in shelters while waiting for a place to live.

Also, the market, even though limited by the ban on foreigners acquiring Cuban real estate, has raised the price of housing. A visit to the online sites where almost everything can be bought and sold on the island—the "Cuban craiglists" Revolico, Cubísima, and Porlalivre—shows that an apartment that sold for around 15,000 to 30,000 CUC in 2011 now costs at least 50,000. In the most expensive neighborhoods, some owners can ask for a quarter million CUC without batting an eye.

In addition, some apartments are bought and sold for conversion into private bars and restaurants. One example is the bar called Azucar Lounge overlooking the Plaza Vieja, operated by a Cuban-Spanish couple in a former apartment with balcony in one of the buildings renovated by the Historian's Office as described in Chapter 16. This variant is most likely what encouraged the owner of that balconied apartment on Calle Obispo to seek a buyer who would pay 160,000 CUC, though the price is far outside the current range for the area. By the same token, however, those who run restaurants or bed-and-breakfasts in multi-family apartment buildings have an incentive to contribute to the upkeep of the buildings' common areas and infrastructure, and to maintain relations of mutual aid with the neighbors. So the cycle of converting some housing units to commercial spaces is not necessarily a vicious one.

Particularly in tourist-heavy Old Havana, privately owned bars have proliferated, some in former apartments bought or rented from their owners, and some in commercial spaces rented from the state. On the other side of the Plaza Vieja from Azucar Lounge sits La Vitrola, owned by a former state restaurant employee, featuring a mid-20th century jukebox as its name implies. A few blocks away on the Plaza de Cristo, the raucous, graffiti-themed tapas bar called El Chanchullero (the wheeler-dealer) is popular with both locals and tourists and can boast of 970 reviews on TripAdvisor in languages from Spanish to English to Korean and Turkish.

With typical barbed Cuban humor, a sign outside the entry door reads (in Spanish) "Hemingway was never here."

***

Popular though bars and *paladares* are with Havanans going out for food and drink, most meals are of course eaten at home. Since the 1990s, nothing has generated more concern and uncertainty for Havanans than food for the week. Although Cuba is the Latin American country where the fewest people live with the threat of starvation, still the years of a state-supported safety net created a degree of expectation and a vision of stability that proved difficult to satisfy. Almost any *habanero* will tell you that food remains an area of discontent.

In the depths of the depression and dislocation of the Special Period, the primary concern was how to find food, period. In the Havana of the 2000s, the issue—as with housing, as with books—is which of the many markets to turn to, and at what price. This represents a drastic change from the environment in which the older generations were shaped: they are used to a hyper-planned structure that regulated the exact quantity of food items in the basic food basket through a ration book issued to every household, administered by the local bodega, alongside a parallel state market offering a wider selection at higher but uniform prices throughout the country. Within that structure, all consumers also operated inside a narrow range of salaries between 100 and 450 pesos a month. In the new Havana, shoppers face a tangled web of markets, products, prices, and currencies that make a week's shopping, on the much wider range of family incomes, an exercise in creative accounting. Let us try to follow a shopper and his or her budget through this maze.

Number one, let's suppose our shopper begins at the corner bodega where their name and ration book are registered. At this bodega they can still buy the assigned "quota," as it's called in common speech, now made up of rice, sugar, vegetable oil, beans, salt, coffee, pasta, and eggs, plus baby food and milk for children and a few other items for the elderly—all at subsidized prices, which are the same regardless of income. The quota no longer covers anyone's necessities for a month, yet it remains a resource that all opinion surveys show the majority is not ready to give up. But once the shopper is done with this step of the journey, there are nine other markets remaining to be tapped.

Next, our shopper might head for the state-run clusters of produce stalls where government-owned farms sell their harvests. Such farms once controlled eighty percent of the arable land, a figure now down to twenty-nine percent. The prices in these markets are not subsidized, but they are capped. The same is true of a third kind of state market, which belongs to the branch of the Armed Forces that runs farms to meet its own needs, and sells the excess to the population. In both of kinds of outlets, shoppers might find plantains, boniatos, beans, lemons, pineapple, pork or lamb, and—in season—mangos, onions, green peppers, papaya, and cabbage.

But for other products they don't find, shoppers must move on to the six kinds of private markets, of which the largest permanent ones are roofed installations with twenty or thirty or more individual stands. These are operated by private sellers and are officially known as "agricultural markets of supply and demand." They have greater variety, sometimes better quality, and always higher prices. Until recently, the one at Cuatro Caminos near the port took up an entire city block, had about 80 stalls, and drew shoppers from across the city in search of the most competitive prices. The one at 19th and B in Vedado is sometimes called the "Whole Foods of Havana" for both its supply of quality produce and its often ruinous prices. In addition, there are private markets run directly by farming co-ops, and others that are run by non-farm cooperatives or individuals that serve as middlemen for farmers. On a smaller scale, there are itinerant vendors who set up their carts in accustomed locales. Less frequently, "agricultural fairs" are set up in parks or city blocks on a Saturday or Sunday to offer much cheaper goods from the countryside. Finally, there is the network of *organopónicos,* urban farms that have been created on vacant lots and that sell their produce in stands alongside these lots.

Within this gamut of nine types of markets, according to official figures, Havana has 138 run by the state, and 24 of the larger supply-and-demand ones. The remaining categories have no official tally.

Havanans setting out to do the week's shopping will start, logically, with the cheapest, then move on to the more expensive, insofar as this is possible given where they live and what means of transport they have. Beyond that, what they do with their food budget will depend on their priorities and means. The range of prices for produce in season can be considerable: onions vary from 4 to 13 Cuban pesos (CUP) per pound; mangos, from 1.50 to 10.00; black beans from 9 to 12, eggplant from 1.20 to 7.00, and pork from 23 to 40. There are similar spreads for papaya, cabbage, boniato, guava, peppers, tomatoes, and squash. In general, the private prices are triple the state ones.

All this, however, comprises only the outlets selling in CUP. Besides the bodegas of subsidized rationed goods, the state possesses a monopoly on the stores at the other end of the spectrum, known popularly since the 1990s as *shoppings*, that sell in the hard-currency-convertible peso, the CUC (which trades for the CUP at a ratio of 1:24). In a *shopping*, a pound of black beans could cost the equivalent of 30 to 35 CUP; a pound of pork, 60; a domestic beer, 24; and a liter of vegetable oil, 50. These stores also sell products such as beef, butter, frozen meats, imported cheese and pasta, canned fruits and fruit juices, and many other processed foods that are generally not available anywhere else. Although many of these products are imported, the domestically produced ones in these stores are not any cheaper.

Besides these ten types of formal markets, Havana also has what's called throughout Latin America and the Caribbean the "informal market." This can be divided into two sorts: gray and black. If a shopper is looking for a kind of fish unavailable in the state CUP fish stores, the logical thing is not to buy it in a *shopping* but to find a freelance fisherman who sells at one fifth of that price. This is a gray market, mildly illegal because the fisherman has no vendor's license and does not pay taxes. The black market, by contrast, consists only of goods diverted from a state warehouse and sold at a discount of 20 to 30 percent below the prices in CUC stores. Examples in the food sector include powdered milk or strawberries. In other sectors, the black market sells such goods as auto parts and elite brands of cigars.

Among all the sources of food products, one stands out for its novelty in the life of the capital: the raised-bed urban farms called *organopónicos*. They arose during the hungry '90s as a practical way to make use of urban and suburban land and to grow crops in the absence of the fuel and chemical inputs that had been crucial to the industrialized state farms. Their long rows of concrete beds are farmed with mostly organic methods, and have changed the city's landscape and the activity of many residents. They also suggest how, with the necessary access and support, city dwellers could contribute to the solution of their own problems.

The *organopónicos'* version of urban agriculture has helped not only with food production but also with cleaning up the city, turning empty lots that had become informal garbage dumps into resources that are cultivated and cared for. The urban farms have increased the green areas of the city and have also provided work for retired people and others outside the labor force. Further, they have stimulated an agrarian culture from which Havana had become divorced, especially among children and teenagers. In the most recent years, the *organopónicos* have gone from being a means to provide particular crops at low cost, to becoming a significant part of the city's food supply and offering alternative employment, frequently in a cooperative. So, as in urban agriculture initiatives and trends elsewhere in the world, urbanites in Havana have begun to ask themselves questions like, "How can we grow plantains or boniatos? When should we plant them? How much irrigation do we need for chard, or lettuce, or cabbage? Which crops can stand the summer heat, and which need shade? Can we grow vegetables and seasonings that are new to most Cuban consumers—broccoli, cauliflower, turnips, tarragon?"

However, although the existence of the *organopónicos* has stimulated awareness of organic food production, even in this sector some attachment to chemical products persists, given the slower effect of biological pest controls and organic fertilizers, and the pressure on producers to respond to short-term demand.

The effects of the new mixed economy are also apparent on Havana's media, information technology, language teaching, live music performance, and any number of other areas. Before moving on, we can return for a moment to where we started this chapter, at the seeming paradox of the bookstores of Obispo. One part of the puzzle, at least, has to do with cultural institutions' resistance to the sway of the market in their particular sphere.

The state bookstores offer most of their wares at subsidized prices, because if they were priced at cost, many users who are already challenged to pay for food or save money for construction or repairs would not be able to buy books. For example, it costs costs sixty CUP to print one copy of a research journal like *Temas*, sold in bookstores throughout the country, yet the magazine's selling price needs to compete with that of a pound of black beans, green peppers, malanga or beets: 10 pesos. If the magazine were sold at cost, only the elite could buy it. The same is true of world literature, contemporary Cuban literature, and other genres of books. But budget constraints mean that press runs are very limited compared to what they were in the 1960s-80s, so the more popular titles sell out quickly, sometimes immediately when they are released at the sprawling Havana Book Fair, held every February and drawing tens of thousands to the grounds and buildings of La Cabaña fortress above the bay. Private bookstores, like all businesses, try to be profitable, so they seek out old books from personal libraries, and they stock up on those of the new titles offered by the state that are likely to quickly sell out. When that happens, the newly out-of-print books are available from the private sellers for prices fifteen or twenty times higher than their original ones— and so are popular books from the past that have not been reissued, or books that have exotic appeal to foreign visitors. This explains why a used book or a practically new one can sell for so much more than it did a year ago at a different and possibly more luxurious store on the same street.

* * *

Life in the capital has evolved in many other ways in the years since 2006, too. Some signal events have included speeches by two new Roman Catholic popes in the Plaza de la Revolución, or the Rolling Stones free concert in the Ciudad Deportiva athletic complex that was attended by an estimated 700,000 fans. In 2015-16 more presidents, prime ministers, foreign ministers, and defense ministers from around the globe visited Havana than ever before, at an average of two per week. Meanwhile, tens of thousands of state-employed doctors and other professionals traveled to Venezuela, Brazil, Central America, and sixty other countries of the global South under government contracts, injecting more cash into the Cuban economy than tourism or sugar. And the highest political office in the capital (first secretary of its Communist Party branch) was occupied by a forestry scientist of mixed Spanish and African heritage, Mercedes López Acea, the second woman to be named to the Political Bureau of the country's ruling party. In the urban landscape, while home internet access remained extremely scarce, Havanans with smartphones and laptops could be seen congregating by day and by night in parks and on sidewalks at the city's forty-some Wi-Fi hotspots which offer full connectivity via cards sold by the state phone company.

Neither the internet nor *la radio bemba*, the capital's well-established rumor mill, however, gave much advance notice of a surprise announcement in 2014. On December 17, the day Cubans celebrate as the festival of Saint Lazarus/Babalú Ayé, the *orisha* in charge of healing the sick, which was also the first day of Hanukah in that particular year, residents of Havana along with others throughout the island were amazed by parallel announcements from Raúl Castro and Barack Obama on their TV screens. The two presidents spoke of an exchange of prisoners and an agreement to begin normalization of relations between Cuba and the United States. After 53 years of intermittent and unsuccessful diplomatic efforts and secret talks involving eleven American presidential administrations (often through unconventional emissaries such as journalists and presidents, novelists and religious leaders), this time normal relations became tangible.

The announcement unleashed a kind of explosion. Many people could not stop hugging one another and cheering in workplaces, schools, and streets across the city of Havana and the whole country. The return of the five Cuban intelligence agents held in U.S. prisons (sentenced to very heavy terms for having infiltrated Cuban-American groups intent on regime change) was a genuinely national cause, beyond ideological alignments or television slogans. Many had dreamed of an end to the tragic saga of their imprisonment, and were jubilant over its happy conclusion. Normalization of relations, however, was hardly anticipated by anybody, whether on the street or in think tanks or specialized academic departments. So many times it had been said that the US would not normalize relations with Cuba while someone named Castro was president, or while a Communist Party ruled in Havana, or until an exile could become Cuba's president. Since the overwhelming majority of Havanans could not remember what Cuba was like without the 52-year-old US multilateral embargo, the sudden expectation of a possible end to the blockade produced a kind of electricity.

As a consequence of the bilateral dialogue and Obama's exercise of presidential powers, licenses to do business with Cuba were issued. Google, T-Mobile, and Verizon began cooperation with the Cuban phone company ETECSA. Starwood, Inc., the parent company of the Sheraton hotel chain, began a joint venture to run the nineteenth century Inglaterra and two more hotels in Havana. Delta, JetBlue, American, and five other commercial airlines were authorized by both governments to fly US customers to the capital and to other cities of Cuba. The Secretaries of Commerce and Health, governors from New York, Minnesota, and Texas, and an increasing number of other official visitors descended on Havana. And, while tourism for pleasure remained illegal under U.S. law, access under the twelve permitted categories ranging from religious and humanitarian motives to "people-to-people" exchange expanded via both the letter of the regulations and the spirit of their enforcement. From 2015 on, the number of U.S. visitors nearly matched the longstanding flow from Canada. In the first half of 2017, "regular" American visitors outnumbered Cuban-Americans for the first time—and many of them stayed in Cuban homes.

None of this, however, closed the biggest gap separating the two societies, which was neither the embargo nor the differing political ideologies, but the long legacy of mistrust. Some Cubans found that this unprecedented new ballgame brought new worries and uncertainties. They had been prepared for generations to confront the historical North American adversary; how, instead, were they to learn to talk and cooperate? Was the United States really committed to respecting Cuban sovereignty for the first time?

Nevertheless, the close encounter between the two peoples looked unstoppable. From the U.S. side, after so many years of Cold War stereotypes, visitors were thrilled with the Havana and the Havanans they found. When the islanders asked them why they chose to visit the city right now, their answer was surprising: they wanted to see the Havana of the Castros, before Fidel and Raúl were gone and McDonald's invaded every corner. The local residents and these new visitors enjoyed each other and got along more rapidly than anyone could have predicted. From the Cuban side, the Americans were welcomed back as if they had not been absent for half a century. "Our Airbnb hosts were beyond helpful," one American backpacker could be heard telling her compatriots in a departure lounge in Havana's airport. "So much more so than in Mandalay."

The event that best captured the contradictory feelings awakened by the re-encounter of the two shores was the visit of President Barack Obama. From the landing of Air Force One under a light springtime drizzle on March 20, 2016, until Obama's departure after attending the opening innings of a baseball game between Cuban stars and the Tampa Bay Rays three days later, the city followed his every step. Obama wanted to come to the island, like Madonna or Leonardo di Caprio had done in preceding years, not as an invited official but "to have direct contact with Cubans."

Unlike those Hollywood figures, the U.S. president's travels paralyzed the normal flow of life and traffic wherever he went. As he and his family followed the typical tourist routes through the old city, the streets near the Plaza de la Catedral, the Plaza de Armas, and the Plaza de San Francisco were taken over by the U.S. Secret Service and Cuban State Security. *Almendrones* ground to a halt, as did horse-drawn carriages, street vendors, motorcycles, buses, pedi-cabs, and open-air three-wheeled "cocotaxis." Cafeterias, amusement parks, pharmacies, and bars all shut down. In Old Havana, inhabited especially by people of African descent, the president did not visit social clubs, *cabildos*, or *babalawos*, but the Archbishop of Havana in the sanctuary of the Cathedral. Soon after, in a meeting in the Gran Teatro de la Habana (the old Teatro Tacón

opposite the Parque Central) televised throughout the island, he spoke
to a group of invitees selected by the U.S. embassy that included new
private-business entrepreneurs, religious figures, bloggers, and only a few
artists and intellectuals, journalists, professors, or scientists.

Reading from a teleprompter, Obama said things that surprised
many in the live and virtual audiences: Why normalization now? Because
what the U.S. had been doing was "not working." "We should leave the
past behind," Obama declared, and "The United States and Cuba are like
two brothers who've been estranged for many years, even as we share the
same blood. . . Our grandchildren will look back on this period of isolation as an aberration, as just one chapter in a longer story of family and
of friendship. . . In the United States, we have a clear monument to what
the Cuban people can build: it's called Miami." Nothing in the past policy
had been wrong or unjust, it appeared—or even worth remembering.
The distance between the President's discourse and the history that many
Cubans knew was striking.

Nonetheless, on the whole, Havanans were grateful for Obama's visit.
No one will recall the phrases so carefully crafted by his talented team of
communication specialists, nor what he said about Cubans or Americans.
What they won't forget is his message of peace and most especially his
determination to be the first president after so many years of war to come
to a city and an island that is both so close and so far.

Eight months later, after the U.S. election of 2016, many in Havana
and the rest of the world feared that the Trump administration would
turn back the clock. On one hand, the rhetoric of President-elect Donald
Trump was very different from his predecessor's, as he threatened to
"tear up the bad deal" that Obama had made. On the other hand, it was
unlikely that the twenty-two accords signed in 2015–16 on such diverse
topics as national security, travel, commercial licenses, embassies, remittances, migration[1], environment, licenses to trade with the Cuban non-
state sector, or cooperation against terrorism and drug trafficking would
be scrapped. As this book goes to press, in the fall of 2017, the result
remains unclear. Meanwhile, one more event that signalled both conti-
nuity and change happened a little more than two weeks after the U.S.

election: the death of Fidel Castro at the age of 90, on November 25, 2016, in Havana.

Fidel's death came sixty years to the day from November 25, 1956, when he and the other eighty-one expeditionaries of the yacht called *Granma* set sail from Tuxpán, Mexico. He did not die from any of the risks he chose to run, nor from the many assassination attempts planned by his enemies. He died in his bed of natural causes. Ten years earlier, when he fell gravely ill, his enemies had celebrated his end, once more in vain. By the time he died, he had survived nearly twenty-five years longer than what a Miami journalist, in a U.S. best-seller of the early '90s, called *"Castro's Final Hour."*

In Havana, most residents heard the news when they woke up the next day, a Saturday. A little before noon, some foreign visitors walking across the Central Park approached a group engaged in a heated argument on one of the benches beside the statue of José Martí. One of the visitors asked one of the debaters what they were talking about, implying that he knew what the answer had to be. The man on the bench answered, "No, my friend, we're talking sports. You know, baseball." The look of surprise on the visitor's face was very telling. Along the Centro Habana axes of Neptuno and San Lazaro, and where they converged at the historic hilltop campus of the university, the flow of traffic and pedestrians looked like that of any other day. In line with official advice, students went to class, and workers to their jobs.

Still, when discussing the milestone event, many did so with an air of sadness. Ordinary activities were called off for Tuesday's memorial ceremony in the Plaza de la Revolución, so that all who wanted to attend could do so. Hundreds of thousands, old and young, went there, and many cried over the ashes. Their reasons were as varied as the population, and equally mixed. The most prevalent common denominator, perhaps, was the feeling that this man had put their country and their city firmly on the world map.

The next day, the coffin carrying Castro's ashes departed for Santiago de Cuba, retracing, in reverse, the route taken by the guerrillas in their advance from Cuba's second city to the headquarters of the defeated army in Havana's Camp Columbia, later Ciudad Libertad. Fidel's remains were buried in Santiago's Santa Ifigenia Cemetery, in the same neighborhood where he had attended elementary school at the Colegio de Dolores, and steps from the mausoleum of José Martí, the most illustrious Havanan buried there.

In his last wishes, Fidel had asked that there be no statues of him nor streets or monuments bearing his name. Thus his figure will not be preserved in bronze like the statue of the Caballero de París in a walking pose next to the Plaza de San Francisco, nor on horseback like that of Antonio Maceo looking over Havana's seafront or Máximo Gomez facing the crowded city. Still, Fidel Castro's death—just like his life—marked the close of one era and the opening of another in the history of the island and of Havana, a city just three years shy of five centuries old. The office of the Historian of the City will celebrate the 500th anniversary of the Key to the Indies on November 16, 2019.

Notes

1 KEY TO THE INDIES

1. Governor and captain-general were originally separate positions, the one civil and the other military, but from the late sixteenth century on they were combined. In our discussion of colonial officials from this time on, we have used the terms interchangeably.

2 THE HOUR OF THE MAMEYS

1. Cuban historian Gustavo Placer Cervera, author of several recent works on colonial military history, suggests that legend may have overtaken fact in the many earlier biographies of Pepe Antonio and accounts of the siege. He points out that the guerrilla leader is likely to have died of the same epidemic of tropical fevers that decimated the British attackers and that archival evidence does not confirm the long-held tradition that he was deprived of his command.

2. In the original Spanish, the women are hiding in *bocoyes de arroz* (casks or barrels for rice), which rhymes with *Dios* (God). In all our translations of songs or verse we've taken liberties to preserve rhyme where appropriate.

3 PARIS OF THE ANTILLES

1. What we are calling the Paseo del Prado, running from La Punta fortress by the seafront south to the Campo de Marte parade ground (since the 1920s the Parque de la Fraternidad) has gone through a succession of official names. It was originally called the "Nuevo Prado," presumably in comparison to the old one in Madrid, which was originally a field

or "pasture" as the name implies. After improvement in the nineteenth century, Havana's Prado was officially renamed Paseo de Isabel II in honor of the Spanish queen. Postindependence, it was again renamed, this time in honor of José Martí. But the old name has stuck, as is the case with many other streets.

At the Campo de Marte began another broad avenue, the Paseo de Tacón, which ran westward to the Príncipe fortress, along the present-day streets Reina and Carlos III, the route of the P-11 and P-12 buses.

5 STIRRINGS OF NATIONHOOD

1. Until we come to our discussion of Domingo Del Monte and his circle, later in this chapter, we are omitting other anticolonial conspiracies and reform efforts mounted by liberal white Cubans. We do not mean to underestimate the importance of such crucial figures in the formation of Cuban national identity and in the fields of poetry, religion, political economy, and education as José María Heredia, Félix Varela, José Antonio Saco, and José de la Luz Caballero.

6 REVOLUTIONS AND RETRIBUTIONS: FROM THE TEATRO VILLANUEVA TO THE MAINE

1. The legendary William Randolph Hearst quote comes from a memoir by James Creelman, who had been a Hearst correspondent in Madrid. When the quote was later picked up by a London paper, Hearst denied having sent such a telegram. The artist, Frederick Remington, and the reporter who accompanied him, Richard Harding Davis, neither confirmed nor denied Creelman's report.

7 MANY HAPPY RETURNS?: U.S. OCCUPATION AND ITS AFTERMATH

1. The suffrage rules included only males over the age of twenty-one who were either Cuban-born or Spaniards willing to take on Cuban citizenship, and who, in addition, could read and write, owned property worth at least $250, or had served in the Liberation Army. The last was a compromise the occupation government could not avoid. Still, given

illiteracy rates, poverty, and the numbers of ex-slaves born in Africa, only about a third of adult Cuban males had the right to vote in these elections.

8 SYMBOL OF AN ERA: ALBERTO YARINI Y PONCE DE LEÓN

1. In some versions of the story the general is not Jesús Rabí but Florencio Salcedo—likewise from Oriente, black, and risen through the ranks of the insurgent army. Either way, the moral is the same.

9 CATCH A FORD ON THE MALECÓN: REPUBLICAN HAVANA'S GROWTH AND DECAY

1. To the confusion of North American audiences, the music of the "rumba" craze that swept the United States in the 1930s was not *rumba* at all, but a mixture of other Cuban genres, especially *son*. U.S. record labels recorded a wide variety of Cuban music, in sessions held both in Havana and in New York, and called all of it *rumba*. Authentic *rumba* never in itself became pop music, even in the Cuban cities where it grew up.

11 RADIO DAYS

1. Stanzas of Martí's *Versos Sencillos* were apparenty first set to the tune and chorus of *La Guantánamera* sometime in the 1950s by the composer Julio Orbón, who taught them to a young Cuban musician-composer named Hector Angulo. In 1962, while Angulo was studying in New York before returning to Cuba for a long and distinguished career, he spent the summer working as a counselor at Camp Woodland, a left-wing summer camp in the Catskills, where Seeger came for one of his annual visits. A recording of Angulo teaching the song to Seeger is available in the Camp Woodland archives at SUNY Albany (Norman Studer Archives, Title ID "Folk Music of the Catskills, July 15, 1962").

14 REVOLUTION WITH PACHANGA: HAVANA TRANSFIGURED

1. Cuba's prerevolutionary communist party had gone by various names, of which Popular Socialist Party was the last. In the 1960s, the 26th of

July Movement, the Revolutionary Directorate, and the PSP merged into a single organization which eventually became the Cuban Communist Party, the ruling party of a Leninist-style single-party state.

16 THE BLACKOUT: HAVANA IN THE "SPECIAL PERIOD" AND BEYOND

1. Translations of Cuban salaries into dollar terms can be misleading, because housing, health care, higher education, and other services that consume a large part of a U.S. salary remain free or cheap in Cuba despite the economic crisis. Still, the comparisons are worthwhile in relation to the products Cubans do have to buy in hard currency or its equivalent.

2. Throughout the period under discussion, the U.S. trade embargo remained in force, except for a loophole voted into law by the U.S. Congress starting in 2001 for cash-only sales of U.S. agricultural goods. Most goods in the dollar stores were imported from Western Europe, Latin America, or Asia. Nonetheless Cuba's new hard-currency sector used the dollar as the standard international medium of exchange, as did all of the country's international trade.

3. There had been a previous and generally popular experiment with farmers' markets in the 1980s, on a more limited scale. They had been closed in the Rectification campaign, on the argument that they were promoting the growth of a class of rich middlemen and diverting personnel and equipment from regular tasks.

4. Since 1959, the Cuban government has taken the position that the perpetually renewable Guantánamo lease is invalid, having been coerced under the terms of the Platt Amendment. The U.S. government, however, has continued to insist on its right to occupy the base.

17 EPILOGUE, 2006–2017

1. After the *balsero* crisis of 1994 (see Chapter 16), successive U.S. administrations followed a policy commonly known as "wet-foot/dry-foot" with respect to Cuban migrants seeking to enter the U.S. without a visa. Those intercepted at sea (wet foot) were returned to Cuba,

the same treatment as would be applied to would-be immigrants from anywhere else. Instead, Cubans wishing to acquire residency in the U.S. were supposed to apply for the quota of 20,000 Cuban immigrant visas to be awarded each year.

However, under an interpretation of the Cold War-era Cuban Adjustment Act passed by Congress in 1966 and additional legislation, those who made it to land (dry foot) were automatically deemed political refugees, admitted to the U.S. as "parolees" with the right to work and receive services, and generally awarded legal residency after a year and a day. Increasingly, the "dry-foot" migrants came not by boat across the Florida Straits, but rather via Central America to the Mexico-U.S. border. In 2015–2016, as the process of normalization raised the spectre of this special treatment being eliminated, the number of Cubans entering the U.S. through third countries, principally Mexico, tripled, reaching 42,000 a year.

One of the last accords reached between the Obama administration and the Cuban government, in December of 2016, ended the dry foot policy. So far, the Trump administration has shown no signs of changing that.

Bibliographic Sources and Suggestions

One of the pleasures of working on this book has been the opportunity to digest a great variety of primary sources, popular works, and scholarly research about Havana—books and articles, nonfiction and fiction, music, pictures, web sites mounted by individuals and institutions in and out of Cuba, maps and tourist guides both intact and disintegrating, memoirs, reminiscences, biographical dictionaries, census documents, and more. In addition we interviewed members of representative families and picked the brains of friends and acquaintances of all sorts. In this bibliographic essay we can't begin to provide a complete list of our sources. What we can do is guide interested readers to some of the historical works and to the sources of most of our direct quotations, and in the process acknowledge our own biggest debts to historians in Cuba, the United States, and elsewhere. A great many of our sources are, of course, in Spanish. Most, even if published in Cuba, are available via inter-library loan from at least a few university or public libraries in the United States.

I. GENERAL WORKS
Comprehensive general works on Cuban history in English include: Louis A. Pérez, Jr., *Cuba: Between Reform and Revolution* (New York: Oxford, 1995) and *Cuba and the United States: Ties of Singular Intimacy* (Athens: University of Georgia, 1997), and Hugh Thomas, *Cuba, or The Pursuit of Freedom* (London: Eyre & Spottiswoode, 1971). For buildings, streets, and other constructions throughout the history of Havana and other Cuban cities, an invaluable resource is Juan de las Cuevas Toraya, *500 años de construcciones en Cuba* (Madrid: Chavín, 2001).

II. COLONIAL ERA (1500–1898)
One key source for our quotations from official records and correspondence, periodicals, and travelers' chronicles throughout the Spanish colonial period is Gustavo Eguren's fascinating collection of primary source excerpts, *La fidelísima Habana* (Havana: Letras Cubanas, 1986). Also very useful throughout this period have been Manuel Moreno Fraginals, *Cuba/España, España/Cuba: Historia Común* (Barcelona: Crítica, 1995) and Eusebio Leal Spengler, *La Habana, ciudad antigua* (Havana: Letras Cubanas, 1988).

For the sixteenth and seventeenth centuries (Chapter 1), a great many quotations and details also come from Irene A. Wright's classic works based on documents in the Archives of the Indies in Seville: *Historia documentada de San Cristóbal de La Habana en el siglo XVI* (Havana: El Siglo XX, 1927) and *Historia documentada de San Cristóbal de La Habana en la primer mitad del siglo XVII* (Havana: El Siglo XX, 1930). In English, readers may also consult her *The Early History of Cuba, 1492–1586* (New York: Macmillan, 1916).

The account of Giovanni Francesco Gemelli Careri that closes Chapter 1 is drawn from Eguren. (The original *Giro del mondo* was published in Italian in 1699, and was published in English translation in the eighteenth century but not since; the section dealing with New Spain has been translated into Spanish, most recently by the Universidad Nacional Autónomo de México in 1976.)

For information on the house of Juana Carvajal we are indebted to the Office of the City Historian of Havana.

The taking of Havana by the English (Chapter 2) has been the subject of many military histories, at that time and ever since. Recent examples include Gustavo Placer Cevera's *Los defensores del Morro* (Havana: Unión, 2003), César García del Pino's *Toma de La Habana por los ingleses y sus antecedentes* (Havana: Ciencias Sociales, 2002), and Sonia Keppel's *Three Brothers at Havana* (Salisbury: M. Russell, 1981). The occupation and its effects have received less attention. Emilio Roig de Leuchsenring, ed., *La dominación inglesa de La Habana: Libro de Cabildos 1762–3* (Havana: Imprenta Molina y Cia, 1929) includes the letter of the Jesuit priest and other primary sources from which we quote, and a useful interpretive essay. Roig has also edited *Cómo vio Jacobo de la Pezuela la toma de La Habana por los ingleses* (Havana: Oficina del Historiador, 1962), containing four chapters from Pezuela's nineteenth century account. *Documentos inéditos sobre la Toma de La Habana por los Ingleses en 1762* (Havana: Biblioteca Nacional José Martí, 1963) includes further documents (including the statement by Benjamin Franklin) and an equally useful essay by Juan Pérez de la Riva. A different interpretation by a Spanish historian is Celia María Parcero Torre, *La pérdida de La Habana y las reformas borbónicas en Cuba, 1760–1773* (Madrid: Junta de Castilla y León, 1998).

For the Marquesa Beatriz de Jústiz and her writings, we are indebted to the work of Luisa Campuzano. See her "Las muchachas de la Habana no tienen temor de dios . . . ," in *Revista Canadiense de Estudios Hispánicos* 16, no. 2 (1992): 307–318, available online at http://www.lajiribilla.cu/ 2001/n17_agosto/516_17.html (accessed June 30, 2006). The texts themselves are also in "Memorial y décimas dirigidos a Carlos III en ocasión de la toma de La Habana por los ingleses," in L. Campuzano, ed., *Yo con mi viveza, pp. 183–194* (Havana: Casa de las Américas, 2003). See, in addition, the chapter "La hora de los mameyes" in Reynaldo González, ed., *El bello Habano*, pp. 4–5 (Vitoria-Gasteiz: Ikusager, 1998).

Levi Redfield's 1799 memoir that includes his participation in the Havana expedition, *A True Account of Some Memorable Events and Remarkable Occurrences in the Life of Levi Redfield*, is available on microfiche. Roswell Park's memoir appears in "A Journal of the Expedition Against Cuba," foreword by Julian Park, *University of Buffalo Studies* I, no. 4 (1920). For more on the role of North American provincial troops in general, see David Syrett, "American Provincials and the Havana Campaign of 1762," *New York History* 49, no. 4 (1968): 375–390. Maj. Joseph Gorham's diary (in its English original) is in *Cinco diarios del sitio de la Habana* (Havana: Biblioteca Nacional José Martí, 1963).

For the nineteenth century (Chapters 3–6), we have drawn on a very wide variety of sources, including those noted above for the colonial period as a whole. Some of these are:

Travel accounts (Chapters 3–6): Frederika Bremer's impressions come from her *The Homes of the New World: Impressions of America*, trans. Mary Howitt (New York: Harper & Brothers, 1853). We have translated comments by Nicolás Tanco, Edward Otto, and others from Eguren. Accounts by U.S. and British visitors (including Samuel Hazard and Richard Henry Dana) can be found in Louis A. Pérez, Jr., *Slaves, Sugar, and Colonial Society: Travel Accounts of Cuba, 1801–1899* (Wilmington: Scholarly Resources, 1992) and *Impressions of Cuba in the Nineteenth Century: The Travel Diary of Joseph J. Dimock* (Wilmington: Scholarly Resources, 1992), as well as in the original books by Hazard (*Cuba with Pen and Pencil* [Hartford, CT: Hartford

Publishing Company, 1871]), Dana (*To Cuba and Back, a Vacation Voyage* [reprint, Carbondale: Southern University Illionois Press, 1966]), Matilda Houstoun (*Texas and the Gulf of Mexico, or, Yachting in the New World* [reprint, Austin, TX: W.T. Taylor, 1991]), and others. The Countess of Merlín (María de las Mercedes Santa Cruz y Montalvo) published her full three-volume account in French as *La Havane* (Paris: Librairie d'Amyot, 1844), and a shorter one-volume edition in Spanish, *Viaje a La Habana*, both 1844; our quotes are translated from the Spanish edition (reprint, Havana: Librería Cervantes, 1922).

Cecilia Valdés (Chapters 3 and 4): We have translated all the quotations from Cirilo Villaverde, *Cecila Valdés o La Loma del Ángel* (Havana: Arte y Literatura, 1977). We have also benefitted from Reynaldo González's critical work on Cecilia and race in nineteenth century Cuba, *Contradanzas y latigazos* (Havana: Letras Cubanas, 1992). After a long absence from print in English, the novel is now available to English-speaking readers in a new translation: *Cecila Valdés, or, El Angel Hill*, trans. Helen Lane (New York: Oxford, 2005).

Afro-cuban societies and religion (Chapter 4): On the *cabildos* and their functions in private and in public, see Philip A. Howard, *Changing History: Afro-Cuban Cabildos and Societies of Color in the Nineteenth Century* (Baton Rouge: Louisiana State University, 1998), Daniel E. Walker, *No More, No More: Slavery and Cultural Resistance in Havana and New Orleans* (Minneapolis: University of Minnesota, 2004), and Judith Bettelheim, *Cuban Festivals: An Illustrated Anthology* (New York: Garland, 1993); the last contains a translation of Fernando Ortiz's classic work on the *cabildos* and the Day of Kings, as well as Ramón Meza's 1891 article in *La Habana Elegante* recalling the celebrations. On the Abakuá, see Tato Quiñones, *Ecorie Abakuá: Cuatro ensayos sobre los ñañigos cubanos* (Havana: Ediciones Unión, 1994). On religious practices deriving from Africa (subject of a recent research boom on the island) we have consulted Joel James Figarola, *Sistemas mágico-religiosos cubanos. Principios rectores* (Havana: Ediciones Unión, 2001) and Lydia Cabrera's classic text *El monte* (various editions) for symbolism including the myths of the *ceiba*.

Social and economic structure in daily life: On the role and place of white women (Chapter 3), see Luis Martínez-Fernández, "The 'Male City' of Havana," in Tamara Hunt and Micheline Lessard, eds., *Women and the Colonial Gaze* (New York: NYU, 2002). The quote from Elga Adman (Magdalena Peñarredonda) is from Luisa Campuzano, "Mirando al norte, viajeras cubanas a los Estados Unidos, 1840-1900," in Rafael Hernández, ed., *Mirar el Niagara* (Havana: Centro Juan Marinello, 2000); it originally appeared in *La Habana Elegante* Year 6, Number 40, September 30, 1888. Most of our examples of black and mulatto families and workers in Chapter 4 are drawn from María del Carmen Barcia Zequeira, *La otra familia: parientes, redes, y descendencia de los esclavos en Cuba* (Havana: Casa de las Américas, 2003) and Pedro Deschamps Chapeaux, *El negro en la economía habanera del siglo XIX* (Havana: UNEAC, 1971). See also Digna Castañeda, "The Female Slave in the Cuba during the first half of the Nineteenth Century," in Verene Shepherd, ed., *Engendering History: Caribbean Women in Historical Perspective* (New York: St. Martin's, 1995). Robert L. Paquette, *Sugar is Made With Blood: The Conspiracy of La Escalera and the Conflict between Empires over Slavery in Cuba* (Middletown: Wesleyan, 1988) also has useful statistics and examples on occupational distribution by color.

Maria del Carmen Barcia's research in social history has also been our main source for the information in Chapters 4 and 6 on prostitutes and their magazine *La Cebolla*, and the descriptions in Chapter 6 of life in the capital during the second Independence War. For the former, see her article "Entre el poder y la crisis: las prostitutas se defienden," in Luisa Campuzano, coordinadora, *Mujeres Latinoamericanas: Historia y Cultura, Siglos XVI al XIX*, vol. 1 (Havana: Casa de las Américas and Universidad de Iztapalapa, 1997); for the latter, *Una sociedad en crisis: La Habana a finales del siglo XIX* (Havana: Ciencias Sociales, 2001).

Rebellion and repression (Chapters 5 and 6): On Aponte, see José Luciano Franco, "La conspiracion de Aponte, 1812," in his *Ensayos históricos*, pp. 143–90 (Havana: Ciencias Sociales, 1974). For La Escalera, as well as Domingo del Monte and upper class *criollo* attitudes toward slavery and independence, see Robert L. Paquette, *Sugar is Made With Blood*, cited above. For Manuel Moreno Fraginals and Jorge Lozano on the attempted Abakuá rescue of the medical students, see, respectively, *Cuba/España* (cited above) and Pedro A. García, "27 de noviembre de 1871: Culpables de cubanía," in *Granma*, November 27, 2001 available at http://www.latinamericanstudies.org/1868/culpables.htm (accessed June 30, 2006). Martí's judgment on the bullfight, from 1878, is quoted in the 1936 pamphlet, *Contra las Corridos de Toros*, digital image available at http://ufdc.ufl.edu/UF00025496/00001/6j. For a judicious account of Evangelina Cossio, see the prologue to Jane McManus, *Cuba's Island of Dreams* (Gainesville: University Press of Florida, 2000).

Cultural ties between Havana and U.S. cities: On the influence of education in the U.S. (Chapter 3), baseball (Chapter 6), and similar matters, see Louis A. Pérez, Jr., *On Becoming Cuban: Identity, Nationality, and Culture* (Chapel Hill: University of North Carolina, 1999). Many further sources on the early history of Cuban baseball may be found there.

Antonio Maceo and Julián del Casal: Two articles on this tantalizing encounter (sources of our description and quotations in Chapter 6) are: Victor Fowler, "Casal disputado y una nota al pie," in the Summer 2002 edition of the internet magazine *La Habana Elegante, segunda época* (www.habanaelegente.com), and Oscar Montero, "Casal y Maceo en La Habana Elegante," in *Casa de las Américas*, no. 225 (October–December 2001) and *Encuentro de la Cultura Cubana*, no. 10 (Autumn 1998) (http://arch1.cubaencuentro.com/pdfs/10/10om117.pdf [accessed June 30, 2006]).

III. OCCUPATION AND INDEPENDENCE (1898–TODAY)

For the complex tapestry of Havana's day-to-day response to the U.S. occupation and its aftermath (Chapter 7), we have drawn extensively on Marial Iglesias Utset, *Las metáforas del cambio en la vida cotidiana: Cuba 1898–1902* (Havana: Ediciones Unión, 2002). A complementary work that also contributed greatly to this chapter is Pérez, *On Becoming Cuban* (cited above).

For the political history of U.S.–Cuba relations and the Platt Amendment, see Pérez, *Cuba and the United States* (cited above), Philip Foner, *A History of Cuba and Its Relations with the United States* (New York: International, 1962), and Emilio Roig de Leuchsenring, *Historia de la Enmienda Platt: una interpretación de la realidad cubana* (Havana, Ciencias Sociales, 1973). The 1823 Thomas Jefferson quote is from a letter to President James Monroe, and that of John Quincy Adams is from a letter to the U.S. ambassador in Spain; for complete citations, see *Cuba and the United States*, p. 276. The letter from General Leonard Wood to President Roosevelt about Juan Gualberto Gómez and the "degenerates" of the Convention may be found in the Theodore Roosevelt Papers (Library of Congress microfilm, Series 1, Reel 12, letter dated April 12, 1901). R.F. Bullard's article on "How Cubans Differ from Us" is in *Century*, November 1907.

Our account of the life and death of Alberto Yarini (Chapter 8) and the barrio of San Isidro comes primarily from Dulcila Cañizares, *San Isidro, 1910: Alberto Yarini y su época* (Havana: Letras Cubanas, 2000), Tomás Fernández Robaina, *Historias de mujeres públicas* (Havana: Letras Cubanas, 1998), and Leonardo Padura Fuentes, "Yarini, El Rey," in his *El viaje más largo*, pp. 231–48 (San Juan: Plaza Mayor, 2002). Quotations from prostitutes are from Fernández Robaina (Consuelo) and Cañizares (Lulú); most quotations from other San Isidro figures are from Cañizares. For a study in English, see Mayra Beers, "Murder in San Isidro: Crime and Culture during the Second Cuban Republic," in *Cuban Studies* 34 (2003): 97–129.

On media-driven anti-black hysteria and the colored community's response, see Alejandra Bronfman, "'En Plena Libertad y Democracia': Negros Brujos and the Social Question,

1904–1919," in *Hispanic American Historical Review* 82, no. 3 (2002): 549–587. On Cuban musicians playing in silent movie theaters, see Ned Sublette, *Cuba and Its Music* (Chicago: Chicago Review, 2004). For Enrique Díaz Quesada and the early history of Cuban cinema, see special issue of *Cuba Update* XIX, no. 1 (October–December 1999), and Arturo Agramonte and Luciano Castillo, "Enrique Díaz Quesada: El padre de la cinematografía cubana" in the Cuban Ministry of Culture's web site La Jiribilla (http://www.lajiribilla. cu/2002/n70_septiembre/memoria.html [accessed June 30, 2006]). See also Alejandro de la Fuente, *A Nation for All: Race, Inequality, and Politics in Twentieth Century Cuba* (Chapel Hill: University of North Carolina, 2001). The most detailed and best-documented history of Cuban filmmaking from its origins to 1990 is María Eulalia Douglas, *La tienda negra. El cine en Cuba, 1897–1990* (Havana: Cinemateca de Cuba, 1997).

Chapter 9, on Havana's growth, decay, and culture in the 1910s–1940s, draws on an eclectic range of sources, including family history interviews which extend through this and the following chapters of the book. Raquel Cañizares and Carlos Larrinaga were interviewed by Dick Cluster and Rafael Hernández in Havana in August 2005. Daniel Motola Roffe was interviewed by Dick Cluster in Havana in December 2004.

A general work on the city's growth, planning, and architectural history is Joseph Scarpaci, Roberto Segre, and Mario Coyula, *Havana: Two Faces of the Antillean Metropolis* (Chapel Hill: University of North Carolina, 2002). More specifically, for *solares*: Carlos Venegas, "Havana between Two Centuries," *Journal of Decorative and Propaganda Arts* 22 (1996): 13–34; sugar industry's role in the city's growth: Oscar Zanetti Lecuona, "La capital del azúcar," in Bernardo García and Sergio Guerra, eds., *La Habana/Veracruz, Veracruz/La Habana* (Veracruz: Universidad Veracruzana, 2002); El Vedado: Mario Coyula, "Más acá del río y bajo los árboles: a la sombra de un Vedado que ya es no más" (manuscript) and Jorge Pavez Ojeda, *El Vedado, 1850–1940. De monte a reparto* (Havana: Centro Juan Marinello, 2003), and "Veinticuatro horas en la vida del Dr Carlos Miguel de Céspedes," *Bohemia,* January 13, 1946. The quotation from Federico García Lorca at the beginning of the chapter is from *A Poet in New York*, ed. Christopher Maurer, translated by Greg Simon and Steven F. White (NY: Noonday Press, 1998), which includes one poem and three letters written in Havana.

On Dulce María Loynaz: Aldo Martínez Malo, *Confesiones de Dulce María Loynaz* (Havana: José Martí, 1999); Ana Cabrera Vivanco, *La voz del silencio* (Havana: Ciencias Sociales, 2000); Dulce María Loynaz, *Fe de vida* (Havana: Letras Cubanas, 1995). A bilingual selection of her poetry is Judith Kerman, translator and editor, *A Woman in Her Garden: Selected poems of Dulce María Loynaz* (Buffalo: White Pine Press, 2002).

On Chano Pozo: Leonardo Padura Fuentes, "La noche triste de Chano Pozo," in *El viaje más largo* (cited above), pp. 277–94; Jordi Pujol, *Chano Pozo: El tambor de Cuba* (Barcelona: Almendra Music, 2001), issued as bilingual book and 3-CD set by Tumbao Cuban Classics, 2001). On the social development of the various genres of Cuban popular music, see Ned Sublette, *Cuba and Its Music,* cited above, Alejo Carpentier, *Music in Cuba,* translated by Alan West-Durán (Minneapolis: University of Minnesota, 2001), and Robin Moore, *Nationalizing Blackness: Afrocubanismo and Artistic Revolution in Havana, 1920–1940* (Pittsburgh: University of Pittsburgh, 1997). A panorama of genres of Cuban dance music from *contradanza* to *timba* may be found in the special issue no. 39–40 of *Temas* (Havana: October–December 2004) devoted to Cuban music. On Los Jardines de la Tropical and the social clubs for people of color, see Eugene Godfried, "Dialogue with Juan Cruz, Past President, Marianao Social Club," on AfroCubaWeb (http://www.afrocubaweb.com/eugenegodfried/juancruz.htm [accessed June 30, 2006]).

Chapter 10, on the revolution of 1933 and its context: Carlos Loveira's *Juan Criollo* can be found in many Spanish editions but has not been published in English. Cira Romero's prologue to the Letras Cubanas edition (Havana: Letras Cubanas, 1987) includes biographical details. For documentary sources on the Cuban labor movement in the nineteenth and twentieth century we drew from *El movimiento obrero cubano. Documentos y artículos* (Havana: Ciencias Sociales, 1977), and on strikes and other events leading up to 1933 from Julio Domínguez Garcia, *Noticias de la República: Apuntes cronológicos 1900–1929* (Havana: Ciencias Sociales, 2003). On twentieth century Cuban feminism, see K. Lynn Stoner, *From the House to the Streets: The Cuban Women's Movement for Legal Change, 1898–1940* (New York: Garland, 1989).

An account of the events of '33 and their context published in the U.S. is Luis Aguilar, *CUBA 1933* (Ithaca: Cornell, 1972). Accounts published in Cuba include José A. Tabares del Real, *La revolución del 30: sus dos últimos años* (Havana: Arte y Literatura: 1971) and Lionel Soto's three volume *La revolución del 33* (Havana: Ciencias Sociales, 1977). The plan for the assassination attempt in the Colón Cemetery is described in the biography of its protagonist Pío Álvarez, Newton Briones Montoto's *Accion directa* (Havana: Ciencias Sociales, 1999). Luis Buch's memoir *Un insurreccional en dos épocas* (Havana: Ciencias Sociales, 2001) describes the underground activity in Havana through 1935, while Olga Cabrera's *Guiteras, La época, el hombre* (Havana: Ciencias Sociales, 1978) analyzes the government of the Hundred Days.

Chapter 11, Radio Days, draws particularly on Oscar Luis López's *La radio en Cuba* (Havana: Letras Cubanas: 1981, 2002), as well as Reynaldo González, *Llorar es un placer* (Havana: Letras Cubanas, 2002) on soap operas, and the two principal magazines of the era, *Bohemia* and *Carteles* (1940–1948), for descriptions of the Constitutional assembly, violent crimes, and other events.

Juan Valdés Paz was interviewed in Havana by Rafael Hernández in June 2005. Various anecdotes about the Caballero de París (Chapter 11 and elsewhere) come from the periodicals *Bohemia* (1945, 1949), *Diario de la Marina* (1944), *Gente* (1949), *Alerta* (1939, 1949) and from María Argelia Vizcaíno's collection "El Caballero de París" (http://freeweb.supereva. com/carlo260/caballero.html?p [accessed June 30, 2006]) on Carlo Nobili's very useful website *Cuba. Una indentità en movimento* (http://freeweb. supereva.com/carlo260/ [accessed June 30, 2006]); there is also a collection called *Yo soy el Caballero de París*, edited by his doctor during the final years of his life, Luis Calzadilla Fierro (Badajoz: Diputación de Badajoz, 2000). The "events of Orfila" are narrated in Oscar Luis López, *La radio en Cuba* (1981) as well as periodicals of the time. Pedro Prada, *La secretaria de la república* (Havana: Ciencias Sociales, 2001) narrates the events surrounding the suicide of Eddy Chibás in the voice of his personal secretary Conchita Fernández.

In Chapter 12, the opening anecdote about Amletto Battisti and the painting stolen from Carlos Miguel de Céspedes is from the same *Bohemia* article of 1946 cited for Chapter 9. Graham Greene's comments on writing *Our Man in Havana* are from his introduction to the edition published by Heinemann and Bodley Head, London, 1970.

J.P. McEvoy's article on Batista's coup appeared in the Spanish edition of *Reader's Digest* in July 1952 and in slightly different form in the English edition of that same month (vol. 62). Batista's statement about the "Monte Carlo of the Caribbean" comes from *Life*, March, 1958. Among many sources on the Mafia in Havana are Robert Lacey's *Little Man: Meyer Lansky and the Gangster Life* (Boston: Little Brown, 1991) and Enrique Cirules, *El imperio de La Habana* (Havana: Casa de las Américas, 1993), available in English as *The Mafia in Havana* (Melbourne: Ocean Press, 2004); contemporary articles in the U.S. press include "Crime: Happy Days in Havana" (*Newsweek*, January 20, 1958) and "Not So Far from the Crowding Mob" (*Saturday Review*, April 19, 1958).

The sex worker's account is from Tomás Fernández Robaina's *Historias de mujeres públicas*, cited above (Chapter 8). Arthur Schlesinger's comment comes from his memoir *One Thousand Days* as cited in Pérez, *Cuba and the United States*. On Burke Hedges, see "Cuba. Ambassador of

Fun," *Time*, September, 1958. Allen Ginsberg's phrases on the Plaza de la Catedral are from his poem "Havana," in *Reality Sandwiches* (San Francisco: City Lights, 1963).

For Chapter 13 and beyond, Verónica Loynaz was interviewed in Havana by Rafael Hernández in October 2005.

Almost all of Fidel Castro's speeches, including the one from Camp Columbia in January, 1959, can be found online in English, translated by the U.S. government's Foreign Broadcast Information Service, at http://lanic.utexas.edu/la/cb/cuba/castro.html (accessed June 30, 2006). The Caballero de París quote on the rebels and their beards is from *Carteles*, May 3, 1959. Carleton Beals on the anti-American mood in Havana in early 1959 is from *Christian Century*, February 4, 1959. On the trials and executions of Batista's officers see *Bohemia* of March 8, March 15, March 22, and April 26, 1959 and *Carteles*, March 22, March 31, April 5, and May 31; *Life*'s report appeared in the January 26, 1959 issue.

Mirta Yáñez's 1976 story "Todos los negros tomamos café" appears in English, translated by Claudette Williams, as "We Blacks All Drink Coffee" in Pamela Mordecai and Betty Wilson, ed., *Her True-True Name* (Oxford: Heinemann, 1989).

Among the many sources on the unfolding of Cuba–U.S. relations in this period, Jane Franklin's *Cuba and the United States. A Chronological History* (Melbourne: Ocean Press, 1997) offers a condensed summary of the events. On the assassination plots directed at Castro, see the 1975 U.S. Senate report, "Alleged Assassination Plots Involving Foreign Leaders" (republished with introduction by Sen. Frank Church, New York: Norton, 1976). The quotation from the CIA trainer of Bay of Pigs expeditionaries is from Peter Wyden, *Bay of Pigs: The Untold Story* (New York: Simon & Schuster, 1979).

The two Dulce María Loynaz poems referred to are both from her *Poemas sin nombre*, numbers XXXV and CXXIV; the latter appears in an English translation in the Judith Kerman collection, *A Woman in Her Garden*, cited above. Much of the information on Operation Peter Pan comes from María de Los Angeles Torres, *The Lost Apple: Operation Peter Pan, Cuban Children in the U.S., and the Promise of a Better Future* (Boston: Beacon, 2003).

In Chapter 14, Alejo Carpentier's opening quote comes from the article he published in the Venezuelan newspaper *El Nacional*, June 17, 1959, reprinted in the magazine *Universidad de La Habana*, September 1984.

The quote from "Violeta" about the closing of brothels is from Tomás Fernández Robaina's *Historias de mujeres públicas*, cited above. On the emigration and expulsion of priests, see John Kirk, *Between God and the Party: Religion and Politics in Revolutionary Cuba* (Tampa: University of South Florida, 1989) and Margaret Crahan, "Salvation through Christ or Marx," in Daniel H. Levine, ed., *Churches and Politics in Latin America* (Chapel Hill: University of North Carolina, 1986). On the conflict over religion see also Aurelio Alonso, *Church and Politics in Revolutionary Cuba* (Havana: Editorial José Marti,1999).

On housing construction, see Scarpaci, Segre, and Coyula, *Havana*, cited above; on film-making and popular music in the 1960s and 1970s, *La tienda negra* and *Temas* no. 39–40, also cited above.

For Chapter 15, Teresita Roca was interviewed in Havana by Dick Cluster in December 2004. For the prior history of the Hotel Montserrat and its site we are indebted to the Office of the City Historian.

The writer Yoss's statement about Russian influence is from his article "Lo que dejaron los rusos," *Temas*, no. 37–38 (April–September 2004). Reinaldo Arenas, *Before Night Falls*, is available in an English translation by Dolores M. Koch (New York: Viking, 1993).

On the social class of Mariel emigrants, see Rafael Hernández and Redi Gomis, "Retrato del Mariel: el ángulo socioeconómico," in *Cuadernos de Nuestra América* III, no. 5 (1986). On emigration as a theme in Cuban cinema, Desirée Díaz, "La mirada de Ovidio. El tema de la emigración en el cine cubano de los 90," in *Temas*, no. 27 (October–December 2001). Our discussion of the crisis of the 1990s and the economic reforms of 1993–96 in Chapter 16 draws on *Temas*, no. 11 (July–September 1997) and no. 30 (April–June 2002), and on Rafael Hernández, "Toward a New Socialist Society? Changes, Crisis, and Social Configurations in Cuba," in his *Looking at Cuba: Essays on Culture and Civil Society* (Gainesville: University Press of Florida, 2003).

Among Daniel Chavarría's recent novels of Havana, *Adios Muchachos* has been published in English, translated by Carlos López (New York: Akashic, 2001). Leonardo Padura's *La novela de mi vida* was published in 2002 by Tusquets (Barcelona) and Ediciones Unión (Havana). Mylene Férnandez Pintado's *Otras plegarías atendidas* (Other Answered Prayers) was published in 2003 by Ediciones Unión (Havana).

Juan Formell's comments on *timba* music and dance come from Robin Davies, "Comenzó La Fiesta: Los Van Van Is in Town," http://www. salsasf.com/features/articles/vanvan01.html (accessed June 30, 2006). The song "¿Y qué tu quieres que te den?" by Adalberto Álvarez y Su Son, appears on their CD *Mi linda habanera* (Bismusic, 2005). For the Havana music market and *timba* in the 1990s, we drew on Emir García Meralla "Hágase la timba" (*Temas*, no. 39–40, cited above). For lyrics to songs by Los Van Van and other Cuban salsa groups, see also http://www.rosariosalsa.com. ar/letras/letras.htm (accessed June 30, 2006).

The Epilogue draws primarily on the authors' interviews, field research, and observations, which are the sources of all direct quotes.

More on the history of Calle Obispo can be found in Reynaldo Montero, *Bajando por la calle Obispo* (Havana: Ediciones Boloña, 2008) and Arturo Pedroso Alés, "La calle Obispo," *Opus Habana* #26, March 30, 2009.

On housing, see *Revista Temas*, #58, April-June 2009, which contains seven studies of the housing situation. For current data, the architect Pedro Vázquez was interviewed by Rafael Hernández in June 2017.

For a discussion of past and present Cuban international migration flows, see Antonio Aja, "La perspectiva migratoria en 2017: ¿Cambio de reglas?" in the website Catalejo, March 6, 2017, at http://www.temas.cult.cu/catalejo/la-perspectiva-migratoria-en-2017-cambio-de-reglas. On possible effects, see "Migración golondrina?" transcript of a panel discussion in the series Último Jueves, March 5, 2015, at http://www.temas.cult.cu/content/migraci-n-golondrina.

On food markets, see Armando Nova, "El mercado agropecuario. Políticas e impactos," in Catalejo, June 30, 2016, at http://www.temas.cult.cu/catalejo/el-mercado-agropecuario-politicas-e-impactos. For a discussion of food spending in relation to family budgets and incomes, see Anicia García and Betsy Anaya, "Gastos básicos de familias cubanas pensionadas y salario-dependientes," *Revista Temas*, # 79, July-Sept, 2014.

On the ceremonies in Havana after Fidel Castro's death, see Jonathan Watts, "Fidel Castro memorial service: crowds gather as dignitaries pay tribute," *The Guardian*, posted on theguardian.com/world, November 29, 2016, and Associated Press, "Fidel Castro's ashes begin 4-day procession to revolution's birthplace," posted November 30, 2016 on cba.ca.

Index